Laudian and royalist polemic in seventeenth-century England

MANCHESTER
1824
Manchester University Press

Politics, culture and society in early modern Britain

General Editors

PROFESSOR ANN HUGHES
PROFESSOR ANTHONY MILTON
PROFESSOR PETER LAKE

This important series publishes monographs that take a fresh and challenging look at the inter-actions between politics, culture and society in Britain between 1500 and the mid-eighteenth century. It counteracts the fragmentation of current historiography through encouraging a vari-ety of approaches which attempt to redefine the political, social and cultural worlds, and to explore their interconnection in a flexible and creative fashion. All the volumes in the series question and transcend traditional interdisciplinary boundaries, such as those between political history and literary studies, social history and divinity, urban history and anthropology. They thus con-tribute to a broader understanding of crucial developments in early modern Britain.

Laudian and royalist polemic in seventeenth-century England

The career and writings of Peter Heylyn

ANTHONY MILTON

Manchester
University Press
Manchester and New York

distributed exclusively in the USA by Palgrave

Published by Manchester University Press
Oxford Road, Manchester M13 9NR, UK
and Room 400, 175 Fifth Avenue, New York, NY 10010, USA
www.manchesteruniversitypress.co.uk

Distributed exclusively in the USA by
Palgrave, 175 Fifth Avenue, New York,
NY 10010, USA

Distributed exclusively in Canada by
UBC Press, University of British Columbia, 2029 West Mall,
Vancouver, BC, Canada V6T 1Z2

British Library Cataloguing-in-Publication Data
A catalogue record for this book is available from the British Library

Library of Congress Cataloging-in-Publication Data applied for

ISBN   978 0 7190 6444 9   *hardback*

First published 2007

16 15 14 13 12 11 10 09 08 07   10 9 8 7 6 5 4 3 2 1

Typeset in 10/12.5pt Scala with Pastonchi display
by Graphicraft Limited, Hong Kong
Printed in Great Britain
by Biddles Ltd, King's Lynn

FOR MY MOTHER

Contents

Contents

Acknowledgements

———◆———

'What a bastard!' was often people's response (usually with a smile) when I told them that I was working on a study of Peter Heylyn. 'But an important bastard', was one Oxford historian's thoughtful addition to the usual antiphonal exchange. I hope that my book demonstrates that Heylyn was both important and interesting. It is for the reader to decide about the noun. I began work on the book with the assurance that I would not fall into the biographer's trap of falling in love with their subject, and I remain unsmitten at the end. But I have emerged from the experience more than ever convinced that we need to take more seriously and strive to understand the people in history who seem less than heroic or agreeable. I also feel that in the end, for all his many faults, Heylyn does not deserve many of the worst epithets, nor the *uniquely* unpleasant status that he has so often been accorded, nor the contempt that usually goes with it. It was an age of angry people who had much to feel angry about, and Heylyn was only one among many who used scholarship both as a tool and as a weapon.

I am grateful to John Morrill, who first suggested Peter Heylyn to me as a possible PhD topic more years ago than I care to remember, and who cheered me on when my PhD took a different direction and (more recently) as I finally found my way back to my original assignment. A number of people have indulged my enthusiasm for studying Heylyn and his milieu and have generously shared references and ideas with me in person and via e-mail. I am very grateful in particular to Cesare Cuttica, Andrew Hegarty, David Scott, Jason Peacey, Tom Freeman, Mark Knights, Barbara Coulton, Robert Mayhew, Peter Lake, Chad van Dixhoorn, Stephen Taylor and especially Ken Fincham and Blair Worden. I am of course solely responsible for the errors and misinterpretations that remain.

I am grateful to the archivists and librarians at all the institutions where I have carried out research, especially the archivists of Magdalen College, Oxford, and the staff of the Centre for Kentish Studies (who replied to a last-minute xeroxing request with understanding and celerity). The legendary efficiency of the staff of the Rare Books Room in Cambridge University Library has been exceeded only by their friendliness and courtesy. I received research funding for this study from the Arts and Humanities Research Board and the British Academy, and I am grateful to both bodies. Alison Welsby could not have been a more encouraging and supportive editor –

Acknowledgements

I am enormously grateful to her for her (apparently!) unfailing confidence in the book and its author.

The book could not have been completed without the guidance and support of my wife, Julia, who has countless times gently dissuaded me when I was heading off confidently in the wrong direction, and nudged me back on to the right one. She has tolerated Peter Heylyn's intrusion into our lives with an indulgence that seventeenth-century people would have struggled to sustain, and has always been ready to discuss ideas, interpretations and findings with me with an open but critical mind. In the last frantic days of writing she has been a priceless source of wise counsel and reassurance. The book is dedicated to a lady who would not have cared for Heylyn's ideas or behaviour but would nevertheless have made him welcome if he had turned up on her doorstep, and whose endurance in the face of afflictions far worse than those suffered by Dr Heylyn continues to inspire love and admiration.

In the text of the book dates are Old Style but the year is taken to begin on 1 January. Of printed works cited below the place of publication is London unless otherwise stated.

A.M.

Abbreviations

AL	Peter Heylyn, *Antidotum Lincolniense* (1637)
AR	Peter Heylyn, *Aërius Redivivus: or the History of the Presbyterians* (2nd edn, 1672)
Ath. Ox.	Anthony Wood, *Athenae Oxonienses*, ed. P. Bliss (4 vols, 1813–20)
Barnard	John Barnard, *Theologo-Historicus, or the True Life of the Most Reverend Divine and Excellent Historian Peter Heylyn* – (16??)
BL	British Library, London
BMA	Peter Heylyn, *A Briefe and Moderate Answer, to the seditious and scandalous Challenges of Henry Burton* (1637)
Bodl.	Bodleian Library, Oxford
BR	Peter Heylyn, *Bibliotheca Regia* (1658)
CA	Peter Heylyn, *Cyprianus Anglicus* (1668)
CE	Peter Heylyn, *Certamen Epistolare* (1659)
CJ	*Journals of the House of Commons*
Coale	Peter Heylyn, *A Coale from the Altar* (1636)
EH	Peter Heylyn, *Examen Historicum* (1659)
ER	Peter Heylyn, *Ecclesia Restaurata* (1661), ed. J. C. Robertson (2 vols, Cambridge, 1849)
EV	Peter Heylyn, *Ecclesia Vindicata* (1657)
Extraneus	Peter Heylyn, *Extraneus Valupans* (1656)
HJ	*Historical Journal*
HLQ	*Huntington Library Quarterly*
HQA	Peter Heylyn, *Historia Quinqu-Articularis* (1660)
HS	Peter Heylyn, *The History of the Sabbath* (1636)
HSG	Peter Heylyn, *The Historie of St George* (1631)

Unless stated, it is the first edition of a published work which is used.

Introduction

———◆———

Writing just twenty years after the death of his subject, the early biographer of Peter Heylyn, George Vernon, was distressed to find that Heylyn's funeral monument in Westminster Abbey had been attacked. 'His Monument has, since the erection of it, had violence offered it by some rude and irreligious hand', he recorded.[1] Few monuments in the abbey have been publicly attacked in this way, and it provides an indication that the animosity that Heylyn had generated in his lifetime continued after he was dead. Other critics restrained themselves to words, but were hardly less hostile. Samuel Coleridge could only exclaim, 'Who being a Christian can avoid feeling the worldly harsh unspiritual Spirit of this bitter Factionary! I scarcely know a more unamiable Churchman, as a Writer, than Dr Heylyn.'[2] The eighteenth-century historian John Oldmixon combined the charge of cynical venality with that of spiteful hostility: 'Heylin wrote for Money as well as Malice, and abuses every Man that comes in his way . . . as dull and impertinent, as he is malicious and inveterate.'[3] To this catalogue of vices the Victorian historian Henry Hallam added that of untruthfulness, remarking censoriously that Heylyn was 'a bigoted enemy of everything puritanical, and not scrupulous to veracity'. The final *coup de grâce* was to suggest that he was not worth reading anyway. Carlyle, commenting on Heylyn's life of Laud, wrote contemptuously that 'the human brain in this stage of its progress, refuses any longer to concern itself with Peter Heylin.'[4]

His contemporaries were equally hostile, and the charges of spite, mendacity and venality were endlessly rehearsed by his seventeenth-century opponents, to be recycled in later centuries. Even the proverbially moderate Richard Baxter declared that people like Heylyn 'speak of blood with pleasure, and [are] as thirsty after more or as designing to make Dissenters odious'.[5] He was 'the bishops darling' who had been trained in 'Billingsgate Colledge'. A chorus of writers insisted that he wrote for money, one commenting that 'all his life he hath loved the world'.[6] Clearly, the wounds that Heylyn had inflicted ran deep.

However, for someone who stirred up such strong emotions, Heylyn has received surprisingly little attention from historians. Partly this may reflect the hostility that he has traditionally aroused, and the assumption not only that such a disagreeable figure is not worthy of study, but also that the writings of such an apparently venal and mendacious writer would not repay serious analysis. But Heylyn's neglect also in part reflects his unfashionable choice of sides. As a supporter of Archbishop Laud and of the royalist cause in the Civil War, Heylyn selected parties which have always received relatively limited historical attention. Royalism has never attracted the energies that historians have lavished on the parliamentarians – partly because they were the losing party in the war, but also because this is often taken to reflect the fact that their principles were outdated and backward-looking. Similarly, Laud's colleagues have always been relatively neglected compared with historians' treatment of their puritan opponents. While Laud himself has always attracted supporters as well as detractors among historians, those lesser clergy involved in his movement have received remarkably little attention. In Heylyn's case, even those scholars of high-church tendencies seem to have been disinclined to devote much attention to someone who seems to have doled out as much invective as he received.

The comparative neglect of Laudianism and royalism has become a more serious anomaly of historical scholarship in recent years, as Archbishop Laud and his policies have been required to bear an ever-increasing weight of responsibility for the outbreak of the Civil War. Most recent work has focused on the Laudian policies themselves, while there have also been studies of the theological backgrounds and principles of those who played a principal role in the implementation of Laudian policies.[7] However, the rationale that was presented to justify these policies has received little detailed examination, and the relationship of Laudianism to royalism remains virtual *terra incognita*.

The relative neglect of Laudian ideology (as opposed to the theological background of its bishops) is all the more serious because it has been suggested most recently by several historians that the Laudian policies themselves were not necessarily as innovative as their opponents claimed, and that individual features of their policies can be found to have precedents stretching well back into the Jacobean period, and even earlier. What is distinctive about the 1630s, it has been argued, is not only the systematic way in which ceremonial and disciplinary policies were enforced but also in particular the rationale with which these policies were imposed. What may have been most crucial was the ideological background which infused with more alarming significance what were forms of church decoration and outward worship which were not in themselves unprecedented or inherently objectionable.[8]

The best recent analysis of the ideology of Laudianism has established an 'ideal type' of Laudian thought.[9] Inevitably, however, this is a picture that smoothes out anomalies and sifts out the inconsistencies between authors, and even within the *oeuvre* of individual writers. There is still a need for a more detailed analysis of where these writers came from, the coherence or otherwise of the views that they expressed in the 1630s, how far these views represented a divergence from their earlier expressed opinions, and how these ideas fed into the royalist writing of the 1640s.

Peter Heylyn would seem to offer an ideal opportunity to investigate these phenomena. Not only did he write copiously before the 1630s, but during the personal rule itself Heylyn was the most important defender of Laudian policies. Unlike the works of most of those who wrote in support of Laudian policies, his writings were in several cases directly commissioned by the king and were published 'by authority'. Just as important, Heylyn continued to write in the 1640s, acting for a while as the editor of the main royalist news-book, *Mercurius Aulicus*, as well as the author of a number of royalist tracts. His writings continued through the 1650s, when he was still described by one opponent as 'the Primipilus among the defenders of the late turgid and persecuting sort of Prelacy',[10] and he greeted the Restoration with three substantial historical works reflecting on the events of the previous hundred years. This sustained productivity, and his consistent high profile, provide us with a unique glimpse of a fully contextualized Laudian career, where his defence of Laudianism in the 1630s can be compared with both earlier and later writings.

But the intention here is not simply to add another Laudian thinker – albeit one with a greater prominence and longer publishing career – to the list of conformist divines who have received biographical studies. Rather, Heylyn merits particular interest, and his career boasts a broader significance, because he was one of the most famous government propagandists and polemicists of the age. Polemical writing was one of the dominant features of the intellectual culture of the age, yet its practitioners have received very little study. This is not only because of a certain distaste for their activities (with the unspoken – or often spoken – assumption that they must have been inherently unprincipled), but also because it is assumed that as mere mouthpieces of the authorities they can have had nothing of interest or originality to say. But this is to assume a simplistic view of the polemicist's work and of the government's control. Pamphleteers who seem to write for a particular side were rarely merely hired pens or hacks. On the contrary, they often led independent lives, writing for a variety of purposes, while their career trajectories may have meant that they slipped in and out of the production of overt propaganda. It was rare for a book to have its content purely dictated by the authorities. A more complex process of voluntary co-option, or proffered assistance, may have lain behind individual works of government propaganda.[11] Moreover, it needs to be considered that, while ostensibly merely providing a justification for government policies, writers like Heylyn were also in a position to shape the government's perceived ideological agenda, and thereby crucially to influence the impact of the policies themselves.

One of the main impediments to detailed studies of polemical authors and the complex processes that lie behind their publications is that often we know little of the authors beyond their published writings. But Heylyn offers a rare opportunity to trace an intellectual and polemical career in detail. This is not just because of his political prominence, and the sheer bulk and regular publication of his writings over forty years, but also because a good deal of biographical material relating to Heylyn was actually presented in the pamphlets themselves, in which he was required to defend his own activities.[12] We are also especially fortunate to possess no fewer than three contemporary biographies of Heylyn – an exceptional number for a conformist divine who never achieved major office in the church.

It will also be argued in the course of this book that it is incorrect simply to brand Heylyn as a government propagandist. In fact, in the context of his writing career, his time as an official apologist for the government was very short, and indeed exceptional. The vast bulk of his writing was not commissioned by the authorities at all. Moreover, it will be demonstrated that for much of his time in government service Heylyn did not act simply as a 'hired pen', supplying printed works to order. Rather, he provided a range of services. Some of these were of the type that has been given the modish term 'knowledge transactions' – presenting critical reports, position papers, calls for action, and syntheses of legal and historical justifications for particular actions.[13] He also acted as a type of government agent in drawing up petitions against the government's opponents. Again, however, Heylyn was not acting here as a mere salaried agent. He drew no official salary, had no formal position at court, and his actions often had a distinct personal agenda to them. As with his printed writings, it is often pertinent to ponder who exactly was using whom in Heylyn's relationship with the authorities.

Given these points, a simple analysis of the content of Heylyn's published writings would represent a missed opportunity. The circumstances of their production, and the context of Heylyn's own career, also require detailed attention. This book therefore seeks to provide an integrated account of Heylyn's career and writings. It is neither a straightforward biography, nor an intellectual study of his works, but seeks to combine elements of both genres in reconstructing the intellectual, political and personal career of one of the most industrious and controversial polemicists of his age. Given the enormous bulk of Heylyn's writings, and the complexity and changing nature of his ideas, it would be easy to produce a very large book indeed. Instead, I have sought throughout to provide a guide to what appear to have been crucial themes and turning points in his career and writings. This has inevitably meant that some of his books have received more detailed treatment than others, but I hope to deal more fully elsewhere with some of the texts that have had to be passed over briefly here. I have also attempted to direct more attention to those works that Heylyn wrote which have been comparatively neglected. Only a tiny portion of Heylyn's works have received detailed scholarly study, and these are often assumed to encapsulate his world-view. A study of his entire output, however, makes it possible to put his more famous works into their intellectual and personal context, and to establish the degree to which they either reflected temporary changes of viewpoint or were shaped by their immediate polemical agenda. As will become clear, Heylyn did not spring forth from university with a single clear intellectual identity. His expressed ideas evolved and shifted considerably over the forty years in which he was a published author.

The neglect of Heylyn by historians has not been total. Of the three biographies that appeared within twenty years of his death, one appeared in a collected volume of Heylyn's works after passing through a number of hands, but the other two – by George Vernon and John Barnard – are independent works. While these suffer from the inevitable hagiographical shortcomings of contemporary lives (especially as Barnard was Heylyn's son-in-law) and their treatment of the chronology of events is sometimes seriously misleading, nevertheless they often offer invaluable information, with the added benefit of providing what are different angles and selections of material.[14] It was not until the twentieth century, however, that Heylyn received further sustained study rather than passing insults. Some of his writings have received brief analysis in a number of books and articles, although these have often tended to focus on the historical works of the last six years of his life.[15] There are more sustained analyses of Heylyn in three useful but neglected PhD theses. The first, by Anne Kendall, was written in 1947, and provides both an overview of Heylyn's whole output (although concentrating on his later histories) and the first positive assessment of his scholarship. John Walker in 1978 provided an excellent study of the practicalities of Heylyn's many publications, combining intensive bibliographical analysis with a broader interpretation of his views. Finally, the latter chapters of Fred Trott's 1992 dissertation 'Prelude to Restoration' provide an incisive analysis of Heylyn's later works in the context of Laudian writings of the 1650s.[16] These dissertations all provide useful ideas and information. I had completed most of my work on Heylyn before consulting them, but although my agenda and my interpretations have often differed from theirs, I have sought to identify what I see as their particular insights wherever appropriate.

NOTES

1 Vernon, p. 290.

2 Coleridge, *Collected Works*, XII, ed. G. Whalley (Princeton NJ, 1984), p. 1097. (Coleridge's marginalia in Heylyn's *Cyprianus Anglicus*). I am grateful to Judith Maltby for this reference.

3 John Oldmixon, *The Critical History of England, Ecclesiastical and Civil* (1724), p. 224.

4 Henry Hallam, *A Constitutional History of England* (3 vols, 1872), II, p. 38; Thomas Carlyle, *Historical Sketches* (2nd edn, 1898), p. 274.

5 R. Baxter, *Church-History of the Government of Bishops and their Councils Abbreviated* (1680), sig. a4r.

6 Thomas Fuller, *An Appeal of Injured Innocence* (1659), iii. p. 33; *EV*, ii. sig. A3r; Hamon L'Estrange, *The Observator Observed* (1656), p. 22.

7 N. Tyacke, *Anti-Calvinists: the Rise of English Arminianism, c. 1590–1640* (Oxford, 1987), chapter 8; A. Foster, 'Church policies in the 1630s' in R. Cust and A. Hughes (eds), *Conflict in early Stuart England* (1989); K. C. Fincham, 'The restoration of altars in the 1630s', *HJ*, 44 (2001), pp. 919–40; A. Milton, *Catholic and Reformed* (Cambridge, 1995).

8 P. Lake, *The Boxmaker's Revenge* (Manchester, 2001), ch. 11, esp. p. 304; J. F. Merritt, 'Puritans, Laudians and the phenomenon of church building in Jacobean London', *HJ*, 41 (1998), pp. 936–60.

9 P. Lake, 'The Laudian style' in K. Fincham (ed.), *The Early Stuart Church, 1603–1642* (1993).

10 *CE*, p. 11.

11 J. Peacey, *Politicians and Pamphleteers: Propaganda during the English Civil Wars and Interregnum* (Aldershot, 2004), esp. pp. 273, 288.

12 Nevertheless, it has proved difficult to track down more than a tiny sample of Heylyn's surviving letters and papers. Within a few years of his death it was already being noted that his son Henry 'has none of his Fathers books' (CUL, Add. MS 4251 (B), No. 237, Arthur Charlott to Edmund Bohun (n.d.)).

13 L. Jardine and W. Sherman, 'Pragmatic readers: knowledge transactions and scholarly services in late Elizabethan England' in A. J. Fletcher and P. Roberts (eds), *Religion, Culture and Society in Early Modern Britain* (Cambridge, 1994).

14 Robertson provides a thorough analysis of the complicated story behind the appearance of these three biographies in his edition of *Ecclesia Restaurata* (*ER*, I, pp. xx–xxviii).

15 Champion, *Pillars*, pp. 64–77; R. MacGillivray, *Restoration Historians and the English Civil War* (The Hague, 1974), pp. 29–41; J. Drabble, 'Thomas Fuller, Peter Heylyn and the English Reformation', *Renaissance and Reformation*, n.s., 3 (1979), pp. 168–88; J. H. Preston, 'English ecclesiastical historians and the problem of bias, 1559–1742', *Journal of the History of Ideas*, 32 (1971), pp. 203–20; R. J. Mayhew, *Enlightenment Geography: the Political Languages of British Geography, 1650–1850* (Basingstoke, 2000);

R. J. Mayhew, ' "Geography is twinned with Divinity": the Laudian geography of Peter Heylyn', *Geographical Review*, 90 (2000), pp. 18–34; R. Mayer, 'The rhetoric of historical truth: Heylyn *contra* Fuller on *The Church History of Britain*', *Prose Studies*, 20:3 (1997), pp. 1–20; R. E. A. Meza, 'Heylyn's theory of royal sovereignty', *Historical Magazine of the Protestant Episcopalian Church*, 55 (1986), pp. 179–202.

16 A. M. Kendall, 'A Royalist Scholar: Peter Heylyn as Historian and Controversialist' (unpublished Radcliffe College PhD thesis, 1947); J. H. Walker, 'A Descriptive Bibliography of the early printed Works of Peter Heylyn' (unpublished University of Birmingham PhD thesis, 1978); F. J. Trott, 'Prelude to Restoration: Laudians, Conformists and the Struggle for "Anglicanism" in the 1650s' (unpublished University of London PhD thesis, 1992).

Chapter 1

———◆———

The making of a Laudian polemicist?

W here do Laudians come from? The origins of puritans seem relatively easy to grasp. There is an established typology of the conversion experience, whereby previously ungodly individuals were spiritually reborn, which is replayed in a whole series of contemporary puritan biographies, culminating in Samuel Clarke's enormous compilations of godly lives.[1] By contrast, there appears to be no simple model of where a committed Laudian should spring from. There is sometimes an assumption that, given the antagonistic relationship between Laudian policies and the predominant religious culture of the age, a future Laudian enthusiast should have been evident in their early years, in pursuing the 'beauty of holiness' and opposing puritanism. However, it is becoming increasingly apparent that some prominent figures in the movement may have gone through an earlier 'Calvinist' phase.[2] Peter Heylyn's case may seem to fit this latter model. As we will see, there is little early sign of the preoccupations of his Laudian writings. Nor can we find a simple Laudian equivalent of a puritan conversion experience. For him, and perhaps for some of the other Laudians of the 1630s, these were convictions that emerged only gradually during the 1620s, and were bound up with their experiences and career development.[3]

HEYLYN'S BACKGROUND

Peter Heylyn was born into a reasonably prosperous provincial family. His biographers have little to say of his father, Henry Heylyn. He was descended from an ancient Welsh family from Montgomeryshire, whose ancestral seat of Pentre Heylyn remained with the family until 1637, and which Peter Heylyn apparently intended to repurchase shortly before his death.[4] Whatever his ancestral background, however, Henry Heylyn would appear to have been the archetypal self-made man, whose will instructed his children to join him in

thanking God 'who of his blessings to me and them hath from a weak beginning and thorough my harde labores inabled me to breede them to what they
now are'.[5] Described as a gentleman in his will, Henry Heylyn had played
a prominent role in local affairs in the town of Burford.[6] Peter's mother
came from a prosperous local family who owned the manor of Lechlade in
Gloucestershire, worth £1,400 per annum, which was eventually settled on
Peter Heylyn's uncle, Robert Bathurst.[7] Bathurst acted as Peter's godfather
and gave him a greater sum in his will than any of Heylyn's siblings. Heylyn
would appear to have kept up his connection with the Bathursts throughout his life: Robert's grandson would be the dedicatee of one of Heylyn's
later works. As we will see, the family link to the Bathurst family may also
have involved Heylyn in curious connections with Robert Bathurst's second
wife, Lady Elizabeth Lawrence, and her son from her first marriage, Henry
Lawrence, who would later serve on Oliver Cromwell's council of state.[8] Heylyn's
immediate family owned land and advowsons in the area around Lechlade,
and he always had close connections with the area. His parents were both
buried in the chancel of Lechlade church, rather than in Burford.[9] Much of
Heylyn's personal life, connections and property were focused in a small area
bounded by Burford (where he grew up) and Lechlade, including the manor
of Minster Lovell (where he would shelter in the late 1640s with his nephew)
and Abingdon (where he lived in the 1650s).

Searching for the origins of a Laudian world view in the early life of Peter
Heylyn, we can find occasional hints of his future predilections. It is often
suggested that Laudianism had a natural affinity with traditional festive culture, and here Heylyn would seem to have the proper qualifications. His birthplace of Burford was a town whose local festive culture was still very dynamic
in this period. Certainly in Heylyn's childhood the town's inhabitants still
had a parade with a giant and dragon through the streets at midsummer.[10]
His early poems include one imaginary game of stoolball with his beloved
(although Professor Underdown would warn us that such games represented
a more individualistic focus than the communal game of football), and
Heylyn's attachment to his local area regularly resurfaces in his writings.[11]

Heylyn also later insisted that his father 'very well understood the constitution of the Church of England, and was a diligent observer of all publick
duties which were required of him in his place and station'. Heylyn claimed
that he 'suckt in as it were with my mothers milk' the basic principles of the
established church.[12] His father would certainly appear to have been strikingly
well read in religion. His study was well supplied with books, which included
an eight-volume set of Augustine's works, six volumes of Nicholas de Lyra
and a volume of 'the Counsells generall and provinciall' – a remarkable
collection of patristic literature for a layman, all of which he gave to his son
Peter in his will.[13] Heylyn also seems to have spent a brief period of time at

Merchant Taylors' School – a seedbed of later Laudians – although the brevity of his sojourn there and his failure to follow the established route from that school to Laud's college of St John's in Oxford would not seem to indicate any decisive influence.[14]

In fact, much of Heylyn's background suggests more puritan connections, and his later insistence on the conformist principles of his parents occurred when he was trying to explain away the more obviously puritan aspects of his education. One of his father's kinsmen was Rowland Heylyn, an alderman and sheriff of London who was a leading light of the puritan Feoffees for Impropriations and a dedicated supporter of a puritan lectureship in Shrewsbury some years before.[15] Henry Heylyn clearly knew Rowland well. He entrusted him with a number of tasks in his will, and also asked him to assign over a cottage to Peter's use. Peter Heylyn himself admitted that his education had had a puritan bent. His tutor at Hart Hall, Walter Newberry, was 'a verie zealous and pragmaticall Puritan' and Heylyn was 'very young and capable of any impression which he might think fit to stamp upon me'.[16] He moved from thence to Magdalen College, which was not one of the more notably 'Laudian' colleges – indeed, it had been dubbed 'a nest of puritans' in the early Jacobean period.[17] One of his friends among the fellows – Thomas Buckner – would become a chaplain to Archbishop Abbot. It was his time at Magdalen College that enabled Heylyn to make contact with his first major lay patron, the earl of Danby, who was a benefactor of the college. Danby had been involved in Protestant military campaigns, and was not a notable patron of conformist divines. While a royalist himself, his brother was to be a regicide.[18] It was Danby, however, who was Heylyn's most important early promoter. Heylyn wrote verses to Danby in the 1620s in which he stressed 'that world of dutie which I owe/Unto your noble bounties'. It was Danby who secured for Heylyn the opportunity to present his first book, *Microcosmus*, to its dedicatee, Prince Charles, at Theobalds in 1621, and in the late 1620s Heylyn would accompany Danby, as his chaplain in all but name, on a trip to the Channel Islands.[19]

Heylyn's ecclesiastical contacts were initially on the moderate Calvinist side of the English church. He was confirmed by Bishop Arthur Lake at Wells Cathedral in 1622, and it was Lake's colleague and friend John Young, dean of Winchester, who helped to present the second edition of *Microcosmus* to King James at court in 1625, and then acted as intermediary when James took offence at a passage in it.[20] Indeed, it was Thomas Buckner – soon to be the Calvinist Abbot's chaplain – who (according to Vernon) persuaded Heylyn in 1624 that he should devote himself to theology.[21]

It would be misleading, however, to seek to typecast Heylyn's religion in his early life. For it is clear that religion was not his most obvious or immediate interest. His autobiographical notes, which he wrote up in the 1640s, do not even mention when he was ordained, but instead retell every occasion when he wrote poems and plays. In his forties he still recorded with pleasure the description of a local football match that he had written in the manner of the history of the destruction of Troy when he was ten years old, and described a series of other poems, songs, comedies and tragedies that he wrote as a student.[22] It was not unusual for budding clergymen to dabble as poets, from Joseph Hall and John Donne to lesser contemporaries of Heylyn such as Peter Hausted, Thomas Pestel, Barten Holyday and Jasper Mayne.[23] Students at university were of course required to develop their literary skills. Typical of a drab but worthy academic exercise is Heylyn's English translation of a recent Latin tribute to the founder of Magdalen College, William Waynflete, which Heylyn dedicated to Langton, the college's president.[24] However, Heylyn's other early poems could not be further removed in style and content from his memorial to Waynflete. There are poems of unrequited love, satirical verses describing events, parodies, memorial poems, doggerel, anagrams and chronograms, and a series of verses addressed to or written about college friends and characters. The most notable absence is devotional verse. Instead, Heylyn was most obviously drawn to satire, doubtless encouraged by college life, but also perhaps inspired by his elder brother's residence at the Inns of Court.[25] Targets for his satire were various. His satirical poems include a mock-heroic account of the behaviour of local people seized by false fears of a Spanish invasion as the local militia marched to Minster Lovell bridge.[26] Another mock-heroic poem presents a vision of the 'late Scullion' of Magdalen College, 'Sir' Kit Strunte, as a knight arrayed with kitchen utensils, doing battle in the fields of Germany in the Thirty Years War. Not surprisingly, Heylyn appears to have had a fascination with the story of Don Quixote, which had recently been translated into English and to which he frequently alludes.[27] He also seems to have been particularly drawn to the Roman satirist Martial. Martial finds his way into poems addressed to Heylyn's *alma mater*, to his friends, to his enemies, and even to Prince Charles. While he regularly quotes fragments of Martial in his other poems, Heylyn also tried his hand at translating some of Martial's epigrams himself, and headed unerringly for the most lewd and tasteless.[28] He would later comment on how 'our late Criticks' marked 'all the wanton and obscene Epigrams in Martial with a Hand or Asterism, to the intent that young Scholars when they read that Author, might be fore-warn'd to pass them over', and yet it was found 'that too many young fellows ... did ordinarily skip over the rest, and pitch on those which were so mark't and set out unto them'. Perhaps he had his younger self in mind.[29]

Heylyn's taste for satire infuses the account of France that he wrote in the mid-1620s, while as late as 1631 he wrote a satirical poem in mock praise of the 'Most Unapparrelled Poet of His Time', Henry Welby, in which he commented that the Roman Catholics would never have embarked upon the Spanish Armada and the Gunpowder Plot if they had known that Welby would write such atrocious verses about them.[30] If this playful satire is less evident in later writings, he nevertheless continued to indulge his interest in verse, although his topics became more sober and political. His last self-composed verses that survive are an elegy on the death of Laud in 1645, although he still inserts verses by others in works published in the 1650s. For all the notoriety of his polemical writings, it must always be remembered that Heylyn regarded himself as a literary writer. He admired and cited the work of Marston, Sidney, Spenser and Drayton in a manner that William Laud could never have done.[31] The flashes of biting satire and parody that are evident in his later controversial works are not simply expressions of hatred and derision but reflect an application of literary techniques that Heylyn was happily developing in his college years.

However, Heylyn's most obvious love in his early career, and the source of his early fame, was the discipline of geography. He worked on geography at different points throughout his life, returning to it in the 1650s. By contrast, he did not publish an overtly theological work until he was in his fifties. His geographical works typically looked to integrate politics and history with topographical description. His first work in this style was his *Microcosmus: a Little Description of the Great World*, first published in 1621 when he was only twenty-two years of age, and the opportunity for his first presentation at court.

One other notable feature of his early career – that seems significant, given his later activities – is early evidence of Heylyn's tendency to create acrimonious controversy and conflict. It is of course dangerous to assume a simple link between public and private life, to expect that a public controversialist was naturally argumentative and must have had a contentious domestic life. Nevertheless, a number of events in Heylyn's early life reveal a person who easily bore grudges and who acted upon them. Many of these clashes reflect the young Heylyn's sensitivity to issues of status. This was of course natural in a younger son, but events at Oxford seem to have intensified such concerns. A particular source of resentment was the fact that he initially entered the university as a 'batteler', meaning that he was essentially on the same level as servitors, carrying out menial tasks for fellows and 'higher grades of students'. Heylyn later insisted that his father had entered him under this status not on grounds of cost but because his elder brother as a commoner at Broadgates Hall 'had been suffered to take too much liberty', but nevertheless Heylyn was emphatic that this was 'very much to my discouragement when once I understood the difference'.[32] Heylyn's resentment over the battelership may also have done little to assist what was clearly a fragile family harmony – his father's will displays a clear anxiety that its contents might be challenged, and he requires his children 'to accept what I have given them without murmure or discontent. And to lyve and love together as brethren and sisters helpful to each other.' Whatever the other family divisions, however, Heylyn seems to have retained good relations with his elder brother Edward, who composed verses for both editions of his *Microcosmus*.[33] Edward's son would later be an important source of support for Heylyn in the years following the Civil War.

A year after the unfortunate affair of the battelership Heylyn went to Hart Hall as a commoner, and from there was chosen a demy at Magdalen College, but here too Heylyn's own autobiographical fragments note further tensions. The fact that he retained the office of 'Impositor of the Hall' for longer than before led to his being called 'the perpetuall Dictator' and 'occasioned a great deal of heart burning towards me, amongst the senior fellows also, which break out into whipping and other base usuage'.[34] It is notable too that Heylyn subscribed a petition (with fifty-three others) to the vice-chancellor (Prideaux) requesting that regent masters should not have to sit bareheaded in the Convocation House 'like boys'.[35] These examples show a particular sensitivity to issues of social status, combined, however, with a readiness to stand up for himself and to refrain from showing deference towards his superiors. His prickly and resentful manner may have prompted another potentially significant clash during his early years as a fellow of Magdalen College. In December 1622, in an event which ironically presages Heylyn's later assaults on the historian John Foxe (and may have added a certain personal piquancy to these attacks) Thomas Foxe, the grandson of the martyrologist, was deprived of commons for three days for 'verba contumeliosa et brigosa in mag. Heylin'.[36]

Especially notable, too, is the introductory preface to Heylyn's first work, the *Microcosmus*. It is not unusual for first authors to be concerned about hostile reviews, but Heylyn displays an extraordinary conviction that the book will be attacked by people whom he already knows. 'I expect hardest measure', he declares, 'where I am best knowne, even in this Universitie, among those, with whom I live and am conversant.' He sees no point in asking for kind acceptance of his book, as 'such as were borne with Criticismes in their mouthes . . . will be allwayes biting in spight of all entreaties'. He would never respect such people. Neither neglect nor contempt can stop their detractions – he wishes that a book nourishing for asses could be made for them. Heylyn removed this section, along with the rest of his preface, from the 1625 edition of the work, but his edgy and defensive aggression remained in his explanation to the reader that to ask for the reader's good opinion was 'a thing infinitly below me'.[37]

Just as significant, though, is the fact that none of these early conflicts seem to have been explicitly ideological. This forms an important contrast with William Laud, who similarly attracted hostility in his early career at university, but this was a hostility that tended to focus on his religious attitudes and expressed ideas.[38] What is clear, however, is that Heylyn was no simple lackey of those in authority. On the contrary, time and again he displayed a sense of embattled distrust towards those in immediate authority that must have given an added edge to his later behaviour, when figures such as John Prideaux and John Williams were involved.

HEYLYN'S IDEOLOGICAL POSITION, 1621–1625

Heylyn's *Microcosmus* of 1621 provides us with an early glimpse of what was (literally) his world view. Given his later Laudian career, it is notable in particular for his strident anti-Catholicism and attachment to the international Protestant cause. His anti-Catholic remarks are directed at familiar targets. The Spanish Inquisition is condemned as 'the greatest tyrannie, & severest kind of persecution under heaven' and the pope described as the Antichrist. Heylyn noted that the description of the Whore of Babylon sitting on the beast with seven heads could be understood only of Rome built on seven hills, and that Pope Joan could be called the Whore of Babylon 'both in a literall and mysticall sense'.[39]

If Heylyn's distaste for Roman Catholicism was conventional, so was his deep interest in the international Protestant cause. Overt advocacy of the desirability of English involvement in the war to defend the Protestant Rhineland Palatinate from the forces of Continental Catholicism was not encouraged at court in 1621. James disapproved of his son-in-law the Elector Palatine Frederick's acceptance of the throne of Bohemia, and looked instead for the resulting war to be resolved by diplomatic means. Heylyn therefore trod carefully in his *Microcosmus* when discussing the Rhenish Palatinate, declaring, 'I say nothing of the deplored estate of this countrey, holding it more fit for my prayers, than safe for my penne.' But his approving remarks that the Elector Frederick had received the crown of Bohemia because of his British marriage 'together with his manifold virtues and religious life' showed where his sympathies lay. Indeed, when his survey reached Bohemia, Heylyn ignored his earlier circumspection and spoke out more strongly. Noting verses which Frederick II had sent Pope Innocent IV that prophesied that a Frederick would defeat the pope, Heylyn reflected that these verses 'had sure some propheticall relation to the sacred person of this Fredericke, and that it may fall out accordingly I beseech the God of battles, and Lord of hosts, to blesse his Troopes with the trophies of victory, that hee may tread upon the necke of the Romish Adder, and outstare the Antichristian Basiliske, till his enemies are made his footstoole'.[40] Elsewhere he offered a surprisingly mild assessment of religious toleration in the Dutch Republic, 'for since all sorts spent their blood, lost their friends, and consumed their estate against the common enemy in warre, good reason they should enjoy the blessings of peace'.[41] When discussing Britain, it is notable that Heylyn's list of great English scholars contains Wyclif, 'who so valiantly withstood the Popish doctrine' and only two post-Reformation divines – John Jewel and the puritan Laurence Humphrey.[42]

All these aspects of Heylyn's viewpoint emerge even more fully and emphatically in the second edition of his *Microcosmus*, published in 1625. The condemnations of the forces of Roman Catholicism are more extended and strident. There is a much lengthier attack on the Spanish Inquisition, the section on the papal Antichrist is significantly expanded, and a new section on the Council of Trent (taken from Sarpi) provides a damning indictment.[43] Also, where the first edition had provided a straightforward account of the different orders of friars and nuns, the second edition provides a lively narrative of their sexual exploits.[44] Heylyn also stoutly defended the Protestant argument against Rome that sought the Protestants' antecedents not within the medieval church but among those sects that opposed it. He inserted in the 1625 edition a new section in which he provides a sustained and sympathetic account of the Albigensians as forerunners of the Protestants. He rejected all charges made against them, declaring emphatically that 'if now the papists aske mee, where was our Church before the time of Luther; I answer, that here it was: that here God was worshipped according to the manner by himself prescribed, and by the reformed Churches followed. Here, I say, were those few Israelites hidden, which had not bowed the knee unto Baal'.[45]

Heylyn's concerns with the fortunes of fellow Protestants abroad also receive much fuller expression in the second expanded edition. There is now a full and detailed section on the massacres suffered by the Huguenots in France. A large new section on the Dutch Revolt provides an emphatic defence of the actions of the Dutch. The tyranny of Alva forced the population into a defensive war which could not be construed as showing any natural Protestant tendency towards rebellion. On the contrary, 'this was a warre of State, not Religion; the most part of the Hollanders being Papists, at the time of their taking of Armes'. Queen Elizabeth had shown herself to be a true Defendress of the Faith by extending her protection to the Dutch, 'not disputing the right of the title, nor intending to her selfe any thing, save the honour of relieving her distressed neighbours'.[46] Heylyn also displayed added enthusiasm for aspects of the Swiss Reformation, adding a new section apparently approving iconoclasm in Berne, and supplementing his earlier praise of Zwingli with the claim that his heart was not burned in the fire with his body, but remained untouched by the fire (a claim which he would later rehearse for Cranmer).[47] His lack of antipathy towards moderate puritan figures was also demonstrated by his applause for William Fulke and Thomas Cartwright's 'learned confutation' of the Rhemish Testament, and in his amended list of England's worthiest divines: he now added the moderate puritans John Reynolds and William Whitaker to Jewel and Humphrey.[48] There was still no sign of Richard Hooker.

Heylyn's opinions were conventional ones for his time. While not overtly 'godly', they nevertheless displayed none of the divisive attitudes and re-servations of the new breed of 'avant-garde conformists' such as Lancelot Andrewes, John Buckeridge, William Laud or Richard Montagu. The conformist remarks that Heylyn did include in *Microcosmus* are relatively unremark-able. He defended the more orderly reformation of the Church of England and contrasted it with the disorder of the Continental Reformation. The Reformation, which God had stirred up Luther and others to perform, 'which in other countries received tumultuously, was here entertained with mature deliberation; the English bearing respect neither to Luther, Zwinglius, nor Calvin, but abolishing such things as were dissonant to Gods word retained such ceremonies as without offence the liberty of the Church might establish'. This Heylyn contrasted with the other Protestant churches which had abolished corrupted ceremonies altogether, although these had been allowed in the primitive church. These reflections were not proto-Laudian – indeed, they were borrowed from Joseph Hall.[49]

Where Heylyn may have been more unusual was in his readiness to support the Spanish match. This is evident not in the *Microcosmus* but in his poetry. He contributed verses to an Oxford volume applauding Charles's safe arrival in Spain in 1623.[50] This is, however, a curious volume. In contrast to the collection of verses published in *Epithalamia Oxoniensia* commemorat-ing Charles's marriage to Henrietta Maria in 1625, all of the poems in the 1623 collection appear anonymously. (It is only the survival of Heylyn's poem in manuscript which allows us to identify his contribution.) If the anonymity of the contributors reflected the contributors' mixed feelings about the match, nevertheless the publication of this volume, and of other pamphlets celebrating Charles's entertainment in Spain, suggests that his-torians may sometimes have overstated the amount of unified opposition to the Spanish match.[51] While Heylyn does not evince any pro-Spanish senti-ments in the pages of *Microcosmus* (and his outspoken support for the Palatine cause would have made this highly unlikely), nevertheless his readi-ness to at least go through the motions of approving the match are an early hint of his vehement insistence in his later works that the Spanish match was the correct policy, and the Spaniards were the natural allies of the English.[52]

Heylyn's enthusiastic comments about the Elector Frederick might perhaps have stirred feathers at the Jacobean court in 1621, but they appear not to have been noticed, and in 1625 such sentiments would have been more welcome as Charles and Buckingham had switched to vigorous advocacy of a war against the Habsburgs. The second edition of *Microcosmus* presents Heylyn as ready to play a more active role in affairs, and 'ready to give over these younger studies . . . for I gazed so long on the porch, that I had almost forgotten to go into the house'. In a new preface addressed to Charles, he presents the book, not as something for his 'recreative retirement', but as a gift to a man of action whose recent travels to Spain had made him 'the greatest and best accomplished traveller'.[53]

If Heylyn was hoping to make a greater impact at court with this new edition, however, his hopes were dashed when the book was presented to King James, who was doing his best to oppose the pro-Palatine war that his son and favourite were eagerly promoting.[54] However, James's concerns were prompted not by Heylyn's advocacy of the Palatine cause but by some incautious references to Edward III describing France as 'the more Famous Kingdom' and granting the French king precedence, which reportedly led James to order the book to be called in. Heylyn's anxious self-justification spared him this dishonour, but he must have felt discouraged from further efforts at courtly advancement for the moment.[55]

Perhaps in partial response to this setback, and to the unknowing role of the French in the debacle, Heylyn took a trip to France. Heylyn's written account of his visit to France circulated in manuscript, but he did not publish it until the 1650s, when pirated copies were being printed.[56] In his *Survey of France*, probably written in late 1625 after his return to England, Heylyn displays a vigorous and scoffing anti-Catholicism as he describes his encounters with French Catholicism. At Dieppe, he describes seeing 'the first Idolatry, which ever I yet saw, more then in my Books', although he blames it on the clergy, 'who will needs impose a new God upon the people'.[57] At Paris he witnessed 'their first superstitions', including the burning of lamps before the altar, which was 'meerly Heathenish'.[58] He mocks religious legends and miracles, encouraging his reader to laugh at 'such ridiculous stuffe', and gives a satirical description of the 'baptizing of Bells'.[59] The ceremonies of a high mass are 'very pretty and absurd', while the worshipping of 'rotten sticks' as portions of the true cross he derides as 'horrible blasphemy, and never heard but under Antichrist!'[60]

But while he found much to mock in the rituals of French Catholicism, Heylyn was not always critical. He praised a plague procession, expressing reservations only over the appeal for saintly intercession in one of the prayers, and carefully stressed that he would honour the relics of martyrs, as long as they were not worshipped.[61] He was also not immune to the beauties of the churches. Amiens Cathedral sent him into raptures. As he described the sumptuousness of its furnishings, the 'excellent Imagery', the gilded statues, the majestic ornaments, the 'richness and glory' of the church, he suggested that his reader 'perhaps will fall into the same extasie that I did'. But the verses that he wrote in praise of the church end with appropriate Protestant complaints: 'But oh good God! How long shall thy decree/Permit this Temple to Idolatrie?/How long shall they profane this Church, and make/Those sacred wals and pavements to partake/of their loud sins . . . ?'

But while Heylyn reserved the right to mock the Catholic rituals, he condemned those French Protestants who had attacked them directly. Throughout his account, Heylyn displays notable hostility towards the Huguenots. He attacks the 'zealous madnesse' with which they had defaced and ruined churches as 'worse than heathenish', and makes direct parallels with English puritan attacks on the cross. Noting the barbarity of the Huguenot attacks on churches, Heylyn declares that 'this I perswade my self had been the fate of most of our Churches, if that faction had got the upper hand on us'.[62] His accounts of Huguenot churches and worship are scathing. The 'foolish opposition' of their first Reformers to all forms of popery had left their churches bare and ragged: 'Painted glass in a Church window, is accounted for the flag and ensigne of Antichrist: and for Organs, no question but they are deemed to be the Devils bagpipes. Shew them a Surplice, and they cry out, a rag of the Whore of Babylon.' Their clergy receive no tithes, having judged them illegal 'in their Schismaticall tracts of Divinity', and are therefore reduced to receiving stipends from the laity, like the puritan lecturers in England.[63] As he turned to describe their form of church discipline, Heylyn seized on the opportunity to mock the institution of lay elders and their humble origins. The lay elders were 'a kind of Monster never heard of in the Scriptures, or first times of the Gospell. These men leap from the stall to the bench, and there partly sleeping and partly stroaking of their beards; enact laws of Government for the Church . . . to these very men, composed equally of ignorance and a trade, are the most weighty matters of the Church committed'. Taking off their aprons, they rushed to council, 'blurted out there a little Classicall non-sense, and passed their consents rather by nodding of their heads then any other sensible articulation, they hasten to their shops'. Again Heylyn warned of how 'the great zelots here in England' had raised great troubles in trying to implement the same system.[64]

For Heylyn, the Huguenots clearly represented the fate that lay in store for the English church if its rulers ever ceased their watch on the presbyterian puritans. It may be that some of the violence of his later attacks on puritanism, and his insistence on the radical agenda that it harboured, were partly prompted by memories of what he had seen and read of the Huguenots in France (although his polemical zeal hardly needed such encouragement).

When touching upon the Huguenots' struggle with the French crown, Heylyn place his sympathies entirely on the side of the French king. If they were obedient to the king, the Huguenots would be safe and receive toleration. It was too much good fortune and tolerance that had made them rebellious. The 'perverse and stubborn condition' of La Rochelle was provoking the king, and the Huguenots had brought ill will upon themselves: when noting the slaughter at Nègrepelisse Heylyn opined that 'the Protestants deserved affliction for their disobedience'.[65]

Heylyn's remarks on the Huguenots represented a reappraisal of his own position in the *Microcosmus*, which he himself acknowledges. Reflecting that King James should not have been censured for failing to aid the Huguenots in their struggle with the French king, Heylyn confessed 'that my self have too often condemned his remissenese in that cause, which upon better consideration I cannot tell how he should have dealt in'. After all, if James had leapt to the Huguenots' assistance King Louis could have supported a rebellion of James's Catholic subjects, while James's failure to provide succour to his own children in Bohemia would have made his actions inconsistent. Heylyn was not quite ready, however, to give James unreserved praise, or to jettison entirely his earlier attachment to the Protestant Cause. 'For . . . denial of his helping hand', he commented, 'I much doubt how far posterity will acquit him, though certainly he was a good Prince.'[66]

Heylyn's *Survey* may reveal the first stirrings in Heylyn's mind of a reappraisal of his world view that had otherwise reflected the anti-Catholicism and enthusiasm for the international Protestant cause that were conventional in this period. Heylyn could satirize forms of godly patriotism in his poems, and occasionally engage in standard anti-puritan gestures. His geographical works also lacked even the limited imperial vision that is evident in writers such as Samuel Purchas – when Heylyn discussed Virginia he offered a short, dispassionate account with no reference to hopes of imperial expansion.[67] Nevertheless, it is only his reflections on the Huguenots in his travel account of France that give any hint of the traits that would become prominent in Heylyn's writings during his Laudian period.

NEW DIRECTIONS AND OPPORTUNITIES, 1627–1632

The later 1620s were an important transitional period in Heylyn's life. He had chosen to favour theology over geography, and had been ordained by Bishop Howson in 1624. Howson was a noted anti-Calvinist, although we should probably not read anything into this event. Howson was the local bishop of Oxford, and there is no suggestion that Heylyn ever sought or gained his patronage.[68] Another significant event was his marriage on 23 October 1628 to Letitia Highgate (whose sister had married Heylyn's elder brother Edward, although that marriage was to prove an unhappy one).[69] This meant the effective end of his fellowship in Oxford, but he seems to have continued to receive his fellow's salary until 1630. He was later accused of having conducted a clandestine wedding so that he would not lose his fellowship.[70] Whatever the truth of the matter, it was only a matter of time before he would have to leave the college. The fact that (according to Vernon) Heylyn never received his wife's promised dowry also raised the need for him to find employment (although he was able to sell the advowson of Bradwell which his father had left him, and still received a rent charge paid out of the manor of Lechlade).[71] He therefore was primed to renew his search for powerful patrons, and perhaps to build on his uncertain start at the court.

Heylyn does not appear to have been someone who was zealously following the activities of the court. His autobiographical notes for the 1620s reveal instead an obsession with Oxford's internal politics, and especially the proctoral elections.[72] Nevertheless, it appears to have been the cat-fights of Oxford University that prompted his fateful alliance with an important rising figure at court. At the heart of this development was a very public clash between Heylyn and the Oxford vice-chancellor, John Prideaux.

Heylyn provides a detailed narrative of his confrontation with Prideaux. According to Heylyn's account, it was in the Schools on 24 April 1627 that Heylyn determined negatively the two theses 'An ecclesia unquam fuerit invisibilis?' and 'An ecclesia posit errare?' On church visibility, Heylyn claimed to have proved his thesis by the fact that the Church of England received no succession of doctrine or government from any of 'the scattered conventicles' of the medieval sects; that the followers of Wyclif as well as the other sects 'held many Heterodoxies in Religion, as different from the established doctrine of the Church of England, as any point which was maintained at that time in the Church of Rome'; and that learned writers in the Roman Church, including Bellarmine, 'have stood up as cordially and stoutly in maintenance of some fundamental Points of the Christian Faith against the Socinians, Anabaptists, Anti-Trinitarians, and other Hereticks of these last ages, as any of the Divines and other learned men of the Protestant Churches'. He ended with the inflammatory remark 'Utinam, quod ipse de Calvino sic semper errasset nobilissimus Cardinalis' (that is, as Bellarmine himself said of Calvin, would that the most noble cardinal had never erred otherwise than he does in this).[73]

This reportedly aroused the furious indignation of Prideaux, who called Heylyn 'Papicola, Bellarminianus, Pontificius' and complained to the younger part of his audience how unprofitable the pains that he had taken among them had been 'if Bellarmine, whom he laboured to decry for so many years, should now be honoured with the Title of Nobilissimus'. Prideaux was particularly angry, Heylyn explained, because in his 1624 Act lecture 'de visibilitate

Ecclesiae' Prideaux and other writers of that time had proved the visibility of the Protestant church (and therefore of the Church of England) 'no otherwise . . . then by looking for it into the scattered conventicles of the Berengarians in Italy, the Waldenses in France, the Wickliffists in England, & the Hussites in Bohemia'. Heylyn reported that he disliked this trend, as undermining the episcopal succession, and therefore 'rather chose to look for a continued visible Church in Asia, Aethiopia, Greece, Italy, yea, and in Rome itself, as also in all the Western Provinces then subject to the power of the popes thereof'. The following Monday, when Heylyn acted as opponent, Prideaux once again proclaimed Heylyn a papist in the public Schools.[74]

What should we make of Heylyn's account of these events? It seems unlikely that Prideaux was provoked simply by Heylyn's assertion of the visibility of the church in established churches rather than in the medieval sects. In fact, Prideaux's 1624 Act lecture on church visibility specifically offered all of Heylyn's suggested forms of church visibility, alongside that of the medieval sects, in answer to the Romanist demand 'Where was your church before Luther?' Prideaux had also been careful to defend the episcopal succession by arguing that the medieval separatist assemblies were under legitimate bishops and pastors.[75] It was Heylyn's view that was the exclusive one. In fact, almost the only example of an exclusively sectarian representation of the Protestants' descent in these years can be found in the discussion of the Albigensians in Heylyn's own *Microcosmus* – he had amplified this in his second edition (as we have seen), and the work was republished in 1627 in the very midst of Heylyn's dispute with Prideaux.

Heylyn therefore undoubtedly magnifies his theological difference with Prideaux. As well as misrepresenting Prideaux's position he may also over-state the audacity of his own arguments, so that they correspond more to his later stance on issues of church visibility. However, the manner in which Heylyn presented his theses may have been calculated to provoke Prideaux. It is still possible that Heylyn had directly implied in his address that he was oppos-ing the Act lecture that Prideaux had given just three years previously. There may have been another intended gibe at Prideaux, too. Heylyn's insistence that Romanists had opposed modern heresies just as well as Protestants had done was one that he regularly repeated in his subsequent works – it was clearly a favourite remark of his. It does not, however, seem to have sprung from any broader interest in Roman Catholic theology. Its use in this con-text mighty conceivably have been partly intended to mock Prideaux, whose Act lecture the previous summer had been concerned with condemning modern heretics in the form of the 'Hetheringtinianos' and others. Stephen Denison had publicly delivered a sermon at Paul's Cross condemning the heretic John Etherington just two months before Heylyn's performance at the Oxford Act, so it may well have been fresh in the minds of his Oxford audience.[76] The implication that Bellarmine had made a better job of refuting modern heresies than Prideaux had managed would easily have aroused the irascible vice-chancellor. Prideaux similarly hurled reproaches at Heylyn when he switched to acting as the prior opponent in the Act, so that Heylyn 'was branded for a Papist before he understood what Popery was'.[77]

It is not clear whether Heylyn was genuinely seeking to align himself with the new anti-Calvinist forces emerging in the country, or whether he had simply relished the opportunity to overstate his case in a polemical fashion in order to make an impact, and to goad the notoriously short-tempered Prideaux. It is possible that he had misjudged the hostility of Prideaux and his supporters. Nevertheless, even if the precise theological difference between Heylyn and Prideaux was small, Heylyn's provocative delivery and Prideaux's furious response, helped along by misunderstanding and considerable personal animosity, had generated a significant public confrontation. Moreover, the debate continued to simmer. Wood reports that several months later, in August, Edward Reynolds, preaching to the university in the chapel of Merton College, 'touched upon the passages which had happened between Prideaux and Heylyn, impertinently to his text, but pertinently enough to his purpose, which was to expose Heylin to disgrace and censure'.[78] Heylyn claims to have sought to defend himself the following November, when he gave his first sermon at court before the king. Here he followed what would become his preferred policy when being attacked for popery by preaching a strongly anti-Catholic sermon. By Heylyn's account, he did this so that Prideaux's charges of popery made against him in the Divinity Schools in April 'should not get footing in the Court before him'.[79]

It is likely that it was Danby rather than Laud who secured Heylyn's preaching opportunity at court. Nevertheless, Heylyn's clash with Prideaux gave him a perfect chance to bring himself to Laud's attention. Heylyn describes having gone to present his services to Laud, apparently for the first time, in February 1628, and claims that it was during this interview that they discussed his clash with Prideaux and Laud recalled his own more unambiguous conflict with Abbot over the succession of the English church during his time in Oxford.[80] It made sense for Heylyn to portray common ground with the rising prelate. The two shared a common enemy in Prideaux, and Laud may well have sympathized with a divine who, like him, had suffered the gibe of 'papist' in the Oxford Schools. It is not clear that Laud offered any immediate support. Heylyn, however, would pursue Laud's patronage determinedly in the following years.

His next opportunity arose when he was invited to accompany his patron, the earl of Danby, to the Channel Islands. Heylyn was ostensibly present on the trip as Danby's acting chaplain, and Danby's concern, as Governor of Guernsey, was to secure the defences of the islands in the face of the military threat from France. Guernsey enjoyed a distinctive form of religious government. Although its church was ostensibly part of the diocese of Winchester, it was run by a presbyterian hierarchy of church assemblies, with each parish having its own consistory (with minister, elders and deacons), supervised by an island colloquy, and above that a synod with the island of Jersey (although this had ceased to meet). King James had expressed a desire in 1613 that both Jersey and Guernsey should be made uniform in their church government with the rest of his kingdom, but this had been implemented only for the island of Jersey.[81] In as much as Danby had any concern with the religious situation in the islands, he strongly believed that it was best left well alone, for fear of stirring up discontent in such a militarily vulnerable area. Indeed, Danby later presented Laud with a series of arguments against the mooted policy of reducing Guernsey's form of government to the English model.[82] Heylyn, however, had plans of his own.

Heylyn seized on the opportunity to ignore the views of his supposed patron, and instead wrote a spine-chilling account of the puritan incursions into the church on Guernsey in order to gain Laud's support. The very lengthy position paper that he sent to Laud seems to have represented the first time that Heylyn had attempted to provide potential patrons with policy advice. In his later preface to the printed version of the work Heylyn made the candid confession that he had sent the account to Laud because 'I had then begun to apply my self to the Lord Bishop of London'. He aimed to let Laud see from the discourse 'that I was not altogether uncapable of managing such publick businesse, as he might afterwards think fit to entrust me with'.[83] Heylyn does not suggest that Laud had requested him to write the report, although Heylyn was appointed a royal chaplain extraordinary in February 1629 – immediately before his departure – and he may have used this opportunity at court to contact Laud. It is notable that at the very beginning of his account Heylyn sought to distance himself from Danby, assuring Laud that he was not Danby's chaplain, 'not otherwise relating to him then as to an honourable friend'.[84]

Heylyn's report was a detailed survey of the forms of civil and ecclesiastical government in the islands of Jersey and Guernsey, which (according to Heylyn) had fallen victim to the schemes of their Elizabethan governors to establish presbyterianism there, so that they could seize the spoil of the deaneries.[85] While James had initially allowed the islands to preserve their presbyterian discipline, he had in time reduced the island of Jersey back into conformity with the Church of England.[86] Heylyn now urged Laud to complete the job by bringing Guernsey under proper control. He attacked its non-episcopal ordinations: while he acknowledged that some churches beyond the seas had legitimately undergone non-episcopal ordination because they were compelled to do so owing to the lack of available bishops, the ministers of

Guernsey could claim no such necessity. Their continued use of ministerial ordination was simply because of their hatred of episcopacy, 'which', he instructed Laud, 'you are bound, if not to punish in them, yet to rectifie'.[87] Failure to do so would discourage the conformity of the ministers of Jersey, and would also run the risk of hardening the obstinacy of those remnants of the presbyterian party who remained in England, who could cite the tolerance of presbyterianism in Guernsey in order to justify themselves. After running through the practical advantages of such a policy, Heylyn felt sufficiently confident in his self-appointed role as adviser in these matters to take it upon himself to recommend individual clergymen who might be appointed to the revived office of dean. He also showed a precocious awareness of the danger of accusations of innovation. Laud should not fear such charges, he emphasized, as it was simply a matter of restoring a discipline, reviving the service of God which had been 'in a Lethargy' and making 'the Jerusalem of the English Empire, like a City which is at unity within it selfe'.[88] Clearly Heylyn was already primed on what would become a fatal Caroline policy of promoting greater unity between the constituent kingdoms of the Stuart monarchy.

Heylyn did not simply seek to provide Laud with the opportunity to defend episcopacy and the English liturgy in Guernsey. He also used the opportunity to warn the bishop of puritan activities in England, and to urge action there too. Heylyn tried to suggest that a number of religious practices and forms of religious organization in England represented stages in the establishment of presbyterianism, 'and may in time make entrance to the rest'. The first English phenomenon that he took aim at was puritan lectureships: 'their lecturers permitted in so many places, what are they, but the Doctors of Geneva? Save only that they are more factious and sustain a party.' The design of the lectureships, Heylyn averred, was to undermine the church's official holy days so that only the days of puritan preaching would be regarded as holy. He also saw sinister intent in those who collected money when such lecturers gave sermons: 'By whose authority stand the Church-wardens at the Temple doors (as I have seen it oft in London) to collect the bounty of the hearers[?]' They were appointed to do so, Heylyn claimed, by puritans who had noted that this duty was prescribed for deacons to perform in the presbyterian system. This view of lay parochial officials – whether church-wardens or vestrymen – as potential lay elders or deacons in disguise was to be frequently aired by Heylyn over the next decade.[89]

Heylyn also observed dangerous puritan activity in the neglect of the church's ordinary fasts and the use of independent fasts in their place. He deplored to Laud how widespread these were, 'a matter certainly worthy of your Lordships care, and of the care of those your Lordships partners in the Hierarchie: that as you suffer not these new inventions, to usurp upon our Churches by violence; so that they neither grow upon us, by cunning or connivence'.[90] Heylyn was clearly hoping to be able to advise Laud on puritan subversion in England as well as the Channel Islands. He concluded his discourse by assuring Laud that he would 'be happy, if in this, or in any other your Lordships counsels for the Churches peace, I may be worthy of imployment'.[91]

It is unclear how far this performance won Laud's attention and patronage. The fact that Heylyn was appointed a royal chaplain in ordinary in January of the following year may well suggest that he had already gained Laud's support. At his later trial, Laud insisted that Heylyn owed the chaplaincy 'under God to the memory of the earl of Danby, who took care of him in the University'. But during his trial Laud was anxiously seeking to dissociate himself from activists such as Heylyn, and may have been hiding behind the technical procedures of such appointments. His claim that Heylyn owed not just the royal chaplaincy to Danby, but also 'that which he got in that service' subsequently, is manifestly untrue, as we shall see.[92] Moreover, Vernon describes Heylyn going to thank Danby for the preferment but being informed by the earl 'that those thanks were not in the least due unto himself, but to the Lord Bishop of London, unto whose generous and active mind the whole of that Dignity was to be ascribed'.[93] This may, of course, reflect Heylyn's own retrospective determination to emphasize his closeness to Laud and to downplay his connection with Danby. The truth may lie somewhere in between – that Danby sought to promote Heylyn, but that Laud was the man whose support was decisive.

If Laud was not yet the prime mover in Heylyn's advancement, however, Heylyn now proceeded to make what would appear to have been his most audacious bid for Laud's support, and (apparently) his most determined break with his past. This was his assault on the puritan Feoffees for Impropriations. The feoffees were a trust established by leading puritans to buy impropriations, advowsons and leases of tithes, and to bestow them on godly ministers. Depending on one's perspective, this might be applauded as a voluntary organization which raised money through charitable donations to supplement the stipends and raise the quality of the church's ministry. Or it could as legitimately be perceived as an attempt by puritan laymen to assert their own control over clergymen and church appointments, to reward nonconformist ministers and to set up a church within the church.[94] The latter interpretation had not been made publicly, however, when on 11 July 1630 – Act Sunday, one of the chief dates in the academic year – Heylyn stepped into the pulpit of the University Church in Oxford, in front of 'that great concourse of People from all parts of the Country', to deliver a sermon on the parable of the tares.[95] This was one of Heylyn's favourite passages of scripture, to which he would frequently return, with a variety of objectives. On this occasion, his objective was to attack puritanism in general, and the Feoffees for Impropriations in particular.

In some respects, Heylyn's sermon offered a restatement of the comments that he had made in his report to Laud from Guernsey the previous year. There are the same complaints that the puritans' solemn fasts were kept while the church's own ordinary fasts were neglected, and that the planting of pensionary lecturers 'uppon daies of common labouer' aimed at supplanting the liturgy and disregarding holy days, so 'that so all pietie and opinion may be fastned, on their daies, & artes of preaching'. But this time Heylyn went further in elaborating the nationwide conspiracy that was only hinted at in his earlier report. He claimed that 'the faction' aimed at dispersing 'their doctrines' and 'have the fautors of their Sect in everie corner; readie for anie desperate service'. He compared them to the ancient heretical Apostolici, in having all things in common.[96]

Turning to the feoffees, Heylyn emphasized that the people entrusted with managing the business were 'most of them, the most active and the best affected men in the whole cause . . . chiefe Patrons of the faction'. The clergymen whom they preferred were 'most of them such as must be serviceable to their dangerous innovations'. They would soon end up with more preferments and dependencies than all the prelates in the kingdom. But Heylyn again saw this, not as the work of a small group, but as part of a nationwide conspiracy. He noted 'those constant conferences which they hold, at all publike meetings, & assemblies; here, at our sister universitie, at the great cittie, that their resorte from all the quarters of the land may be lesse suspected', their purpose being 'to receive intelligences, to communicate their counsailes, & confirme their partie'. The puritan faction had insinuated themselves 'into the bosoms of our gentrie and our Commons: and made themselves so strong a partie, that the maine counsailes of the state are crossed or carried by them; accordinge as they see it suitable to their occasions'. Attacking episcopacy and condemning any who opposed them as papists and time-servers, they thereby drew 'the greatest ministers of state, I will not saie the king himselfe, into discredit with the people'. Having completed his assault, Heylyn made the characteristic apology that perhaps he had said too much, 'more I am sure, then maie become a stander by'.[97]

If Heylyn's message is clear, it is less apparent precisely why he chose to deliver it at this time and in this way. Was it an independent move to attract Laud's support, or was Heylyn acting under Laud's instructions in giving the sermon? Heylyn certainly had every incentive to make a pitch for the bishop's patronage, as Laud had been appointed chancellor of the university less than three months earlier, and Heylyn may have lobbied for his candidature.[98] The feoffees were certainly a natural target for Laud, and he appears to have become aware of their existence in 1629. They are alluded to in a draft version of the 'Considerations for the Better Settling of the Church-Government' which he and Harsnet submitted to the king in 1629.[99] Nevertheless, there is no direct evidence to suggest that Laud specifically instructed Heylyn to make his assault. Given his usual eagerness to emphasize his closeness to the archbishop, it is unlikely that Heylyn would not have mentioned any direct encouragement from Laud in the matter if he had received any. It seems more plausible, given what we have seen of Heylyn's earlier manoeuvres, to present his sermon as a further bid to bring himself to Laud's attention by presenting another manifestation of puritan subversion. Heylyn's own later account of the sermon reports how 'some honest and well-meaning men' among his auditors pitied his misfortune 'in being put (as it was then generally, but falsly, thought) on that odious task by some higher power'. But, in the face of puritan threats, Heylyn sent a copy of the sermon to Laud 'and signified in a Letter therewith sent, that he [Heylyn] was both able and ready to make good his charge, whensoever it should be required'.[100] If Heylyn's account distorts events, it may be in the implication that he was disconcerted by the puritan response and sent a copy of the sermon to Laud only in self-defence. This may have been the ruse, but the version of the sermon that was sent to Laud was a presentation copy bound in vellum.[101] This surely suggests a deliberate plan on Heylyn's part.

It seems fairly clear that Heylyn regarded the sermon as a prime opportunity to bring himself to Laud's attention once more. But the attack upon the feoffees was not a random attack on an anonymous puritan target. On the contrary, they were an institution with which Heylyn had some personal acquaintance, although the precise details are difficult to substantiate fully. To begin with, one of the prominent members of the feoffees was his father's friend and kinsman Rowland Heylyn, with whom Peter must have had some direct dealings when carrying out the provisions of his father's will. Another possible contact may be the treasurer of the feoffees, the London grocer John Gearing. Heylyn's eldest sister (and Rowland's niece) was married to one John Gearing of Lechlade, and while this was clearly not the same man as the feoffee, it seems likely that they were related.[102]

A further intriguing and suggestive event is described by Heylyn in his autobiographical notes. Heylyn records that on 28 April 1628 he heard in London of a plot by the puritans of Lechlade to put the minister, William Phipps, out of his vicarage. Heylyn immediately warned Phipps of this 'for he came to Towne with me', and after a further discovery of a puritan plot against his life Phipps brought 'the principall Actors' into the court of Star Chamber. There is some evidence for Heylyn's account. The chance survival of a note listing cases to be heard in Star Chamber in 1628 shows that a number of people were charged by William Phipps with 'Confederacies, Conspiracies, bribing of witnesses ... and other Offences' although nothing more of the case has been unearthed. What is particularly striking is the identity of some of those being charged, whose names Heylyn suppressed in his own notes on the affair. The first name is 'Lady Elizabeth Lawrence widow' who was in fact Heylyn's aunt (being Robert Bathurst's second wife), whose grudges against Phipps may have included his having acted as a witness to Bathurst's revised will in 1623 that had been grudging in its attitude towards her and made no bequest at all to her son from her former marriage.[103] Two other people cited by Phipps were John Gearing and Simon Gearing.[104] Were these Heylyn's Lechlade relatives? Or were the John and Simon Gearing who were cited actually associated with the feoffees? It is notable that a Simon Gearing made annual donations to the feoffees in 1627 and 1628.[105] Certainly, it was later claimed against the feoffees that they had intrigued against ministers and plotted to evict them. They were formally accused of having conspired in particular to force out one John Burgen, the curate of St John Baptist in Cirencester (only a short distance from Lechlade).[106] Intriguingly, Heylyn later claimed that he first became aware of the feoffees because he travelled frequently to 'a Town in Gloucestershire' where the Feoffees had established a new lecture and filled it with a nonconformist minister. This was Cirencester, and Heylyn specified that it was 'Geering, one of the Citizen Feoffees' who was the man personally responsible for their activities there.[107] After their success in expelling Burgen, were the feoffees now seeking to control the impropriation of the neighbouring town of Lechlade?

Whatever the truth surrounding these rather murky events, it is clear that Heylyn knew for some time of the behaviour of the feoffees, and cannot have been unaware of the involvement of one or more of his relatives in the organization. His assault upon the feoffees in the sermon was therefore in part a burning of his boats with prosperous branches of his own family. He also appears to have played a role in the government proceedings against the feoffees that followed. He later asserted that he 'was commanded to deliver a particular of all such passages as he had observed in the carrying on of this design' to Attorney General Noy, who conducted the formal prosecution of the feoffees. The official accusations against the feoffees in 1633 include a number of points that follow those specifically made by Heylyn in his sermon.[108] This was to be one of many occasions on which Heylyn played a direct role in supplying information for attacks on the government's opponents, and it was not the only time that he worked in close co-operation with Noy.

While Heylyn's sermon is particularly famous for his attack upon the feoffees and their association with a nationwide puritan conspiracy, it is also notable for Heylyn's comments on other conforming clergy of the Church of England, and here in particular we can note a more exclusively Laudian note which distinguishes his work from the more standard forms of anti-puritanism. Part of the message of Heylyn's sermon was that the puritan threat had been dangerously neglected. While the church was threatened by both Rome and the puritans, the puritans were 'the more reserv'd and secret adversarie' who sought to capture the sovereignty of their country by undermining the church, 'by practising upon the people; by the pretence of libertie, the preservation of religion & the state'.[109] These puritan tares had been sown because of 'a general negligence; both in the Prelates & the people'. The cause of this neglect was not simple carelessness, however; Heylyn saw its root in an insidious 'popularity', whereby the ecclesiastical establishment indulged the puritan menace because of a desire not to provoke the opposition of the people. His remark 'that possiblie there cannot be a greater mischeife in the churche of God; then a popular Prelate' is underlined in the original manuscript, possibly by Laud himself (Heylyn would reproduce the phrase verbatim in his life of Laud, written some thirty years later).[110] Heylyn went on to complain that the clergy were willing to betray the church to the puritans 'yf by that meanes we may preserve our selves in love & safetie'. They were 'fearefull to give offence, loathe to take notice of these tares; which in the end (unlesse the Lorde prove gracious to us) will be the ruine of this churche'.[111] Similarly, he explained some of the errors in the late medieval church as the result, not of a corrupt and overweening clergy, but rather of a negligent episcopate who simply wanted to live quietly in the love and good opinion of their people.[112] This sense that many of the church's problems had been created by weak, 'popular' conformists became a common theme in Heylyn's writings, especially in the 1650s.

After Heylyn's sermon against the feoffees, it becomes more clear that Laud rather than Danby was now acting as Heylyn's patron. Just seven months after the sermon, it is especially noteworthy that it was Laud (rather than Danby) who presented Heylyn and his new book, *The Historie of St George*, to its dedicatee, King Charles, in his bedchamber at Whitehall Palace.[113] Heylyn's choice of topic also gave him an ideal opportunity to kowtow to the nobility. Heylyn distributed bound copies of the book 'to all such Knights of the Order [of the Garter] and men of eminencie as were about the Towne' – his later opponent Thomas Fuller jeeringly noted that each copy had 'a written letter prefixed to every one of them'.[114] It is not clear, however, that this helped Heylyn to win any noble patronage. On the contrary, the earl of Exeter (as Heylyn himself reported) 'snapped me up for a begging scholar which he was after much ashamed of, when it came to be knowne'. Youth and inexperience may partly explain Heylyn's poor treatment. His personal presentations may indeed have seemed the actions of a 'begging scholar' – the earl of Rutland insisted on Heylyn taking 'two twenty shilling peeces in Gold' for his pains, much to Heylyn's embarrassment.[115] If Heylyn conspicuously failed to win the patronage of the nobility, however, his book seems to have been more successful in winning the crucial backing of Laud and the king. Heylyn had clearly been targeting the king for some time. He had contributed three poems to *Britanniae Natalis* – Oxford's collection celebrating the birth of the future Charles II.[116] His *Historie of St George* was dedicated to the king, and its frontispiece was adorned with an engraving of the monarch. The Order of the Garter was an institution close to Charles's heart, and the book gave Heylyn an ideal opportunity to endear himself to the monarch. When he presented the book to the king, Heylyn reported that Charles 'held some conference with me about the Argument'. Later the same year, Heylyn moved quickly to present the king with a copy of verses celebrating Charles's recovery from smallpox, which the king read and sent to the queen. In them, Heylyn wrote obsequiously that 'in the closing of a good kings eyes/Not a man onely, but a nation dies/ . . . for 'tis no profanation,/To say, in him we live and are a nation'.[117] Two years later Heylyn had his new son christened Charles.[118]

The *Historie of St George* was in some ways Heylyn's most successful work. His controversial pamphlets may be better known, and secured his reputation as the regime's official polemicist, but it was probably the *Historie* that secured Charles's early patronage, and it was presumably Heylyn's role as semi-official historian of the Order of the Garter that led him to expect to be appointed to a prebendal stall at Windsor when one became available in 1633.[119] The *Historie* was undoubtedly a bid for secular patronage, and is a useful reminder that Heylyn's first writings for the court were not concerned with explicitly religious matters. Here he was the historian and geographer, rather than the religious controversialist. Nevertheless, his choice of topic led him to cross swords with Calvin and the puritan John Reynolds,[120] while his polemical requirements pushed him towards a remarkably positive reading of the English past.

Part of the logic of the *Historie* was the same as that of Mathew Parker's defence of the succession of the archbishops of Canterbury, and Francis Godwin's *Catalogue of the Bishops of England*.[121] Heylyn's basic task was to defend both the existence of St George (against those who claimed that he was fictional) and the church's high opinion of him (against those who claimed that he did exist but was an Arian heretic). This made it vital for him to emphasize the integrity of the church traditions that had commemorated him in the medieval period, and to downplay the suggestion that such devotions merely reflected the foolish superstitions of popery. A defence of the historical continuity of religious institutions thus necessarily required the author to play down implicit criticism of the forms of Roman Catholic religion, and potentially to be in a position of critical dissent from the activities of the early Reformation. The polemical agenda of the work obliged Heylyn to amass evidence of the high regard in which St George was held in the medieval church (in order to refute the claims of the puritan John Reynolds that George was an Arian).[122] But this required Heylyn to devote time to compiling stories of saintly apparitions, of devotion to relics and of churches and monasteries founded in George's honour – all to be glossed in as positive a manner as possible.[123] Thus the magnificent monasteries dedicated to St George reflected 'the fruitfull devotion of those times'.[124] He defended his extensive use of Roman Catholic liturgies with their prayers to St George. They could be relied upon for points of 'Historicall faith' without implying an approval of doctrines of saintly intercession, but instead offering proof that 'St George was constantly commemorated, and in his proper course, as a noble Martyr'. The existence of superstitious corruptions in the Roman liturgies was clear evidence that purer ceremonies must have existed earlier.[125] Heylyn did at various points seek to insert qualifications (such as his suggestion that Richard I's alleged vision of St George was a 'kingly fraud' to encourage the crusader troops), but he regularly had to defend the essential value of these particular forms of commemoration, even if they had later been abused.[126] His polemical purpose also created a framework in which the position argued by Protestant authors was inevitably that of the 'enemy'. Heylyn did of course do his best to exploit those Protestants whom he could cite in support of the existence of St George, and none did he use with more delight than John Foxe.[127] Yet the basic thrust of his work was the rejection of a host of English and Continental Protestant divines, from Reynolds, Calvin and Chemnitius to Perkins, Crakanthorp and Polanus.[128]

It was Heylyn's attacks upon Calvin and Reynolds that partly explain the hostility that greeted the work. Archbishop Abbot made it clear to Heylyn that he disliked the argument, while Wood reports that George Hakewill (a close ally of Heylyn's enemy John Prideaux) wrote a discourse attacking Heylyn's work. Hakewill's work was stopped before it reached the press by the Oxford vice-chancellor, who passed the work on to Laud, who in his turn notified Charles of it. The origins of the second edition of Heylyn's *Historie* lie in Charles's apparent instructions to him to work on a refutation of Hakewill's arguments, while expanding his study of the Garter records (in which Heylyn received the assistance of Matthew Wren).[129] If Heylyn was stung by these criticisms, there is no evidence that he felt the need to moderate his approach. On the contrary, in the second edition of the *Historie*, far from taking the opportunity to delete those sections that had aroused antipathy, Heylyn was actually more outspoken in his hostility to Reynolds, and in his determination to uphold the reputation of the *Golden Legend*'s author and of the Middle Ages in general.[130] He certainly felt less need to appease the supporters of Reynolds. A reference to Reynolds's 'so learned and celebrated worke' was pointedly changed to 'his so celebrated worke' in the second edition, and a further reference to Reynolds as 'this great and famous Scholler' is removed entirely.[131] He also dwelt much longer on the unfortunate reception in England of Calvin's erroneous view of the saint.[132] Hakewill's complaint that 'where he [Heylyn] hath occasion to speak of the Roman writers, especially the legendaries, he magnifies them more, and when he mentions our men he vilifies them more than he did in the first Edition' is entirely accurate.[133]

It is difficult to believe that Heylyn was not encouraged by Charles, Laud and others to maintain this combative stance – either by direct instruction or by perceived encouragement of these lines of argument. If gifts of his first edition to members of the Order had fallen flat, Heylyn's decision to present inscribed copies of the second edition to members of the episcopate perhaps reflected a broader shift in his preoccupations.[134] In his text, Heylyn had presented the honouring of St George as the work of an alliance of kings and prelates, knitting accounts of their actions together so that 'the devout performances of the Prelates, may be defended by the power and countenance of their Soveraigne Princes'.[135] This was precisely the alliance of church and monarch that Heylyn would champion in the ecclesiastical sphere.

A final publication which may have been intended by Heylyn for Charles's eyes, but was not explicitly presented in such a manner, was a curious work which he published anonymously in 1632, entitled *Augustus, or An Essay on those Meanes and Counsels, whereby the Commonwealth of Rome was altered, and reduced unto a Monarchy*. It provides an apparently dispassionate historical analysis of the strategies that Augustus deployed in destroying the Roman republic and establishing his imperial rule. There is an obvious temptation to see the work as a body of instruction to Charles as he embarked upon an absolute monarchy. Heylyn, however, claimed that the essay had been written 'long since' for his 'private satisfaction', and there is some reason to accept this suggestion that the work was a private essay written back in the 1620s. To begin with, it must be stressed that Heylyn does not offer a crude endorsement of Augustus's policies. He reflects that Sextus should have made the best use of his opportunity to kill Augustus, and notes that Augustus suffered himself to be ruled by his wife Livia and used a variety of women.[136] Some reflections also do not fit the attitudes that Heylyn expressed in the 1630s and beyond, thus he notes approvingly that Augustus allowed the people liberty of speech even though some pasquils were written against him, noting that libels are best ignored rather than stormed against.[137] Perhaps the playwright in Heylyn did approve of how Augustus kept people happy about the governmental changes by entertainments and stage plays.[138]

Nevertheless, there are some pieces of political observation that sit well with Heylyn's later expressed views. Thus he noted how Augustus removed all urban liberties, because the greatest and most populous cities are prone to faction and sedition. He also opined that many dangerous sort of men under pretence of 'Ancient Liberty' 'were apt to any bold attempt; and sodaine altera-tion'.[139] Such reflections seemed to give endorsement to Heylyn's other obser-vations: that Augustus did not refer all to Precedent, but more to Precept, that Augustus prescribed laws and orders to the commons in their *comitia* 'as himselfe listed', and that the emperor had resisted attempts to restore the old powers of the tribunes because they would have frustrated his hopes 'of altering the forme of Government'.[140] However, Heylyn's mixed conclusion to the work makes the balanced observation of Augustus that 'it had beene an ineffable benefit to the Commonwealth of Rome, if eyther he had never dyed, or never beene borne'.[141]

This was not a simple clarion call for absolutist government, then. But Heylyn's decision to publish the book at a time when Charles's personal rule was becoming established must surely have been prompted in part by the hope that some of his remarks would strike home. If observations of Augustus's absolutist style of government were not applied directly to cur-rent events, nevertheless the timing of the publication would seem to invite application to some aspects of Charles's personal rule. In this respect, Heylyn may have felt that the balanced and neutral tone of many of the observations – if indeed they dated from a time when he was not expecting a public, much less a royal, readership – served a useful purpose by not imply-ing that the author was simply urging absolutist policies upon the king. The decision to publish anonymously was another means of avoiding such charges. These were prudent considerations in the circumstances. Not only was there pressure for a new parliament to be called in 1631–32 in the wake of Gustavus Adolphus's military successes in Germany, but King Charles himself seemed anxious to avoid suggestions that he intended any novel changes in government. The earl of Clare had been proceeded against in the aftermath of the 1629 parliament for having in his possession a copy of a paper originally composed in 1614 which had urged the king 'to bridle the impertinency of Parliament' by undertaking a military *coup*, establishing garrisons in every town with mercenary troops and imposing new taxes solely on the authority of the crown. Sir Francis Kynaston and Sir Robert Filmer similarly seem to have been discouraged by the king from publishing their own vindications of more absolutist styles of government. Indeed, Laud stated at his trial that several absolutist tracts had been written but denied publication during the personal rule.[142] In this context, it may be significant that *Augustus* was licensed on 5 November 1631 by Laud's chaplain, William Haywood, just two days after Heylyn had been granted a prebendal stall at Westminster.[143] Was it perhaps Laud who advised Heylyn to publish the book anonymously?

If *Augustus* may in places have suggested that Heylyn was running ahead of his new patrons, his publications of the early 1630s nevertheless imply that

Heylyn was becoming familiar with what Charles and Laud wanted to hear. In the 1630s these were very valuable skills indeed, and Heylyn would come into his own.

NOTES

1 Samuel Clarke, *The Marrow of Ecclesiastical History* (1675); W. Haller, *The Rise of Puritanism* (1957), pp. 93–114; T. Webster, 'Writing to redundancy: approaches to spiritual journals and early modern spirituality', *HJ*, 39 (1996), pp. 35–56.

2 N. Tyacke, 'Archbishop Laud' in K. Fincham (ed.), *The early Stuart church* (Basingstoke, 1993); *idem*, 'Lancelot Andrewes and the myth of Anglicanism' in P. Lake and M. Questier (eds), *Conformity and orthodoxy in the English church, c. 1560–1660* (Woodbridge, 2000); 'The creation of Laudianism: a new approach' in T. Cogswell, R. Cust and P. Lake (eds), *Politics, Religion and Popularity* (Cambridge, 2002), p. 176.

3 I have argued more generally for seeing Laudianism partly as a process through which divines passed, or a 'moment' in which they participated, in my 'Creation of Laudianism' and 'The Laudian moment: conformist trajectories in early Stuart England' (forthcoming).

4 Vernon, pp. 3–4.

5 TNA, Prob. 11/140, fols 273r–276v.

6 R. H. Gretton, *The Burford Records* (Oxford, 1920), pp. 213, 325, 368–9, 403.

7 Vernon, pp. 4–5.

8 TNA, Prob. 11/142, fol. 407r–v; *PT*, sigs A2r–v, B3v.

9 *Memorial*, pp. xiii–xiv, xvii.

10 D. Underdown, *Revel, Riot and Rebellion* (1985), p. 46.

11 BL, Add. MS 46885A, fol. 2r–v; Underdown, *Revel*, pp. 75–6. In his poem the lovelorn Heylyn is the bowler, but manages to hit his beloved in the face with the ball.

12 *PT*, sig. B3v–B4r.

13 TNA, Prob. 11/140, fols 273r–276v. Henry had also acted as an overseer of the will of the vicar of Sherborne, Alexander Ready (Gretton, *Burford Records*, pp. 368–9).

14 Heylyn is noted as attending 1611–12: E. P. Hart (ed.), *Merchant Taylors' School Register, 1561–1934* (2 vols, 1936). I am very grateful to Andrew Hegarty for alerting me to Heylyn's attendance at Merchant Taylors', which is not mentioned by Heylyn himself in his diary, or by any of his seventeenth-century biographers.

15 B. Coulton, 'Thomas Hunt of Shrewsbury and Boreatton, 1599–1669', *Transactions of the Shropshire Archaeological and Historical Society*, 74 (1999), pp. 33–4.

16 *Memorial*, p. xii; *PT*, sig. B3v–B4r.

17 H. R. Trevor-Roper, *Archbishop Laud, 1573–1645* (2nd edn, 1962), p. 115.

18 Macray, *Register*, III, p. 151; *ODNB*.

19 BL, Add. MS 46885A, fols 20v–21r; *Memorial*, p. xvi; *ODNB*.

20 Vernon, pp. 14–24; Barnard, pp. 94–101.

21 Vernon, p. 15.

22 *Memorial*, pp. xi–xii, xii, xiv, xvi, xviii. It is important to note that the surviving manuscript of Heylyn's autobiographical notes may not be a full copy: it is Wood's notes 'Out of an account of Dr Heylins life, written by him self to Apr. 8 1645', which his son Henry Heylyn lent to him on 8 July 1673 (Bodl., Wood MS E.4, fol. 20r).

23 L. J. Mills, *Peter Hausted* (Bloomington IN, 1944).

24 *Memorial*; Magdalen College Oxford Archives, MS 224.

25 P. J. Finkelpearl, *John Marston of the Middle Temple* (Cambridge, 1969).

26 BL, Add. MS 46885A, fols 9v–10v; W. Braekman, 'Peter Heylyn's holograph collection of poems', *Studia Germanica Gardensia*, 13 (1971–72), pp. 140–3.

27 BL, Add. MS 46885A, fols 12r–13v. See also *EH*, ii. sig. A2v.

28 BL, Add. MS 46885A, fols 7r–v, 18v; Braekman, 'Collection', pp. 135–7; Magdalen College, Oxford, MS 224. A quotation from Martial even ends Heylyn's memorial to Waynflete.

29 *EH*, i. p. 94.

30 BL, Add. MS 46885A, fols 35v–36r.

31 *Microcosmus* (1625), pp. 394, 475; *HSG* (2nd edn), p. 303. Heylyn was invited to Drayton's funeral: *EH*, i. p. 69.

32 S. Porter, 'University and society' in *The History of the University of Oxford*, IV, *Seventeenth Century Oxford*, ed. N. Tyacke (Oxford, 1997), pp. 36–7, 53.

33 TNA, Prob. 11/140, fols 273r–276v; *Microcosmus* (1621), sigs ¶¶2v–3r; *Microcosmus* (1636), sig. ¶4r–v.

34 *Memorial*, pp. xiii–xiv; Bodl., Wood MS E.4, fol. 22r–v.

35 A. Wood, *History and Antiquities of the University of Oxford* (2 vols, Oxford, 1792–96), II, p. 337 (cf. p. 317).

36 Macray, *Register*, III, p. 143.

37 *Microcosmus* (1621), sigs ¶¶1v–2r; *Microcosmus* (1625 edn), sig. ¶3v.

38 *ODNB*.

39 *Microcosmus* (1621), pp. 51, 105.

40 *Ibid.*, pp. 154, 166.

41 *Ibid.*, p. 140.

42 *Ibid.*, p. 250.

43 *Microcosmus* (1636), pp. 51–2, 178–80, 297–8.

44 *Ibid.*, pp. 198–201.

45 *Ibid.*, pp. 112–13.

46 *Ibid.*, pp. 79–80, 250–4.

47 *Ibid.*, pp. 282, 284.

48 *Ibid.*, pp. 121, 471–2.

49 *Microcosmus* (1621), p. 249. The only overtly anti-puritan remarks occur in a brief passage where Heylyn wondered why presbyterianism was 'importunately desired' in England, and in a comparison of the alleged Japanese obsession with inverting Chinese customs with 'our factious Puritans' wilful opposition to all things used by Romanists (*ibid.*, pp. 249, 360).

50 *Votiva, sive ad Serenissimum . . . Iacobum . . . Regem . . . De auspicato . . . Caroli, Walliae Princeps, etc., In Regiam Hispaniam Adventu . . . Oxoniensium Gratulatio* (1623), p. 15; J. P. Hudson, 'Peter Heylyn's poetry notebook', *British Museum Quarterly*, 34 (1969–70). The only named piece is the 'Oratio Panegyrica' by John King.

51 I hope to document this in more detail elsewhere.

52 See below, chs 5 and 6.

53 *Microcosmus* (1636), sigs ¶2r–v, ¶3v.

54 T. Cogswell, *The Blessed Revolution* (Cambridge, 1989).

55 Vernon, pp. 18–24.

56 See below, ch. 5.

57 *Survey*, pp. 11–12.

58 *Ibid.*, pp. 93–5.

59 *Ibid.*, pp. 21–2, 54–6, 97–8, 175–6.

60 *Ibid.*, pp. 135–6, 138.

61 *Ibid.*, pp. 57–8, 100–2, 194–5.

62 *Ibid.*, pp. 136–7, 163.

63 *Ibid.*, pp. 242, 244.

64 *Ibid.*, pp. 242–4.

65 *Ibid.*, pp. 233, 234–9, 241–2.

66 *Ibid.*, pp. 240–1.

67 D. Armitage, *The Ideological Origins of the British Empire* (Cambridge, 2000), p. 85; *Microcosmus* (1621), p. 408; *Microcosmus* (1625), p. 792.

68 Barnard, p. 93; Vernon, pp. 15–16.

69 Edward Heylyn's will of 1640 includes a remarkable attack upon his wife, declaring that 'shee hath done me wrong. God forgive her. Joincture I intend her none: because shee hath so often disloyally forsaken me', although he admits that 'she hath bin traduced by rascalls' (TNA, Prob. 11/185, fol. 293r).

70 *CE*, pp. 136–8; *Memorial*, p. xx; Bodl., Wood MS E.4, fol. 26r–v. Heylyn's son-in-law firmly rejected what he saw as Vernon's attempts to defend Heylyn's claim that his marriage was not clandestine, without seeming to realize that Vernon was essentially summarizing Heylyn's own self-defence. Barnard emphasized that the fact that the marriage was clandestine was 'a general known Truth, believed by every one in the University, affirmed by all'. Neither the president nor the fellows knew that the marriage was taking place, and though they were invited to the wedding dinner 'they took the invitation to a merriment, and not to a Marriage'. The marriage was 'expresly against the Laws and Statutes of the Colledg-Founder; and much more for a married Fellow to keep his Fellowship after' (Barnard, pp. 17–21).

71 Vernon, p. 34. His college friend John Allibond, who conducted the marriage, duly became rector of Bradwell.

72 *Memorial*, pp. xviii–xix.

73 *EH*, ii. appendix, sigs P3v–P4r.

74 *Ibid.*; Barnard, pp. 105–9; Wood, *Ath. Ox.*, III, col. 553.

75 Prideaux, *Viginti-duae Lectiones*, i pp. 130, 136–9, 140, 142.

76 *Ibid.*, i. pp. 95–6; P. Lake, *The Boxmaker's Revenge* (Manchester, 2001), p. 2.

77 *EH*, ii. appendix, sig. P4r.

78 Wood, *Ath. Ox.*, III, col. 553.

79 *EH*, ii. appendix, sig. P4r.

80 *CA*, pp. 175–6.

81 D. M. Ogier, *Reformation and Society in Guernsey* (Woodbridge, 1996), pp. 87–157.

82 *CSPD Addend., 1625–1649*, p. 556 (printed in F. B. Tupper, *The Chronicles of Castle Cornet, Guernsey* (2nd edn, Guernsey, 1851), pp. 45–6). Danby argued that the Guernsey church's close association with the French Reformed church was a positive benefit, not only because they could provide succour to fleeing Huguenots but also because they could receive useful intelligence.

83 *Survey*, sig. a2r.

84 TNA, LC 5/132, pp. 87, 165, 166; *Survey*, p. 283. The college accounts, however, describe Heylyn as being granted six months' absence to serve as Danby's chaplain: Bloxam, *Register*, V, pp. 46–8.

85 *Survey*, pp. 325–6, 334–5.

86 *Ibid.*, pp. 379–411.

87 *Ibid.*, pp. 415–16.

88 *Ibid.*, pp. 417–22.

89 *Ibid.*, p. 376.

90 *Ibid.*, p. 377.

91 *Ibid.*, p. 422.

92 Laud, *Works*, IV, p. 294; K. Fincham, 'William Laud and the exercise of Caroline eccle-siastical patronage', *JEH*, 51 (2000), 69–93. At his trial Laud also stated that there was no proof presented that he promoted John Pocklington or even knew William Beale, but clear evidence exists that he preferred Pocklington, while Beale not only knew him but kept him secretly informed of the University of Cambridge's plans to oppose his rights of visitation: see A. Milton, 'The Laudians and the Church of Rome, *c.* 1625–1640' (unpublished Cambridge University PhD thesis, 1989), p. 7 n.

93 Vernon, p. 36.

94 On the feoffees see C. Hill, *Economic Problems of the Church* (Oxford, 1956), pp. 252–67; I. M. Calder, *Activities of the Puritan Faction of the Church of England, 1625–1633* (1957).

95 *CA*, p. 210.

96 Magdalen College Oxford Archives, MS 312, p. 38.

97 *Ibid.*, pp. 38–42. Compare this with Heylyn's comment after his extraordinary attack on King James in *Observations*: 'but I know not what temptation hath drawn this note from me' (p. 14). The charge that the feoffees had deliberately targeted market towns that were either very populous or had the power to elect MPs is not made in Heylyn's sermon, but appears later: *CA*, pp. 209–10; *EH*, i. p. 210.

98 Heylyn records in his diary being awoken in his chamber 'verie early' on 11 April 1630 by a fellow of St John's with the news of the death of the earl of Pembroke 'and that there was an hope of the Lord Bishop of London to be Chauncellour of the University etc' (Bodl., Wood MS E. 4, fol. 26v). Laud was elected the following day. Heylyn was too obscure a figure to have played any major role, but he makes the telling comment that 'Laud's friends not only in St Johns, but in other Colledges, so bestirred themselves, that before noon there was a Party strong enough to confer that honourable Office on him' (*CA*, p. 208). The group of academics who procured Laud's election included the master of Heylyn's college, Accepted Frewen (K. Fincham, 'Oxford and the early Stuart polity' in Tyacke, *Seventeenth Century Oxford*, p. 199). It is at least clear from Heylyn's account that it was assumed that he would be a supporter of Laud's, and his friendship with a fellow of Laud's ex-college of St John's is suggestive. I am grateful to Andrew Hegarty for reminding me of this passage in Heylyn's diary.

99 G. E. Gorman, 'A Laudian attempt to "tune the pulpit": Peter Heylyn and his sermon against the Feoffees for the purchase of Impropriations', *Journal of Religious History*, 8 (1974–75), pp. 336–8.

100 *CA*, p. 211.

101 Laud's copy of the sermon survives as Magdalen College Archives MS 312. See also W. Prynne, *Canterburies Doome* (1646), p. 386.

102 TNA, Prob. 11/140, fols 273r–276v; 11/278, fols 373–4.

103 TNA, SP 16/159/28; Prob. 11/142, fols 406v–407v. Elizabeth Lawrence was the widow of Sir John Lawrence and clearly preferred to use her earlier name (with its attached title). Bathurst refers to her in his will as 'Lady Elizabeth' and even 'Lady Laurance'. Among limited grants, he required her to provide surety to his executor for £100 within three days of his decease if she wished to purchase his household goods, and stipulated that if she refused to do this 'then shee shall not have nor inter-meddle with the said goodes'. Her son Henry Lawrence is merely noted in the will as owing Bathurst £300 – an amount which he is still required to repay in full, although the final instalment of £100 is to be given to his mother. The fact that the will is a revised one leads one to suspect that it reflects a recent decline in relations between Bathurst and his wife and stepson.

104 *Memorial*, p. xix; TNA, SP 16/159/28.

105 Calder, *Activities*, pp. 30–1.

106 *Ibid.*, pp. xix, 40, 55, 80–1. The attorney-general specifically used the word 'conspiracy' to describe this activity (p. 80).

107 *CA*, p. 210; *EH*, i. pp. 210–11; P. Seaver, *The Puritan Lectureships: the Politics of Religious Dissent, 1560–1662* (Stanford CA, 1970), pp. 88–9; Calder, *Activities*, pp. xv, xxi.

108 *CA*, p. 212; Gorman, 'Laudian attempt', pp. 348–9.

109 Magdalen College Oxford Archives, MS 312, pp. 24, 36–7.

110 *Ibid.*, p. 27; *CA*, p. 170.

111 Magdalen College Oxford Archives, MS 312, p. 41.

112 *Ibid.*, pp. 30–2.

113 *Memorial*, p. xx; Bodl., Wood MS E.4, fol. 26r.

114 *Memorial*, pp. xx–xxi; Bodl., Wood MS E.4, fols 26r–v; Thomas Fuller, *The Appeal of Injured Innocence* (1659), p. 28. Fuller claimed to have seen copies of these dedicatory letters in Heylyn's hand, in copies addressed to the earl of Lindsay and the earl of Danby. (He would have presumably been shown the latter by Danby's brother, the regicide Sir John Danvers, who was a patron of Fuller's.) Copies that still survive with Heylyn's written dedications include those given to the earl of Northumberland and to Prince Charles: see below, n.134.

115 *CE*, pp. 329–30.

116 *Britanniae Natalis* (1630), pp. 46–7.

117 *Memorial*, pp. xx–xxi; Bodl., Wood MS E.4, fols 26r, 27r; BL, Add. MS 46885A, fols 37v–38v.

118 Bodl., Wood MS E.4, fol. 27r. This surviving version of Heylyn's diary does not mention the birth of any of his other children.

119 *Memorial*, p. xxi. Heylyn's failure to gain the prebendal stall reflects the fact that he could not always count on Laud's support. The man appointed instead – Christopher

Potter – wrote to Laud in October 1633 thanking him for 'your last favourable medi-
ation to his Majesty in my behalfe, for a prebend in Windsor' (Prynne, *Canterburies
Doome*, p. 356).

120 See *HSG* (2nd edn), pp. 37, 41–2, 48, 52 and *passim*.

121 See Milton, *Catholic and Reformed*, pp. 284, 337 n.

122 *HSG* (2nd edn), pp. 41–2.

123 *Ibid.*, chs 5–8.

124 *Ibid.*, pp. 271–3.

125 *HSG* (1st edn), pp. 206–8.

126 *Ibid.*, pp. 288–94; (2nd edn), pp. 297–301.

127 E.g. *HSG* (2nd edn), pp. 163, 197–8.

128 *Ibid.*, pp. 39–43.

129 *Memorial*, p. xxi; Barnard, pp. 124–5; Wood, *Ath. Ox.*, III, cols 558–9; Bodl., Wood
MS E.4, fol. 26r–v; SUL, Hartlib MS 29/2/5v. Heylyn had attacked the comments
on St George that Hakewill made in his *Apologie of the Power and Providence of God*,
e.g. *HSG* (1st edn), pp. 50–2.

130 Thus a passage in the first edition condemning the 'Fabulous' period of the high Middle
Ages that 'delighted only in the miracles and apparitions of the Saints . . . the fruits
of superstitious fancies' (1st edn, pp. 151–6) was removed in the second edition (2nd
edn, pp. 12–13), where Heylyn inserted instead a sentence applauding the author of
the *Golden Legend* (2nd edn, p. 13). He also removed an attack on the *Golden Legend*
(1st edn, pp. 40–1) and inserted in its place an attack on Baronius (2nd edn, pp. 34–5).
An additional section (2nd edn, pp. 19–21) defended the idea of dragons.

131 Compare *HSG* (1st edn), p. 48, and *HSG* (2nd edn), p. 41.

132 *HSG* (2nd edn), ch. 3. Heylyn also includes a new section emphasizing the disagreement of Reynolds and Calvin, against the charge that he had sown a false division
'betweene bosome friends' (pp. 45–8).

133 William Sanderson, *Post-haste: a Reply to Peter (Doctor Heylin's) Appendix; to his
Treatise, intituled Respondet Petrus* (1658), p. 13. Hakewill dismissively added, 'but the
matter is not much, what he saith of the one, or of the other, the condition of the
man being such, as his word hardly passeth, either for commendation, or a slander'.

134 See the copy of the second edition inscribed to Bishop Corbet: BL, shelfmark
4825.c.24. Heylyn also kept some copies of the book in reserve, presenting a copy to
Prince Charles in June 1638: John Rylands Library, Manchester, shelfmark 20634.

135 *HSG* (1st edn), p. 260.

136 *Augustus*, pp. 49–50, 225–6.

137 *Ibid.*, pp. 147–9.

138 *Ibid.*, pp. 142–3.

139 *Ibid.*, pp. 153, 163–5.

140 *Ibid.*, pp. 141–3.

141 *Ibid.*, p. 227.

142 L. J. Reeve, *Charles I and the Road to Personal Rule* (Cambridge, 1989), pp. 158–62; P. R. Seddon (ed.), *Letters of John Holles, 1587–1637* (3 vols, Thoroton Society, 21, 25–6, 1975–86) I, pp. lxix–lxxi; Sir Robert Filmer, *Patriarcha and other Writings*, ed. J. P. Sommerville (Cambridge, 1991), p. viii; E. S. Cope, *Politics without Parliaments, 1629–1640* (1987), pp. 27–8; Laud, *Works*, III, p. 400.

143 TNA, SP 16/203/6.

Chapter 2

'Civill warres amongst the Clergy', 1632–1640

Writing to Sir Gervase Clifton in 1637, one of his correspondents remarked on the outbreak of what he called 'the civill warres amongst the Clergy, whose pennes are their pikes and so they fight dayly between the Table and the Altar, whose severall battayles are set forth in diverse books'.[1] Contemporaries were struck by the violence and acrimony of the religious pamphlet disputes of the 1630s. These were civil wars that pre-dated those of the laity in the 1640s, and were fought with pens rather than swords, but nevertheless they were exchanges whose content spilled over into the religious debates of the early years of the Long Parliament, and allowed battle lines to be drawn up at an early stage.

Heylyn was one of the most prominent soldiers in these civil wars. He was, indeed, a commissioned officer, and was to be found wherever the battle was hottest. The 1620s had seen him manoeuvre himself into the orbit of the court, and the outbreak of hostilities among the clergy finally gave him the opportunity to deploy his writing skills in defence of the regime. Verses that he addressed to Laud in November 1633 spelt out the danger from puritanism and assured the new archbishop of Heylyn's support. The poem concentrates on how Laud was libelled by 'Lewd scandals'. It has become 'a gainefull Art' to attack the church and its rulers, but the archbishop is assured that he will 'survive their Plots, & Prophecies' and the 'desperate malice' of those 'who yf words could kill/Would not have any left to crosse their will'.[2]

Heylyn's readiness to defend the Laudian reforms and to portray their opponents as dangerous extremists provoked hostile comment at the time. One diarist remarked scathingly that Heylyn was 'rather to be marked with a black coale, he careth not who fall so that he may rise, a busy braine'.[3] But if Heylyn was ready to bend his ideas and behaviour to support the regime in his search for advancement, he was certainly not alone. The same diarist commented in 1628 that many scholars were bending their studies towards Arminianism 'because that such are preferred'.[4] The list of clergymen who adapted their views to support the Laudian regime of the 1630s is a long one. Many clergymen who had attacked Arminianism in the 1620s became outspoken supporters of Laud's policies of the 'beauty of holiness' in the 1630s, including two of the British delegates who had attended the Synod of Dort (Walter Balcanquahall and Thomas Goad).[5] Few executed a more blatant *volte-face* than Heylyn's Oxford contemporary Humphrey Sydenham. Sydenham had violently attacked the new Arminians in a collection of sermons published in the 1620s, where Arminians were condemned as 'desperate cut-throats and enemies to the Truth'. But in a sermon in February 1626 he had complained pointedly that learned divines in the universities 'lie mouldring for non-employment, and dashed for slownesse of promotion'. By the 1630s he was dedicating a set of sermons to one of those 'Arminians', William Laud, in which he thanked Laud for his favours and encouragement, urged the archbishop to work harder to ensure 'a Generall Harmony . . . in the publike practice of our Church', earnestly praised the 'sacred sensualitie' of church music, and violently attacked puritan forms of piety.[6]

Heylyn's activities in support of the regime rapidly came to focus on its religious policies, but it should be noted that he did not initially embrace such a narrow remit. His *Historie of St George* and *Augustus* show that he was still commenting on broader issues in the early 1630s, and his first directed employment involved his amassing of evidence against William Prynne's notorious attack on stage plays, *Histriomastix*, which did not comment directly on religious policies at all. In the early 1630s he also appears to have developed close links with Attorney General Noy, with whom he worked in the prosecutions of Prynne and the Feoffees for Impropriations.[7] While Noy is known to have been an ally of Laud's, it is notable that Heylyn seems to have developed an independent relationship with Noy, and sometimes notified Laud of what Noy had revealed to him.[8] Indeed, Heylyn records having stayed with Noy over Whitsuntide in 1634, when the attorney-general showed him all the ship money precedents that he had accumulated in 'a great wooden Box' and a 'larg paper book . . . about the priviledges & jurisdiction of the Ecclesiasticall Courts'. Heylyn advised the ailing attorney to go to Alresford (where Heylyn now had a living) for his health, but after Noy's death a few months later, there is no evidence that Heylyn was able to develop any links with other ministers in Charles's government, and his fortunes and advancement henceforward became tied ever more exclusively to Charles's new archbishop, William Laud.[9] For all of his closeness to Laud, however, Heylyn never became his chaplain – a point to which we shall return.

Another point to which we will consistently return is that, while Heylyn is famous for the pamphlets that he wrote defending government policies in the 1630s, he did not actually perform the role of a print propagandist until

1635, when he had already received most of his rewards from the government, and had already launched systematic attacks on his and the regime's opponents. His time as a pamphleteer in support of the government would also only last a brief two years. This is not to say that he was not active as an apologist of the regime, and a diligent servant of its interests, for the entire decade. Rather, his role as a public polemical writer was only one of those he was called upon to fill. For Heylyn, government service amounted to much more than a handful of printed pamphlets.

HEYLYN UNLEASHED: ATTACKS ON OPPONENTS, 1631–1635

Heylyn's assaults on the church government of Guernsey and the Feoffees for Impropriations had already revealed his readiness to launch his own attacks on apparent enemies of the regime in order to secure his own advancement. His first direct employment by the regime would appear to have been, not as a historian or propagandist, but as an agent to intrigue against its perceived enemies. In many cases, these were tasks where Heylyn's personal and professional duties would appear to have happily coincided. As figures with whom he had already clashed came to be marked opponents of the regime, so Heylyn was diligently employed in mustering evidence against them. It is often unclear precisely when Heylyn was acting under orders, or how far he was playing on the regime's evident hostility towards these figures for his own benefit.

One early task which he was given was the amassing of evidence against Prynne's notorious attack on stage plays, *Histriomastix*. Vernon recounts that Heylyn was called to the council table on 27 January 1633 and commanded to read over *Histriomastix* and to collect 'all such passages, as were scandalous or dangerous to the King or the State'. Heylyn seized the opportunity with relish. Assigned a fortnight to complete the task, he completed it in less than four days, gave a copy of his papers to the attorney-general, and also wrote a small tract on the punishments due by law to offenders such as Prynne. It was Heylyn's collections that provided Council's case against Prynne at his trial.[10] Heylyn's basic task was to provide the most hostile possible gloss on Prynne's writing, and Prynne's conviction for sedition provided ample evidence of his success. If Prynne was indeed guilty of pursuing a more radical agenda, Heylyn's ability to identify that agenda can have been little more than a lucky guess. His collection against Prynne relied on seizing upon decontextualized passages in order to suggest that implicit attacks were being made upon the king. Prynne's noting the deaths of princes who loved stage plays, for example, showed that 'thoughe not in expresse tearmes, yet by examples and other implicite meanes, hee laboures to infuse an opinion into the people, that for acteinge or beinge spectatours of playes or maskes it is just and lawfull to laye violent handes upon kinges and princes'. Prynne later complained with some justice of how Heylyn had maliciously selected 'scattered fragments or dimidiated sentences' from the book, 'annexing such horrid, seditious, disloyall, false glosses, applicacions, construccions and inferences, as none but heads intoxicated with malice, disloyalty and private revenge could ever fancye'. He also claimed that Heylyn had 'reported to diverse that he had found high treason in it . . . and that he hoped he should have my life and head for it'.[11] If Prynne was right in claiming that there was a 'private revenge' motivating Heylyn on this occasion, it was presumably the fact that a brief passage in the *Histriomastix* had attacked his *Historie of St George*. The attorney's charge managed to mention this point early on as evidence that Prynne's book was 'nott onely scandalous to the whole State but alsoe most idle', leading a provoked Prynne to protest that Heylyn was guilty of worse treason 'in his Geography and S. George, as I could easily prove'.[12] But Heylyn would not have needed personal animosity in this case to spur him on in his eagerness to supply the worst possible gloss on the words of the regime's perceived opponent, and Prynne's complaint that Laud in particular had not read his works but had relied on Heylyn's extracts was probably true.[13] One minor oddity of the proceedings against Prynne of which Heylyn at least would have been conscious was the fact that one of the defendants in the case was his erstwhile friend Thomas Buckner. It was Buckner who had reportedly advised the young Heylyn to turn to theology in 1624, but it was Buckner who stood charged with licensing part of Prynne's book, for which Laud successfully urged his imprisonment.[14] As we have seen, this was not the only occasion when the tergiversations of Heylyn's career placed him in an antagonistic relationship with former friends and relatives.

'Private revenge' may have played more of a role in Heylyn's activities against another figure who had come to be identified as an enemy of the regime, John Williams, bishop of Lincoln and dean of Westminster. Heylyn had been appointed to a prebendal stall in Westminster as early as November 1631. This was presumably a reward for his *Historie of St George*. But the appointment is also quite likely to have been a deliberate attempt to plant an unscrupulous government agent at the heart of Dean Williams's power base in the capital (all the more necessary as Laud had vacated his own prebendal stall at Westminster in 1628 on becoming bishop of London). Dean Williams's relations with the crown had been deteriorating for some years. After being dismissed from his post as lord keeper in 1625 he had been accused of betraying privy council secrets in 1627 and a charge against him had been pending in Star Chamber since 1628, accompanied by attempts to force him to resign the deanery. The appointment of Heylyn was all the more apt a move on the king's part as Williams (in his capacity as bishop of Lincoln) had only just refused to institute Heylyn to the living of Hemingford Abbots in

Huntingdonshire, to which the king had sought to present him. The precise reasons behind Williams's actions are unclear, but it seems likely that this event marked the beginning of Heylyn's personal animosity towards the bishop, which complemented that felt by Charles and Laud themselves.[15]

Heylyn attended his first chapter meeting on 22 December 1631 and by July 1632 he was already offering information to the secretary of state, Sir John Coke, against Williams that he had wheedled out of the civil lawyer Dr William Spicer.[16] This first move against Williams involved a series of remarks that Spicer was alleged to have made in a conversation with Heylyn at his house in Westminster on 22 July 1632. According to Heylyn, Spicer reported a number of comments delivered in his hearing by Williams during and after dinner at Buckden around the 12th of the same month. Finding Spicer 'somewhat contractable in certaine propositions made unto him' (presumably in business concerning the library), Williams said to Spicer 'with greate scorne and laughter . . . that he would crosse him out of the Catalogue of his freinds as the king had crossed him (the saide Bishop) out of the list of his privie Counsell'.[17] Williams was also said to have remarked during the same meal 'that the Lords of the Starre-chamber could leape a statute when they pleased'. Potentially more incriminating, however, were the remarks made afterwards to Spicer by the bishop in private. Williams was alleged to have said:

> that howsoever he had had some troubles in the Courte, and that the king was made against him: yet he had made himselfe so strong, and stood so firmely that he did not care for any of them all. And as for those which had so made the king against him, they had donne the king none of the best offices: for should there come a parliament (which newes, saide he, yf thou hadst brought mee, thou hadst bene a wellcome man indeed) then should such things be called to an account, that both the king and they should have cause to repent of medling with him: or to that effect.

Here were prophetic words indeed, and ones which were not entirely implausible for Williams to have uttered. Heylyn sought to make the most of them. He gave a sworn account of Spicer's alleged words to Secretary Coke on the 26 July, stressing (as he put it) that Williams's reported speech included 'some passages which to mee did seeme to tend to the dishonour of his majestie, and to the preiudice of his affaires, yf time should serve'. 'Which', Heylyn added sanctimoniously, 'being a sworne servant of his majestie, I doe conceive all other obligations sett aside, that I am bound both by oathe & duetie to make knowne unto him'.

That Heylyn was acting alone, rather than in league with Spicer, is made apparent by the account which Spicer himself was then required to provide. Spicer went out of his way to minimize the damage. He admitted that Williams had said that the king had discharged him from the privy council, and that the lords of the Star Chamber leapt over statutes, but said that Williams had specified that he would call 'Sir John Lambe and others into question' if there were a parliament (with no word of the king). Moreover, where Heylyn had claimed that the speeches were made in a 'scornefull manner', Spicer averred that they 'were spoken in ordinary passage with a great deale of modestye as I then and yet conceived it without any taunting scoffing or repining etc'.[18] Spicer also failed to mention the alleged remarks about a parliament threatening the king when repeating Williams's words in the hearing of another of the prebendaries, Dr Lewis Wemyss, on the 25 July. Despite prompting by Heylyn, Spicer allegedly 'paused, and answered, that he durst not tell all the passages which were betweene them'.[19]

Spicer's coyness undoubtedly helped to ensure that these charges progressed no further. Nevertheless, Williams was left in little doubt of Heylyn's intentions. Williams had allegedly informed Spicer that he had told him things in private conference which he dared not repeat before Heylyn, 'nor held it safe for him [Spicer] so to doe'.[20] Williams can hardly have been surprised when he was confronted by a set of articles drawn up against him in the name of the prebendaries two years later, and can have had no doubts as to their true author. Williams's chaplain and later biographer, John Hacket, was certainly convinced that Heylyn was behind these charges, 'whom I have heard call'd General Wrangler, the Challenger that undertakes all Modern Writers, of as much ingenuity as Tertullian's Hermogenes, *Maledicere singulis officium bonae conscientiae judicat*'.[21] Certainly, it was Heylyn who provided a Latin translation of the articles, and who was chosen as advocate by the prebendaries at the hearing of the commission into the grievances. The thirty-six articles against Williams deal with a number of issues ranging from precedence and dress protocol to corruption and maladministration. Several of them seem to reflect Heylyn's characteristic preoccupations, and some of the contents seem to take us back to Heylyn's college days. There was the usual resentment of an ecclesiastical superior, and demands for more dignified treatment: it was complained that the prebends should be regarded by the dean as 'brethren' but that he 'hath manye tymes miscalled and vilified them to their discouragement & discredite', telling one that he was 'a sawcie fellowe', another that he was 'crackbrained', and so on. Heylyn would appear to have been the prebend who had allegedly read 'a short Remonstrance unto his Lordship in the Chapter', to be met with the response that he was 'a sawcie felowe to dare to tell him of his oathe'. Williams's response to the formal charge was to declare that 'the Deane might hold it a sawcie parte for a yonge man a Mr of Artes & a Prieist, to challenge his Deane . . . of periurye'. There were several complaints about diet and seating precedence. But there was also a charge that Willliams had undermined the authority and reputation of the abbey by secretly entering into a treaty with the town of Westminster to establish an incorporation.[22]

It was later reported that, after Heylyn had presented his speech concerning the prebendaries' right to sit in the 'great pew', after a long pause Williams made the brief but telling (and indeed prophetic) response: 'If your Lordships will hear that young fellow prate, he will presently persuade you that I am no Dean of Westminster.'[23] While the articles failed, Heylyn was not a loser thereby. Hacket's remark that 'every one of his Adversaries had a Recompence given them, like a Coral to rub their Gums, and make their Teeth come the faster' is not far from the truth.[24] Heylyn's teeth were certainly soon in action again. The crucial point is that when Heylyn and Williams crossed swords in pamphlet controversy, this was merely the latest stage of what was already a long-running campaign that had nothing to do with issues of religious policy *per se*.

A further example of Heylyn's ability to use the divisions of the 1630s to secure the humiliation of his opponents related to his old *bête noire* of the 1620s, John Prideaux. Prideaux had already been severely checked by the king (prompted by Laud) in 1631 at Woodstock for his apparent encouragement of anti-Arminian and anti-ceremonialist sermons by younger fellows who had flouted the vice-chancellor's jurisdiction,[25] and was thus a very obvious target for the increasingly ascendant and well connected Heylyn. A further crossing of swords was inevitable, and occurred in 1633, when Heylyn presented his theses for his DD. While it is the personal animosity of the two men that provides a crucial element in explaining their clash, it is nevertheless significant that Heylyn (just as in 1627) again managed to imply that their exchanges revealed Prideaux's religious heterodoxy.

Heylyn's three DD theses were all concerned with the authority of the church – maintaining that the church had authority in determining controversies of the faith, in interpreting scripture, and in determining rites and ceremonies – and again Prideaux and Heylyn were involved in hostile exchanges. The precise nature of these exchanges is unclear. It was afterwards charged against Prideaux that he had maintained that the church was 'mera chimera', that it could neither teach nor determine anything, and that all controversies were more appropriately referred to the universities than to the church, as the universities' schoolmen could determine all controversies better than the bishops. It was also charged that on the mentioning of 'the absolute decree' (of predestination) Prideaux 'brake into a great and long discourse, that his mouth was shut by authority, else he would maintain that truth contra omnes qui sunt in vivis, which fetched a great hum from the country ministers that were there'. In reply to these charges, Prideaux claimed to have approved Heylyn's theses, and that the positions he was charged with maintaining were 'impious and ridiculous' – they were merely 'oppositions, according to my place proposed for the further clearing of the truth to which the respondent was to give satisfaction'. In response to the particular charges, Prideaux argued that he had said that it was Heylyn who made the church 'mera chimera' by his answer, that Prideaux had argued only that the church in abstract did not teach or determine controversies, and that universities had fitter opportunities merely to discuss controversies and to prepare them for determination by ecclesiastical assemblies, which themselves enjoyed the superior authority. He had spoken about the absolute decree only because another respondent had commented upon it 'but bent, as I took it, against somewhat I have written in that behalf' so that Prideaux 'was put upon it to shew in what sense I took absolutum decretum'. Prideaux completed his defence with a protestation of his subscription to the doctrine and discipline of the Church of England, and a heartfelt plea that he be left in peace to continue his duties as regius professor and that 'my [academic] sons especially be not countenanced in my declining age to vilify and vex me'.[26]

These responses of Prideaux to the charges – which had been sent on to him by Laud at the specific command of the king – were delivered in the king's presence as, just as in 1631, Prideaux was summoned to appear before the king at Woodstock Manor to defend himself. Heylyn later claimed that he was not present at this hearing, from which Prideaux would appear to have emerged relatively unscathed. Subsequently a manuscript containing Prideaux's responses was drawn up with the title 'The Answer of D. Prideaux to the Information given in against him by D. Heylyn'. Heylyn claimed that Prideaux himself denied authorship of this account and 'commonly imputed it to one of Trinity Colledge, whom he conceived to have no good affections to him', although it was 'coppied out and disperst abroad by some of his own party and perswasions, to keep up the credit of the cause'. Heylyn complained that 'The Answer' gave a misleading account of the exchanges, most particularly in that it omitted some of the 'extravagant expressions' that Prideaux had used against him on the day. In essence, Prideaux presented the events so that he would appear as the moderate, and Heylyn the aggressive extremist (the charges against him, of course, had sought to present Prideaux as the dangerous opponent of the church and Heylyn as the upholder of orthodoxy).[27]

In a later self-defence Heylyn focused on another alleged aspect of their exchanges at the Act which was not raised in the initial charges against Prideaux. This was the claim that Prideaux had accused Heylyn of falsifying the Church of England's public doctrine concerning the text of Article 20, which Heylyn had quoted as declaring that the Church of England 'hath power to decree Rites or Ceremonies, and authority in Controversies of Faith'. Prideaux allegedly read out from a version of the Thirty-nine Articles to demonstrate that this sentence was not in the original article. Deducing that Prideaux was reading out the text from the 1612 Geneva edition of the *Harmony of Confessions* – which followed the Edwardian book of articles in omitting this sentence – Heylyn claimed that he had sent a friend (formerly his chamber fellow at Magdalen College) to get a copy of the Thirty-nine Articles from the bookshop. At this point Prideaux said that he was willing to drop the point and move on, but Heylyn (characteristically) insisted on freeing himself from calumny. He publicly read out the article from the newly purchased book, and then theatrically passed the book around the auditory. It was claimed that the provoked Prideaux had then delivered himself of a series of hostile remarks on Heylyn's theses.[28]

It is impossible to know precisely what transpired at the Act. Nevertheless, it does seem unlikely that Prideaux would have maintained the precise positions that he was accused of in the initial charges, except (as he maintained) as notional oppositions in the process of examination. However, not only was Prideaux a known opponent of Laudian policies, but he was also notoriously short-tempered on these occasions, and Heylyn was an old opponent who was plainly more than happy to provoke him. It seems more than likely that Prideaux levelled incautious accusations of his own, and he may well have used the 'extravagant expressions' and participated in the stand-off over Article 20 that Heylyn complained of. Certainly, in his self-defence Prideaux conspicuously failed to deny the charge that he had complained that his mouth was 'shut by authority' on the issue of predestination.

Whatever the truth of the precise events, this latest clash between Heylyn and Prideaux displays a number of notable features. Firstly, it was clearly a highly public event, and was manifestly perceived by those persons involved as a struggle between two sides. Heylyn had made sure that he had his supporters present, and those attending included the queen's almoner. A hearing of DD theses had turned into a public debate over the right of the church to change its rites and ceremonies, at precisely the time when the Laudian church was poised to bring in significant changes, and Heylyn had once again managed to imply that Prideaux was opposing the authority and doctrines of the church. Secondly (if Heylyn's report is accurate) the problem of identifying the true text of a foundation document of the Church of England's own reformation was raised in dramatic fashion, and the dangerous excesses of the Edwardian Reformation were identified. These were issues that would inform much of Heylyn's later writings. The fortunes of Prideaux and Heylyn in 1633 also reflect how far Heylyn had risen – on this occasion the browbeaten Prideaux found himself hauled before the king and required to respond to Heylyn's charges (although his apparent escape may reflect the degree to which Heylyn's position at court was not yet secure). Another significant feature is the degree to which these conflicts made use of a free-floating public sphere of manuscript publication – the different factions in Oxford were diligently circulating their own accounts of events, to each other's mutual disadvantage.

This was not, however, the end of the matter. Heylyn later claimed that the Book of Articles that was published the next year at Oxford in Latin still omitted the crucial section from Article 20 (having followed either the *Harmony* or perhaps a corrupt 1571 edition) 'to the great animation of the Puritan party, who then began afresh to call in question the Authority of the Church in the points aforesaid'. This was supposed to have been done on Prideaux's encouragement, with the result that he received a reprimand once again from Laud (acting as chancellor) and the printers were forced to reprint the book – or at least that part of it – according to 'the genuine and ancient Copies'.[29] Heylyn would seem to have continued to keep Prideaux in his sights for possible further attacks. In 1637 he may well have been responsible for a paper which found its way into the state papers collection, which provides a characteristically selective and misleading set of extracts from Prideaux's newly published collection of *Certaine Sermons*. Prideaux's attacks on atheism at court and sacrilege in the church are noted in one sermon (although without alluding to the fact that the sermon in question was preached in 1614), as is an assault on the 'stateliness' and arrogance of prelates whose aloof carriage provoked puritanism.[30] While the extracts may have been made with hostile intent, nevertheless the depiction of Prideaux as an implacable opponent of Laudian policies was not fanciful: it was reported in 1634 that 'Prideaux is writing a treatise proving the unlawfulness of cringing or bowing to the tables & says rather die than do it & that the martyrs die for far less matters'.[31]

Heylyn also found another cunning way of wreaking his revenge on Prideaux in the year following their confrontation at the Oxford Act, when he effectively recruited Prideaux into the defence of the newly reissued Book of Sports. Heylyn had noted that in a collection of Prideaux's lectures published in 1625 he had made a number of significant criticisms of aspects of puritan sabbatarianism. In the context of the 1630s these could be read as offering potential support to the government's anti-sabbatarian programme. Heylyn decided to publish his own anonymous translation of this lecture, with Prideaux's authorship proudly declared on the title page. This was a ruse that made sense only because Prideaux had so comprehensively undermined his position with Charles and Laud that he would reap no advantage from seeming to support government policy. In fact, the whole strategy presupposed Prideaux's popularity with the puritan 'cause' instead. If Prideaux's apparent espousal of the Book of Sports might lead his godly supporters to look more kindly on the government policy, then all was well. If, on the contrary, they were enraged by Prideaux's apparent betrayal, then this would serve the equally useful purpose of undermining Prideaux's role as a focus of opposition to the government of the church.

Just to make sure that there was no mistaking the pamphlet's intent, Heylyn appended his own extended preface to the work in which he spelt out how the lecture's author defended Sunday recreations. His gloss on Prideaux's position in the preface undoubtedly misrepresented his attitudes. Where Prideaux, having asserted that people were permitted recreations on Sundays 'to refresh our spirits, and nourish mutuall neighbourhood amongst us', emphasized the four properties of solemn festivals, those of 'Sanctitie, Rest from labour, Cheerefulnesse, and liberalitie', Heylyn's summary of his position emphasized cheerfulness to the exclusion of the other properties, and slipped in his own endorsement of wakes, dancing, shooting and wrestling.[32] Where Heylyn's preface hurled abuse at extreme puritan positions and stressed that such 'Judaizers' separated themselves 'from all that are called Christian', Prideaux stressed instead that he was concerned 'not so much . . . to abate their zeale, but (if it may be done) to direct it rather'.[33] Nevertheless, there was enough in Prideaux's text that corresponded to Heylyn's position – from his insistence that the fourth commandment pertained only by analogy to the Lord's day to his condemnation of 'Schismaticall Stoicisme' and 'the Sabbatarians of this Age, who by their Sabbath-speculations would bring all to Judaisme' – for Heylyn's strategem to work.[34]

The resulting pamphlet had a considerable impact, going into three impressions within a year. Prideaux's puritan supporters certainly found the work uncomfortable, although one noted that the preface was 'very dangerously written with a great shew of learning . . . & so cunningly'.[35] The puritan William Twisse wrote nervously that 'Dr Prideaux his Lecture was neither delivered (as I am perswaded) by word of mouth, nor afterwards set forth in print to strengthen so sharpe proceedings aganst the Ministers of God as now are in course'. He also complained of 'the immodest and unreasonable carriage of this Prefacer, who would obtrude the contrary opinion upon Doctor Prideaux, as it were, in despite of him; And indeed, it is thought that hee owed him a spight, and to pay that hee owed him, he came to this translation'.[36] Part of the interest in the pamphlet stemmed from the fact that it was in effect the first publication discussing the Book of Sports, and the opening salvo in the sabbatarian controversy.

A review of Heylyn's various attacks on the regime's opponents in the first half of the 1630s reveals a number of interesting features. Firstly, Heylyn was not a bullying henchman of the government firing his shots at the humble poor. On the contrary, Heylyn aimed his weapons most aggressively towards those who were in immediate authority over him. The resentful 'batteler' was finally exacting his revenge on those above him. This provides a useful reminder that Laudianism was not simply involved in upholding notions of hierarchy – its adherents could be just as active in assaulting figures of local authority. Secondly, not one of all these different attacks on the enemies of the regime up to 1635 took the form of printed propaganda. Rather, Heylyn worked by a combination of formal charges, petitions, reports and insinuations. These had been enough to win him considerable rewards. By 1633 he was already tipped for a prebendal stall at Windsor to add to the one he had received in 1631 at Westminster, and in 1633 he finally received the prosperous living that Charles had first promised him in 1631.[37] It was only in 1635, when Heylyn had already won his spurs from the government (and considerable rewards) that he began to compose the formal works of polemic in defence of government policies for which he is most remembered.

WRITING FOR THE GOVERNMENT, 1635–1637

The years 1635–37 witnessed an explosion of printed works discussing, opposing and defending the religious policies of Archbishop Laud. It is not entirely clear how far the government consciously orchestrated a propaganda drive in support of its policies, or how far it was simply happy to endorse the efforts of a series of divines who were keen to seek promotion by supporting the government's policies. There is a suggestive surge in the publication of visitation sermons in the years 1636–37 which concentrated on vindicating the government's policies and extolling the beauty of holiness.[38] The fact that the policies were generating opposition, partly in the form of manuscript and sometimes printed pamphlets, helped to give further justification for those clergymen venturing into print. There had been pamphlet controversies in the 1620s, with multiple attacks on Richard Montagu's *Appello Caesarem* and John Cosin's *Collection of Private Devotions* – although neither publication received sustained support from the government. There had also been a minor flurry of exchanges in the early 1630s over the works of Giles Widdowes, which had included heated debate over the practice of bowing at the name of Jesus. But it was only in the mid-1630s that the government's religious policies received both direct support from government polemicists and targeted opposition. As specific debates developed with puritan critics, so a number of authors sought to enter into the ranks of government apologists – most notably John Pocklington and Christopher Dow. But the pamphlets of Peter Heylyn occupied a special position in this body of literature. Heylyn had been serving as a government hit man against the regime's opponents for several years. When he entered the ranks of government propagandists, therefore, it was with the explicit support of the regime.

The first controversy to which Heylyn contributed was that surrounding the Book of Sports. The rigours of English sabbatarianism had prompted some pamphlet exchanges over the previous decade, most notably between Richard Byfield and Edward Brerewood, and also in the pamphlets of Thomas Broad. Prideaux's lecture had been expressive of a broader unease with some of the excesses of puritan sabbatarianism, a concern which was only intensified by the publication by Theophilus Brabourne in 1628 of his *Discourse upon the Sabbath Day*, followed by his *Defence of that most ancient and sacred Ordinance of Gods, the Sabbath Day* (1631), in both of which he presented the case for the continuing obligation on Christians to observe the Saturday sabbath. Brabourne's work would perhaps in other times simply have been passed over. However, it offered an easy target for those concerned by the Judaical extremes of puritan sabbatarianism. It was Francis White, bishop of Ely, who drew up a defence of the church's position which also provided a justification for Charles's recent reissuing of the Book of Sports, which permitted lawful recreation on a Sunday after the Prayer Book services had ended.

The Book of Sports prompted an outraged response from the godly, especially when ministers were required publicly to read it to their congregations. Opposition focused in particular on the insistence that people were still bound to obey the fourth commandment as a moral law, and to refrain from any recreation, work or other profanation of the Lord's Day sabbath. As Heylyn later explained, the authorities exercised deliberate and careful control over the publication of works supporting the government's policy. The plan was that White would cover 'the Argumentative and Scholasticall part', whereas Heylyn would cover 'the Practical and Historical' elements of the debate – with both books being completed by Michaelmas term 1635.[39] This plan meant that another author had to wait his turn. Christopher Dow had independently composed his own defence of the Book of Sports and submitted it for publication late in 1634, but had to wait for a year until White's book was complete, when his own book was finally entered and licensed for the press on 18 November 1635. White's *Treatise* was entered on 13 July 1635 and went through two editions in that year, and a further edition in 1636. Heylyn's own contribution was entered at the Stationers' on 12 September 1635, and licensed the following month. It seems to have been published very rapidly, as Heylyn was dispatching a copy of the second edition of the work to Sir Thomas Wentworth by 19 February 1636.[40]

Heylyn's work – the *History of the Sabbath* – was ostentatiously dedicated to the king. Heylyn specifically flagged the courtly origins of the work in his dedicatory epistle, where he explained to Charles that he had partly developed the work when preaching to the king at court, and 'in part, fashioned at those times, which by your Majesties leave, were borrowed from attendance on your sacred person'.[41]

For all its polemical intent, it is important to note that the *History of the Sabbath* was specifically presented by Heylyn as not being a work of controversy. In his preface he claimed that he wrote 'not out of any humour or desire of being in action, or that I love to have my hands in any of these publike quarrels, wherewith our peace hath beene disturbed'. Avoiding issues of argument and disputation, he instead simply sought to study the sabbath in 'the point of practice, which is matter of fact'. Heylyn's *History* therefore provides an account from Genesis onwards of when and how the Jewish sabbath was first observed, and then a discussion of the authority by which the Lord's Day was instituted and how it was observed from the early church up to the present day. Heylyn was still presenting himself as, in effect, the author of *Microcosmus* and the *Historie of St George*, rather than as a controversial theologian or polemicist. That being said, the *History* is of course a sustained piece of special pleading (a 'purposive history', in Kendall's phrase)[42] aimed particularly at the arguments of the puritan Nicholas Bownde in his *Doctrine of the Sabbath* (1595) while vindicating the Book of Sports. Heylyn's essential argument ran that the sabbath was not kept before the time of Moses or engrafted in the law of nature; that the Jews never considered the sabbath commandment to be moral, natural and perpetual; that the Lord's Day was established by the church's authority without being based formally on the fourth commandment; and that the Lord's Day only very gradually came to be observed with any severity, and was never esteemed a sabbath day until recent puritan authors 'deserted the whole practice of the Christian Church . . . for the space of 1600 yeeres'.[43]

It has been common in recent years for historians to present Heylyn's work on the sabbath simply as a malicious distortion of the past. Certainly, he ignored considerable evidence for the use of the term 'sabbath' and the rigours of sabbatarian observance, not just in the medieval church but also in the post-Reformation Church of England.[44] Nevertheless, it seems clear that Heylyn's identification of a new puritan sabbatarianism in the 1590s was at least partly accurate. If writers before that time had generally accepted that the sabbath was 'partly moral and partly ceremonial', Bownde and later authors such as Gouge, Dod and Cleaver departed significantly from this position by arguing that the fourth commandment was 'in no part ceremoniall' but rather was entirely moral and of the Law of Nature.[45] Bownde may only have been intensifying existing trends in puritan sabbatarianism but his denial that the fourth commandment had any ceremonial component crossed an important boundary. Heylyn leapt to the other extreme by insisting that the sabbath law had no moral content whatsoever, and was wholly ceremonial. But his consistent concern would actually appear to have been to emphasize the equal importance of holy days, and of the church's right to institute them.[46]

Heylyn undoubtedly provided a seriously misleading account of previous sabbatarian practice in England. By disregarding earlier sabbatarianism, however, he was able to associate its emergence more exclusively with puritanism. The appearance of Bownde's interpretative shift at precisely the moment when the presbyterian movement was defeated thus enabled Heylyn to draw a direct connection, and to postulate a puritan strategy to regain the lost ground by cultivating sabbatarianism as a way of undermining the holy days (and hence the authority) of the church.[47] There is a sense that Heylyn had gone massively beyond his remit to defend sabbath recreations, and had created an enormously detailed but often severely distorted history of the past based on a deliberately polarized view of the issues in dispute. Nevertheless, in the process of building his polemical structure he had identified a novel puritan development.

Heylyn speedily issued a second edition of the *History*. This was not because the book had suffered any printed attacks, but because he wished to insert new material.[48] There was no alteration of the argument. On the contrary, it was intensified with the addition of new Edwardian and Elizabethan material (particularly their respective Injunctions) and also updated with more recent Oxford theses defending sabbath recreations. He also inserted new material on the allegedly lax observance of the sabbath in Scotland, which he claimed was based on information supplied 'by sundry natives of that Kingdome, of good faith and credit', and added (with some relish) the reports of the supposed recantations of the Saturday sabbatarians Traske and Brabourne.[49]

After the second edition of the *History* Heylyn made no further contribution to the sabbath controversy, although further books on the government's side emerged from John Pocklington, Robert Sanderson and Gilbert Ironside the following year, while Francis White took it upon himself to respond to the attacks in Henry Burton's *Lord's Day Sabbath Day*.[50] Heylyn's refraining from further writing on the sabbath did not, however, represent any reluctance on his part to tackle adversaries – indeed, he was already fully engaged elsewhere.

It was the altar controversy that saw Heylyn's most famous polemical interventions. The altar policy was one of the most controversial of the Laudian reforms. Moves to place the communion table altarwise at the east end of the church behind altar rails gathered momentum during the early 1630s, with Archbishop Neile imposing a railed altar on the northern province in 1633, to be followed by a number of bishops in the southern province, supported ultimately by a metropolitical order from Laud in 1635.[51] Such ceremonial innovations naturally aroused opposition, and that opposition increasingly found a useful store of polemical ammunition in a letter composed to the vicar of Grantham by John Williams as bishop of Lincoln back in 1627. Called upon to mediate in a conflict between vicar and alderman over the former's decision to place the communion table at the east end of the chancel (and his threat to build an altar of stone there), Williams claimed to have stayed up most of the night to produce a letter that proposed a solution.[52] Rather than the communion table being an altar fixed at the east end of the church, Williams resolved that the table should not be called an 'altar', should not stand 'along close by the wall' at any time, and that it should not be fixed in the higher part of the chancel, but (as the canons directed) should at the time of communion be moved to the place where the minister would be most conveniently heard by the congregation (presumably in the body of the church or chancel).[53]

Even if the origins of Williams's 'Letter to the Vicar of Grantham' were apparently contingent and pastoral, the letter soon assumed a more import-ant public role. The development of the altar policy by the Laudian bishops in the 1630s meant that Williams's 'Letter' assumed a new importance. The 'Letter' was reportedly discussed in the House of Commons (presumably in the debate in the 1629 session on Bishop Neile's innovations concerning the altar, in which the actions of the vicar of Grantham were mentioned). Allegedly Prideaux spoke publicly of the 'Letter' in reverential tones, and it was also fully discussed at the St Gregory's hearing in 1633, where the east-end altar policy was debated in the presence of the king.[54] Its fame resulted in the rapid spread of manuscript copies, although the 'Letter' itself was not printed. It was reportedly being used as an authority by opponents of railing in altars, and sold among Drury Lane booksellers in written copies. Heylyn later reported that it was Matthew Wren who first brought Williams's letter to the government's attention, although Vernon reports that it was John Towers, dean of Peterborough and prebendary of Westminster, who engaged Heylyn to answer Williams (although the king himself approved it). Given Laud's per-sonal animosity towards Williams, and Heylyn's readiness to be employed against his dean, it seems unlikely that Heylyn did not act with Laud's full knowledge and support.[55]

This was the first time that Heylyn had been involved in a public, printed pamphlet debate with another divine, and it is notable that initially he con-tinued to assume the more shadowy role that he had adopted in his earlier government services, typified by his role as the anonymous translator of Prideaux's sabbath lecture. His refutation of Williams's 'Letter' took the form of an anonymous supposed letter to a clergyman who was being required to move the altar to the east end but who had changed his mind about the lawfulness of doing so after reading Williams's 'Letter', 'though it be now exacted of you by your Ordinarie'.[56] The pamphlet – entitled *A Coale from the Altar* – takes the form of a debate with the 'Epistoler' about the actions of the vicar of Grantham in the 1620s, but is ultimately applied to vindicate what is now a national policy (as Heylyn flags at the beginning and end of the pamphlet). Heylyn's pamphlet was printed anonymously under the motto of 'a judicious and learned Divine'. Williams proved more than happy to continue with this shadow boxing. He published his reply – *The Holy Table Name and Thing* – anonymously, claiming to be merely 'a Minister in Lincolnshire' (although the book did bear Williams's imprimatur, in which he declared the book, written by 'some Minister of this Diocesse' to be 'most Orthodox in Doctrine, and consonant in Discipline, to the Church of England'). Heylyn finally revealed his own identity in his reply to *The Holy Table* – entitled *Antidotum Lincolniense* – which was published with the full panoply of authorial name and dedication to the king in 1637. Williams never identified his adversary in the *Holy Table*, although he ironically dubbed him 'Dr Coale' and pretended that he was responding to 'D. Coal, a judicious Divine of Q. Maries dayes', thereby mischievously implying that Heylyn was Henry Cole, the zealous Roman Catholic provost of Eton (and prebend of Westminster), who had preached before the burning of Thomas Cranmer.[57] Similarly, Heylyn never attacked Williams by name, even claiming of the 'Letter' that 'I am confident it can be none of his who is pretended for the author'.[58]

That being said, it would be naive to suggest, as one recent historian has done, that Heylyn 'really believed this', and was genuinely unaware that Williams was the author of both *Letter* and tract.[59] The true authorship of the works in the dispute seems to have been a fairly open secret. Heylyn's authorship of the *Coale* was public knowledge by September 1636 (almost a year before he openly acknowledged it in the *Antidotum*) and Williams was commonly said to have avowed his authorship of the 'Letter', while Laud was commenting as early as 5 April 1637 that 'the world says' (and he agreed) that Williams was the author of the *Holy Table*.[60] Both authors also dropped heavy hints that they knew each other's identity.[61] If Heylyn really did think that Williams's work was by the radical puritan John Cotton, then he was the only person in England who seemed to be under that impression. His readiness to level accusations against Williams on the basis of the least whisper of wrongdoing makes it simply implausible that Heylyn would not have sought to father the 'Letter' and subsequent treatise upon Williams. Rather, Heylyn was pursuing other polemical objectives. Ingenuously granting the anonymity of the tract allowed Heylyn to adopt a combative tone that would not otherwise have been appropriate for dealing with his ecclesiastical superior. It also permitted him to imply that Williams's views were so extreme that they *must* be those of a separatist. Heylyn could be confident that the public would not assume that Williams was therefore not the author (he was well understood everywhere already to be such), but that instead they would detect the apparently puritan potential in the position that Williams was adopting.

Adopting this polemical tactic made it possible for Heylyn to father the most unlikely political and religious radicalism on Williams's text. While his *Coale* directly stressed at several points that the author of the 'Letter' belonged to the popular puritan party,[62] the *Antidotum* made the supposed similarity of the works of the author of the *Holy Table* and those of the puritan firebrand Henry Burton its central framing device. Having provided a table at the beginning of the work comparing the two authors, and having accused Williams of swapping notes with Burton, Heylyn made constant scornful allusions to 'your deere disciples', 'your brethren', 'your holy brethren', 'the brethren of your partie', and 'your Partizans'.[63] The author was ready to go on the next ship to New England, to join 'your good friend I[ohn] C[otton]'.[64] The *Holy Table* itself had been carefully timed in its publication, 'calculated like a common Almanack . . . with an intent that it should generally serve for all the Puritanes of Great Brittain'.[65] Even Williams's reference to bishops as being of apostolical institution was seized upon as betraying malicious and radical intent: the failure to describe them as being *iure divino* revealed that Williams had 'a good mind to betray the cause' and was ready with 'your holy brethren' to get rid of bishops.[66] Every attempt was made to link religious radicalism with political radicalism. Williams's description of the *Coale* as a 'licensed libell' was thereby an attack on the lord treasurer and Star Chamber, who were responsible for the licensing process. 'How great a Royalist soever you pretend to be', Heylyn commented, 'you love the King well, but the Puritans better.'[67]

Such comments all served the broader policy of Laud towards his moderate, episcopalian opponents.[68] In the case of Prideaux, he was partly co-opted so that he would seem to speak in favour of the Book of Sports. But Williams's overt hostility and courting of popular support made co-option impossible, and in such cases efforts were directed instead towards marginalizing them. Rather than it being a work that offered a moderate critique of Laudian policy from the middle ground of English Protestantism (and from a bishop at that), it was therefore crucial for the *Holy Table* to be represented as a more radical publication, and thereby discredited.

In his turn, Williams sought to maintain his claim to the middle ground by depicting Heylyn himself as an anti-episcopalian radical. The *Coale* was, Williams claimed, 'but a libel against a Bishop', and he systematically threw Heylyn's arguments back at him. Heylyn's championing of the vicar of Grantham's actions against those of the bishop enabled Williams to compare Heylyn with John Cotton and Thomas Cartwright, and to accuse him directly of puritanism. He compared Heylyn's high-handedness to the writings of the presbyterian Cartwright, who 'from his Presse at Coventry, was wont to send abroad much of this stuff in Martin Marprelates dayes'.[69] The vicar of Grantham he shrugged off as being mentally unstable – another example of Williams's determination to use all the stock materials of conformist defenders of the *status quo* against dangerous radicals.[70] Just as Heylyn had used Williams's anonymity to brand him a radical puritan, so Williams returned the compliment.

Williams's chaplain, John Hacket, was the man who was ultimately caught out in these elaborate games. During a sermon given at his archidiaconal visitation of Bedfordshire in 1637, Hacket seized on the opportunity to con-demn the author of the *Coale from the Altar*, 'shewing how the Coale, in a most rancorous sort, and knowing the Author, yet had most despitefully and virulently abused the Bishop; as the Jesuites dealt with K. James his booke, which they pretended not to know in their Answeres'. In suggesting that the 'Letter' had been written by John Cotton, Heylyn had written 'quite against his own conscience'. If a presbyter publicly wrote against an episcopal act and inveighed against it, declared Hacket, he was guilty of puritanism, 'though it come forth cum licentiâ' (thereby repeating Williams's complaint). Hacket concluded in emphatic manner that he knew of a case in France where a man had shot his enemy with an arrow, but had claimed falsely that it was a hunting accident: 'he pretended he tooke him to bee a wolf but he suffred as a murderer'.[71]

It was Hacket, however, who was the one to suffer: he found himself berated for opposing royal policy on the information of a local clergyman, Jasper Fisher. On hearing the sermon, Fisher (who had recently fallen foul of Williams) hastily penned an account of it to another of the bishop's new enemies, John Pocklington (who had himself written against Williams on the altar con-troversy). Pocklington swiftly informed Laud, and Hacket was eventually driven to make a humble petition to the archbishop.[72] Hacket's treatment provides clear evidence that Heylyn was writing to official orders: an attack on Heylyn's anonymous work was construed as an attack on government policy. Laud himself made a point of attacking the *Holy Table* in his speech at the censure of the puritan 'martyrs' Burton, Bastwick and Prynne. While refraining from identifying the author, Laud stressed that 'in the judgment of many learned men, which have perused this book, the author is clearly conceived to want a great deal of that learning, to which he pretends'. His main concern, though, was to emphasize that Heylyn's detection of the author's radical intentions was correct. 'For my own part, I am fully of opinion', Laud declared, that 'this book was thrust now to the press, both to countenance these libellers [Burton, Bastwick and Prynne] and, as much as in him lay, to fire both Church and State'.[73] There could be no clearer official endorsement of the argument of Heylyn's *Antidotum Lincolniense*.[74]

Even in a period notorious for the venomous style of its polemic, Heylyn's exchanges with his dean exhibit remarkable reserves of vitriol. The fact that the two antagonists knew each others' identities all too well, and had already built up a substantial amount of personal animosity, surely helps to explain the bitterness of their exchanges. However, this was a battle which was not to be decided by the power of the pen, however poisonous its ink. Williams was apparently preparing a response to Heylyn's *Antidotum* when the Star Chamber case (appearing in the same month as the publication of the *Antidotum*) led to the seizure of all his books, leaving him unable to mount an effective reply.[75] Heylyn was not involved directly in the final Star Chamber prosecution of Williams for subornation of perjury, although he was doubtless an enthusiastic observer.[76] Williams's removal did, however, clear the way for Heylyn to play a more direct role in the running of the abbey.

As with the sabbatarian controversy, there were other defenders of the government's stance, most notably John Pocklington's *Altare Christianum* (a response to Williams's *Holy Table*, which went through two editions) and also works by Joseph Mede.[77] Again, the puritan replies for the moment had to circulate in manuscript, although the more audacious William Prynne dared to print his own *A Quench-coale* in 1637. Prynne takes aim at a number of writers in his work, but particularly directs himself at Heylyn. He admits that the *Coale from the Altar* is 'the maine Treatise I here encounter, which fires all these fortifications at once'. Heylyn had been too ashamed of the work to put his own name to it, 'though as impudent, as shamelesse, as active an instrument of mischiefe & as great an incendiary for his yeares as any living in our Church, if he on whom some have fathered it be the man'.[78]

The final polemical work that Heylyn produced appeared with no hidden allusions or disguised authorship, but with clear government approval. This was his *Briefe and Moderate Answer to the seditious and scandalous Challenges of Henry Burton*. Although it did not bear a dedication to the king or declare itself on the title page to be 'printed by authority', Heylyn nevertheless explained in his preface that he had been 'commanded by authority' to return an answer to Burton's two sermons entitled *For God and the King*. There had been a flood of pamphlets from Prynne, Bastwick and others, but Burton's work was targeted for refutation because it was 'the leading Libell, in respect of time . . . and that those which may have followed are but a re-petition of, and a dilating on those points which are there conteined'. The assump-tion was that if Burton were to be effectively answered 'the rest would perish of themselves'.[79] Nevertheless, Heylyn's book did where appropriate engage with charges made against the bishops in *Newes from Ipswich*. In essence the book was intended to serve as a wide-ranging response to the flurry of 'odious Pamphlets' that had appeared, attacking all different aspects of the Laudian programme.

As with his *History of the Sabbath*, the timing of the publication of Heylyn's *Briefe and Moderate Answer* was carefully controlled by the auth-orities. Heylyn's work had to wait for several months so that it could be pub-lished simultaneously with another work with which it was closely connected, Laud's *Speech at the Censure of Burton, Bastwick and Prynne*. Laud's speech in Star Chamber at the prosecution of the three puritan 'martyrs' offered a careful justification of his religious policies and a refutation of some of the charges made against him. It was observed at the time that Laud spoke for two hours 'out of a note booke prepared for that purpose against Burton's aunsweare' (although Laud's speech is more generally concerned with the charges made in *Newes from Ipswich*).[80] It is possible that Heylyn may have provided some of the materials for Laud's speech – particularly perhaps the discussion of the omission of part of Article 20, which on Heylyn's account he had already pursued in detail in his clash with Prideaux in 1633.[81] Heylyn's *Answer* and Laud's *Speech* were both entered in the Stationers' register on the very same day (that of the execution of the sentence against the three puritans), and one assumes that the two works were meant to be read in parallel – they appear to some extent to have divided up puritan charges and books between themselves, and Laud refers to Heylyn's book when explaining that Burton's book 'shall presently be answered . . . at large, to satisfy all well-minded people'.[82] Nevertheless, Heylyn's work is not only a great deal lengthier than Laud's printed speech, but also a great deal more intemperate in its expression.

As it was required to respond fully to Burton's work, Heylyn's *Answer* ranged widely through all aspects of the ecclesiastical policies of the 1630s and the range of controversial ceremonialist literature produced in the 1630s. As Burton had depicted a sinister popish plot behind all these phenomena, so Heylyn needed to exonerate all the policies and the individuals involved, from Laud and the diocesan bishops down to individual pamphleteers. He was also obliged to say much more about royal authority and state affairs than he had done in his other controversial works. Where Burton tried to distinguish attacks on ecclesiastical authority from attacks on royal authority, however, Heylyn insisted that the two were indivisible. Nevertheless, Heylyn did perpetrate some incautious turns of phrase regarding the king's powers which he seems to have tried to adjust between the printings of this edition.[83]

Whatever the similarities in their arguments, the difference in tone between Laud and Heylyn's works against the puritan 'martyrs' is striking and doubtless deliberate. Where Laud's speech is polished, dignified and restrained in the manner appropriate to a court of law, Heylyn's is witty, railing and deriding. Laud commented piously of his puritan opponents that 'it becomes not me to answer them with the like either levities or revilings', but he clearly felt that it became Heylyn (and perhaps this is what he thought Heylyns were for).[84] While Heylyn's response to Burton was not fuelled by the levels of personal animosity that were present in his pamphlets against Williams, Heylyn was nevertheless able to muster a striking level of satirical venom. His chosen method of attack was ridicule, and implied association with radical sectaries, and there were sufficient prophetical gestures in Burton's book to make his work easy for him. Thus he noted Burton's 'opinion of some extraordinary calling from above, the same perhaps that Hacket was possessed with in Queene Elizabeths reigne . . . and how know wee, but that in some of his spirituall raptures, he might faine an hope, that his dread name should be as famous in the stories of succeeding times, as Muntzers, or King John of Leidens'. When the pursuivants came to arrest Burton, 'Bold men, that durst lay hands upon a Prophet of such an extraordinary calling, who if his power had been according to his spirit, would have commanded fire from heaven, to have burnt them all, or sent them further off with a noli me tangere'.[85]

Heylyn's two most official works – the *Antidotum* and the *Briefe and Moderate Answer* – were thus published to seal the authorities' defeat and punishment of the authors concerned.[86] They both mark how 1637 was the year of Heylyn's greatest triumph. The official spokesman of government policy in two major works published by authority, he had also witnessed the final humiliation of his enemy Bishop Williams and the punishment and incarceration of his puritan opponents.

HEYLYN'S FORTUNES AND THE IMPACT OF HIS WORKS

Heylyn's extraordinary run of government-sponsored publications meant that he was now a prominent figure in the public eye. He had directly profited. Having received the prebendal stall in Westminster in 1631, he was further given the parsonage of Houghton in Durham (worth £400 p.a. by the 1680s) by the king in 1633.[87] This was presumably as a reward for his services against Prynne, Williams and the feoffees, but also the king had supposedly assured him in 1631 that he still owed him a living after his failure to be instituted to the living of Hemingford Abbots. As this promise pre-dated his actions against Prynne and Williams, we can assume that it was his *Historie of St George* that had initially prompted it. This did not mean, however, that the king was not appreciative of his other activities. A few hours after Heylyn had been given the parsonage of Houghton, Charles instructed him through Laud that he should exchange Houghton 'for some other Living nearer hand, and more for the convenience of his Chaplain, his Majesty conceiving that he might have frequent occasion to make use of his service, and therefore was unwilling that he should have any Preferment that was so far distant from his Court'.[88] Heylyn therefore exchanged it for the parsonage of Alresford in Hampshire (which was let for £350 p.a. in the 1640s). In addition, in the later 1630s the Westminster chapter (with Williams out of the way, and a royal commission in control) offered Heylyn the parsonage of Islip, which he exchanged for South Warnborough (just eight miles from Alresford). Building up a substantial library to support his writing, Heylyn appears subsequently to have divided his time between stays at Westminster and the court and his country rectory of Alresford. While not occupying any position of authority or added dignity in the church, Heylyn had nevertheless accumulated a very prosperous portfolio of livings. He would later comment that the ecclesiastical preferments that he had accumulated before the Civil War provided him with an income of more than £800 per annum – an enormous sum for a junior clergyman.[89]

This is not to imply that all was peaceful in Heylyn's domestic life. In fact, the self-righteous aggression and stubbornness that Heylyn displayed towards Bishop Williams was also evident when he dealt with other ecclesiastical superiors, such as his diocesan Walter Curll, bishop of Winchester, who struggled to deal with his junior colleague's peremptory demands in two letters 'by way of challeng' over his right to claim trees from the bishop's woods.[90] Heylyn was also involved in legal proceedings against the local man, Arthur Lipscombe, to whom he demised the glebe and tithes of the parsonage of Old Alresford.[91]

If Heylyn's books did not gain him the immediate favours that his other services before 1633 had secured, nevertheless it is clear that they had a remarkable impact on contemporaries. His translation of Prideaux's lecture and his *Coale from the Altar* both went through three editions in little more than a year, while his *Antidotum* and *History of the Sabbath* almost immediately went into second editions. It was reported in 1637 that his *Briefe and Moderate Answer* (and Laud's speech) 'doe sell apace' and that in his *Antidotum* 'Doctor Heylin hath so answered the Byshop of Lincolnes booke that it is held punishment ynough for his Lordships attempt on that subject'.[92] His books were read by Laudians doubtless anxious to find support for their policies, including William Juxon, as well as ministers of state such as Sir Francis Windebank.[93] His pamphlets were also read and annotated by the earl of Bedford, and his *History of the Sabbath* and *Coale* were purchased by the fifth earl of Huntingdon.[94] Hostile readers also acquired the books,[95] and a range of authors from James Ussher and George Hakewill to Richard Bernard, William Twisse, John Ley and Hamon L'Estrange committed responses to paper, if not yet to print.[96] Sir William Drake, that incorrigible observer of intellectual fashions analysed by Kevin Sharpe, was eagerly seeking Heylyn's acquaintance in the 1630s because he esteemed his historical scholarship but also (and revealingly) because he admired his 'seconding the humour of the time' in his *Historie of St George* and *History of the Sabbath*.[97]

Heylyn was clearly recognized as the spokesman of the Laudian movement. That is not to say, however, that some of those who supported Laudian policies of the 1630s did not have concerns that the arguments of Heylyn and other writers were going too far. Certainly, Joseph Mede voiced his concern that some of the books printed in defence of altars justified them on 'dangerous Grounds' and risked leading to idolatry, while John Cosin and Robert Sanderson expressed their dissent from the more extreme antisabbatarian positions being presented in the 1630s by the government's apologists (with Cosin attacking Heylyn directly).[98] Nor did the other polemical apologists for Laudianism in the 1630s always echo Heylyn's precise arguments. Richard Bernard correctly noted that Heylyn's arguments on the sabbath sometimes differed from those of Pocklington and Dow.[99] In fact, the explanations and defences of Laudian policies in the 1630s varied considerably from each other on points of detail and interpretation, and Heylyn was not able to create a single Laudian 'orthodoxy'.[100] Nevertheless, Heylyn was the only polemicist of the 1630s apart from Bishop Francis White who consistently published with the direct support of the authorities. Even when he seemed to go beyond what the authorities wished, therefore, he could be taken to predict the direction of policy. When Williams complained that no bishops commanded what Heylyn was arguing, he made the rueful addition that Heylyn's words were therefore a prophecy of what he intended to do when he became a bishop.[101]

CHANGING AGENDAS, 1637–1640

Heylyn published nothing further after the *Briefe and Moderate Answer* for four years. This public silence after the extraordinary avalanche of publications over the previous two years requires explanation – after all, the tumultuous events of these years surely invited more comment than those of the previous two.

There are a number of possible explanations for Heylyn's silence in these years. One relates to his health. Vernon records that Heylyn's whole family was afflicted around this time with 'a contagious Fever' that threatened Heylyn's life, leaving him much weakened afterwards, and then returned so violently a year later 'that all his Friends together with himself supposed him fallen into a deep Consumption'.[102] Heylyn also became engrossed at this time in a new project (begun in September 1638) of writing a history of the Church of England since the Reformation. This led him to make extensive use of Sir Robert Cotton's library, but also to conduct a thorough survey of the records of Convocation. A copy of the extracts that he made from the Convocation registers still survives, and reveals Heylyn's concern to trace Convocation's dealings from the very beginning of the Henrician period until well into Elizabeth's reign.[103] Heylyn's desire to highlight the role played by Convocation in the English Reformation was to become one of the features of his later writings, and his researches fed significantly into his perception of events in 1640 and after the Restoration, as we shall see.

Another straightforward reason for Heylyn's silence is the fact that he was evidently not being invited to write anything by the authorities. His *Antidotum* and *Briefe and Moderate Answer* had been 'commanded' responses, but the punishment of Burton, Bastwick and Prynne had put a temporary halt to puritan publications in England. The emerging crisis in

Scotland, on the other hand, was one which Charles seemed determined to solve in his own way. Despite the flood of Scottish pamphlets seeking to persuade the English of the justice of the Covenanters' cause, there seems to have been no attempt by the English authorities to recruit the pens that had been writing in support of English Laudianism.[104] The principal official response to the Covenanters came in the form of the king's formal answers and declarations, the most substantial of which was the folio volume entitled *A Large Declaration concerning the late Tumults in Scotland* (1640). This was ghost-written, not by Laud or Heylyn, but by Walter Balcanquahall, the Dort delegate and son of a Scots presbyterian exile, who had back in the 1620s been presenting himself as one whose advancement would gain credit among the government's opponents, and who in the 1630s had wanted his friends to consider him as someone maligned by Laud.[105] There was an obvious rationale to the use of a Scottish minister in this case. But it also reflected a broader policy change by Charles's ministers, who sought to co-opt a number of unimpeachably orthodox figures into the defence of the Scottish bishops and the condemnation of the Scottish rebellion. Thus the Calvinist bishop Thomas Morton's sermon against the rebellion was 'published by his Majesties speciall command' in 1639, and the Irish bishop Henry Leslie (who like Morton had been a vociferous opponent of Arminianism in the 1620s) wrote a *Full Confutation of the Covenant* – printed in the same year – which was also declared on its title page to be 'published by authority'.[106]

The central plank of the authorities' defence of bishops was supplied by Joseph Hall, in his tract *Episcopacie by Divine Right Asserted* (1640). This did not reflect the eclipse of the Laudian party – they were still very much in the dominant, as the 1640 convocation would show. Hall's defence of episcopacy in his treatise was in fact very strictly patrolled by Archbishop Laud, who stiffened the arguments and sharpened the language of Hall's proposed work. Laud insisted that Hall should emphasize that episcopacy was of divine rather than merely apostolical institution, that the presenting of episcopacy as a separate order was 'the very main of the cause', and that Hall should avoid the concession that presbyterianism could ever be of use where episcopacy could not be had. Hall himself admitted that he had 'put a drop or two of vinegar more into my ink in two several places' in order to meet Laud's wishes.[107]

This did not mean, of course, that the Laudians were silent during the Scottish crisis, and in unpublished court sermons they provided an aggressive response. Heylyn delivered a court sermon on 27 January 1639 which made pointed allusions to 'Covenants and Combinations against lawful government' and 'perverse resistance against [the] just Authority of your supreme Lord, as well in temporal matters as Ecclesiastical'. 'Some amongst us though not of us', Heylyn observed, 'have set on foot those Doctrines, and pursued those practises, which are become a scandal to our Reformation and further will dishonour it, and in time subvert it, if care and order be not taken to prevent the mischief.'[108] Heylyn thus primed his audience for the so-called First Bishops' War against the Scots. The failure of that campaign, which resulted in Charles being forced reluctantly to agree the Pacification of Berwick with the Scottish rebels, did not tame the Laudian voice of the chapel royal. Preaching before the king in September 1639, John Pocklington warned that a king could be 'too good to thinke any evill of his native Subjects', condemned the flattering speeches of obstinate and rebellious spirits who were 'able to poison whole kingdoms', and averred that 'religious Princes may conceive hopes, that there gracious endeavours to bring all there subiectes to agree in one set uniforme and right service of God will take effect in Godes good tyme, though they seeme, as farre asunder as North & South'.[109]

Neither of these sermons was published. Heylyn had never published any of his sermons delivered in the 1630s – it is notable that while many Laudian visitation sermons were published in the mid-1630s, one that Heylyn delivered in Winchester was not – and therefore it is not overly significant that this particular sermon remained unpublished.[110] Nevertheless, the dearth of printed Laudian responses to the Scottish events, and the new official recognition of Leslie, Morton and Balcanquahall, points to an obvious shift in government tactics, and for a time at least there was no obvious place for the provocative Heylyn. It was not (yet) that Heylyn was in disfavour, but clearly the preferred response to the Scots crisis was to parade the government's Calvinist credentials in order to wrong-foot their Scots opponents. Instead, Heylyn turned to other forms of scholarly service. Even when he was publishing his official pamphlets in the 1630s he had put together a private paper of advice for the bishop of Winchester, supplying him with historical precedents to support the official requirement that preachers' prayers before the sermon should be merely exhortatory.[111] Now he had other tasks to perform. According to Vernon, Heylyn was asked by Laud at this time to make a Latin translation of the Scottish prayer book, with the idea that this would accompany a printed 'Apology' that would vindicate Laud and Charles's policy. The plans for the 'Apology' would seem to have gone no further, however, although there remains among Laud's papers a manuscript tract which may well have been related to it. The tract is entitled 'A Brief Survey of the Times and Manner of Reformation in Religion of the Churches of England and Scotland, and of the Liturgy, Rites, Ceremonies, and Discipline therein used or controverted; and how far the Present agrees with the Former'.[112] A number of the points made in this tract correspond to those which Heylyn would make in his later writings. The Joseph of Arimathea story of England's conversion is endorsed, and the puritans are described as pursuing a policy of token conformity under King James while instilling in the people through lectureships a dislike of church government, liturgy and established doctrine. It is explained that the fruits of such 'Presbyterial Courses' were manifested in the libellous writings of Burton, Bastwick and Prynne, and the tract provides a chronological history of puritan opposition and a summary of their objections, together with a chronology of the emergence of the English liturgy. Nevertheless, the manuscript that survives does not appear to be in Heylyn's hand, and while its author clearly shared many of Heylyn's ideas (and may have been inspired partly by him) some of its sources and arguments do not correspond to Heylyn's other writings.[113]

Heylyn does appear to have assisted in providing materials for Laud's expanded second edition of his *Conference with Fisher* (printed in 1639), which the archbishop hoped would establish irrefutable evidence of his own Protestant loyalties. Wood reports that Heylyn wrote two short tracts in 1637 – 'A Discourse of the African Schism' and 'The Judgment of Writers on those Texts of Scripture on which the Jesuits found the Popedom and the Authority of the Roman Church' – to contribute materials for the relevant sections of Laud's work.[114] Such working practices further strengthen the case for assuming that Heylyn's *Briefe and Moderate Answer* provided some of the materials and arguments for Laud's *Speech at the Censure*, rather than the other way round.

If Heylyn was providing the archbishop with material for Laud's attempt to fend off accusations of popery, he was also active in mounting his own self-defence at this time in his court sermons. He had already used the court in 1627 to defend himself from Prideaux's charges of popery, and he later explained that by 1636 he had decided once more to use the court pulpit to proclaim his Protestant credentials. This was because 'hardly a libel' was published at the time 'in which I was not openly accused of Popery, or at the least of being an under-factor unto those who had the chief managing of that design'. If we accept the sermons which Heylyn later printed to be authentic in content and dates, then it seems clear that he attempted to disarm his enemies by offering them a traditional brand of Elizabethan or Jacobean anti-Catholicism, with its emphasis on the charge of idolatry, on the pope's identity as Antichrist and the descent of the 'true church' in the Middle Ages through a sequence of heretical sects.[115] These were all positions that he had opposed in his *Briefe and Moderate Answer*, published just the year before. While Heylyn hereby performed something of a *volte-face* in returning to the anti-Catholic themes of his early *Microcosmus*, his sermons nevertheless always retained an anti-puritan sting in their tail, which was usually slipped in towards the end of the sermon. Although the anti-puritan passages could be brief, they were often deadly. Thus in one sermon Heylyn demanded, 'when we behold men factiously bent to oppose the Church, seditiously inclined to disturb the State, disloyally resolved to resist the Sovereign ... may we not certainly affirm, that they have hearkened to the Doctrines of Knox and Cartwright, and their successors in the cause?'[116] Another sermon, delivered on 21 January 1638, managed to sneak in most of the text of Heylyn's 1630 sermon against the feoffees.[117]

Perhaps Heylyn's most outspokenly anti-puritan performance of these years was an extraordinary sermon that he delivered at the consecration of his friend John Towers as bishop of Peterborough at Lambeth Palace on 13 January 1639.[118] Consecration sermons typically presented models of the bishop either as a preaching pastor or as a custodian of order.[119] Heylyn's sermon is (unsurprisingly) in the latter category. But it stands out from other sermons of this type by its extraordinarily aggressive and defiant tone. Heylyn may have had to adjust some of the language of his court sermons in the changed circumstances of the late 1630s, but with a Laudian audience he was able to speak more freely. The sermon itself takes its text (Acts 20:30–1: 'Also of your own selves shall men arise speaking perverse things, to draw away Disciples after them; Watch therefore') as a warning of 'popular and seditious risings' against the civil magistrate and the church and of 'civill Warre'.[120] There are direct allusions to the Scottish uprising,[121] but Heylyn's principal concern is with England, and the chief danger to the church is seen as coming from within: 'the Church was never overcome but by the Church'. Heylyn does not merely mean to allude to ministers teaching false doctrine and gaining parties to themselves (although he can see that this can easily be observed) but to bishops. Heylyn returns to his favourite theme of the danger of 'popular prelates' who draw the people to them and are involved in uprisings. There are barely veiled allusions to the imprisoned Bishop Williams in the form of the early Christian heretic Novatus, who rebelled soon after he became a bishop and was the founder of the Cathari 'as they (in some respects) of our English Puritans'.[122] Heylyn's condemnation of lukewarm conformist fellow-travellers extends even to the translators of the King James Bible. He suggests that they substituted the word 'overseer' for 'bishop' in their translation of Acts 20:28 'because they were afraid to offend the people'.[123] Heylyn ends by warning bishops that they need to be on their guard, not just against wolves and heretics, but especially 'subtle practisers, and such as would fain rise in the Churches fall'.[124]

Even if he saved his most outspoken performances for other venues, Heylyn was certainly not retiring from the court. On the contrary, he combined his court sermons with attempts to cultivate the next royal generation. When Charles's son, the future Charles II, was instituted to the Order of the Garter Heylyn seized on the opportunity to ingratiate himself by presenting the young prince in June 1638 with a copy of the second edition of his *Historie of St George*. In a flattering written dedication Heylyn encouraged Prince Charles to read in the book the catalogue of heroic princes that had gone before him in the Order, and (significantly) 'the succession of those Prelates and other Officers, which have done service thereunto'. Suggesting that among all the great members of the Order the prince should choose to emulate his father, Heylyn signed himself 'your highness most obsequiously devoted'.[125]

Heylyn played his most prominent public roles in 1640. He was appointed a justice of the peace for Hampshire in February 1640,[126] and just two weeks before the Short Parliament began he preached a sermon on Passion Sunday in Westminster Abbey. The sermon is relatively emollient compared with his extraordinary consecration sermon of the previous year. He touches upon some familiar topics. He deplores the neglect of official fast days, where works of Christian humiliation were not just ignored 'but branded and defamed as superstitious, if not somewhat worse'.[127] He insists that the power of church government and correction is committed only to bishops, and that if it were extended to every minister it 'would doubtless prove the greatest tyranny, that ever the poor Church of Christ did suffer under', and notes from Andrewes (writing against du Moulin) that the title of 'pastor' first belonged only to bishops. He notes that while the bishop as a good shepherd should use his pipe more often than his staff 'yet the Sheep become unruly, and will not hear the Shepherds-pipe, pipe he never so sweetly; he must needs take his staffe in hand, there's no other remedy'. But Heylyn immediately (and uncharacteristically) cuts himself off, stressing 'I touch onely on these Controversies, and so passe them by'.[128] There is perhaps some irony when his text leads him to reflect that we should be ready to die for Christ 'when our spirituall necessities, and the extremities of his Church, shall so require . . . Thus must we be resolved, if ever, as God knows how soon, there should be occasion.'[129] But there is little sense that Heylyn was really seeing current events in these terms. His moderate tone may reflect a broader official desire to project a conciliatory mood at the dawn of the new parliament. But Heylyn's actions in the concurrent Convocation represented anything but a retreat from the Laudian agenda.

Heylyn played a major role in his first-ever Convocation, which accompanied the Short Parliament which met in April.[130] This convocation was in many ways Heylyn's finest hour and the apogee of the Laudian movement. He seems to have played a prominent part in three important aspects of the convocation, namely the decision to prolong the meeting after the parliament had been dissolved, the drafting of the canon on church ceremonies, and the drawing up of a standard set of visitation articles for the country.

Of these, the most controversial was the decision that Convocation should remain in session after the hasty dissolution of the Short Parliament. Heylyn later asserted that Convocation would have been dissolved too if it were not for how 'one of the Clergy' (clearly himself) acquainted Laud with an Elizabethan precedent of 1585 for raising a subsidy through Convocation without parliament, 'directing to the Records of Convocation where it was to be found'. This clearly drew on the research that Heylyn had recently been undertaking on the English Reformation, and was the precedent that was presented in justification of Convocation's subsequent actions.[131]

If Heylyn had acted as the official apologist for the regime in his printed works of polemic, Convocation witnessed him again acting as the figure chosen to defend and explain the Laudian ceremonies in person. When a committee of the Lower House of Convocation was appointed to draw up the canon on ceremonies (which would establish a number of the Laudian reforms, including the placing of the altar at the east end), Heylyn was deliberately placed last around the table 'of purpose that he might answer all such arguments, as had been brought against any of the points proposed, and were not answered to his hand'.[132] He also allegedly drew up a paper offering 'a mutual Conference by select Committees between the House of Commons and Lower House of Convocation' so that the clerical representatives could give satisfaction to the Commons on the disputed ceremonies (again, one assumes, with Heylyn providing the lead).[133] The king's commission confirming the canons that had been passed also closely follows the arguments that Heylyn had presented in the 1630s to defend the non-canonical ceremonies that were being reintroduced, and may reflect his direct influence. Specifically addressing the arguments that had been used against them, the commission argued that some of the recently disputed ceremonies had been used by some of the Reformers, but that they had not been imposed under Elizabeth because they were sufficiently widespread not to need legislation to enforce them, although they had subsequently been neglected as 'Foreign and unfitting usages' had crept in in their place. Most of them, however, had been retained in the chapel royal, and the commission argued (as Heylyn did against Williams) that attacks on ceremonies used in the chapel royal were actually aimed at Charles's royal person, implying that he was guilty of superstition.[134]

The drawing up of a single national set of episcopal visitation articles represented a further attempt to establish uniformity of church government with a pronounced Laudian slant. Heylyn later made it clear that it was he who raised with the prolocutor the need for 'one uniform body of Articles to be used in Visitations', and that he himself was then required to compile such a set 'in pursuit of his own project'. After some suggested changes, he read out his version to the house, where it was accepted, and also brought in a canon for requiring this book to be used in all parochial visitations, to ensure uniformity in the outward government of the church. Again, Heylyn's task was partly to provide a justification for what was proposed, in this case providing marginal references to every appropriate canon, rubric, law, injunction 'or other Authentick Evidence' which supported each article.[135] While supposedly simply a work of synthesis, Heylyn's choice of visitation articles in fact included many recent Laudian novelties, such as the insistence on confirmation before communion, the practice of confession, the railing in of the altar, and the requirement that the congregation should stand at the creed 'and other parts of divine service'.[136]

The Convocation of 1640 in a sense represented the final act in Heylyn's unofficial role as apologist for the Laudian regime. His pamphlet defences of the ceremonial innovations of the 1630s had become the approved form in which they were justified, and he had played a significant hand in drawing up the compulsory set of visitation articles that enshrined the new Laudian order. He also sat on the committees drafting other canons, and even drew up one canon himself, for the celebration of the king's accession day.[137] Most important of all, his historical researches had provided the justification for the fateful decision to continue the meeting of Convocation after the dissolution of the Short Parliament. The Convocation provides an important reminder that Heylyn was not simply a pamphleteer – in making proposals, tendering historical advice, drafting canons and papers, and in actively arguing his case in person, Heylyn was still exercising a decisive influence over the outward face of the Laudian church as late as the spring of 1640.

NOTES

1 Nottingham University Library, Clifton Correspondence MS 309. I am grateful to Julia Merritt for this reference.

2 BL, Add. MS 46885A, fol. 39v.

3 Bodl., MS Top. Oxon. C.378, p. 283. I am grateful to Ken Fincham for this reference.

4 *Ibid.*, p. 247.

5 Milton, 'Creation', p. 176; Walter Balcanquahall, *The Honour of Christian Churches* (1633); Bodl., Tanner MS 68, fol. 45; A. Milton, 'The Laudian moment: conformist trajectories in early Stuart England' (forthcoming).

6 Milton, 'Creation', p. 176; Humphrey Sydenham, *Five Sermons preached upon Several Occasions* (1627), pp. 37, 53–4, 64, 66, 67, 69, 154–5; *idem, Sermons upon Solemne Occasions* (1637), ep. ded., pp. 14–32, 269–70. Not all ministers found that they could attract Laud's support by appealing to his anti-puritanism. One minister who tried to deflect criticisms by claiming that his accusers were a company of puritans won only temporary remission: he claimed that Laud had initially promised him support, although Laud later condemned him (presumably having found that the charges were accurate): *Reports of Cases in the Courts of Star Chamber and High Commission*, ed. S. R. Gardiner (Camden Society, n.s., 39, 1886), p. 197.

7 For Heylyn's working with Noy over the prosecution of Prynne see D'Ewes, *Journal*, pp. 186–7.

8 *Memorial*, p. xxii.

9 *Observations*, pp. 121–2; *Memorial*, p. xxii; Bodl., Wood MS E.4, fol. 27v. Noy's book 'about the Ecclesiasticall Courts' was presumably related to the 'booke of Ecclesiastical Jurisdiction in favour of the Ecclesiastical part' which he is listed as borrowing from Sir Robert Cotton's library on 15 January 1631 (BL, Harl. MS 6018, fol. 179v). Vernon dates the beginning of Heylyn and Noy's friendship to the day upon which Heylyn had the prebendal stall at Westminster bestowed upon him by the king (presumably it was Noy who conveyed this message to him): Vernon, p. 42.

10 Vernon, pp. 50–1. The paper which Heylyn prepared for Noy survives as TNA, SP 16/534/71, a notebook entitled 'The Passages against the King and State in Historiomastix. Such also as occurre against the Church & Clergie in the same Author'. See also Heylyn's description of this paper, and his insistence on its centrality to the case against Prynne, in *CA*, p. 230. The surviving copy does not include the section of passages 'against Church & Clergie', which Noy explained at the trial was 'lefte outt of the Information' (S. R. Gardiner (ed.), *Documents relating to Proceedings against Willliam Prynne in 1634 and 1637* (Camden Society, n.s., 18, 1877), p. 2). However, the surviving copy of 'Passages against the King and State' also includes a collection of 'Tytles of Honour bestowed by Mr Prynne upon the Puritans their Innocency, Loyaltie and Pietie' (fols 133v–134r) which were likewise omitted from the formal charge but which Noy could not resist alluding to.

11 Gardiner, *Documents*, pp. 13, 32, 43. For the list of errors accumulated by Heylyn see pp. 3–13.

12 William Prynne, *Histrio-mastix* (1633), pp. 671–9; Gardiner, *Documents*, pp. 3, 43.

13 Gardiner, *Documents*, pp. 32, 36–7, 43.

14 Vernon, p. 15; Gardiner, *Documents*, pp. 15, 17, 21, 23, 26; Laud, *Works*, VI, p. 234.

15 Barnard, pp. 129–33; Vernon, pp. 41–2. The royal mandate for Heylyn's installation as prebend of Westminster, dated 4 November 1631, was endorsed by Williams on 7 November, authorizing any of the other canons to execute it: WAM 53333.

16 WAM, Chapter Act Book II, fol. 52v; TNA, SP 16/221/41, 42.

17 TNA, SP 16/221/41.

18 TNA, SP 16/221/42.

19 TNA, SP 16/221/41.

20 *Ibid*.

21 Hacket, *Scrinia Reserata* (1693), ii. p. 91. For Hacket's account of the articles see *ibid*., pp. 91–3.

22 WAM 25095; C. S. Knighton, 'The Lord of Jerusalem: John Williams as dean of Westminster' in C. S. Knighton and R. Mortimer (eds), *Westminster Abbey Reformed, 1540–1640* (Aldershot, 2003), pp. 251–5. The charge of supporting a lay plot against the abbey's interests seems to have been based on an attempt to draw a highly misleading parallel between the incorporation attempt of 1633 and an earlier and very different incorporation attempt in 1607. For an authoritative account of this matter see J. F. Merritt, *The Social World of Early Modern Westminster* (Manchester, 2005), p. 98. The controversial use of dubious historical parallels deriving from archival materials would seem to fit Heylyn's *modus operandi*.

23 Vernon, p. 80.

24 Hacket, *Scrinia*, ii. p. 92.

25 Bodl., Jones MS 17, fols 300r–309v; Laud, *Works*, V, pp. 56–70.

26 Laud, *Works*, V, pp. 87–91. See a contemporary copy in Bodl., Rawlinson MS D.353, fol. 104r–v.

27 *EH*, ii. appendix, sigs P2r–P3r.

28 *Ibid.*, sigs P4v–P5r.

29 *Ibid.*, sig. P5r–v.

30 TNA, SP 16/406, fols 167r–168r.

31 SUL, Hartlib MS 29/2, fol. 48r.

32 John Prideaux, *The Doctrine of the Sabbath* (3rd edn, 1635), preface, i. pp. 13–14, ii. p. 40.

33 *Ibid.*, preface, i. p. 11, ii. p. 5.

34 *Ibid.*, ii. pp. 19, 30–1, 41.

35 SUL, Hartlib MS 29/2, fol. 9r.

36 William Twisse, *Of the Morality of the Fourth Commandement* (1641), sig. C4r, p. 93. Twisse generally tiptoes around Prideaux's arguments and tries to interpret them in the best possible light: see pp. 187, 191, 224 and *passim*.

37 Vernon, pp. 41–3, 51–2.

38 The year 1636 saw the publication of visitation sermons delivered in 1635 and 1636 by Edward Boughen, John Featley, Jasper Fisher, John Pocklington, William Quelch and Alexander Read, and sermons and controversial works by John Browning, Peter Hausted, Peter Heylyn, Christopher Dow and Edmund Reeve. The year 1637 saw the publication of 1636 visitation sermons by Samuel Hoard and Richard Tedder, other sermons by Thomas Lawrence, Humphrey Sydenham, Anthony Sparrow, William Watts and John Yates, and further controversial works by Heylyn, Dow, Pocklington and Gilbert Ironside. It is also notable that a remarkable number of Laudian works were published by the London stationer John Clark, although it is not clear how far this is evidence of an orchestrated campaign.

39 *CA*, p. 296.

40 Walker demonstrates (pp. 86–8) that the work was distributed among several printers.

41 *HS*, sig. A5r–v.

42 A. M. Kendall, 'A Royalist Scholar: Peter Heylyn as Historian and Controversialist' (unpublished Radcliffe College PhD thesis, 1947), p. 138.

43 *HS*, sig. ar.

44 K. L. Parker, *The English Sabbath* (Cambridge, 1988), pp. 197–216.

45 Nicholas Bownde, *The Doctrine of the Sabbath* (1595); William Gouge, *The Sabbaths Sanctification* (1641), p. 1; John Dod and Robert Cleaver, *A Plaine and Familiar Exposition of the Ten Commandments* (19th edn, 1662), pp. 118–20, 122; J. H. Primus, *Holy Time: Moderate Puritanism and the Sabbath* (Macon GA, 1989), pp. 72–81.

46 Primus, *Holy Time*; A. Milton, review of K. L. Parker, *The English Sabbath*, in *JEH*, 41 (1990), pp. 491–4.

47 *HS*, ii. p. 250; Primus, *Holy Time*, pp. 85–6, 91, 94, 99.

48 Walker errs in describing the second edition as simply a 'reprint' (p. 93). New sections of text are inserted in the preface and also later parts of Book 2.

49 *HS* (2nd edn), ii. pp. 328, 240–2, 248, 260, 264, 268.

50 John Pocklington, *Sunday no Sabbath* (1636); Robert Sanderson, *A Soveraigne Antidote against Sabbatarian Errours* (1636); Gilbert Ironside, *Seven Questions of the Sabbath briefly Disputed* (Oxford, 1637); Francis White, *An Examination and Confutation of a lawlesse Pamphlet* (1637).

51 On the timing and nature of the altar policy see K. C. Fincham, 'The restoration of altars in the 1630s', *HJ*, 44 (2001), 919–40.

52 Many of the details of Williams's account of events in Grantham are queried in a notable anonymous manuscript response to his *Holy Table* that is based on detailed personal knowledge of the people and events. This response survives in a volume of Heylyn's papers (Bodl., Rawl. MS D.353, fols 139–42), and was presumably sent on to Heylyn while he was known to be working on his *Antidotum Lincolniense*, although it would appear to have reached him too late for use in that volume.

53 [John Williams], *The Holy Table, Name and Thing* (1637), pp. 5–20. I have throughout used the edition (STC 25725.6) printed in facsimile in *The Work of Archbishop Williams*, ed. B. Williams (Abingdon, 1979).

54 Williams, *Holy Table*, pp. 5, 58; *Commons Debates for 1629*, ed. W. Notestein and F. H. Relf (Minneapolis MN, 1921), p. 52 (cf. p. 133). Hacket, *Scrinia*, ii. p. 102. Prideaux's published Act lectures (*Viginti-duae Lectiones de totidem Religionis Capitibus* (Oxford, 1648)) do not refer to Williams's 'Letter' directly. Nevertheless, his 1631 lecture 'De missae sacrificio' does make a number of points very similar to those made in the 'Letter', especially in the interpretation of Hebrews 13:10 (compare *Lectiones*, i. p. 252, with Williams, *Holy Table*, p. 17). Prideaux was quite capable of using these lectures to make implicit attacks on Laudian policy: see Milton, *Catholic and Reformed*, pp. 116–17.

55 *CA*, p. 314; Vernon, pp. 89–90. Hacket also suggests that the 'Letter' was raised by Williams's enemies at this point in order to injure his case in Star Chamber: *Scrinia*, ii. p. 101.

56 *Coale*, p. 2.

57 D. MacCulloch, *Thomas Cranmer: a Life* (New Haven CT, 1996), pp. 600–1.

58 *Coale*, p. 3.

59 Williams, *Work of Williams*, p. 93 (and comments on 'Text 2' at end [unfoliated]).

60 John Winthrop's correspondent Robert Ryece reported in a letter of 9 September 1636 that the author of the *Coale* 'is an notable flatterer of the Courte one Dr. Heylyn': *Winthrop Papers*, III, *1631–1637* (Massachusetts Historical Society, 1943), p. 303. See also [W. Prynne], *A Quench-coale* (1637), pp. 187, 194; Laud, *Works*, VII, p. 337.

61 Heylyn's *Coale* (pp. 20–1) digs out examples of the Marian dean of Westminster (Hugh Weston) and one or other of the Marian bishops of Lincoln calling the protestant communion tables 'oyster boords', a sally which Williams clearly understood and complained of (*Holy Table*, p. 98), to which Heylyn even more plainly replied, 'there is (as you have now discovered him) one Bishop of Lincoln and Deane of Westminster, that calls it standing Altar-wise, by the name of Dresser': *AL*, i, p. 98. At one point (*ibid.*, i. p. 77) Heylyn slips into quoting the text of the 'Letter' against the author of the *Holy Table*, implying that both works were written by the same author. Note also Williams's sneering reference to princes having their powers profaned by 'bunglers ... and Chaplains (to shew how ready they are, at the very first call, to be dealing in matters of State) ... puddling in studies they do not understand': *Holy Table*, pp. 22–3. Heylyn was of course a royal chaplain.

62 *Coale*, pp. 42, 47–8, 77–8.

63 *AL*, i. preface, and pp. 41, 42, 86, 99; ii. 8, 11–12, 26, 28.

64 *Ibid.*, i. pp. 3, 16 (cf. ii. p. 11).

65 *Ibid.*, i. p. 3.

66 *Ibid.*, ii. pp. 7–8.

67 *Ibid.*, i. pp. 2, 36.

68 A. Milton, 'Licensing, censorship and religious orthodoxy in early Stuart England', *HJ*, 41 (1998), pp. 646–9.

69 Williams, *Holy Table*, pp. 58, 70–1, 73–4, 75.

70 E.g. Williams, *Holy Table*, pp. 8, 59, 78. Cf. A. Walsham, '"Frantick Hacket": prophecy, sorcery, insanity and the Elizabethan puritan movement', *HJ*, 41 (1998), pp. 62–4.

71 LPL, MS 1030, Nos 58, 67 (cf. Nos 65–6). Among the Jesuit publications that Hacket presumably had in mind was Robert Parsons' *Judgment of a Catholicke English-man* (1608) – an attack on King James's *Triplici Nodo, triplex Cuneus*, which Parsons claimed to believe to be the work of Thomas Morton rather than the king: P. Milward, *Religious Controversies of the Jacobean Age* (1978), pp. 109–10.

72 *Ibid.*, Nos 58–9, 65–7. On Williams's clash with Fisher a few months previously see Nos 51, 53.

73 Laud, *Works*, VI, p. 63. Hacket complained that Laud make the accusations 'reading out of his Notes', implying that these 'Notes' were provided by Heylyn: *Scrinia*, ii. p. 129.

74 Laud also approvingly sent a copy of the *Antidotum* to Viscount Wentworth: *Works*, VII, p. 372.

75 Hacket, *Scrinia*, ii. pp. 109–10.

76 Heylyn was presumably involved in Laud's attempts to have Williams prosecuted for writing the *Holy Table*, and may have composed the paper described in Hacket, *Scrinia*, ii. p. 129.

77 Joseph Mede, *The Name Altar anciently given to the Holy Table* (1637); *idem*, *Churches, that is, Appropriate Places for Christian Worship* (1638).

78 Prynne, *Quench-coale*, p. 72 (and pp. 8, 44, 147, 151–3, 167, 169–70, 172, 181, 182, 187, 190–1). He later reports less ambiguously that the author of the *Coale* was 'Doctor Heylyn as most give out, and some Circumstances discover' (p. 187).

79 *BMA*, sig. dɪv.

80 Gardiner, *Documents*, pp. 75–6.

81 Laud, *Works*, VI, pp. 64–8. Compare also *ibid.*, pp. 50, 53 and 59, with *BMA*, pp. 149–50, 157–8 and 137 respectively.

82 Laud, *Works*, VI, p. 68. Given the date of the entry in the Stationers' register, and Heylyn's emphasis that his book remained unpublished because it was not intended to be released 'till the execution of the sentence', I am unable to understand the logic behind Walker's claim (pp. 116–17) that the book must have been distributed in shops 'according to plan . . . about the middle of June' in time for the start of the trial.

83 See below, ch. 3.

84 Laud, *Works*, VI, p. 69.

85 *BMA*, sigs B4v–C2r.

86 Again, Burton's work had met with another opponent in the shape of Christopher Dow, but, unlike his pamphlet on the sabbath, Dow's *Innovations Unjustly Charged* may have sneaked through ahead of the publication of Heylyn and Laud's official responses. (At least, it was entered at the Stationers' on 19 June, during the trial.) But while Dow may have gained Laudian patronage after the event, there is no evidence that his work was officially solicited in the manner that Heylyn's was.

87 Barnard, p. 142.

88 Vernon, pp. 51–2.

89 *Extraneus*, p. 50. Heylyn adds that in addition his 'Books, Plate & moveables' had a value of at least £1,000.

90 Bodl., Rawl. MS D.353, fol. 100v: Curll to Heylyn, 11 February 1636.

91 The opinions of Sir Robert Heath and Thomas Malet (the latter dated 20 April 1638) in favour of Heylyn in this case (which related to the payment of tax for the king's household from the tenants of the tithings leased from the parsonage of Alresford) are contained in Bodl., Rawl. MS D.353, fol. 102r–v. WAM 1194 contains a note of a related court case dated 7 May 1638: one version of the report reads that by John Glyn's counsel Heylyn prepared a bill in which he set forth 'an agreement that by his Majesties especiall favour the plaintiff is collated by the Lord Bishop of Winchester' to the rectory. Clearly Heylyn was keen to emphasize his receipt of royal patronage wherever possible.

92 *HMC De L'Isle*, VI, pp. 109, 114.

93 T. A. Mason, *Serving God and Mammon: William Juxon, 1582–1663* (Toronto, 1985), p. 155. Sir Francis Windebank owned copies of Heylyn's *Historie of St George*, the *History of the Sabbath*, the *Briefe and Moderate Answer* and *Microcosmus* (TNA, SP 20/9, fols 12v, 13v, 14v). It is of course possible that Juxon's and Windebank's copies were gifts from the author. Among the booklists of delinquent royalists' libraries in the 1640s 'Mr Heath' also had a copy of the *History of St George* (fol. 34r). References simply to 'Heylin' in the booklists of 'Mr Mostyn of the Temple' and Dr Richard Steward (fols. 8v, 29v) presumably refer to the *Microcosmus*.

94 D. Duggan, '"London the ring, Covent Garden the jewell of that ring": new light on Covent Garden', *Architectural History*, 43 (2000), pp. 152–3, 161; Huntington Library, San Marino CA, Hastings MSS, HAF 12.10. (I owe this last reference to Ken Fincham.)

95 E.g. the puritan James Crowther; see an apparent inventory of his books drawn up after his death in August 1637: Claydon House MSS, microfilm reel 3 (1635–38). See also M. M. Verney (ed.), *Memoirs of the Verney Family* (2 vols, 1907), I, pp. 102–3.

96 *The Judgment of the late Primate of Ireland* (1658); George Hakewill, *A Dissertation with Dr Heylyn: touching the Pretened Sacrifice in the Eucharist* (1641); idem, *A short but cleare Discourse, of the Institution, Dignity and End, of the Lords Day* (1641); Richard Bernard, *A Threefold Treatise of the Sabbath* (1641); John Ley, *Sunday a Sabbath* (1641); Hamon L'Estrange, *Gods Sabbath before the Law, under the Law and under the Gospel* (1641); William Twisse, *Of the Morality of the Fourth Commandement* (1641). For pre-1640 references to some of these works being in circulation, along with other refutations of anti-sabbatarian works (conceivably including Heylyn's *History*) written by Thomas Ball, Thomas Lydiat and John White of Dorchester, among others, which were not subsequently published, see SUL, Hartlib MS 29/2 fols 9v, 36r, 51v; 29/3, fols 19r, 20r, 36v, 37v, 44r, 49r; Bodl., Tanner MS 65, fol. 83r: William Twisse to Archbishop Ussher, 9 June 1640; Henry Burton, *For God and the King* (1636), p. 127. See also below, ch. 4.

97 K. Sharpe, *Reading Revolutions* (2000), p. 93.

98 *The Works of Joseph Mede*, ed. J. Worthington (1664), p. 1041; Robert Sanderson, *A Sovereign Antidote* (1636) in *The Works of Robert Sanderson*, ed. W. Jacobson (6 vols, Oxford, 1854), V, pp. 1–2, 10–12; *The Works of . . . John Cosin*, ed. J. Sansom (5 vols, Oxford, 1843–55), V, pp. 529–37.

99 Richard Bernard, *A Threefold Treatise of the Sabbath* (1641), p. 114.

100 Milton, 'Creation', pp. 180–1. I hope to discuss this issue in more detail elsewhere.

101 Williams, *Holy Table*, p. 69.

102 Vernon, p. 94.

103 *Ibid.*, pp. 94–5, 194; LPL, MS WD 54, pp. 89–226. This collection of Heylyn's extracts, in a copy later made by Stanhope, contains materials from sessions of Convocation between 1529 and 1583. I am very grateful to Gerald Bray for bringing it to my attention.

104 J. Raymond, *Pamphlets and Pamphleteering in Early Modern Britain* (Cambridge, 2003), pp. 171–87.

105 TNA, SP 16/49/40 (cf. 16/52/55); Robert Baillie, *Ladensium Aytokatakpισις: the Canterburian's Self-conviction* (3rd edn, 1641), p. 14; Milton, 'Laudians and the Church of Rome', p. 9 n. 30.

106 Thomas Morton, *A Sermon preached before the Kings most excellent Majestie, in the Cathedrall Chutrch of Durham . . . the fifth Day of May 1639* (Newcastle upon Tyne, 1639); Henry Leslie, *A full Confutation of the Covenant, lately Sworne and Subscribed by many in Scotland: delivered in a Speech . . . 26th of September 1638* (1639).

107 Thomas Morton, *Sermon*; Laud, *Works*, VI, pp. 573–8; Hall, *Works*, X, pp. 540–3; Milton, *Catholic and Reformed*, pp. 460, 468–9, 489.

108 *PT*, pp. 113–14.

109 Bodl., Rawl. MS E.21, fols 164r, 165r–v, 168r.

110 *The Diary of John Young*, ed. F. R. Goodman (1928), p. 106.

111 This was his *Brief Discourse*, finally published in the *Ecclesia Vindicata* in 1657.

112 LPL, Lambeth MS 731 (printed in William Nicholls, *A Supplement to the Commentary on the Book of Common Prayer . . . To which is added an Introduction to the Liturgy of the Church of England* (1711)).

113 For example, the author discusses Thomas Hutton's tracts responding to the West Country ministers' objections to subscription which Heylyn does not ever seem to refer to in his accredited writings: Nicholls, *Supplement*, pp. 26–37.

114 Vernon, pp. 95–6; Wood, *Ath. Ox.*, III, col. 567. Cf. Laud, *Works*, II, pp. 191–4.

115 *PT*, sig. A4r, pp. 65–7, 70–1, 75, 105–12. See also *CE*, p. 141.

116 *PT*, pp. 82–3. Cf. pp. 113–14.

117 *Ibid.*, pp. 45–56.

118 *Ibid.*, pp. 311–36.

119 K. Fincham, *Prelate as Pastor* (Oxford, 1990), pp. 251, 276–8.

120 *PT*, pp. 315–16, 318.

121 *Ibid.*, pp. 325–6.

122 *Ibid.*, pp. 319–22.

123 *Ibid.*, pp. 332–3.

124 *Ibid.*, p. 334.

125 John Rylands University Library, Manchester, shelfmark 20634.

126 Vernon, p. 96; TNA, C231/5, pp. 279–405.

127 *PT*, p. 365.

128 *Ibid.*, pp. 353–6.

129 *Ibid.*, pp. 364, 366.

130 For accounts of the Short Parliament convocation see J. Nalson, *An Impartial Collection of the Great Affairs of State* (2 vols, 1682–83), I, pp. 351–74; J. Davies, *The Caroline Captivity of the Church* (Oxford, 1992), pp. 251–87.

131 *CA*, pp. 429, 440, 443. It is interesting to note, however, that Heylyn's surviving notes on Convocation go up only to 1583 (LPL, MS WD 54, pp. 89–226).

132 *CA*, p. 434.

133 This is described only in Vernon, p. 97, but given that Vernon essentially follows *Cyprianus* on the Convocation (where this is not mentioned) it may not be accurate.

134 See the text in *CA*, pp. 424–5. The link with Heylyn is suggested in Trott, 'Prelude', p. 332.

135 *CA*, pp. 436–7, 441.

136 Fincham, *Visitation Articles*, II, pp. xxvi–xxvii, 222–44.

137 LPL, MS 577, p. 273; *CA*, p. 427.

Chapter 3

The voice of Laudianism? Polemic and ideology in Heylyn's 1630s writings

Heylyn's publications were the most obvious source for contemporaries to go to for an explanation of the rationale and justification of the religious policies of the 1630s. While Laud's speech at the censure of Burton, Bastwick and Prynne offered a brief self-defence, and Francis White wrote defending the Book of Sports, there were no other apologia of the policies offered by any prominent member of the ecclesiastical establishment, whether bishop or dean. Other minor authors wrote to defend royal policy on the altar (Pocklington, Mede) and the sabbath (Dow, Pocklington, Ironside, Primerose, Sanderson), and against the broader charges of Burton (Dow), while a number of published visitation sermons and other works defended the beauty of holiness and condemned its critics. But it was only Heylyn whose writings covered all the areas in dispute and who also published explicitly with the approval of those in authority – most clearly in his *History of the Sabbath*, *Antidotum Lincolniense*, and the *Briefe and Moderate Answer*.

If Heylyn was then the official spokesman for the Laudian movement, what broader ideology did he present in his works? This chapter is intended to scrutinize the dominant themes in his published works of this decade, relating in particular to the nature of the English Reformation, puritanism, Roman Catholicism, and the foreign Reformed churches. We will seek in part to determine whether these reveal a unified and consistent vision, or whether tensions and ambiguities can be observed. Given that the best picture that historians now have of Laudianism is one that has consciously synthesized a collective 'ideal type', there is a particular value in analysing the perhaps less coherent and more contingent body of opinions that a single Laudian author expounded.[1]

One feature of such a focused study, however, must be to note the ways in which the specific polemical demands being made on a particular text may have altered the tone or balance of an argument. Heylyn did not compose unified, comprehensive statements of Laudian principles. Rather, each one of his works (with the partial exception of the *History of the Sabbath*) was written in response to the writings of others, and often engaged in point-by-point rebuttal of the opponent's arguments. This meant that the agenda and the subject matter of discussions was in most cases being set by the opponent. Therefore, for example, Heylyn provided very little discussion of Arminianism and doctrines of predestination, because (unlike the 1620s) these did not feature prominently in the debates over Laudian policy. Much of Heylyn's agenda was fixed on the rejection of charges of innovation, for which his opponents had mustered a series of examples mostly from the ecclesiastical and political history of the previous hundred years – it is therefore often the recent history of the church, and of the Church of England in particular, that is the focus of debate. Moreover, his opponents Burton and Williams both took up a stance of defending the established church settlement and the *status quo*, arguing that it was the Laudians who were the innovators. While it was in Heylyn's polemical interest to associate their positions with radical puritanism, nevertheless his opponents' polemical stance meant that Heylyn was generally not obliged to defend most features of the Elizabethan settlement on their own terms.

Heylyn also had his own specific polemical agenda that he was working to in each of his publications. Thus in his edition of Prideaux's *Doctrine of the Sabbath* his chief aim was to embarrass Prideaux into seeming to support the Book of Sports (preferably in its most radical form). His *History of the Sabbath* essentially aimed to provide a historical justification for the toleration of sabbath recreations in the Book of Sports, and therefore to undermine the evidence for sabbatarianism in the Church of England in particular by presenting it as a recent puritan innovation. *A Coale from the Altar* aimed to justify the actions of the Grantham minister against the specific criticisms of Williams, but also to discredit opposition to the current altar policy in general, and to harm the reputation of Williams himself in particular. The *Antidotum Lincolniense* represented the first time that Heylyn had responded in print to a work specifically written against him – it was therefore even more crucial for him to defend everything that he had written in the *Coale* and to associate Williams with extreme puritanism (he may also have received even more direct encouragement from the authorities to humiliate Williams). The *Briefe and Moderate Answer* sought to refute all the specific criticisms made in Burton's *For God and the King* – which went well beyond the altar and sabbath controversies – but was also intended to justify royal policies against what was perceived as a broader campaign of puritan criticism. Of all these works, it was only the *History of the Sabbath* where Heylyn was free to provide a more comprehensive account of his thoughts on the issues in hand, and even here he had specifically agreed not to tackle the moral and theological aspects of the matter. The differing agendas of these works inevitably altered the tone and content of some discussions, as we shall see.

While the intention is to study Heylyn's public printed works of this period, his unprinted works of these years (the short tract on the prayer before the sermon, his court sermons and the sermon against the feoffees) will be noted wherever their content is pertinent. Sometimes, as we shall see, it can throw important light on our interpretation of passages in his printed works.

THE CHURCH OF ENGLAND AND THE REFORMATION

The basic appeal of Heylyn's Laudian tracts is to England's Reformation. The essential justification of Laud's policies was that, as the archbishop himself put it, they were returning the Church of England 'to the rules of her first reformation'. Heylyn echoed these words. All the things that puritans claimed to be innovations were simply 'a restitution of those ancient orders, which were established here at that Reformation'.[2] Laud's general aim, Heylyn instructed Burton, was 'to restore this Church to its antient lustre; and bring it unto that estate in which it was in Queene Elizabeths first time, before your predecessours in the faction had turned all decency and order out of the publicke service of Almighty God'. The innovations were all on the puritans' side. The task of Laud therefore was actually to suppress the innovations which Burton and 'those of your discent' had introduced into the church.[3] It was only because the rules of the Reformation had been ignored for so long that their revival appeared to be an innovation.

The question, however, was to which part of the Reformation settlement the Laudians were appealing. There had been many 'rules' in the different stages of the church's reformation under Henry VIII, Edward VI and Elizabeth. And at what point and why had the 'rules of her first reformation' been disregarded? Heylyn was one of the first Laudian writers who attempted to answer these questions, and to offer detailed explanations of what was necessarily a selective appeal to the past history of the Church of England and its reformations. He did not offer a systematic overall interpretation of the reformation of the Church of England – that had to wait for his later years. But his pamphlets responded to and reflected the fact that a general appeal to the 'rules' of the Church of England's reformation was proving highly problematic. Some aspects of the Reformation, it was emerging, could very easily be used to condemn aspects of the Laudian programme. Heylyn's treatment of the Reformation and the 'rules' of the Church of England therefore tended to vary. Sometimes Heylyn appealed to the letter of the law regarding precisely which aspects of the Reformation legislation could be deemed to be still legally binding; at other times he appealed to the practice of the chapels royal and cathedrals, or to the early events in the Reformation, as providing a truer account of what was intended, regardless of what was specifically now required.[4] In polemical works of this type there was plainly a utilitarian and opportunistic motivation impelling Heylyn to treat different aspects of the Church of England's reformation in what were often inconsistent ways. Nevertheless, in Heylyn's need to address the conflicting evidence of England's reformations we can discern consistent themes. The need regularly to disregard aspects of the English Reformation that seemed to conflict with the Laudian reforms prompted Heylyn to move towards what was (at least in embryonic form) a broader reinterpretation of the nature of the Reformation and the subsequent development of the Elizabethan church.

One significant change may be noted in Heylyn's presentation of the origins of the Reformation. Where his *Microcosmus* had emphasized the role of medieval heretical sects such as the Albigensians as forerunners of the Reformation, and as evidence of the location of the Protestant church before Luther, Heylyn now rejected this position entirely, insisting on the continuity that the Church of England had maintained in its reformation with the medieval Catholic church. Moreover, Heylyn did not merely reject the sectarian account of the Protestants' ancestry, he also implied that this was the exclusive preserve of the puritans. Burton and his friends had another pedigree 'from Wicliffe, Hus, the Albigenses, and the rest which you use to boast of' but he told them to 'keepe it to your selfe . . . the Church of England hath no neede of so poore a shift'.[5] Heylyn did not make any further attacks on Wyclif yet – these would appear in the future – but his disregarding of Wyclif along with the other opponents of the medieval church showed how his mind was working. The Laudians seem generally to have avoided targeting Wyclif directly at this point (although Richard Montagu is an exception).[6]

When discussing the English Reformation, Heylyn hinted at a readiness to be sceptical about the orthodoxy and authority of its foremost historian, the martyrologist John Foxe. When Williams cited a marginal note from Foxe's work, Heylyn retorted 'I trust you will not justifie all the marginall notes in the *Actes and Monuments*'.[7] Rather than attacking Foxe directly at this stage, however, Heylyn was keener to utilize his testimony in polemical debate when it suited his argument, given that his opponents deferred to Foxe's authority (as Heylyn told Williams, Foxe was 'Your Author').[8] Thus, having triumphantly invoked Foxe as a defender of the historicity of St George, Heylyn warned his English Protestant opponents that if they rejected what Foxe said of the plausibility of the martyr St George it would allow Roman Catholic authors to question many of the martyrs whose sufferings Foxe recorded while averring that he was both writer and witness.[9]

Turning to the English Reformation itself, Heylyn provided little discussion of the Henrician reformation. His opponents were not citing it, so there was no need to engage directly with it, although his reference to 'the first reformation of religion in K. Edwards time' implied that there had been little reformation under Henry VIII.[10] He did, however, move to correct Burton's attempt to use the Submission of the Clergy to argue his erastian claim that the bishops required the authority of the king confirmed by letters patent to carry out their episcopal jurisdiction.[11]

It was the Edwardian Reformation that consistently offered more of a challenge to Laudian apologists, with its iconoclasm, erastianism, increasingly radical reform of religious worship, and emphatically Reformed doctrine.[12] Laudian discussion of the Edwardian reform had perforce to be selective in its reading of which reforms should be embraced and which rejected. Heylyn was determined to identify under Edward, not a radical reformation, but a consistent policy of moderate reformation on the part of the Edwardian reformers. He stressed: 'I' was not the purpose of those holy men in King Edwards time to make a new Church, but reforme the old; and onely to pare off those superfluities, which had in tract of time beene added to Gods publike service. In which regard, they kept on foote the Priesthood and Episcopate, which they had received; with many of those rites and ceremonies to which they were before accustomed: not taking either new orders, or bringing in new fashions, never knowne before.'[13]

For Heylyn, this restraint was encapsulated in the First Edwardian Prayer Book. This liturgy had a particular appeal for Laudian enthusiasts. It provided important precedents for some of the Laudians' favoured non-canonical ceremonies, and Heylyn himself cited it in defence of standing at the gospel, for the use of a prayer before the sermon that puritans accused of teaching prayer for the dead, and especially (in the altar controversy) for references to the 'sacrament of the Altar'.[14]

The fate of the First Edwardian Prayer Book was, for Heylyn, emblematic of the more general fact that the moderate reformation intended by the reformers had been subverted by other forces. The fact that the Edwardian prayer book had been superseded by a second, more thoroughly reformed, version obviously required explanation. Heylyn sought to discredit the Second Edwardian Prayer Book, and the rejection of the First, by attributing that act to the malign influence of foreign divines, and specifically John Calvin. In the face of Williams's denials, Heylyn's *Antidotum* provides a fuller account of Calvin's influence, noting his letters to Protector Somerset demanding further reforms, and his subsequent letters to Cranmer. While Somerset was removed from power and eventually executed before the Second Prayer Book was drawn up and ratified, Heylyn still insisted that Calvin had supplied the momentum for the reform of the Prayer Book, although it was carried out under the government of the duke of Northumberland, who was influenced by the unreliable Bishop Hooper just as Somerset had been by Calvin.[15]

Heylyn's chief concern in these pamphlets was to present the retention of altars and continued use of the term in the early stages of the Edwardian Reformation as the considered policy of the reformers, and to argue that their abandonment after 1550 therefore must have represented Calvin's interference. He was equally anxious to deny Williams's worrying suggestion that the removal of altars was prompted by pressure from below. Williams had claimed that the Edwardian church had removed altars because people in country churches were scandalized by Romanist superstition, and beat down their altars *de facto*, and then the supreme magistrate by 'a kind of law' put them down *de jure*, and set communion tables in their place. Heylyn instead set himself to demonstrate the popular enthusiasm for the retention of altars.[16]

The practical execution of the more radical reformation was, Heylyn argued, the work of 'the King and State', and while Calvin incited them to this work,[17] the other malign force that Heylyn identified in the Edwardian Reformation was the greed and erastian instincts of the Edwardian court. Again, Heylyn was prompted to present this argument partly by one of his opponents, in this case Henry Burton. Burton partly (as we have seen) wished to cite Edwardian statutes to suggest that the bishops were acting illegally by exercising their ecclesiastical jurisdiction under their own names, without the king's letters patent. The government was sufficiently concerned by this accusation that Charles charged the chief justices to make a formal judgement showing this law to have been repealed under Mary, and its revival at the beginning of James's reign to have lapsed.[18] Nevertheless, Burton was also able to note Edwardian statutes which forbade the election of bishops by deans and chapters, instead authorizing the king to confer bishoprics by letters patent. In the face of this erastianism, combined with the statute's Edwardian insistence that the church courts were kept solely by the king's authority, and that all jurisdiction derived from the king's authority, Heylyn was obliged to adopt a more general condemnation of the erastian councillors in Edward's court. He did not at this stage condemn King Edward himself (this he would do only in his history of the Reformation, published after the Restoration) but he did emphasize that during Edward's minority 'there was much heaving at the Church, by some great men which were about him, who purposed to inrich themselves with the spoyles thereof'.[19] Ultimately, of course, Burton made for a very implausible erastian. Nevertheless, his attempts to deploy the Edwardian statutes against the bishops' jurisdiction had obliged Laudians like Heylyn to detach themselves more directly from some aspects of the Edwardian Reformation.

In contrast to the excesses of the Edwardian Reformation, the Elizabethan settlement was the standard to which Laud and Heylyn essentially appealed. Some of the tactical restraint of the early Elizabethan settlement could be invoked to justify Laudian alterations. Thus Heylyn could defend the dropping from the 1630s fast book of a clause referring to the country's liberation from superstition and idolatry by appealing to the precedent of the Elizabethan liturgy's omission of a passage from the Edwardian liturgy which prayed 'from the tyrannie of the Bishop of Rome, and all his detestable enormities, from all false doctrine etc. Good Lord deliver us'.[20] Nevertheless, as presented by Heylyn, the decline in standards of public worship set in very soon after the Elizabethan settlement was established. In some areas the decline occurred almost simultaneously with the promulgation of the Elizabethan statutes. Other decline was more incremental. The best evidence for the decay of public worship could be found by looking at the ceremonies that were still performed in the cathedrals and chapels royal. These had preserved the authentic religion of the early Reformation which had declined and disappeared in the parish churches. 'Were it not for those Cathedralls', Heylyn declared in his *Coale*, and repeated verbatim in the *Briefe and Moderate Answer*, 'we had . . . before his time beene at a losse amongst ourselves, in the whole forme and order of divine service, here established.'[21]

Having asserted that cathedrals and the chapel royal had preserved the true Elizabethan religion, Heylyn could then accept with equanimity the charge that in most of the country the practices that the Laudians advocated were not in use.[22] As evidence that they had once been practised in country churches, however, Heylyn sometimes invoked popular traditions and folk memory. Old people could still remember having performed ceremonies that had only recently disappeared. When discussing sabbatarianism, for example, he claimed that folk memory could attest to a more tolerant earlier practice of sabbatarian discipline: 'old wives' in parishes could remember 'with what harmlesse freedom they used to behave themselves, that day, in their yonger times'.[23] For bowing towards the east and the altar, Heylyn asserted that 'old people use it still, both men and women; though now it be interpreted as a curtsie made unto the Minister'.[24]

The reasons for the decay of worship in the Elizabethan and Jacobean churches lay partly in simple neglect, but also in the spread of puritanism, although Heylyn did not at this stage credit the all-consuming influence to puritanism that he would in his later writings. While the early Elizabethan period represented the apogee of authentic English Protestantism, the puritans' preferred forms of worship, by contrast, emerged only in the later years of the reign. It was only then that the puritan lectureships emerged, and the new sabbatarian doctrines of Bownde and others. The lectureships were 'the greatest innovation in this Church, that possibly could be projected' and reflected a broader puritan plot to undermine the English church and bring it closer to Geneva.[25] Heylyn mocked Burton's claims that the English church had constantly observed preaching on fast days: the puritan could cite only Jacobean and Caroline statutes as precedents, which, as Heylyn commented, hardly made for proof of the antiquity of the practice, but actually confirmed it to be an innovation.[26]

The problem for Heylyn, however, was that the same charge could easily be levelled against some of his own preferred doctrines. When he wished to deny the novelty of the claim that episcopacy derived *jure divino* from Christ, Heylyn cited the writings of Richard Bancroft, Thomas Bilson and Adrianus Saravia to show that 'this is no new saying devised but yesterday'.[27] The *jure divino* doctrine of episcopacy was of course scarcely any older in the Church of England than the sabbatarian doctrines of Bownde. But if his appeal was to a minority of right-thinking divines in the 1590s, at this point Heylyn was not prepared to present them as a minority. While he may have been limited to the authority of Bilson, Saravia and Bancroft when defending the *jure divino* status of episcopacy, Heylyn nowhere implied that this was not the belief of the majority of divines in the Elizabethan Church of England. On the contrary, he claimed that if, when Burton referred to 'our Divines' he meant 'those worthies of the Church, who have stood up in maintenance of the holy Hierarchie against the clamours and contentions of the Puritan faction; or such as are conformable unto the Articles and orders of the Church of England' – then none of these divines had ever suggested that episcopal authority was not derived from Christ and the apostles, and their ordination therefore *jure divino*. Anyone who had ever maintained the contrary 'is one of yours, Travers, and Cartwright, and the rest of your Predecessours; men never owned for hers by the Church of England'.[28] In effect, this was to brand as alien presbyterians all Church of England divines before Bancroft and Bilson. Heylyn may by 1662 have developed more fully a sense of estrangement from dominant trends of thought in the Elizabethan church, but there is little explicit evidence of such attitudes in his 1630s writings.[29]

THE CHURCH OF ROME

There is little trace of strong anti-Catholicism in Heylyn's 1630s writings, so that his anxiety to protect himself against charges of popery by preaching anti-Catholic sermons at court in the later 1630s is perhaps understandable.[30] The only notable example where he deployed more harsh language towards Roman errors – particularly deploying the charge of 'judaism' – appears in his *History of the Sabbath*, but this is very much the exception that proves the rule. He condemns later medieval ceremonies and vestments in the church as 'jewish', but this is so that he can place them within the same general movement as the more vigorous sabbatarianism of the later Middle Ages (and hence with the puritan sabbatarianism of his own time).[31] In his 1630s works there are no passages scoffing at Roman ceremonies of the sort that pepper his *Survey of France* – Heylyn's task is to instil greater concern for ceremony in worship, and an attempt to justify Laudian ceremonies by juxtaposing them with attacks on the extremes of Romanist worship was presumably regarded as counterproductive.

Heylyn's writings were so bound up with the problem of puritanism, and arguments over Reformation and post-Reformation developments in England, that the Church of Rome did not really feature in his discussions. His only conspicuous comments on the Church of Rome occur in his tract against Burton, and here the polemical context is critical. Burton was making a series of charges of insidious moves towards popery in the church, on the basis of several remarks published in 1630s tracts by pro-Laudian figures, and the amendment of anti-Catholic allusions in official prayer books. These were all charges that could have been rejected with little further comment. The suspiciously 'popish' remarks in works by Thomas Choun, Robert Shelford and others could have been dismissed as irrelevant, as they were the works of private men who were not part of the Laudian establishment. Heylyn was ready to do this in the case of the irenical works of Franciscus a Sancta Clara, who had demonstrated how the Thirty-nine Articles could be made compatible with the decrees of the Council of Trent, in order to promote the reunion of the Church of England with Rome. In this case Heylyn simply denied that Sancta Clara's writings were pertinent, rejecting as hearsay the reports that the work had been presented to the king by a prelate.[32] But in the case of the other authors Heylyn swung on to the offensive in his *Briefe and Moderate Answer*, not just agreeing with the remarks that had been objected to, but restating them and hurling them back at the puritans.

Thus he defended the assertion (by Choun) that the Church of England did not differ from the Roman Church in 'fundamentals', but then took the point further by launching an additional defence of Rome. 'The Church of Rome' (he declared) 'doth hold as fast on that foundation [the 'rock' of St Peter] as you, or any Zealot of your acquaintance; and hath done more against the Hereticks of this Age, in maintenance of the Divinitie of our Lord and Saviour, then you, or any one of your Divines, be hee who he will.'[33] He defended Shelford's argument that the pope was not the Antichrist, explained away references from the Homilies (that Burton had urged) as not being spoken 'positively and dogmatically', and undermined a century of Protestant argument by reproducing the stock Catholic response that St John had said that the spirit of Antichrist does not confess that Christ had come in the flesh, so that unless Burton could find a pope denying Christ's incarnation 'you have no reason to conclude that hee is that Antichrist'.[34]

When discussing the alteration made to the prayer book for 5 November, which had rephrased the condemnation of those 'whose Religion is rebellion, whose faith is faction' to read those 'who turne Religion into rebellion, and Faith into faction', Heylyn defended the change and did not deny Burton's claim that it both avoided the charge against Rome but also by implication extended it to the puritans.[35] Heylyn's basic point was that Burton erred in not distinguishing between the official doctrines of a church and the particular arguments of private men who were members of that church. He could have left it at that. But again he went further and mounted a defence of Romanists' loyalty. He emphasized that adherence to the Church of Rome was not in itself rebellion, 'though somewhat which hath there beene taught may possibly have beene applied to rebellious purposes'. He emphasized that the Oath of Allegiance was not refused by all seminary priests and lay papists, commenting that 'some have written very learnedly in defence thereof'. When Burton challenged the papists to name any Protestant who had ever committed treason against a king, Heylyn again did the work of a Romanist controversialist by emphasizing that he could think of many. He noted that the Genevans had expelled their bishop; the Calvinists in Emden had expelled their earl; Calvin, Pareus and Buchanan had justified the deposing of princes; and Burton himself had condemned 'absolute' obedience.[36]

A similar amendment to a passage in the fast book, where a reference to the country's deliverance from superstition and idolatry had been deleted, had raised Burton's fears that the authorities did not want popery to be called superstition and idolatry. Heylyn defended the change, compared it with a similar amendment made by Elizabeth to the Edwardian liturgy, and argued that accusations of superstition and idolatry gave 'a very great scandall and offence' to English Catholics.[37] If this implied a sense that Catholics could be enticed into the Protestant church by moderation and tact, it was reinforced by Heylyn's suggestion that cathedrals had played a major role in keeping Catholics within the Church of England.[38] However, Heylyn did not explicitly argue that Laud's policies were directed at attracting Catholics back into the Church of England, still less that there was any hope of reunion with the Church of Rome – these were reflections born of the different polemical circumstances of the 1650s.

Wherever Burton noted an apparent softening of an anti-Catholic position and saw it as insidious popery, Heylyn in each case sought not to reassure his opponent that nothing sinister was intended, but instead seized on the opportunity to denounce the anti-Catholic tenet, to defend the Roman church and to contrast its behaviour with that of the puritan faction. This was hardly calculated to soothe puritan fears, but that of course was not one of Heylyn's objectives. The fact that Heylyn made such outspoken attacks on forms of conventional anti-popery revealed both a polemical energy that was ready to avoid more orthodox answers, and also a conviction that such attacks would be looked upon favourably at court. It was presumably a sense of the changed tone of the court, in the wake of Charles's declaration against Roman proselytizing there, which prompted Heylyn's court sermons (unpublished in the 1630s) to indulge in all the most outspoken forms of anti-Catholicism that he had only just berated in Burton. Where his *Briefe and Moderate Answer* had condemned accusations of superstition against Rome, and the calling of the pope Antichrist, Heylyn seems to have indulged in precisely these accusations against Rome in court sermons delivered between January 1638 and January 1639.[39] If the text of these sermons (which Heylyn published in 1659) is authentic, they would suggest that the moderate tone that he adopted in the *Answer* was simply prompted by the anti-puritan polemical context. While some members of the Laudian movement adopted a genuinely irenical posture towards Rome, and explored the possibility of reunion, this does not appear to have been a preoccupation of Heylyn's at this stage.[40]

THE FOREIGN REFORMED CHURCHES

Heylyn's writings of the 1630s represent something of a departure from the Reformed internationalism evident in early editions of the *Microcosmus*. A more critical attitude towards the Reformed churches is evident, most notably in the tone in which he discusses Calvin's alleged interference in the Edwardian Reformation. There was nothing new in conformist divines attacking Calvin, but Heylyn's determination to associate Calvin in particular with the revision of the First Edwardian Prayer Book foreshadowed some of his later thinking.[41] There were hints, too, that he was ready to question the instinctive identification of the Church of England with the Reformed churches abroad. When Burton referred to the fact that 'Our Divines' opposed the doctrine of *jure divino* episcopacy, Heylyn commented pointedly that his opponent must mean 'the Genevian Doctors, Calvin and Beza, Viret and Farellus, Bucan, Ursinus, and those others of forreine Churches, whom you esteeme the onely Orthodox professours'.[42] Against such thinking, Heylyn was ready (like Bancroft and others before him) to urge the example of those other foreign Protestants, the Lutheran churches, for their support for episcopacy, and their preservation of altars.[43] His 'Brief Discourse on the Form of Prayer appointed to be used by Preachers before their Sermons' (written *c.* 1636 but not published until 1657) also notes how the Lutheran churches do not use a form of invocation in their prayer before sermons, emphasizing instead the distinctiveness of the Genevan church in contrast to all others in Christendom.[44] Generally, however, Heylyn did not urge the Lutherans as an alternative Protestant party to the Reformed, or suggest that the Church of England really had a closer identity with them. Typically, having noted that the Lutherans had retained standing altars, Heylyn immediately added to his opponent Williams that 'in those other Churches of the Reformation, some of the chiefe Divines are farre more moderate in this point, than you wish they were' (citing Oecolampadius and Zanchius).[45] He was also conscious that the Lutherans had only limited polemical value. When citing the testimony of the Saxon Confession in the second edition of his *Historie of St George*, Heylyn anticipated that 'they of Calvins partie' would say that the Lutherans 'are but a kinde of semi-Papists, and image-worshippers at the least, if not idolaters: neither their Churches to bee reckoned as reformed, nor the men as Orthodoxe'.[46]

There was as yet no specific indication that Heylyn perceived Calvin and his followers to be an overwhelming international threat to the governments and churches of Europe, and no systematic disengagement from the foreign Reformed churches. He still depicted the principal errors as being those of native puritans. Heylyn did note that 'generally those divines of forraigne Churches are contrary in the point of Discipline, unto the Hierarchy and rites of the Church of England: which some implicitely, and some explicitely, have opposed and quarrelled. Which ... is the onely reason why you would have them studied in the first place, that so young students might be seasoned with your Puritan principles'.[47] Nevertheless, in his *History of the Sabbath* Heylyn laid particular emphasis on how the Reformed churches of the Continent did not follow the precepts of England's sabbatarians.[48] On this issue it was the English puritans who threatened to infect foreign churches with their errors rather than vice versa.

There was an obvious value in embarrassing the puritans with the fact that the divines and churches from whom they drew so much of their inspiration held significantly different views from them on this matter. Heylyn declared with relish in the preface to his *History of the Sabbath* 'that whereas those who first did set on foot these Doctrines, in all their other practises to sub-vert this Church, did beare themselves continually on the authority of Calvin, and the example of those Churches, which came most neere unto the Plat-forme of Geneva: in these their Sabbath-speculations, they had not onely none to follow; but they found Calvin, and Geneva, and those other Churches, directly contrary unto them'.[49] But this reflected the conventional polemical manoeuvres used in the past by Bancroft and others, which ultim-ately revolved around treating the English presbyterians as distinctively extreme compared with their Continental counterparts.[50] While pointing to the malign influence of foreign presbyterian thought, Heylyn was still not overtly condemning the doctrinal influence of the Reformed churches, specifically their doctrine of predestination. This was mostly a consequence of the agenda set by the 1630s controversies (as we have noted), but never-theless Heylyn did not use the opportunity of his brief exchange with Burton on predestinarian issues to make an attack on Calvinism (although his need to uphold the impartiality of the King's Declaration would have militated against this anyway).[51]

PURITANISM

The venom of Heylyn's anti-puritanism was infamous in his lifetime. His depiction of puritanism in the 1630s displayed several notable features, and tended to propose a more all-embracing range of doctrines and practices than had been the case in earlier conformist thought. While this unquestionably served polemical ends, however, these were not random charges, and the radical puritan voices that he claimed to detect were not always mere fabrications, as we will see.

Heylyn claimed to detect greater extremism in the more recent puritan writers than had been evident in their forebears. While there was nothing new in the faction's charges, nevertheless the recent puritans cried out with 'farre more malice than their fathers did', levelling accusations simply 'because they can no longer be permitted to violate all the orders of Gods Church, here by Law established'.[52] Nevertheless, Heylyn was generally most keen to emphasize the continuity of his current opponents with the puritanism of the past. He constantly compared the behaviour and arguments of his opponents with those of Martin Marprelate, and noted that many of Burton's arguments had already been refuted by late Elizabethan conformists such as Richard Cosin.[53] Elsewhere, he taunted Burton with references to 'Travers, and Cartwright, and the rest of your Predecessours'.[54]

Heylyn was eager to portray the existence of a unified puritan conspiracy, rather than a handful of aggrieved pamphleteers. This always strengthened his polemical hand. Partly it enabled him to associate any individual puritan, no matter how moderate their stated stance, with the most radical puritan sectaries. Thus he constantly referred to Burton as 'brother Burton' and alluded to his and Williams's 'brethren', their 'friend' John Cotton and their 'brethren' in New England.[55]

One of Heylyn's favourite methods was to find similar ideas or phrases in the work of more outspoken puritan pamphleteers. This was a particular concern when he was attacking the establishment figure of Williams, who had generally sought to avoid the directly inflammatory and oppositionist comments of Burton and Prynne. Heylyn's *Antidotum* went to particular lengths in its preface to demonstrate systematically that Williams and Burton must have been taking ideas directly from each other. He was also delighted to uncover similar phrasing and citations in Williams's 'Letter' and a tract by Prynne.[56] But while Williams's case particularly required this treatment, Heylyn was more generally concerned to prove collusion between puritan authors in order to boost his claim that there was a broader conspiracy at work. Thus he was eager to note that Burton had taken some of his arguments from John Bastwick.[57] Heylyn was also happy to emphasize how the notorious presbyterian writer Alexander Leighton had alluded to Burton having preached against episcopacy at a general fast.[58] He also seized upon Prynne's citation of Leighton's *Speculum belli sacri* as a way of associating Prynne with Leighton's explicit anti-episcopalianism and subversive potential.[59]

The puritan plot itself was never laid out systematically, but was invoked in order to depict any puritan complaints in the worst possible light. Heylyn also often avoided using the term 'puritan' directly – his allusions instead tended to be to 'the faction' or 'the brethren' who were aiming to overthrow the Church of England, the bishops and (ultimately) the monarch. In fact, Heylyn made most use of the notion of a puritan plot when he was seeking to attribute sinister potential to what seemed outwardly inoffensive phenomena. Thus the use of extempory invocatory prayers before the sermon by puritan preachers was deliberately 'contrived, and set on foot by the Puritan Faction' as part of their plot 'to overthrow the publick service of this Church'. When Burton complained of long cathedral services without preaching, Heylyn accused him of trying to 'bring all piety and the whole worship of God, to your extemporary prayers and sermons'.[60] The introduction of sabbatarian doctrines represented a plot by 'the Brethren, who before endeavoured to bring all Christian Kings under the yoke of their Presbyteries; made little doubt to bring them under the command of their Sabbath Doctrines'. They thereby hoped 'to bring all higher Powers, what ever, into an equall ranke with the common people, in the observance of their Jewish Sabbatarian rigours'.[61] Heylyn also made his customary attack on the plot behind the puritan lectureships. They were 'a new and late invention borrowed by Travers and the rest towards the latter end of Queene Elizabeths time, from the new fashions of Geneva', which had been brought in from Geneva 'that by degrees, insensibly wee might bee brought more neere that Church' – 'the greatest innovation in this Church, that possibly could be projected'.[62]

Heylyn insistently linked this puritan plot with 'popularity'. This was not in itself a novel theme in anti-puritan writing, which had often sought to present puritanism as an inherently subversive and democratic ideology.[63] Nevertheless, the charge of 'popularity' is particularly prominent in Heylyn's 1630s pamphlets, and is all the more remarkable for the fact that the charge was here being made against a bishop of the church (Williams) and a former royal chaplain (Burton). In both cases, Heylyn accused his opponent of seeking the support of the people after he had been excluded from the court. Burton exemplified the fact that 'most men, whom the Court casts out; that they doe labour what they can, to out-cast the Court'.[64] For such men, puritan populism had a natural appeal. Heylyn therefore seized upon every example of such 'populism' in Williams's writings, in line with his more general determination to deplore the insidious phenomenon of 'popular prelacy'. Where Williams urged 'charity' towards parishioners, Heylyn asserted that the bishop intended to violate all the orders and ceremonies of the church rather than 'give offence unto the Brethren'. This was merely 'a trick to please the people, and put the reines into their hands, who are too forwarde in themselves to contemne all Ceremonie, though in so doing they doe breake in sunder the bonds of Charitie'.[65] Heylyn was therefore particularly appalled by Williams's suggestion that 'the Countrey people' had reformed the church: 'This is fine Doctrine, were it true, for the common people, who questionlesse will hearken to it with a greedy eare; as loving nothing more than to have the sovereignty in sacred matters: and who being led by a Precedent, more than they are by a Law or Precept, thinke all things lawfull to be done, which were done before them'.[66] Where Williams referred to the name and form of altar being taken away from 'us, the Children of the Church and Commonwealth', Heylyn decided not only that Williams was referring to the puritans, but also that by saying 'commonwealth' rather than 'kingdom' he was making a distinction 'betweene the well-fare of the King, and the Common-weale'.[67] Burton was similarly accused of political disloyalty in coming near 'the Puritan tenet that Kings are but the Ministers of the Common-wealth, and that they have no more authority then what is given them by the people'.[68]

The populist aspects of puritanism enabled Heylyn to emphasize the magnitude of its threat. The puritans might be a minority, but by playing on the desires and weaknesses of the people they could easily win almost universal support. While he sometimes sought to marginalize 'the Brethren', Heylyn at other times treated them as a dominant force. The neglect of the ceremonies which the Laudians sought to revive was itself evidence of the puritan success. Similarly, the rejection of the church's appointed times of fasting 'is reckoned a chiefpoint of orthodox doctrin, in the present times'.[69]

There was an element of irony in the charge of 'popularity'. In some of his writings Heylyn was not averse to emphasizing and praising the opinions and actions of people who had opposed the wishes of the ecclesiastical authorities. In his *History of the Sabbath* he regularly emphasized approvingly the opposition of the population to the attempts by the authorities to impose stricter forms of sabbatarianism.[70] While he was appalled by Williams's suggestions that the common people had thrown down altars, Heylyn was, however, equally happy to invoke a popular conservatism which the Edwardian authorities felt that they had to appease, and noted the Western Rising as evidence that, far from pulling down altars spontaneously, the people were actually opposing such policies.[71]

Heylyn also claimed to identify a distinct anticlericalism in the puritan party. The polemical context required him to present the clergymen Williams and Burton as promoting this lay dominance, but this enabled Heylyn to suggest that they were traitors to their own profession ('a mans enemies are those of his owne house').[72] It was the vestries that attracted Heylyn's particular attention, and he repeated the charges and concerns that he had first expressed in his letter to Laud from Guernsey and his sermon against the feoffees. Thus his *Coale* accused Williams of pandering to 'the Vestry-doctrine of these dayes; in which the Church-wardens, & other Elders of the Vestry, would gladly challenge to themselves the Supreme disposing of all Ecclesiasticall matters in their severall Parishes: leaving their Minister (in Townes Corporate especially) to his Meditations'.[73] Where Williams described having appointed churchwardens 'whom it principally doth concerne under the Diocesan' to settle the Grantham dispute, Heylyn complained that this was 'another smack of the said Vestry-doctrine: & was there placed in front to delight the people, who need, God wot, no such incouragements to contemne their Parsons, being too forward in that kind of their own accord'.[74] Williams was trying to suppress his clergy 'by putting them into the hands of the Vestrie Elders'.[75] As so often with Heylyn, his claims that parish officials were behaving as the equivalents of lay elders and deacons had a grain of truth in them, however paranoid his assumptions of crypto-presbyterianism. When the Westminster Assembly debated the creation of the presbyterian system, it was suggested that 'in the church of England ther is some vestige of ruling elders in church wardens' and 'debate about the deacons & church wardens doing that which belongs to the overseers & churchwardens'.[76]

This point may also serve to warn against the temptation to present Heylyn's depiction of 'puritanism' as simply a fanciful polemical construct. It has been argued that the Laudians' anti-puritan paranoia generated a radical puritan opposition that had not been there, so that Heylyn's polemical unveiling of puritan radicalism became a self-fulfilling prophecy.[77] There can be little doubt that Heylyn deployed every polemical weapon that he could find, and deliberately misrepresented and exaggerated Burton's and Williams's positions. Nevertheless, however partisan, malicious and extreme Heylyn's take on puritan behaviour may have been, it must be stressed that Heylyn's anti-puritan gestures were not purely fanciful. Unlike other conformist divines, he had seen the presbyterian system at work at first hand during his time in France and Guernsey. He had also been a diligent observer of puritan preachers in London, where, as recent research is revealing, there were many very radical voices to be heard in the Caroline period.[78] When he reported that before their sermons London puritan preachers would declare 'that the words which they should speak, might not be entertained as the words of a mortall man, but as they were indeed the words of the immortal, and Living God', Heylyn added, 'for in that very stile I have heard it often'. When he was later accused of inventing the puritan sermon which he claimed to have heard at Sergeant's Inn in Fleet Street where it was taught 'that temporall death, was at this day to be inflicted, by the Law of God, on the Sabbath-breaker', Heylyn protested that his report was true and that the sermon in question had been delivered by 'Father Foxley, Lecturer of St Martins in the Fields'. Foxley, he insisted, had preached in his hearing that sabbath-breakers should be executed, and had warned lawyers that they deserved death.[79]

There is a danger, too, that in rejecting Heylyn as an obviously partisan commentator historians may take Heylyn's opponents too easily at their own word. In fact, there is suggestive evidence that Henry Burton was already an anti-episcopalian of separatist tendencies when he made his attacks on Laudianism. It was already being claimed that he had preached the removal of bishops at a fast sermon in London.[80] Burton also makes an extremely improbable erastian, despite his attempts to accuse the Laudian bishops of infringing on the royal supremacy. His temptations towards self-referential millenarian prophecy – which would become so prominent in his later years – were already evident in 1636, and Heylyn's mockery of his pretensions and assimilation of Burton's position to that of more radical puritan prophets was malicious, but not entirely misplaced.[81]

Heylyn's association of Williams with John Cotton of Boston was more obviously fanciful in one sense. But his suggestion that the prelate was toying with 'popularity' and flirting dangerously with puritan opposition to Laudianism as a means of regaining his political position was far closer to the mark than his critics have often suggested. It may be true that Williams's opposition to the forced imposition of the Laudian 'beauty of holiness' showed a sensitivity to the pastoral problems that such a policy would engender among evangelical but conformist figures such as the town elite of Grantham. There may well also have been an instinctive sympathy on Williams's part for a more pastorally engaged, sensitive approach – it would certainly have appealed to his political pragmatism. Nevertheless, Williams's remarks in his *Holy Table* concerning the Franciscan priest Sancta Clara make it quite clear that he was not simply seeking to provide sober advice on ecclesiastical tactics which the manuscript distribution of the 'Letter' had forced him to make public. Having primed his readers to be wary of Heylyn's references to the 'Good work now in hand' and the 'speciall inclination of these times, to a peculiar kinde of pictie', Williams slyly commented that 'I should therefore reasonably presume that this *Good work in hand*, is but the second part of Sancta Clara'.[82] Williams's reference to Sancta Clara here is clear evidence that, as well as chiding the approach adopted by Laud, he was manifestly seeking to question the doctrinal probity of the government, and to imply that the new policies were linked with a broader plan to reconcile the Roman and Protestant churches. He may not have tossed around the epithet 'popish' as freely as Prynne or Burton did, but his remarks concerning Sancta Clara amounted to very much the same thing.[83]

In this sense, Williams's determination to present himself as a moderate mainstream churchman provided a gloss on what was actually a consciously 'oppositionist' position. He can hardly have been unaware that his opposition to Laud would enable him to position himself favourably in the eyes of the next parliament, whenever that might be called. Williams's reported remarks to Spicer in 1632 make it clear that this was an active consideration of his, and certainly Laud was regularly fearful that a parliament might indeed be imminent.[84] It is certainly true that Williams's subsequent prosecution by the government made him a martyr in the eyes of many in the country. His prosecution in Star Chamber excited national interest. One hostile commentator had reported in October 1635 how 'the eyes of all the kingdom are set upon this cause as the determining cause betwixt Puritans and loyal subjects', with Williams regarded as the champion of the puritans 'and the only man that dare oppose his Majesty's government'.[85]

Heylyn was not, then, the only man playing to an audience in his polemical exchanges in the 1630s, and the 'popular' puritan clothing of his enemies was not entirely imaginary, even if his anti-puritanism displayed a remarkable venom and lack of discrimination.

HEYLYN AND LAUDIAN ORTHODOXY

Was the position that Heylyn presented in these tracts really that of the government? It is certainly the case that Laud seems to have made use of Heylyn's work, while Heylyn constantly referred to and lauded the policy makers of the 1630s, and wrote with authority of what their policies intended. Heylyn clearly felt authorized to offer personal defences of those involved in implementing the religious policies of the 1630s. Of Laud, Heylyn solemnly told Burton that 'both for the sinceritie of his conversation, as a private man, and for the pietie of his endeavours as a publicke person, you would be shrewdly troubled to finde his equall in this Church, since the first reformation of religion in K. Edwards time'.[86] 'Can you remember', he asked Williams, 'any Metropolitan of and in this Church ... which hath more seriously endeavoured to promote that uniformity of publicke Order, than his Grace now being?'[87] When Burton attacked the Laudian bishops White, Montagu and Wren, Heylyn retorted that they were men 'who both for their endeavours for this Churches honour, fidelity unto the service of the King, and full abilities in learning, have had no equals in this Church, since the Reformation'.[88] He also lauded the great example that Charles set for his people in his religious carriage, which was a sermon in itself. 'When did you ever finde a King, that did so seriously affect Church-worke; or that hath more endeavoured to advance that decency and comlinesse in the performance of divine Offices, which God expecteth and requires, than his sacred Majestie?'[89]

Heylyn's readiness to enthuse about his superiors and the magnitude of their deeds may have led him to emphasize the novelty of their performance more than they would have wished. Despite all the claims of the authorities that they were not guilty of innovation, Heylyn's reference in *Coale from the Altar* to 'the piety of these times' was seized upon by Williams as evidence of the novelty of current practices. Heylyn made no attempt to deny the charge, but rather amplified this claim in the *Antidotum*, where he praised the 'speciall inclination of these times to a peculiar kind of piety, differing from the piety of former times'. He chided Williams: 'finde you not the "piety of these times" inclinable in a higher degree to that uniformity [in divine service] than any of the times before?'[90] In these passages, the notion that the Laudians were actually returning the church to its position at the time of the Reformation itself was implied more directly, with Heylyn delighting in the sight of 'Churches more beautified and adorned *than ever since the Reformation*'.[91]

That being said, while Heylyn was usually content to raise historical precedents in order to refute charges of innovation, he was occasionally careful to deny that the Laudians were responsible for some of the innovations that they were charged with. Thus he made no attempt to defend the erection of images and crucifixes, but claimed that there was no proof that the bishops had given any orders for setting them up.[92] He insisted that the church was encouraging bowing *towards* the altar, but not *to* the altar. Other writers defending the Laudian policies were not always so careful. Also, where writers such as Pocklington provided elaborate symbolic defences of the placing of the altar and the erection of communion rails, exalting the powers of the priests ministering 'in the most holy place of all' and stipulating that rails were needed 'to preserve it entire and apart for the Priests to officiate in', Heylyn ultimately rested with the 'minimum' Laudian position on church order, insisting that 'the disposeing of Gods Table, rather to one place than another, . . . is not considerable in itselfe, or otherwise materiall in his publick worship, further than it conduceth unto Order and Uniformitie'.[93]

Similarly, Heylyn did not necessarily see himself as bound to defend all those books defending Laudianism in the 1630s that were accused by Burton of innovations in doctrine. Thus he maintained that 'the opinions of some private men, prove not in my poore Logick an Innovation in the Doctrine of the Church delivered, though contrary unto the Doctrine so delivered'. In practice, he did selectively defend writings by Thomas Jackson, Richard Browne, John Cosin, Anthony Stafford, Edmund Reeve and Robert Shelford – he clearly saw little if anything to disagree with in their work.[94] Unlike Christopher Dow, however, he specifically did not defend the irenical publication of Sancta Clara.[95]

Heylyn did also seek to defend the administrative record of the much criticized Bishop Wren. In responding to complaints of suspensions of puritan ministers in Norfolk and Suffolk, Heylyn went to the diocesan registers to collect the precise figures of those censured or suspended, and also verified that there had been no deprivations of ministers in Surrey for not reading the Book of Sports.[96]

If Heylyn sometimes strikes a more restrained note than some of the more enthusiastic private defenders of Laudian policies, this may have reflected the need for more care in a writer whose works (unlike those of Dow, Pocklington and the rest) were proclaimed as being published 'by authority'. Nevertheless, although Heylyn did not wallow in the exuberant sacerdotal imagery and lavish symbolic language in which other Laudian authors indulged,[97] it would be misleading to suggest that he was a relatively 'moderate' author. The historical revisionism of his *History of the Sabbath* sought to marginalize what had been mainstream opinions, and his readiness to damn as subversives those who only acknowledged the apostolic (rather than the simply divine) origins of episcopacy represented a remarkable narrowing of what would pass for orthodoxy in the Laudian church. He may generally have kept his own radical policy proposals for private papers, but they do also sometimes make an appearance in his published works. Thus, when in the second edition of his *History of the Sabbath* Heylyn noted that in 1 Eliz. c. 2 the same penalty is imposed on those not coming to church on holy days as on those not coming on Sundays, he reflected that, if this law were executed as it should be, the holy days might soon regain the credit that they had lost.[98]

Heylyn was never simply the mouthpiece of the authorities, although his publications bore the mantle of official approval. Rather, within limits, these publications gave him the opportunity to associate his own ideas and attitudes directly with the regime, and to shape the form of Laudian orthodoxy.

CONCLUSION

The Laudian reforms of the 1630s had an enormous impact on contemporaries, and generated profound concern that the foundations of true religion were being threatened. While some of the divines associated with the movement can be shown to have had ideas that were significantly different from what had passed for orthodox in the Elizabethan and early Jacobean period, however, it should be evident from the foregoing discussion that the pre-eminent apologist of the Laudian movement in the 1630s did not present a coherent alternative world view behind these policies. There were undoubtedly some shocking and highly unusual ideas and opinions expressed in Heylyn's tracts, but while a rather different perspective on the nature of England's Reformation is implied, there is no systematic and coherent alternative reading being offered. There are implied attacks on Foxe, and on the Second Edwardian Prayer Book, but these are not necessarily followed up. Of course, as the government's chief apologist, Heylyn could not necessarily slay too many sacred cows when seeking to explain and vindicate the official policies being pursued. Nevertheless, Heylyn displayed sufficient readiness to challenge existing assumptions about the errors of the Roman church, or the status of episcopacy, to suggest that he was not cravenly seeking to provide a moderate and reassuring account of the government's objectives.

The lack of a coherent theoretical and historical underpinning to Heylyn's expressed position in his 1630s pamphlets reflects in part the contingent and disjointed polemical contexts in which his different works originated. But this also surely represents the fact that Heylyn's own ideas and opinions were shifting during this period, as his apparent backtracking in his court sermons at the end of the decade would suggest. The evolving nature of Heylyn's own position was there for all to see because of a publishing curiosity of the 1630s, namely that his *Microcosmus* continued to be published essentially in the form of its 1625 edition.[99] Preserved in the *Microcosmus* were very different views of Continental Calvinism, the Protestant succession and the errors of the Church of Rome. These 1630s editions of *Microcosmus* would appear to have been published without Heylyn's overview, but their publication simultaneously with his controversial writings for the government presents a strangely schizophrenic figure. It would not be until the 1650s that Heylyn would expound a more systematic and coherent ideology, but even then (as we shall see) his position was not always entirely consistent.

NOTES

1 Lake, 'Laudian style'; P. Lake, 'The Laudians and argument from authority' in B. Y. Kunze and D. D. Brautigam (eds), *Court, Country and Culture* (Rochester NY, 1992); Milton, 'Creation', p. 164.

2 *BMA*, sig. d1v.

3 *Ibid.*, p. 82.

4 E.g. *Coale*, pp. 58–9, 62–3; *Antidotum*, i. pp. 40–2, 45–6, 53–4, 57–8, 94–7; *BMA*, pp. 171–3.

5 *BMA*, p. 72.

6 Milton, *Catholic and Reformed*, pp. 305, 313–14.

7 *AL*, p. 93. Note also his passing comments on the bitterness of the Magdeburg centurists: *HSG* (1st edn), p. 188; (2nd edn), p. 194.

8 *AL*, p. 129. For examples of his citing of Foxe see *Coale*, pp. 9, 34, 36–7; *AL*, pp. 87–99, 122–5, 126. It should also be noted that throughout his career Heylyn always had to use Foxe as his basic source for the ecclesiastical history of the English Reformation.

9 *HSG* (2nd edn), pp. 197–8.

10 *BMA*, p. 78.

11 *Ibid.*, p. 97. Heylyn similarly rejected the claim of Henry VIII's supreme headship on the grounds that it had subsequently been repealed: *ibid.*, pp. 97–100.

12 See most recently D. MacCulloch, *The Tudor Church Militant* (1999).

13 *BMA*, pp. 71–2.

14 *Ibid.*, pp. 123, 138; *Coale*, pp. 16–17.

15 *AL*, i. pp. 110–21.

16 *Coale*, p. 36; *AL*, i. pp. 121–6.

17 *AL*, i. p. 121.

18 *BMA*, pp. 93–103.

19 *Ibid.*, p. 100.

20 *Ibid.*, pp. 157–8.

21 *Coale*, p. 27; *BMA*, p. 175.

22 E.g. *Coale*, p. 26.

23 *BMA*, p. 51.

24 *Ibid.*, p. 137.

25 *Ibid.*, pp. 130, 163–4.

26 *Ibid.*, p. 55.

27 *Ibid.*, p. 64.

28 *Ibid.*, p. 67.

29 See below, ch. 7.

30 See above, ch. 2.

31 *HS*, ii. p. 129.

32 *BMA*, p. 123. Milton, *Catholic and Reformed*, pp. 239, 250–1.

33 *BMA*, p. 125. Note also the parallel between these remarks and Heylyn's alleged words in his conflict with Prideaux in 1627 (see above, ch. 1).

34 *Ibid.*, pp. 127–9; cf. Dow, *Innovations*, p. 53.

35 *Ibid.*, pp. 153–7.

36 *Ibid.* Heylyn had denounced Rome's practice of canonizing men like Anselm and Becket, who rebelled against their king, in his *Historie of St George* (*HSG*, 2nd edn, pp. 53–4).

37 *BMA*, p. 158.

38 *Ibid.*, p. 175. The comments of the French ambassador Marquis Rhosny that Heylyn quotes here would frequently occur in his other works.

39 *PT*, pp. 65–8, 69–71, 75, 105–12.

40 Milton, *Catholic and Reformed*, pp. 353–69.

41 For earlier attacks on Calvin see Milton, *Catholic and Reformed*, pp. 427–34.

42 *BMA*, pp. 64–6.

43 Milton, *Catholic and Reformed*, p. 394 n., 442.

44 *EV*, pp. 341–2.

45 *AL*, i. p. 131; *Coale*, pp. 28, 33–4.

46 *HSG* (2nd edn), p. 196.

47 *BMA*, p. 120.

48 E.g. *HS*, ii. pp. 173, 181, 186–7. See also Heylyn's comments in Prideaux, *Doctrine of the Sabbath*, preface, pp. 5–6, 10. Heylyn does, however, criticize the French and Genevan churches for alienating potential converts by their restrictions on dancing: *HS*, ii. pp. 187–8.

49 *HS*, preface [unfoliated].

50 Milton, *Catholic and Reformed*, pp. 450–2.

51 *BMA*, pp. 45–9, 122–3.

52 *Ibid.*, sigs c4v–d1r.

53 *Ibid.*, pp. 12–15.

54 *Ibid.*, p. 67.

55 E.g. *AL*, i. preface, pp. 41, 42, 86, 99; ii. pp. 8, 11–12, 26, 28; *BMA*, p. 39.

56 *Coale*, pp. 20–1. See also *AL*, i. pp. 78, 98; ii. p. 11.

57 *BMA*, p. 94.

58 *Ibid.*, p. 88; Francis White, A *Treatise of the Sabbath-Day* (3rd edn, 1636), sig. **2r [marg.]; Alexander Leighton, *An Appeal to the Parliament, or Sions Plea against the Prelacie* (1628), p. 331; Foster, *Notes from the Caroline Underground* (Hamden CT, 1978), p. 50.

59 TNA, SP 16/534, fol. 131v.

60 *EV*, p. 338; *BMA*, p. 165.

61 *HS*, ii. p. 252.

62 *BMA*, pp. 163–4.

63 See P. Lake, 'Anti-puritanism: the structure of a prejudice' in P. Lake and K. Fincham (eds), *Religious Politics in post-Reformation England* (2006). I am grateful to Professor Lake for allowing me to see this article before publication.

64 *Ibid.*, sig. b1r.

65 *Coale*, pp. 57–8.

66 *Ibid.*, p. 40.

67 *Ibid.*, p. 42.

68 *BMA*, p. 26.

69 *Ibid.*, p. 161.

70 *HS*, ii. pp. 94, 123, 139–42, 264–5.

71 *Coale*, pp. 38–41; *AL*, i. pp. 108–9, 123.

72 *AL*, ii. p. 25.

73 *Coale*, p. 11. See also *AL*, ii. pp. 24–9.

74 *Coale*, p. 12.

75 *AL*, ii. p. 26.

76 Minutes of the Westminster Assembly, I, fol. 212v; III, fol. 69r – transcribed in C. van Dixhoorn, 'Reforming the Reformation: Theological Debate at the Westminster Assembly, 1643–1652' (unpublished PhD thesis, University of Cambridge, 2004), IV, pp. 346–7; VI, p. 121. I am very grateful to Dr van Dixhoorn for these references.

77 Foster, *Notes*.

78 P. Lake, *The Boxmaker's Revenge* (Manchester, 2001) D. R. Como, *Blown by the Spirit: Puritanism and the Emergence of an Antinomian Underground in pre-Civil War England* (Stanford CA, 2004).

79 *EV*, p. 340; *HS*, ii. p. 254; *CE*, i. p. 34. On Foxley see Merritt, *Social World*, pp. 345–6.

80 See above, pp. 93–4.

81 S. Rowlstone, 'Religion, Politics and Polemic in early Seventeenth Century England: the Public Career of Henry Burton, 1625–1648' (unpublished PhD thesis, Canterbury Christ Church College, 2006); *BMA*, p. 88.

82 Williams, *Holy Table*, pp. 84–5. See also the reference (p. 71) to 'these judicious Divines that tamper so much in doctrine with Sancta Clara'.

83 Williams's claim in his recantation that he had not intended to make people fear that 'there were an intent or preparation to introduce the Romish religion. Or that those that are entrusted and employed therein under your sacred Majesty endeavoured the same' (Williams, *Work of Williams*, p. 104) needs to be read in the context of his use of Sancta Clara and comments on 'the piety of these times'.

84 E.g. Laud, *Works*, VII, p. 502.

85 LPL, MS 1030, No. 38 (quoted in Williams, *Work of Williams*, p. 47).

86 *BMA*, p. 78.

87 *AL*, i. p. 86.

88 *BMA*, p. 84.

89 *AL*, i. pp. 84–5.

90 *Coale*, p. 4; Williams, *Holy Table*, pp. 82–6; *AL*, i. p. 84.

91 *AL*, i. p. 86 (my italics).

92 *BMA*, p. 172.

93 *Ibid.*, pp. 136–8; *Coale*, p. 31; John Pocklington, *Altare Christianum* (1637), pp. 68, 128, 132. On the 'maximum' and 'minimum' Laudian positions on authority see Lake, 'The Laudians'.

94 *BMA*, pp. 123–7, 169–70.

95 *Ibid.*, p. 123; Dow, *Innovations*, p. 44.

96 *BMA*, pp. 112–15.

97 Lake, 'Laudian style'.

98 *HS* (2nd edn, 1636), ii. p. 242 (cf. the inserted material in ii. p. 148).

99 Heylyn declared in 1652 that all six of the post-1625 editions had appeared 'without my perusal or super-vising', and that it was only on revising the work after the Civil War that he became aware of the many mistakes in it (*Cosmographie*, sig. A3v; and see below, ch. 5). It certainly seems unlikely that Heylyn would have continued knowingly to publish work which contradicted his own arguments so directly. There are a number of changes of wording in the post-1625 editions that are too significant to have been random printers' errors – these include careful rewording of some of the passages regarding the Albigensians and the visibility of the church (see *Microcosmus* (1636 edn), pp. 112–13, 178, 183, 260, 470, 479). These are almost certainly amendments made by the licenser, as he sought to soften the impact of these passages rather than removing them entirely (which Heylyn himself would surely have done by the 1630s). On this style of censorship see A. Milton, 'Licensing, censorship and religious orthodoxy in early Stuart England', *HJ*, 41 (1998), pp. 629–32.

Chapter 4

Prosecution, royalism and newsbooks: Heylyn and the Civil War

ON THE DEFENSIVE: HEYLYN AND THE LONG PARLIAMENT, 1640–1642

Preaching from the pulpit of Westminster Abbey on 13 December 1640, Heylyn could hardly have failed to notice that among the congregation, listening intently to his sermon, was the dean, John Williams, newly released from the Tower and bent on revenge. Three days earlier, when they had met in the Jerusalem Chamber, Williams had given Heylyn 'a freindly compliment' that 'he had me now fast enough'. As Heylyn now preached his sermon in front of his adversary he was suddenly interrupted by Williams, who jumped up, knocked on the pulpit with his staff and exclaimed 'No more of that point!' Convinced that he had finally trapped his opponent, Williams demanded a copy of the sermon that Heylyn had just preached.[1] The event soon became famous. The following year it was alleged against William Grant, minister of Isleworth in Middlesex, that he condemned a visiting preacher by saying 'that if he had been as nere the Pulpit as the Bishop of Lincolne was to Doctor Heylin, he would have pulled him out of the Pulpit'.[2]

This very public interruption of Heylyn by his dean symbolized the dramatic reversal of ecclesiastical fortunes that was occurring in the last months of 1640. Those imprisoned or suppressed under the Laudians were now released, and Laud and his supporters were the chief targets. In this context, Heylyn himself, as the regime's most notorious propagandist, was directly in the line of fire, not least as his immediate superior had been one of his most prominent victims.

It was the failure of the Second Bishops' War which had precipitated this sudden change of events. The collapse of the English campaign against the Scots, and the Scots' occupation of Newcastle, had helped to force a new parliament on a reluctant Charles I. With the king for the first time effectively obliged not to dissolve the parliament, MPs were finally in a position to press home their grievances and to ensure that the abuses of the personal rule would not happen again. High on the list of parliament's grievances were the policies of Archbishop Laud, and everyone knew that Laud would be an immediate target.

Certainly Laud himself had no illusions. He had in the past confided to Wentworth his fears over what a parliament would mean for his policies, and during the first month of the Long Parliament he spent his time sorting out the arrangements for his charitable bequests in Reading and the gifts of his manuscripts to Oxford. Clearly he was assuming at best an impending demotion or suspension.[3] The expected storm soon broke. In the early weeks of the Long Parliament there were systematic attacks on those responsible for the church policies of the previous decade, with petitions against members of the clergy, and on 18 December the impeachment of Laud himself on a charge of high treason.

What Laud may not have predicted was the speed with which Charles himself seems to have withdrawn his support from his archbishop. While the reasons are not entirely clear, the change of behaviour was abrupt and unmistakable: Laud's personal account book shows that gifts to him from Charles ceased in November 1640 and never resumed. He certainly felt that the king had abandoned him, and commented in his diary on Charles's betrayal of the earl of Strafford that the latter had fallen because he served a king 'who knew not how to be, or to be made, great'.[4]

Charles was not alone in withdrawing his support. Some other erstwhile supporters of Laud found the time ripe for a change of sides. The Laudian bishop Juxon's chaplains, John Hansley and Thomas Wykes, switched from licensing Laudian works for Juxon during the personal rule to licensing anti-Laudian works under the Long Parliament. Civil lawyers such as Robert Aylett and Thomas Eden, who had been notorious enforcers of the Laudian reforms as diocesan chancellors in the 1630s, became firm supporters of parliament in the 1640s. Most famous of these perhaps was Nathaniel Brent, Laud's own chancellor, who had been notorious for his harsh imposition of Laudian conformity in the 1630s (and was knighted for his pains in 1639 and subject to impeachment proceedings in 1641) yet swung violently to the parliamentary side and testified vigorously against Laud at the archbishop's trial. Even the outspoken John Pocklington complained to parliament that his books in support of Laudian policies had been published without his 'procurement, motion or knowledge' and that he had only 'composed them for his own satisfaction'.[5] Robert Sanderson, who had enthusiastically dedicated sermons to Laud in 1637 'preached by appointment of your grace', gave a visitation sermon at Grantham in 1641 in which he specifically distinguished the Church of England's position from those who had busied themselves and troubled others with putting forward new rites and ceremonies with scandal and without law, using the church's name for the serving of their own purposes.[6] How would the pragmatic Heylyn respond in this time of anxious allegiance swapping and denial?

Heylyn certainly knew that there were dangerous times ahead. Such a prominent apologist for Laud's policies was clearly going to be a target of parliament's animosity – indeed, given his absence from London at the beginning of the Long Parliament, rumours swiftly spread 'in City and Country' that Heylyn had already fled for fear of prosecution.[7] He did not flee, but the prosecution would come soon enough – he was swiftly summoned by a parliamentary committee. He was also singled out for attack in parliamentary speeches. He was condemned in the opening week of the Long Parliament, 'his bold Pamphlets' being taken as key evidence for the 'secret worke in hand' (the phrase that Williams had objected to) to 'drawe the Religion to olde Ceremonies'.[8] Sir Edward Dering's speech on presenting the Kent petition against episcopacy alluded to Heylyn's phrase 'the piety of these times', while the future royalist Lord Falkland singled Heylyn out for ridicule in a parliamentary speech that was subsequently printed.[9] Alongside all this he had generated enormous popular hostility. Heylyn himself later remarked that he was 'most despitefully reviled and persecuted with excessive both noise and violence' by members of the public who thronged the doors of the parliamentary committee concerned with investigating Prynne's prosecution.[10]

He was soon attacked in print as well. A flood of pamphlets attacking Laudian policies (many of them composed during the 1630s) poured from the press in 1641, and in most of these Heylyn's writings were picked over and refuted.[11] Only one work – George Hakewill's *Dissertation with Dr Heylyn* – singled out Heylyn's writing exclusively for a book-length refutation; Heylyn would later boast that his *Briefe and Moderate Answer* and *History of the Sabbath* had never received book-length answers.[12] Nevertheless, he was unquestionably a marked man, and was in the gun-sights of two men in particular – John Williams and William Prynne.

Of these two enemies, Williams was undoubtedly the more immediate and worrying threat. With the calling of the Long Parliament Williams was free finally to play the role of the pivotal mediator between the crown and its opponents to which he had so often aspired. Fifteen years later, Heylyn could still remark bitterly of how at his release Williams was feted, 'his person looked upon as sacred, his words deemed as Oracles'.[13] Heylyn had a right, not just to be bitter, but also to be fearful. Williams had already indicated to William Spicer back in 1632 that, given the chance, he would not be charitable towards his enemies, and Heylyn was undoubtedly someone whom the vengeful dean would have had in his sights. It is also clear that Heylyn had more enemies surrounding him in Westminster than he was entirely aware of – and some in his close circle who were now happy to inform against him. Thus, after Heylyn told the committee examining the prosecution of Prynne that he no longer possessed any of his notes relating to the events, the committee privately received information that Heylyn had in fact subsequently shown such notes to friends at the house of 'Mr Levet' (presumably the lawyer with whom he had travelled to France, and the dedicatee of *Augustus*). Heylyn was therefore obliged to bring the 'little booke full' of notes to the committee. At the same meeting of the committee, Prynne 'showed divers printed bookes' in which Heylyn had libelled him by name, 'and in his sermons impliedlie'. Heylyn had published no sermons, which suggests that someone in his auditory – either at court or at the Abbey – had informed against him.[14]

The most detailed account that we have of the public clash between Heylyn and the newly released Williams is Heylyn's own, and it therefore needs to be treated with some caution. Heylyn was prompted to write the account some sixteen years later by the accusation that, having trampled on and insulted Williams in the 1630s, Heylyn had gone crawling to Williams in servile fashion once the bishop was released from the Tower.[15] Nevertheless, the account repays careful study, and when supplemented by other sources provides an intriguing glimpse of Heylyn's state of mind at this crucial stage in his career.

Heylyn claimed that he did not attend on Williams after the dean's release from the Tower, but only saw him at the next chapter meeting, where he 'gave him as few words as might be the common civility of a complement, for his return unto the College'. It was the Sunday following his appearance before the parliamentary committee for the courts of justice that Heylyn's sermon was famously interrupted by the dean's call of 'No more of that point'. In Heylyn's account, the preacher explained to his auditors that he had virtually finished the present point, but would proceed to the next as he was bid.[16] Williams's intervention would appear to have been prompted by a passage of the sermon in which Heylyn deplored that people no longer harkened to the voice of the church, 'what schism in every corner of this our Church! . . . some rather putting all into open tumult, than that they would conform to a lawful government, derived from Christ and his Apostles to these very times'. According to Heylyn's son-in-law (who seems to have had access to his father-in-law's sermon notes) Heylyn then moved on to more tactful generalizations, condemning others 'combining into close and dangerous factions, because some points of speculative divinity are otherwise maintained by some than they would have them'. This led him to a pious denial 'that a difference in a point of judgment must needs draw after it a disjoining of the affections also, and that conclude at last in an open schism. Whereas diversity of opinions, if wisely managed, would rather tend to the discovery of the truth than the disturbance of the church, and rather whet our industry than excite our passions.' He ended with the lament that, if only 'we' had observed due moderation and not ignored patristic admonitions that people should not be suspended from the communion of the church, 'we had not then so often torn the Church in pieces, nor by our frequent broils offered that injury and inhumanity to our Saviour's body, which was not offered to his garments [by those that crucified him]'.[17]

Heylyn's hypocrisy was palpable here. Nevertheless, the fact that Heylyn could openly admonish his hearers 'that we are so affected with our own opinions, that we condemn whosoever shall opine the contrary' also provides a useful reminder of just how widely deployed and easily adopted the language of moderation and irenicism was in this period. It would have been ludicrously foolhardy for Heylyn to have attacked his puritan opponents too directly. Nevertheless, by intervening before Heylyn had provided a more pacificatory gloss on his words, Williams clearly felt that he had finally nailed his opponent. After Heylyn's sermon was over Williams moved swiftly: summoning another prebend as witness, he demanded that Heylyn give him a copy of the sermon that he had just preached. Heylyn claimed that he did so, and that he gave Williams 'the whole book of Sermons that he then had with him'. Coming out of the service on the same evening, Williams sent one of his gentlemen to desire the sub dean (Newell), Dr Thomas Wilson and Heylyn to come to his lodging. Heylyn answered 'in a full Cloyster' that he would not go; he would meet Williams in parliament, the law courts, or the abbey's public chapter house and answer charges, 'but that he would never shuffle up the business in the Bishops lodging, or take a private satisfaction for a publick Baffle'. Having disrobed, Heylyn then passed the time with his friends Robert Filmer (the theorist of absolutism, who lived in the grounds of the abbey) and John Towers (the fiercely Laudian bishop of Peterborough and fellow prebend of Westminster) and in their presence the sub-dean came back from Williams, returning the book of sermons that Heylyn had delivered to him. Heylyn stoutly refused to accept the book, stating 'that the Book was taken from him in the sight of hundreds, and that he would not otherwise receive it, than either in the same place or a place more publick'. He then (so he claimed) urged Williams to read over all the other sermons and find what he could against him, and 'that as he did not court his favours, or expect any thing from him, so neither did he fear his frown, or any further mischief which he could do to him, equall to what he had done already; And finally, that he was more ashamed of the poorness of this prostitution, than at the insolencies of the morning.' The sub-dean in response simply threw the book into the room and left.[18]

Heylyn confessed that some people subsequently thought 'that he had carried it with too high a hand'. As relations continued to be frosty, the sub-dean finally met with Heylyn in the Common Orchard and urged him in Williams's name 'to apply himself to the Bishop, as being better able to help or hurt him than any other whatsoever'. After consulting with friends, Heylyn finally waited on Williams on a Saturday evening. Meeting alone in Williams's private gallery and, 'after some previous expostulations on the one side, and honest defences on the other, they came little by little unto better terms, and at the last into that familiarity and freedom of discourse, as seemed to have no token in it of the old displeasures'. This was clearly a cease-fire rather than a real reconciliation – Heylyn explained that he never met Williams again except when he later visited the bishops imprisoned after their presentation of a protestation in December 1641.[19]

What should we make of Heylyn's account? As we have stressed, he was undoubtedly keen to emphasize as much as possible his hostility towards Williams and his refusal to kowtow to him, largely in order to refute the charge of craven hypocrisy. Nevertheless, the account of his behaviour (allowing for overstatement) does seem to fit with what we have already seen of Heylyn's often truculent character. Heylyn's natural determination to defend his interests would have been reinforced by the fact that he had every reason to be on his guard against Williams, who was quite clearly bent on revenge. Heylyn had already received information that Williams had talked in private with Heylyn's other professed enemy, William Prynne.[20] Moreover, those involved in another publication against Williams's *Holy Table* met instructive fates. Pocklington was proceeded against for his *Altare Christianum*, which was burnt and the licenser William Bray forced to preach a recantation sermon simply for his involvement in the book's publication.[21] The proceedings against Pocklington were particularly savage: the House of Lords directed on 12 February 1641 that he be deprived of all his ecclesiastical livings, disabled from ever holding any place in the church, have his two books to be publicly burnt, and be forbidden from ever coming within the verge of the court again.[22] This judgement, and especially the final point, which was so clearly aimed at purging the chapel royal of the influence of a Laudian chaplain, must have made Heylyn – himself a royal chaplain – dread his own fate.

The prosecution of Bray and Pocklington makes it all the more remarkable that Heylyn did not receive the same treatment. It is true that there was a certain arbitrariness in who attracted parliament's interest. Thus one of Laud's chaplains, John Oliver, writing to Edward Hyde on 12 January 1641, expressed his surprise that 'I have not been cald upon yet in any manner, and searching every corner of my actions, I can not tell why I should; but the time is curious, and you know the place I have lived in'.[23] Nevertheless, Heylyn was more of a special case. He had written two books against Williams on the altar, which had both gone into more than one edition and had been more prominent publications than that of Pocklington.[24] Both Williams and Prynne had a right to bear personal grudges against Heylyn, and there was plenty of material in his printed tracts, let alone his manuscript sermon book, which could have been used against him.

How, then, can we account for Heylyn's remarkable escape, and the astounding self-confidence that he mustered in his dealings with Williams, and the dean's own backtracking? Two possibilities present themselves. The first would be that Heylyn was energetically working to cut a deal with the parliamentary committee. He was certainly capable of performing sudden somersaults of opinion and allegiance, as his early career testifies. His accounts of how the committee of inquiry into the prosecution of Prynne treated him are suggestive. He claimed that 'though he made his first appearance with all those disadvantages of prejudice and prepossession, which commonly obstruct the way to an equal hearing, yet got he so much ground on them, by his own modest confidence on the one side, and the want of fit proofs on the other, that in the end he was dismissed, not only with cheerfull countenance from them all, but with expression also of esteem and favour from divers of them'. Heylyn also claimed that the violently anti-Laudian John White, who was a member of the Prynne committee (and 'most eagerly bent against' Heylyn 'at his first appearance') and had attended his abbey sermon, yielded to Heylyn's request to read out Heylyn's account of the sermon to the committee, testified to the truth of Heylyn's account, and thereby won the unanimous support of the Prynne committee for Heylyn's sermon and a condemnation of the behaviour of Williams. This sounds highly implausible, of course, but Heylyn's later account matches what he appears to have written in his private diary nearer the time, and his appeal to the testimony (if it were to be required) of 'not only Mr Prynne himself, but several members of that Committee, who are still alive' is significant.[25] It is also suggestive that Heylyn does not appear in John White's *The First Century of Scandalous, Malignant Priests* (1643), in which the behaviour of so many Laudian divines was upbraided. Moreover, the account of one committee member (Sir Simonds D'Ewes) of the committee's behaviour suggests that Heylyn was being pacificatory. He noted that under cross-examination 'Dr Helin excused all malice' and D'Ewes was reduced to commenting that if only Heylyn 'had proceeded with the spirit of Christian Mansuetude hee might have prevented Mr Prinns punishment'.[26] At the committee's meeting on 23 December Heylyn also felt confident enough to raise the question of whether he was actually being called as a delinquent or whether he was simply called as a witness.[27]

Clearly, moreover, the committee was most concerned to incriminate Laud himself, rather than to see the blame attached to a minor official such as Heylyn. On 15 December the committee all agreed 'that the now Archbishop of Canterburie had a hand in this prosecution of Mr Prinne as deepelie as Dr Helin'.[28] The notes of John White's committee on the Feoffees for Impropriations are similarly suggestive in that, while they mention 'Dr

Heylin's Act Sermon', they emphasize that it was Laud who procured the crushing of the feoffees, and that he had bragged that he was the man who had set himself against it (a report that could only redound to Heylyn's favour).[29] Whether Heylyn was actively trying to detach himself from Laud is unclear; at least he does not seem to have been dissuading the parliamentary committees from doing this. Later rumours of Heylyn's grovelling before Williams may reflect such attempted repositioning. As we have seen, Heylyn would certainly not have been the only divine seeking to distance himself from the archbishop.

This does not provide a complete explanation, however. Things did not proceed as smoothly as Heylyn would have us believe. The Prynne committee *did* find Heylyn guilty as a delinquent, and if his case then disappeared in the committee on religion this was explicable partly by the sheer pace of political events and work load of the committee concerned. If Heylyn had indeed cut a deal, then it is unlikely that he would not have been used more publicly, or that the news would have circulated more widely. A more likely solution is suggested by Heylyn's anxiety to present himself to the Prynne committee as a mere 'employee' acting under the instructions of the attorney-general in amassing evidence against Prynne. The fact that when Williams was pursuing him for his Westminster sermon Heylyn made a point of sending an account of his sermon to the king is also highly suggestive.[30] It is Heylyn's determination to link his activities very directly with the king which seems the most likely explanation of why his opponents drew back from their engagement. Williams in particular did not want to jeopardize his new relationship with the king. It was later reported that when Williams demanded as part of his reconciliation with Heylyn that the latter should publicly acknowledge his error in publishing the *Antidotum Lincolniense* and have the book called in, Heylyn refused, and maintained 'that he received his Majesty's royal command for the writing and printing of that book'.[31] Heylyn's own account of his actions is conspicuously silent on the subject of the king, but with Laud already in the Tower there was no one else obvious whose support he could invoke.

Events at the end of January 1641 provide further evidence for this interpretation. On 30 January 1641 the Prynne committee finally delivered their verdict on Heylyn, finding him 'a delinquent, in having been a promoter and furtherer of the suite against Mr Prinne in the Starre-chamber and having since preached and written in his printed bookes libellouslie against him Dr Bastwicke and Mr. Prynne'.[32] The day before this final judgement (and presumably having advance knowledge of the committee's broadening of the charge to include his later pamphlets) Heylyn wrote an anxious letter to the courtier Endymion Porter, whom he had met that morning. Heylyn saw their meeting as miraculous (it made him willing to believe 'that God beginnes to be in love with miracles againe') and he declared that God had brought the two of them together providentially 'for no other end, then the redresse of my affaires'. Heylyn was clearly panic-stricken, reflecting that 'it cannot be worse with me, than it is alreadie'. Heylyn's urgent request was for some form of written attestation from the king of his support for Heylyn's actions. He emphasized 'how much it doth concerne the king in honour to iustifie the intimacion of his owne commands' (presumably the royal prompting to write his *Briefe and Moderate Answere* against Burton, which the Prynne committee was now intending to charge him with, and which had declared itself to have been 'commanded by authority'). At the same time, Heylyn was anxious to emphasize that 'the Attestation which I now desire . . . cann no way conduce to the disservice of his Majestie, or the dishonour of his Ministers'.[33] The complete silence of Heylyn and his biographers on this matter in their accounts of Heylyn's actions is all the more telling.

There is little to suggest that Heylyn enjoyed a close friendship with Porter at this point. He would have known him from his times as royal chaplain, and Porter was a famously affable figure who may later have supported Heylyn's bid for the deanery of York.[34] Heylyn's particular interest in Porter presumably partly reflected the fact that he knew no one else at court who could put his case to the king at this juncture. But he may also have been prompted by knowledge of the king's successful intervention on Porter's behalf less than three weeks earlier when the East India Company was seeking to prosecute the courtier. Charles had been able to persuade the Company to drop their petition to parliament against Porter by emphasizing that Porter was acting on his instructions.[35]

Heylyn's readiness to invoke the king's direct involvement in his activities may have helped to secure lenient treatment, at least temporarily, and it may be a reflection of his renewed confidence that a few days later Heylyn attended his first meeting of the Westminster chapter since the return of Williams.[36] Nevertheless, the increasing readiness of parliament to confront the king made any promise of royal support a declining asset. In April 1641 the Commons was once more referring Heylyn to the Committee for Religion for promoting the suit against Prynne. It is not clear, however, that any further prosecutions occurred. Heylyn's biographers imply that after some of these hearings he was given leave by the chairman of the committee to retire to the country, on condition that he would be sent for if needed. Heylyn reportedly told friends that he would go to Alresford and not return to Westminster while these 'two good friends' of his (i.e. Williams and Prynne) dwelt there. Indeed, Heylyn did not sign the minutes of any Westminster chapter meetings between May 1641 and February 1642. Heylyn's initial release was not unique: he himself later noted how John Cosin, William Haywood, and John Squire were all petitioned against, but released after examination.[37]

Parliament had too much business to be able to pursue all of its prosecutions immediately. This did not, however, mean that Heylyn, like the others, would not receive severe punishment when the Commons was ready to act.

Given the need to protect himself against the attacks of Williams and parliament, Heylyn was not in a position to do much to defend the Church of England with his pen against the increasing attacks being levelled against it by puritans in parliament and the press. Moreover, there was a sense that the church itself was anxious to dissociate itself from Heylyn. Prominent figures in the church were now looking to distance themselves from the excesses of the Laudians and to reform the church itself. A series of new appointments to bishoprics in the years 1641–43 included a number of Calvinist divines who had either been in trouble with Laud or had mustered little obvious enthusiasm for his reforms.[38] Among these new episcopal appointments was Heylyn's old enemy John Prideaux.[39] Of the list of Lenten preachers at court in 1642, more than one-third had been either unenthusiastic or positively hostile towards the Laudian reforms of the 1630s.[40] Another new bishop, Thomas Westfield, had provided a very selective defence of bishops in a sermon at St Paul's in 1641, deploring how evil reports on individual bishops brought disgrace on the function as a whole, and defending anti-Arminian bishops such as Morton, Abbot, Ussher and Hall.[41] The future royalist George Morley wrote a more explicit condemnation of the Laudian establishment. In his *Modest Advertisement* of 1641. Morley defined himself very specifically at the end of the work against those who would not accept changes to episcopacy. He stated unequivocally that it would be a sin not to harken to the voice of the people's complaints. It was the church's deafness to such complaints that was the cause of God's current chastisement. In particular, Morley appealed for a more rigorous observance of the sabbath, urged 'that pietie and godlinesse (the substance of Religion) be more attended than rites and ceremonies', and argued against arbitrary church government, and clergymen 'hunting after secular imploiment'.[42]

In 1641 those exercising most authority over the church were seeking to appease some of the puritan objections and to embark upon reform of the church. This partly reflected the influence of Heylyn's nemesis John Williams, and also of the Calvinist archbishop of Armagh, James Ussher, both of whom had been welcomed back into the king's counsels. Ussher encouraged schemes for a 'reduced episcopacy', where more of the episcopal powers would be exercised with the assistance of the leading godly ministers of the diocese. This is a scheme that would continue to engage the hopes of moderate conformists searching for accommodation throughout the next twenty years, with Ussher's proposals being reprinted in 1656 and 1660. Heylyn, remarkably, never seems to have commented directly on these schemes, but his hostility can be taken for granted. Meanwhile, Williams chaired a new committee to reform the Book of Common Prayer and the ceremonies of the church. The committee was specifically empowered, not just to remove recent 'innovations', but to contemplate the reform of the liturgy itself. Early papers from the committee – whose members included a number of prominent puritans – include firm rejections of many of the positions urged by Heylyn in the 1630s, and especially the claim that the Church of England had real rather than just metaphysical altars – a position explicitly described as having been argued by 'Dr Heylin and others at this last Summers Convocation'.[43]

In these circumstances no clergymen were printing explicit defences of Laudian policies or attempting to refute anti-Laudian pamphlets, although some works appear to have circulated in manuscript.[44] It is hardly surprising, then, that Heylyn did not throw himself into a series of works defending Laudian policies and condemning the assaults being made on the established church, or even publish refutations of pamphlets that attacked his own work.[45] Not only was he struggling to save his own skin, but his own church would seem to have disowned him and his ideas. Nevertheless, he did still continue to write and publish in these difficult years, albeit in a more circumspect way.

One intriguing work that he published in 1641, at the height of his troubles, was an apparently uncontroversial work, which presented itself as an 'Index' or 'Manual' rather than a piece of argument. This was *A Help to English History*, which simply provides a set of lists and catalogues demonstrating the succession of kings, bishops and noblemen in England since Saxon times. As an apparently neutral listing, it later became one of Heylyn's most popular works, with owners of the book inserting their own updates of material, and new editions being published until 1786.[46] It might seem what we would expect from a cowed Heylyn in 1641, retreating into uncontroversial scholarship in the face of parliamentary attacks. But there is more to the publication than that. Certainly it was not written to make money – Heylyn later claimed that he made no conditions at all with the undertakers for the printing of the book, and that he received only a few copies by way of payment.[47] Moreover, for such an apparently unobjectionable work, Heylyn went to extraordinary lengths to disguise his authorship. This was the first of his works since the *Coale from the Altar* that he had published anonymously. In this case, he used the pseudonym 'Robert Hall, Gent'. – disguising both his name and his profession with no elaborate anagrams – and for good measure the book's dedication claimed that 'Hall' was already dead. It was Heylyn's friend and undertaker Henry Seile who put his name to the dedication to Prince Charles (just as he had done in the earlier anonymous work *Augustus*). The explanation for Heylyn's subterfuge is more apparent in the preface to the work, which declares the work's intention to be more controversial than it might have appeared. Heylyn explained that he had written the book 'to satisfie the mindes of those (if any thing will satisfie them) that either are the enemies of Regall or Episcopall power'. In the case of the former, 'whereas some conceive that Kings were instituted by the people, on sight perhaps of such confusions as had beene noted and observed in a popular government', the catalogues of royal succession that the book provided 'will make it evident and apparent, that in this Countrey there was never any other government then that of Kings either in any part thereof, or the whole together'. In the case of the bishops, 'whereas it is factiously given out by others, that the Episcopall authority and regiment in and of the Church, is not the proper and peculiar government of the same, but violently obtruded on it by the power of man: the Tables of Episcopall succession will make it evident, that the said forme of Government, is of as long a standing in the Church it selfe; Religion and Episcopall jurisdiction being brought into this Land together'.[48] The inclusion of lists of the succession to noble titles in the same work also helped to create the impression that the tables of royal, episcopal and noble succession were in some way related, even interdependent. An attack on the bishops must therefore surely become an attack upon the others. This was therefore a conscious entry into the debates on royal and episcopal authority.

The increasingly radical assaults on the church gradually seem to have drawn Heylyn back into the ranks of its defenders. Even if prominent figures in its ranks had opposed the Laudian innovations, they were soon themselves the recipients of puritan attack. Thus Richard Dey's *Two Looks over Lincoln* (1641) attacked Heylyn's *Coale from the Altar* but was mostly concerned to condemn Williams's *Holy Table*, which in the changed context of 1641 no longer appeared the godly publication that it had seemed in 1637.[49]

It was in the defence of episcopacy – increasingly coming under attack in press and parliament – that Heylyn could still find common cause with the newly dominant forces in the Church of England. Eschewing the world of public named pamphlets, he returned to his *modus operandi* of the first half of the 1630s, offering papers of private advice, private meetings, and anonymous publications. Firstly this took the form of a paper prompted by the trial of the earl of Strafford by the House of Lords, when the bishops were excluded from the house on the grounds that 'no bishop should be of that committee for the preparatory examinations in the . . . case, under colour that they were excluded from acting in it by some Ancient Canons, as in causa sanguinis, or the cause of blood'. Heylyn's brief treatise instructed the bishops to stand to their rights of peerage, and was presented to Laud and 'some other bishops'. It is possible that the king also had a view of this work – he certainly seems to have been primed in 1641 to insist on the historical validity of bishops' sitting in the Lords, and asserted that they had had voices in parliament 'even before the conquest'.[50] This soon became an issue of more

fundamental importance as the exclusion of the bishops from voting in the
trial of Strafford was followed by a bill from the Commons to exclude bishops
altogether from the House of Lords. When a broader pamphlet dispute then
developed around the right of bishops to vote in the House of Lords on any
issue, the main defence of the bishops' position was Bishop Williams's *An
Abstract of those Answers which were given . . . unto the Nine Reasons sent up from
the House of Commons*, which did not mention their historical validity.[51]

Heylyn's reported visit in December 1641 to the twelve bishops imprisoned
by parliament for having claimed that parliamentary sessions which they had
forcibly been prevented from attending were invalid may also have conceivably
been an attempt to supply them with specific advice and historical justification
for their stance. Heylyn's efforts – whether or not they were formally requested
– were in vain. Indeed, he later voiced his disgust that the bishops made no
use of his defence of their sitting in the Lords at Strafford's trial. 'This', he
later remarked, was 'the first degree of their Humiliation', as the bishops'
failure to defend their interests encouraged their adversaries to deprive them
of their votes in parliament, and then to destroy the order altogether.[52]

Heylyn contributed a more substantial defence of episcopacy in 1642
in the form of an anonymous printed work, his *Historie of Episcopacie*, which
he published under the pseudonym 'Theophilus Churchman' The cloak of
anonymity, or perhaps the wrongfooting of moderate episcopalians, may have
given Heylyn the confidence in the preface to this work to give voice to what
must have been long-nursed resentment at the ways in which churchmen
had flirted with 'reduced episcopacy' and indulged in anti-Laudian attacks
in the first year of the Long Parliament. He particularly attacked George
Morley's *Modest Advertisement*. Men such as Morley, Heylyn complained, 'under-
tooke to answer them [the Presbyterians] upon equall termes [and] parted for
ought I can see on the same termes also, complying with them in some points
of no small importance, out of a silly hope to obtaine the rest: and thereby
letting them perceive how much was to bee got by confident and continuall
clamour'. He condemned the calumnies that authors such as Morley had
visited upon the Laudian clergy 'whether out of a conceit, that to bestow a
dash upon the Prelacie, would make the businesse tast the better; or that they
held it an high point of Policie not to goe so farre, but that they might retire
with safetie in the change of times'. They had acted 'as if there were no
better way to justifie the government of Bishops, then by traducing of their
persons, nor any safer meanes to be devised for vindicating the Church, then
by calumniating the Clergie'.[53] Morley was his specific target, but Heylyn may
also have resented Bishop Hall's readiness to repeat without correction
the Calvinist Bishop Potter's attack on the Laudian ceremonies, noting his
'vehement dislike of some innovations, as the turning the Table to an Altar,
and the low crindging towards the Altar so erected'.[54]

Ostensibly though, Heylyn's work was simply a contribution to a unified episcopal position that Hall had defended. Heylyn explained that he had refrained from defending episcopacy against its opponents as long as Joseph Hall was in the field – and Hall had been effectively a lone voice from 1638 through to 1641 as his initial defence of *jure divino* episcopacy was attacked by the quintet of puritan writers going under the name of 'Smectymnuus'.[55] Heylyn's initial absence from the debate may well have been a matter of instruction rather than self-restraint, as the authorities clearly conceived that the defence of episcopacy would be more effective in the hands of respected Calvinist bishops than in those of Laudian enthusiasts. Hall had announced his retreat from the fray in 1641, inviting younger challengers to take over, and Heylyn was more than ready to fill the breach.[56]

His *Historie* was not only printed anonymously, but also avoided an overtly disputational format. Hall had despaired of settling the argument, and Heylyn therefore insisted that he had proceeded by a different method from that which had been used thus far in the conflicts between Hall and the Smectymnuans, 'not in the way of Argument, or of Polemicall discourse . . . but in the way of an historical narration, as in point of fact; in which the Affirmative being made good by sufficient evidence, it will bee very difficult, if not impossible, to prove the negative'. This had of course been his preferred method in his *History of the Sabbath*, and he would deploy it increasingly often in the following two decades. Thus, while the preface to the *Historie* makes it clear that his main opponent is Smectymnuus, the book itself makes virtually no reference to his opponents' arguments, although all the issues in dispute – from bishops' sole powers of ordination to their exercising of secular powers – make their appearance in the historical narrative. The book concerns itself purely with providing a history of episcopal government in the first three centuries of the church, the argument being the traditional conformist one that Christ himself had established an imparity of ministers in the church, and that the apostles followed his example in ordaining the three orders of ministry of bishops, priest and deacons.[57]

Heylyn's treatment of the origins and nature of episcopacy is also relatively conventional. Although he follows the more recent Laudian insistence that episcopacy is a separate order of the priesthood rather than merely a higher degree of it, there is none of the outspoken extremism of Jeremy Taylor's *Of the Sacred Order and Offices of Episcopacy*, published in 1642, which is even more assertive than Heylyn in its insistence that episcopacy is crucial to the very being of a church (suggesting that it is not just a separate order of the priesthood, but actually the only true priesthood). Nor does Heylyn adopt the position argued a few years later by Henry Hammond, who maintained that, rather than there having been originally three orders of the clergy (bishops, presbyters and deacons) there were only two (bishops and deacons), with the bishop also being referred to as a presbyter. Only gradually had 'secondary presbyters' been introduced (in other words, the bishops were the only original ministers).[58] Taylor's was probably the first work in defence of the Church of England's episcopal order to deny explicitly the validity of the clerical orders of the foreign Reformed churches. Again, Heylyn does not attempt to argue this inflammatory point in his *Historie*, although he would go on effectively to deny the foreign Reformed churches' orders in his later publications.[59]

Heylyn's relatively conventional treatment of the issues in dispute, the lack of an overt controversial edge, and Heylyn's use of a pseudonym, may have partly been responsible for the fact that his own work appears to have made little impact on contemporaries. While a presentation copy was reportedly given to the king by Secretary Nicholas, the book itself does not seem to have sold very well.[60]

A similar work that Heylyn seems to have worked on at this time was his *History of Liturgies*. Heylyn later claimed that the book was 'required' by someone in authority, but their identity is unclear. According to Vernon it was sent to London and received by the bookseller but not printed.[61] Presumably, it too would have been submitted under a pseudonym – it would not be published until 1657. The 1657 text partly reflects later rewriting, but it nevertheless seems clear that its early version must have mirrored the style of the *Historie of Episcopacie*. Like the *Historie*, it seeks to provide a dispassionate, 'factual' account – this time of the existence of set liturgies in the early church, in reaction to the puritan attacks of the early 1640s. But, in common with his other histories, the fundamental distortion lies in the way in which the issues are formulated by Heylyn at the beginning. Where the Smectymnuans attempted to distinguish between an order of divine worship and the imposition of set forms Heylyn simply ignored the distinction, and took any record of a ceremony to represent the existence of a fixed liturgy.[62]

A notable feature of both histories is their preoccupation with the early church. This reflected the polemical agenda of his puritan opponents in the early 1640s. His works of the 1630s, and later of the 1650s, were aiming to convince opponents whose acceptance of the legitimacy of the established English church and the Elizabethan settlement could be taken for granted, so that Heylyn's essential task was to demonstrate that the Laudians were not guilty of 'innovation' but were in fact more faithful adherents to the principles of the Reformation. The more radical puritan critics of the 1640s were, however, urging the wholesale reshaping of the government and liturgy of the English church.

Heylyn had retreated to Alresford, and seems not to have been present when Westminster Abbey itself came under attack in late 1641.[63] Nevertheless, he could not have been unaware of the declining political situation, and soon afterwards he became briefly involved. In January 1642 the king fled London in the face of the hostile popular response to his failed attempt to arrest the five members. Charles initially moved to Windsor, and it seems to have been there that Heylyn joined what must have been a very depleted court, serving his usual duties as royal chaplain for the month of January. A sermon survives that he apparently delivered before the king at this time (on 25 January).[64] Preached on the text of Christ as the shepherd (John 10:27), it is most emphatically not a call for vigorous action or for taking up arms against opponents. Rather, the tone is one of resignation and contemplation. Christ expects meekness, lowliness and humility from his sheep, and readiness to be corrected. They must also be prepared to retire and contemplate his teachings, and to take up their cross to follow Christ.[65] Following Christ, Heylyn is also clear, means following his example of forgiving enemies: 'in all Morall duties whatsoever, as Prayer, and Fasting, and Alms-deeds, in pardoning such offences as are done unto us, and humbling our selves under the mighty hand of God; in these he hath commanded an obedient imitation, and in all those we ought to follow him'.[66] At this point at least (if Heylyn's later printed text is reliable) Heylyn would seem if anything to have been encouraging the king to re-engage with parliament, rather than rousing him to fight his foes. Given the king's situation at the time, it could well have seemed to Heylyn that Charles had no other choice.

It is not clear that Heylyn remained with the king beyond his monthly course of duties. He presumably returned to his living of Alresford, although he seems to have travelled to Westminster in February and May of 1642, where his presence is recorded at chapter meetings.[67] He was not able in his Hampshire rectory to avoid the impact of the deteriorating ecclesiastical situation or the attentions of parliament, however: in February 1642 the Commons ordered him to admit a lecturer chosen by his parishioners at Alresford.[68]

With the outbreak of war Heylyn would appear to have been a marked man again, and one whom parliament was apparently keen to see imprisoned. Sir William Waller's forces swept through Hampshire in the early days of the war, and Heylyn's Alresford living lay right in their path. According to Vernon, Waller sent eighty soldiers to be quartered in Heylyn's house, 'with full commission to strip him naked of all that he had'. Heylyn was brought before Waller by his provost-marshal, and Heylyn was told by Sir William that he had been commanded by parliament to seize him and send him prisoner to Portsmouth. Vernon claimed that Heylyn 'by his powerful reasoning did so far prevail upon the General, as to be dismissed in safety'.[69] The claim that Heylyn's powers of persuasion disarmed the parliamentarian general would, however, appear to be wishful thinking. A later Chancery case makes it clear that Heylyn fled arrest.[70] His bailiff and other servants also seem to have been forcibly ejected from the parsonage.[71]

HEYLYN AS ROYALIST PROPAGANDIST, 1642–1645

It seems clear that Heylyn fled from Alresford to the royalist court at Oxford, although Heylyn's own later account simply reports that he waited on Charles there as part of the normal course of his attendance as royal chaplain-in-ordinary in the winter of 1642. He had not been there a week when he received the king's command through the Clerk of the Closet to attend Secretary Nicholas and receive directions from him relating to the king's future service. At the end of his normal chapel attendance he was charged not to leave Oxford without special leave.[72] The following August a letter sent by the king to a number of Heylyn's parishioners in Alresford, which was then back under the control of royalist forces, commanded them to collect Heylyn's tithes, reap and house his corn and account for the proceeds, because of Heylyn's being 'by Our speciall command detained and imployed in Our Service at Our Court at Oxford'.[73]

For the first time since 1637 Heylyn was instructed by the government to write, and throughout 1643 and 1644 he composed a series of works, although none of them was published under his own name. This writing took different forms. Most famous (in recent scholarship) is his work as the first editor of the royalist newsbook *Mercurius Aulicus* – this was the special employment that he was charged with by the king (through Secretary Nicholas). In this, perhaps more than in any of his other work, Heylyn was a hired pen. But his newsbook responsibilities did not dominate his time in Oxford, where he was based between January 1643 and May 1645. He had ceased to act as editor of *Mercurius Aulicus* by September 1643, and well before then his successor John Berkenhead had been playing a major role in its composition. For the majority of his time in the royalist capital Heylyn wrote other things – short news pamphlets, several treatises (some unpublished at the time), and a series of sermons that he published only some fifteen years later. In none of these writings was Heylyn simply acting as a mouthpiece of royalist opinion, not least because there was no single, unified royalist opinion that was awaiting expression.

The royalist press was famously able to control its output more carefully and systematically than its parliamentarian opponents.[74] But this did not mean that a single message emerged from royalist Oxford. On the contrary, there were important divisions of opinion in royalist circles on many theoretical issues – on the role of the king, his relation to parliament, the role of the Oxford Parliament, and the basis of royal authority – as well as on practical and strategic matters (most fundamentally, from 1644 onwards, on whether the king should seek support from foreign troops, either Irish Catholics or Scottish Covenanters). These were not divisions of opinion that fed into simple ideological camps, of 'constitutionalists' versus 'absolutists', or of 'ultras' versus 'moderates'. Rather, they were divisions based partly on practical strategy and partly on personality.[75] In practice, this meant that royalist writing on political matters was often shifting and incoherent, with many ambiguities. Royalist publications should therefore be thought of partly as independent attempts to mould what the received royalist opinion would be. Even more than in his Laudian writings, then, Heylyn was seeking to construct an orthodoxy rather than reflecting an existing one.

Heylyn's writings as editor of *Mercurius Aulicus* do not, however, necessarily take us to the heart of these divisions. On the contrary, in reporting royalist successes and glossing over the failures Heylyn was able to express views that all royalists would have agreed upon. Similarly, his news 'supplements' often focused on the affronts to people's liberties being perpetrated by their parliamentarian opponents, so that Heylyn could even appear as the champion of liberty and freedoms, condemning 'blind obedience' and warning of the threat of servitude for 'we of this brave free-borne nation'. He could even pose as the defender of parliament, declaring, 'let Parliaments recover their good old Priviledges, these are all our Birthrights, and hath bin that which hath made the happiness and freedom of the English Nation loved and envied through Christendome'.[76] Certainly, editorship of the newsbook gave Heylyn the opportunity to glory in the successes of Sir Ralph Hopton's forces. His very first report also dealt with events in his birthplace of Burford, and attention to local matters frequently gives an added edge to his accounts of events.[77] But Heylyn's editorial work also provided him with the opportunity to settle some old scores. For example, *Mercurius Aulicus* is notably perfunctory in describing the death in battle of that iconic royalist figure and scourge of Laudians Lord Falkland (while in the privacy of his own diary Heylyn commented more baldly: 'this day died Lord Falkland, in whom the church lost no great friend – I am sure I did not').[78] Other news pamphlets enabled Heylyn to indulge in the popular fashion of subverting and imitating genres for polemical effect.[79] His *Lord have Mercie upon Us* uses the genre of the plague pamphlet in order to expand on what became one of Heylyn's favourite themes – the guilt of the City of London for the sufferings of the country because of the Civil War. In this case it is the plague of war, which has spread from London into the surrounding countryside. Heylyn places the blame for the war squarely at the feet of Londoners, and proposes that a cross and 'Lord have mercy' should be painted on the doors of the disaffected. He also used biblical analogies for the Londoners' behaviour. Noting how Londoners had celebrated the king's formal entry into the city in the autumn of 1641, only to drive him out in the New Year, Heylyn suggested New Testament parallels: those who had lately cried 'Hosanna' on the king's return now cried 'Crucifige'.[80]

Heylyn might be expected to have relished his role as intelligencer for the king's side. He had, after all, been one of the few writers before the Civil War to use the term 'royalist' in a positive sense, and here he was the undisputed spokesman of the royalist party, providing the factual information to sustain the cause. One would assume that this would have delighted a man who had always tried to find ways of putting his scholarship at the practical service of the authorities. In fact, however, it is quite clear that Heylyn deeply disliked his editorial duties. Vernon reports that he undertook the work with great reluctance, while Heylyn's own autobiographical notes record with relief how in September 1643 'I cleared myself of my employment of under Secretary' in writing the newsbook. The post was instead given to John Berkenhead, but Heylyn admitted that Berkenhead had already been playing a major role in writing the newsboook, and 'had of late so interlaced his expressions and intelligences that I could hardly call it mine'. Berkenhead's modern biographer has suggested that his influence may actually be traceable much further back, as early as the fourth week of the newsbook's publication.[81]

Why was Heylyn so averse to this position? Partly it would seem to have been a matter of status. Certainly his later son-in-law was outraged when his biographer Vernon recounted Heylyn's activities in editing *Mercurius Aulicus*, regarding it as 'unworthy to be mentioned'.[82] Heylyn always considered himself a scholar, and the journalism served only to diminish his status. Living in his old university, the contrast between his journalistic duties and the world of scholarship must have seemed all the more acute, even if earlier his times in Oxford had hardly been those of the detached scholar. It may also be that he was uncomfortable with the overt partisanship of the post. Heylyn was of course happy to write very distorted histories, but the virtue of scholarly impartiality was one that he constantly and seriously invoked. This leads us to another reason for his distaste for the work – he does not seem to have been very good at it. Contemporaries and later historians seem to agree that Berkenhead was a much more able journalist. Thomas contrasts Berkenhead's 'racy phrasing and spicy humour' with Heylyn's 'mannered writing, with its Latinistic phrasing, its pedantic turns of thought, and its occasional heavy-handed humour'.[83] This partly may reflect a generational change in what passed for wit, but for Heylyn to be accused of lacking 'racy phrasing and spicy humour' shows that his style had changed from the irreverent satire and humour evident in his early college poems and his *Survey of France*. Age and assumed dignity may have curbed his humour, although Heylyn was still not incapable of swingeing satire. But he seems to have been unwilling to deploy it over such serious events, where his instincts seem to have been to play the dispassionate historian rather than the scathing journalist. When he did employ satire in the newsbook, it was weighed down by a leaden, scholarly didacticism that was far removed from Berkenhead's lightness of touch. Unencumbered by the aspirations to scholarly reputation that Heylyn nursed, Berkenhead was ready to treat his readers to more knockabout fare.

It should also be emphasized that the editorship of *Mercurius Aulicus* was not necessarily the ultimate mark of royal favour. It did not reflect a close connection of Heylyn with the king. Heylyn was never personally close to Charles even in the 1630s, but in the 1640s there is no real evidence of any intimate contact with the monarch at all, after Charles had promptly abandoned Heylyn's main patron, Laud. While he had first come to royalist Oxford to fulfil his monthly duties as royal chaplain, and continued to serve as such, Heylyn was not one of those royal chaplains who worked with the king or whose counsel was sought in later negotiations. When the king did communicate with Heylyn, it would appear to have been via Secretary Nicholas.

Also, while Heylyn appears to have known the duke of Richmond, Lord Digby and Endymion Porter, he seems to have lacked a true patron among the lay royalists. While Secretary Nicholas clearly knew him well (perhaps from his time as a fellow resident of Westminster in the 1630s), it is unclear that Heylyn had many dealings with the grandees of the royalist party. He had known Lord Digby earlier through Magdalen College, noting in his diary that Digby 'was pleased to hold great correspondence with me, whilst he continued in the College', but it is not clear that this correspondence continued after Digby's student days were over, and Digby was no friend to the Laudian clergy in the early months of the Long Parliament.[84] There is certainly no evidence that Digby performed any services for Heylyn during his time in the royalist capital.[85]

It also seems clear that Heylyn was not a popular figure even among fellow royalists. Like many royalists, he had struggled to secure appropriate lodgings in Oxford. In January 1643 he had taken a vacant chamber in his *alma mater* after receiving the king's instructions to remain in Oxford. But Heylyn then discovered soldiers in the process of taking possession of it five months later, on behalf of the person who had succeeded to the rights of the deceased former owner. Heylyn told Secretary Nicholas and petitioned the king, who gave instructions that Heylyn should be resettled, only for the chancellor of the university, the Marquess of Hertford, to intervene. Hertford called on Heylyn to attend him, but finding that the king had already intervened he withdrew from the case, then dined with Heylyn and enjoyed a friendly correspondence with him thereafter. That at least is Heylyn's account, and Heylyn's later dedication of his *Theologia Veterum* to Hertford would suggest that a reconciliation had been effected. Nevertheless, resentful accounts that told of how Heylyn, when disturbed in his lodgings, had petitioned the king, calling himself His Majesty's creature, and how Hertford had checked him for this, were still circulating late in the 1650s, when Henry Hickman inserted them into a work against Heylyn.[86]

In fact, in 1643 Heylyn could have been forgiven for feeling that he was not among friends when he joined the royalist party. He would have been all too conscious of the fact that there were men in the royalist party who had not only been happy to see the downfall of Laud and his policies, but had willingly participated in their overthrow. Laud had dreamed presciently in November 1642 that 'the Parliament was removed to Oxford; the Church undone; some old courtiers came in to see me, and jeered'. While Laud himself remained in the Tower, nevertheless the church was indeed 'undone', and there were plenty of courtiers at Oxford who had jeered at the archbishop and his followers.[87] Lord George Digby and Sir John Culpepper had presented grievances against Laudianism to parliament, and Digby had proposed to the Commons that evidence should be gathered against all those ministers responsible for the policies of recent years.[88] The royalist hero Sir Francis Wortley had pleaded that men should save the Church of England by punishing those of her sons who 'have dishonoured her by Pride, Tyranny, or Covetousnesse'.[89] Royalists had also made broader attacks on the forces of clericalism. Lord Falkland had launched a systematic attack on Laudian clericalism as the price for impeding the Root and Branch petition against bishops, condemning the Laudian obsession with preaching 'the sacrednesse of the clergie' and how they had worked to create 'a blind dependance of the people upon the clergie'. The Laudian bishops and their adherents were, he proclaimed, guilty 'of the destruction of unitie under pretence of uniformity: to have brought in superstition, and scandall, under the titles of reverence, and decency; to have defil'd our Church by adorning our Churches'. Falkland depicted the Laudian clergy as ultimately being of popish beliefs: some were 'so absolutely directly and cordially Papist, that it is all, that fifteene hundred pounds a yeare can doe to keep them from confessing it [popery]'.[90] Even when the House of Lords initially refused to exclude bishops from the house in June 1641, they had happily agreed (royalist peers among them) to the exclusion of clergy from the court of Star Chamber, from the privy council, from temporal courts and from being JPs (a provision which would have been particularly pertinent to Heylyn, who had only just been appointed a JP for the first time in 1640). Members of the royalist party also now included Edward Bagshawe, who had headed the attack on Laudian clericalism through his condemnations of the canons of 1640 and the *ex officio* oath, his attack on *jure divino* episcopacy and his complaint that the Laudian bishops had 'perverted the ways of godliness'.[91]

If some royalists had indulged in anti-Laudian behaviour in the early 1640s, there also seem to have been much broader lay/clerical tensions at work within royalism. There was clearly talk in royalist Oxford, as royalist fortunes declined and peace negotiations became more urgent, that it was only clergymen who were concerned in seeking to uphold episcopacy, which had become one of the obstructions to a settlement with parliament. It was said that those who insisted on the need to preserve episcopacy simply preferred 'the interests of some inconsiderable men before the inconveniences and com-mon wishes of all'.[92] Heylyn was not alone in distrusting the devotion of the royalist high command to upholding episcopacy. Griffith Williams, a former chaplain in the 1630s to the lord chamberlain, Pembroke, and whom Heylyn would have known as a fellow Westminster prebendary, was forthright in his denunciation of the behaviour of lay royalists towards the church. He stated bluntly in his *Discovery of Mysteries*, published in 1643 (despite Falkland's attempts to block it), that he now feared the secret enemies of church and state who lurked at the court more than those enemies who lay in the earl of Essex's camp.[93] Williams traced a plot against church and state dating back to the beginning of the Long Parliament, but saw the plot still at work in the *royalist* camp, especially among those around Charles who supported an attack on the government and patrimony of the church, who 'pretending great loyalty unto him . . . either to raise or to secure their owne fortunes, would perswade S. Paul to part with S. Peters keyes, so he may still hold the sword in his hand; or to speake more plainly, to purchase the peace of the Common-wealth with the ruine of Gods Church'.[94]

In fact, some of the most important defences of episcopacy written in this period were composed in order to prevent fellow royalists from sacrificing it in peace agreements. Henry Ferne wrote a whole tract specifically against those who felt that episcopacy might be abandoned without prejudicing their reli-gion and their devotion to the king's cause.[95] Similarly, Henry Hammond's *Considerations of Present Use concerning the Danger resulting from the Change of our Church Government* (1645) was specifically aimed at those who believed that episcopal government was lawful but yet thought that to sacrifice it was not a change of religion. Hammond targeted the 'sonnes of this Church' who thought church government 'so unconsiderable a thing, and so extrinsecall to Christianity' that it could be surrendered 'merely out of intuition of our own secular advantages'.[96]

Heylyn's concerns over royalist erastianism and anti-Laudianism can be glimpsed in several of the writings that he undertook after he had finished his duties on *Mercurius Aulicus*. Two works which he published anony-mously in 1645 are particularly notable here. The first is an act of homage to his former mentor, William Laud, when he was executed by parliament. Heylyn swiftly composed *A Briefe Relation of the Death and Sufferings of the Most Reverend and Renowned Prelate* (1644/5). Heylyn can hardly have been unaware that the king had expressed little regret at Laud's death. A number of royalist MPs had been happy to see the archbishop committed to the Tower in 1641, and the erastian attitudes of others would have meant that few would have mourned the death of his policies, if not of the prelate himself. The emphatic tone of Heylyn's eulogy may well therefore have been prompted by defiance as well as grief.[97] There is certainly implied criticism of Laud's royalist opponents in Heylyn's reflection that it was the attack on bishops which had necessitated the subversion of the fundamental laws, and that the committal of Laud to the Tower was a breach of the subject's liberties which supplied the precedent for all the later troubles. All of the later misfortunes would have been avoided 'had the Subject made his Case their owne'. 'They who doe so gladly sell the bloud of their fellow Subjects', Heylyn remarked darkly, 'seldome want Chapmen for their owne in an open Market.'[98] This was surely directed at fellow royalists.

While historians have noted the martyr cult that developed around Charles I, it should also be emphasized that Heylyn's pamphlet attempted to do the same for Laud, while pre-dating the Caroline cult by several years. Heylyn presented the treatment of Laud as the presage of all the country's later troubles. In describing Laud's execution, Heylyn declares that the scaffold was 'a Throne whereon he shortly was to receive a Crowne, even the most glorious Crowne of Martyrdome'. Like Samson, 'he gave a greater blow unto the enemies of God and the King at the houre of his death, than he had given them in his whole life before'. But Heylyn did not compare 'this glorious Martyr' only with Samson. Sir John Clotworthy's baiting of Laud on the scaffold he compared to the scribes and Pharisees proposing questions to Jesus, while Heylyn noted that the sun shone while Laud prayed at the block but went behind a cloud as soon as the blow was given, just as occurred at the execution of St Stephen. At his execution Laud's soul ascended on wings of angels into Abraham's bosom. The archbishop had exchanged his mitre for a crown, and in his final elegy Heylyn proposed that Laud's name should be placed as a fixed rubric in the Prayer Book calendar – 'And let this silence the pure Sects' complaints/If they make Martyrs, we may make a Saint'. The elegy concludes even more strikingly with an appeal to the newly sainted Laud to 'let us have thy prayers' – an allusion that was removed in the second London reprint of the work (presumably without Heylyn's agreement, as he retains this phrase in the version of the elegy with which he concludes his later life of Laud, *Cyprianus Anglicus*).[99] Heylyn's memorial to Laud – 'the last publique Office I shall do him', as he himself called it – provides a useful reminder that, while Heylyn often changed ideas and support – and was very far from being an uncritical admirer of King Charles – he would appear to have been consistently loyal to Laud.[100]

Heylyn's anxieties concerning the erastian instincts of prominent royalists may also partly lie behind a curious work published by Heylyn in 1645 entitled *Parliaments Power in Lawes for Religion*. This was not a work prompted by the royalist authorities. Its ostensible background was that a friend of Heylyn's (George Ashwell, of Wadham College, according to Wood) was troubled by the Roman Catholic charge that the Church of England's religion was essentially a parliamentary religion. Heylyn responded by composing a short treatise which nevertheless represents one of the most emphatically clericalist readings of the English Reformation that he ever mounted. Determined to deny that parliament played any role in the Reformation, Heylyn displayed his usual powers of overkill by producing an interpretation of the Reformation that placed the responsibility for every stage of the process in the hands of Convocation and the clergy:

> The proceedings of this Church in the Reformation were not merely Regall (as it is objected by some Puritans) much lesse that they were Parliamentarian in so great a work, as the Papists falsely charge upon us, the Parliament for the most part doing little in it, but that they were directed in a justifiable way, the worke being done Synodically, by the Clergie only, according to the usage of the Primitive times, the King concurring with them, and corroborating what they had resolved on.[101]

Heylyn also took particular delight in arguing that in Henry's reign parliament was used only to impede the reformation.[102]

Heylyn later insisted that this tract was written 'on an occasion really given'.[103] Certainly there had been conversions to Catholicism in the royalist court at Oxford. Moreover, George Ashwell was apparently a friend of another fellow of Wadham, Tristram Sugge, who was clearly entertaining serious reservations about the conduct of the English Reformation which he expressed in a number of manuscript notebooks. It seems very likely that Heylyn and Sugge were at least aware of each other through their mutual friend. (They also shared the same enthusiasm for the patriarchalist writings of Robert Filmer.)[104] Nevertheless, Heylyn's arguments also may well relate to continuing disagreements on the royalist side. The insistence that it was the church and not parliament that had reformed religion in England may have refuted Roman claims, but this was also a very opportune moment to be reminding royalists of the same thing as the Uxbridge negotiations got under way.

Similar concerns are apparent in some of the court sermons which Heylyn continued to deliver while he was at Oxford. Thus a sermon given at Christ Church on 26 September 1643 gives several examples praising church fathers standing up to the laity: 'St Ambrose was resolved not to submit his judgement in a point of faith to the decisions and decrees of a Lay-Tribunal, though nothing but apparent ruine was to be expected on his refusal of the same . . . An equal courage unto which we finde in Chrysostom' (and he also urges the courage of Luther before Charles V).[105] He stresses the importance of the church retaining the power of excommunication, and of binding and loosing: 'And to what end serves "Dic Ecclesiae", if the poor Church have power to hear, but not to censure?'[106] He condemns people's failure to assist the Laudians when they had tried to suppress the puritan menace before it was too late: 'How few made offer of their service, when occasion was; I say not to root out, but suppress those tares which threatned then such imminent dangers, and have since brought so sad a desolation on this Church of Christ?'[107] There is still the implication, then, that those around him in royalist Oxford had not supported Laud. He notes 'how few made offer of their service' when an attempt was made to root out the tares that have now brought desolation on the church, he warns of popular iconoclasm and condemns the 'monstrous Paradoxes in Divinity' that have been vented in the Westminster Assembly, he appeals that the church should have the power to censure vice effectively, and warns of how 'the zeal of some Reformers hath eaten up many of the Houses of Almighty God'.[108]

Many of these concerns are also evident in one of Heylyn's most interesting and revealing works from this period which he wrote in Oxford but which he did not manage to have published. This was his treatise entitled *The Stumbling Block of Disobedience and Rebellion*. Heylyn seems to have encountered unfamiliar problems in publishing his writings during this time, which may reflect the new and possibly cumbersome royalist system of pre-publication censorship that was introduced in 1644. He revised his *History of Liturgies* in 1645 in response to the parliamentary ordinance of January of that year reducing all set times of public worship to one, but this revised version remained unpublished.[109] The failure to publish the *Stumbling Block* is surprising. It is not clear that the work was directly blocked. Vernon reports that it was written in late 1644, and that Lord Hatton, Bishop Duppa, Sir Orlando Bridgeman and Richard Steward perused the whole treatise. The king had approved its contents, and commanded Lord Digby to consider the book, 'in whose hands it did for a long time rest'.[110] Inertia and increasing practical restrictions on royalist printing may mostly explain the fact that Heylyn's work lay dormant. But as this would have been his first extended, controversial treatise to have been published with official endorsement since 1637, it is worth pausing over its content. There are undoubtedly aspects of the work which would not have endeared themselves to some bodies of royalist opinion.

One issue on which Heylyn may have raised eyebrows was his explicit attack on the king's *Answer to the Nineteen Propositions*. Charles's *Answer to the Nineteen Propositions* – apparently written by Falkland and Sir John Culpepper – had argued that, rather than the three parliamentary estates consisting of the secular lords, the bishops and the commons, they actually consisted of the king, lords and commons, with the king therefore performing a role in which he was co-ordinate with the other constituent groups of parliament. The intention was to argue that parliament was therefore not capable of doing anything when one of its constituent elements – the king – was absent. But the argument could, of course, cut both ways, and gave parliamentarian pamphleteers the opportunity to argue that, as two of the three estates remained with them, they might still pass legislation in this emergency. The king now ran the risk of being demoted to being merely one of three equal estates in parliament, which were co-ordinate equals in the making of law.[III] Another aspect of the disagreement over the estates that was of direct concern to Heylyn and other clergymen was the fact that the *Answer to the Nineteen Propositions* could be taken to endorse the absence of the bishops from parliament, as they were no longer taken to constitute a separate estate. The *Answer* also contained worrying concessions on the reform of the church and the toleration of nonconformity.[112]

Aspects of the *Answer to the Nineteen Propositions* had been rejected by implication in a number of royalist works. Heylyn's own pamphlet *The Rebells Catechism* (1643) had attacked the notion that the king's power was 'co-ordinate' with that of parliament, although it did not suggest that this position had been granted by royalist writers.[113] Others had written as if bishops were one of the three estates: Bramhall was clearly writing with gritted teeth when he remarked that he assumed that there was a good reason for removing the bishops' votes in the Lords, but he did not doubt that there would be other good reasons for restoring them again.[114] Other royalist clergymen implicitly disagreed with the *Answer* by counting bishops as one of the three estates.[115] Heylyn's *Stumbling Block* was more unusual in specifically condemning other royalist writings. He complained directly of how the argument that the king was one of the three estates had been 'presented to the world in some publick writings . . . A fancy by what Accident soever it was broached and published, which hath no consistence either with truth, or ordinary observation, or with the practice of this Realm, or any other'. It implied that the king's power must be co-ordinate with the Lords and Commons, and that therefore the two could overrule the king, 'which dangerous consequents whether they were observed at first by those who ventured on the expression, or were improvidently looked over, I can hardly say'. Heylyn chose his words carefully here, but he made it clear in a later anonymous work that he assumed that Charles himself was responsible for this concession in the *Answer to the Nineteen Propositions*, which had obliged royalist writers to accept the idea of co-ordinate power. In the *Stumbling Block* Heylyn also explicitly condemned Henry Ferne's *Conscience satisfied*, published in Oxford in 1643, for 'improvidently' urging this model of co-ordinate power. 'Certain I am', Heylyn balefully concludes, 'it gave too manifest an advantage to the Antimonarchical party in this Kingdome, and hardned them in their proceeding against their King.'[116]

Heylyn's *Stumbling Block* differed from prominent royalist writings in other ways. Heylyn offered a more emphatic defence of royal authority, not only in denying parliament any share in sovereignty, but also in insisting that the king had sole legal sovereignty through the Normans' right of conquest. Rather than using biblical or patriarchal arguments for royal authority, Heylyn turned to history. He noted that 'when the Norman Conqueror first came in, as he wonne the Kingdom by the sword, so did he govern it by his power: His Sword was then the Scepter, and his will the Law.' Any subsequent grants of liberties did not detract from the basic fact of the king's absolute sovereignty, established by right of conquest. This meant that 'the power of making Laws . . . is properly and legally in the King alone'.[117]

The basic thrust of the whole treatise reflects another aspect of Heylyn's attempts to rewrite the royalist position, and this related to the perceived position of Calvin and the foreign Reformed churches. Heylyn's *Stumbling Block* is specifically aimed at Calvin's remarks in chapter 20 of Book 4 of the *Institutes*, where he states that while people must never rebel against anointed kings, nevertheless where popular officers had been ordained to restrain the power of kings (such as the three estates in every kingdom) those officers were bound in conscience to restrain kings whenever necessary. This was a concession that had long created anxiety, and that David Owen had attacked explicitly as early as 1610.[118] For those who were keen to invoke Calvin as an authority against rebellion it was tempting simply to ignore this passage, and that is what Thomas Morton in his sermon against the Scottish rebels in 1639 and Walter Balcanquahall in the King's own *Large Declaration* in 1640 had done. They and later royalist writers had in fact been anxious to emphasize that Calvin condemned rebellion, and that the foreign Reformed churches condemned the activities of the Scottish Covenanters and the English parliament. King Charles for one was not fooled by this partial reading of Calvin. He intervened directly in 1639 to change the text of Morton's sermon in advance of publication. Where Morton had written that there was not 'any one syllable in Calvin out of which they shalbe able to prove their conclusion of opposing the Higher Powers', Charles ordered this passage to be deleted because of the King's 'sight & reading divers Sayings in Calvins Institutions (lib. 4.)'.[119] Heylyn differed from this approach of careful selection or knowing omission by confronting Calvin's concession head-on and denouncing it. Rather than seeking Calvin's support, he was happy to depict Calvin and his followers as the source of all the popular rebellions of the previous hundred years. In his *Rebells Catechism* Heylyn had already attacked Calvin and Buchanan for endorsing ideas of popular sovereignty and of the king's two bodies respectively.[120] In the *Stumbling Block* Heylyn declares that all the wars and miseries of recent years have derived from Calvin's fatal words, notes that Calvin never retracted them in later editions of the *Institutes*, and announces that his book is bringing the Genevan reformer at last to a public trial.[121]

But it is Heylyn's concerns with anticlericalism – on the royalist as well as the parliamentarian side – that form one of the striking features of the *Stumbling Block*. Heylyn was happy to develop the notion that royal power in England was invested with the right of conquest of the Norman kings, but he was also concerned to curb the erastian instincts of prominent royalists. While the

Stumbling Block is usually read simply as a defence of royal authority, it should be noted that one-quarter of the work – some seventy-three pages – is effectively a separate tract defending the right of bishops to sit in parliament, and also asserting the more general right of clergymen to exercise secular political authority.[122] Amassing authorities for the latter point takes Heylyn back not just to the Old Testament, but also to ancient Egypt and the Druids. Just as his *History of Liturgies* sought to identify a basic ritualistic tendency in human nature, so Heylyn endeavoured to establish here that in all human societies the priesthood exercised secular powers. Moreover, Heylyn insisted that the removal of bishops from parliament deprived the clergy of proper representation, and meant that the clergy had become the only members of the political nation who were not represented in parliament. This Heylyn equated with slavery.[123]

All this went well beyond Heylyn's immediate task in the *Stumbling Block* of denying the model of the three estates and the right of parliamentary bodies to resist their sovereign monarch. It also went beyond even the associated point that, by making the bishops no longer one of the three estates, the *Answer to the Nineteen Propositions* could be construed as supporting the Bishops' Exclusion Act – a contentious piece of legislation that was physically enacted every day that the Oxford Parliament met with no bishops present. Again, it seems that Heylyn's message was directed at royalists just as much as parliamentarians. Indeed, Heylyn concluded the whole treatise by admitting that, while he had pleaded the cause of kings in the book, he had 'added somewhat in behalf of the Church of England, whose Right and privileges I have pleaded to my best abilities'. He ended with the pious hope that, as kings received their authority from God, 'so they may use [it] in the protection and defence of the Church of God', and therefore God would 'save them from the striving of unruly people'. Given that earlier in the tract Heylyn had deplored how the Bishops' Exclusion Act had been 'extorted' from the king under pressure, and was therefore legally invalid, these closing remarks were perhaps rather more than a pious platitude.[124] There was surely a veiled threat that God's protection would be removed from the king unless he started to defend the church properly.

IN RETREAT, 1645–1648

According to Heylyn's own account, he finally departed from the royalist capital in early May 1645. He claimed that he had the king's leave to depart, but in truth there was little to keep him in Oxford. Apart from a brief period in June 1644 he had long ago ceased to edit *Mercurius Aulicus* – the main reason why Charles had first required him to remain in the city. There is little indication that he had had many direct dealings with the king during his years in Oxford, nor does he seem to have developed close relations with other prominent royalists. Relieved as he was to be no longer serving as editor of *Mercurius Aulicus*, his lack of a salary may have left him struggling all the more to secure appropriate accommodation. As Heylyn later described events, his departure from Oxford was not prompted by any wish to promote royalist objectives elsewhere – he simply wished to leave the city and instead to immerse himself in scholarly retirement.

There were, however, recent events which may well have bred in Heylyn a sense of profound resentment and alienation from the court. Heylyn was clearly furious that in November 1644 he had been passed over for the deanery of York, despite having been recommended to the king by the duke of Richmond, Secretary Nicholas and 'M.E.P.' (presumably 'Mr Endymion Porter'). He grumpily entered in his diary that the post had been given to Dr Marsh 'one who had never lived before above the life of Curate'. Heylyn blamed Bishop Duppa for having acted against him.[125]

The failure to gain the deanery would have been a particular blow to Heylyn, as he urgently needed the income. Because of his residence in Oxford he had been voted a delinquent by parliament in November 1643, when the Committee for Sequestrations had ordered the County Committee to inventory his books at Alresford. As the area had been retaken from Waller by royalist forces, the sequestration order could not be implemented, and Heylyn had continued in reasonable prosperity, owning a coach and horses among other trappings of affluence. According to Heylyn's diary, it was not until 27 March 1644 that a parliamentary order was sent to the committee at Portsmouth to sequester Heylyn's estate and seize his goods. It was the taking of Reading by the earl of Essex on 26 April that then enabled the sequestration of Heylyn's estate to be effected. After the taking of Alresford by parliamentary forces Heylyn's goods, corn, cattle and money were seized, and his books carried away to Portsmouth. Heylyn had attempted to have his goods removed from Alresford in time, but either through ill luck or the treachery of his neighbours, the cart with all the goods was seized by parliamentary soldiers. Heylyn blamed his losses on the behaviour of a royalist colonel who would not send a convoy of horse to guard the goods, although Newcastle had given an order for it.[126] Heylyn was not, of course, the only loser in the events around Alresford – the withdrawal of the royalist garrisons from Reading and Abingdon was part of a disastrous series of military blunders by Charles that almost resulted in his falling into enemy hands, and which led him secretly to flee Oxford temporarily for Worcester at the beginning of June.

Heylyn petitioned the king for reparations out of the estate of the parliamentarian Colonel Norton (whose hand was on the warrant of sequestration), but without success: his first petition was simply denied, and the second one merely put off.[127] Heylyn was now effectively destitute. He sold his only remaining possessions – his coach and horses – and survived on charity, sending his wife to live in London.[128] Given that all of Heylyn's troubles had been inflicted because of his enforced residence at Oxford at the king's command, the rejection of his petitions for reparations and then the king's decision to pass over his suit for the deanery of York must have instilled a deep sense of betrayal. When Charles himself left the city in May 1645, planning ultimately to meet up with Montrose in the north, Heylyn may well have felt that his obligations towards the king and the royalist cause were now at an end. Impoverished because of his support for the king, but unable to gain any royal patronage to support himself, the only course of action left was to leave Oxford and try to live with friends and kinsmen. Whatever the precise reason for his departure, it is difficult to dismiss the suspicion that for Heylyn it reflected a desire to abandon his direct involvement in the struggles of the royalist party, and to look to his own resources. As Heylyn later described events, his departure from Oxford was not prompted by any wish to promote royalist objectives elsewhere – he simply wished to leave the city and instead to immerse himself in scholarly retirement. In this context, the final sentences of the last surviving sermon that he delivered in Oxford, less than two months before his departure from the royalist capital, may be revealing. Ironically it would appear to have been the only time that he spoke as part of the Lenten roster of court preachers, but if this honour was intended to appease him for his losses it was unsuccessful. The sermon ends in notable fashion. Addressing the faithful soul as it prepares for the final judgement, Heylyn writes:

> Come then thou blessed Soul into the place of thy rest; Thou hast been long a wearied Pilgrim on the face of the earth, tossed from one station to another, spent with continual travel, and worn out with labours, yet all this while couldst find no rest for the sole of thy foot: Here is an everlasting rest provided for thee, Enter thou good and faithful Servant into the joy of the Lord; Thou hast been faithful in a little, employed thy Master's Talent to the best advantage, and for so doing hast been reviled and beaten by thy fellow-servants, wounded and shamefully intreated by those Husbandmen to whom the Lord let forth his Vineyard; and slain in fine, in hope, the Lords Inheritance would be shared among them.[129]

It may not be fanciful to suspect a self-referential element in these words of farewell from Oxford. Heylyn was not, after all, one to bear his oppressions lightly.

Departure from Oxford at this point was certainly not in itself a trouble-free option. The city was surrounded by parliamentarian forces soon after Heylyn left it. Heylyn's son-in-law provides an elaborate account of the dangers and humiliations of the subsequent weeks and months. According to Barnard, Heylyn left Oxford 'walking as a poor traveller in the country, not knowing well whither he should go'. Disguised in name (taking the aliases of Barker and Harding) and clothing, Heylyn was nevertheless betrayed by one Mrs Munday, a zealous 'she-Puritan', in Oxfordshire at his first setting out. Having barely escaped, Heylyn then travelled through various royalist safe houses, while his wife and children stayed among relatives and friends. After 'God' (or more likely relatives) sent him supplies of money, he settled with his wife and eldest daughter in the house of a Mr Lizard in Winchester. The calamitous royalist defeat at Naseby in June meant that Heylyn received only temporary respite, however. When parliamentary forces seized Winchester later that summer Lizard temporarily hid Heylyn in 'a private room', possibly a priest hole, for a short period of time, but soon Heylyn fled Winchester, leaving his wife and daughter behind there. He was briefly caught and manhandled by soldiers as he left, but managed to reach 'a private friends house in a Parish of Wiltshire'.[130] It is unclear how far Barnard may have embellished this account, or how true was the supposed report that Heylyn received from an MP that parliament intended to execute him in revenge for the punishment of Prynne. Nevertheless, there seems little doubt that for some of this time Heylyn went in fear of his life, and that he was always conscious that his Laudian notoriety would have made him a sought-after prisoner. If he appears at times a more cautious figure in the 1650s, anxious to avoid offending the army, then it is important to bear in mind his own sufferings and dangers in the 1640s.

With the end of the war Heylyn was free to compound for his sequestration. He 'waded through' his composition (in his own words). On 6 December 1646 he was fined at a tenth, £112, and all his personal estate was taken from him.[131] He was fortunate that his time in Oxford meant that he was able to profit from the articles made at the surrender of Oxford in 1646, which saved him from further prosecution, and also gave him a guarantee that if he continued to compound he would be freed 'from Oaths, Engagements and Molestations . . . except an engagement by promise, not to beare Armes against the Parliament, nor wilfully do any act prejudiciall to their Affaires'.[132] As Heylyn later noted, this freed him from having to swear the Covenant and Negative Oath.[133] Heylyn's decision to compound was not entirely unusual. Prominent lay royalists such as the earl of Dorset, the marquess of Hertford and the marquess of Dorchester compounded under the Oxford Articles, as did a number of royal chaplains (including Bruno Ryves, William Fuller, Griffin Higgs and William Brough) and Humphrey Henchman.[134] Nevertheless almost none of the churchmen in the Hammond/ Sheldon circle of 1650s 'Anglicanism' compounded, and Robert Skinner was virtually the only bishop who did so. Heylyn's decision to compound under the Oxford Articles did not necessarily alienate him from other royalists, but it did distinguish him from the more prominent 'Anglican' clergymen.

Having, as he later described, 'fixed my self on a certain dwelling near the place of my birth' in Oxfordshire in mid-April 1647 (possibly the house of his friend Dr Kingsmill), Heylyn from thence removed to Minster Lovell in Oxfordshire, the seat of his deceased elder brother, in 1648, 'which he farmed of his nephew Colonel Heylyn for six years'.[135]

The years following the end of the war were ones of increasing anxiety for the future of the church. During 1647, when there was a possibility that Charles might form a temporary alliance with the Independents and the army, a number of clergymen dispatched letters of advice to Charles over how legitimate it was for him to offer temporary religious toleration to dissenters. Those involved were the bishops Brian Duppa, Ralph Brownrigg, James Ussher, Thomas Morton, John Warner, William Juxon, John Prideaux, and William Piers, and the royal chaplains Robert Sanderson, Gilbert Sheldon, Richard Holdsworth, Henry Hammond, Brian Walton and Jeremy Taylor. Heylyn, who had been a royal chaplain longer than a good number of these men, was not involved.[136] Neither was he one of those chaplains called to attend on Charles during his final months.

Heylyn did not turn his back on the church completely, however. Even with the war still raging in April 1646, he was writing a letter of recommendation to his friend Bishop Towers for one Dr Alcorne, 'a very able scholar and a honest churchman', to a disputed living in Berkshire.[137] In 1647 he also completed what was his only publication between 1645 and 1652, which was printed the following year under the title of 'P. H. Treleinie, Gent'. (an anagram of his name). Thus was his short tract *The Undeceiving of the People in the point of Tithes*. It is notable that Heylyn chose to portray the author of his tract as a gentleman rather than a clergyman. He had of course been deprived of his cure of souls at this point, so there was some truth to the appellation. But the argument of the tract is also essentially that of a layman. Its greatest stress is on common law, and on a topic that had generated some notably extreme and clericalist readings by Richard Montagu and others, its tone is moderate and restrained. While Heylyn's *Observations* of 1656 represent an occasion when Heylyn's anonymity as an author seems to have freed him to make more outspoken comments, it is notable that in his anonymous tracts of the 1640s the sense of vulnerability that led him to adopt a pseudonym would also seem to have drawn him to an uncharacteristically moderate style of argument. His tract on tithes would be reprinted in 1651, when parliament once more debated the issue.

Nevertheless, Heylyn was no longer involved with events at court, nor was he permitted publicly to exercise his ecclesiastical office. Before the end of the first Civil War, Heylyn would already seem to have ceased to play the public role to which he had so long aspired. His movements during the Second Civil War are unclear. He had had sufficient contact with the underground royalist movement during the months after his flight from Oxford to have doubtless been aware of royalist activities in the area. He was certainly in contact with family members living in London, his nephew the royalist colonel, and with Sir Robert Filmer in the summer of 1648.[138] The only tantalizing hint of his possible involvement in the revived royalist movement of these months is Barnard's report that he shielded the parliamentarian turncoat Marchamont Nedham during the latter's brief career as the editor of the royalist *Mercurius Pragmaticus*. Barnard claims that Heylyn 'preserved him in a high room' (presumably at his nephew's manor house at Minster Lovell), from which place Nedham 'continued writing his weekly *Pragmaticus*'. If this story is true, it seems unlikely that the ex-editor of *Mercurius Aulicus* would not have discussed the content of the new royalist newsbook with its author, although Nedham's later apostasy to the republican cause would have made Heylyn reluctant to acknowledge this. Certainly, Barnard notes that Heylyn 'could never after endure the mention of his name, who had so disobliged his country and the royal party by his shameful tergiversation'. It seems likely that in the Second Civil War and its aftermath Heylyn's chief contribution was to offer the clandestine hospitality from which he himself had profited in the years 1645–46. He and his family had already suffered sufficiently at the hands of parliament and the army, and received little acknowledgement from the king, for Heylyn to have been ready to risk further punishment by playing a more overt role in royalist resistance.

NOTES

1 *Memorial*, p. xxii; Wood MS E.4, fol. 27v.

2 *The Petition of the Inhabitants of Istleworth . . . against William Grant* (1641), p. 5; CUL, MS Mm/1/45, p. 35.

3 *ODNB*, s.n. 'William Laud'.

4 *Ibid.*; Laud, *Works*, III, p. 443.

5 Milton, 'Creation', pp. 183–4; *idem*, 'Laudian moment'; B. P. Levack, *The Civil Lawyers in England, 1603–1641* (Oxford, 1973), pp. 147, 207, 213, 227; Matthews, *Walker Revised*, p. 50; W. W. Greg, *Licensers for the Press to 1640* (1962), p. 106.

6 P. Lake, 'Serving God and the times: the Calvinist conformity of Robert Sanderson', *Journal of British Studies*, 27 (1988), pp. 103–4, 108.

7 Vernon, p. 106.

8 *The Journal of Sir Simonds D'Ewes from the Beginning of the Long Parliament to the Opening of the Trial of the Earl of Strafford*, ed. W. Notestein (New Haven CT, 1923), p. 6 and n.30. For Heylyn's awareness of these attacks see his *Extraneus*, p. 55.

9 M. Jansson, *Proceedings in the Opening Session of the Long Parliament* (6 vols, Rochester NY, 2000–), II, p. 187; *The Lord Faulkland his learned speech in Parliament*,

in the House of Commons, touching the Judges and the late Lord Keeper (1641), p. 5. Ironically, Falkland and Heylyn were natives of the same town: Falkland was born at Burford Priory and had inherited the town and manor (Gretton, *Burford Records*, p. 274).

10 Heylyn, *Cosmographie* (1652), sig. A3v.

11 E.g. Richard Bernard, *A Threefold Treatise of the Sabbath* (1641); William Twisse, *Of the Morality of the Fourth Commandement* (1641), esp. pp. 22–3, 42, 91–3, 105, 153; George Hakewill, *A Dissertation with Dr Heylyn: touching the Pretended Sacrifice in the Eucharist* (1641); idem, *A Short but Cleare Discourse, of the Institution, Dignity and End, of the Lords Day* (1641); Hamon L'Estrange, *Gods Sabbath before the Law, under the Law and under the Gospel* (1641), esp. pp. 21, 32, 67, 69, 72, 74, 75, 79, 82, 98.

12 *CE*, pp. 46–7.

13 *Observations*, p. 217.

14 D'Ewes, *Journal*, pp. 186–7.

15 *Extraneus*, pp. 43, 53–4.

16 *Ibid.*, p. 58. Heylyn's full account appears on pp. 58–66.

17 Barnard, pp. 192–4.

18 *Extraneus*, pp. 58–61. Barnard's account of the events differs in some details: Barnard, pp. 195–6.

19 *Extraneus*, pp. 63–5.

20 *Ibid.*, p. 56.

21 *EH*, i. pp. 242–3. *LJ*, IV, pp. 180, 183, 219.

22 *LJ*, IV, p. 161.

23 Macray, *Register*, IV, p. 182.

24 Pocklington was also proceeded against for his *Sunday no Sabbath*, but Heylyn's *History of the Sabbath* was no less intemperate in its argument, and also went into two editions. Williams's reported exclamation in the committee on religious innovations (sitting in the Jerusalem Chamber) that all books should be publicly burnt that had disputed the morality of the Lord's Day sabbath would undoubtedly have been aimed at Heylyn just as much as Pocklington: *EH*, i. p. 243.

25 *Extraneus*, pp. 57, 62–3. Heylyn recorded in his diary for 13 December that because of the reports raised by Williams's interruption of his sermon he had decided 'to send a copie of the whole passage as it should have been spoken, both to my friends at Court & enimies in parliament' (my italics), and under an entry two days later records 'the Bishop of Lyncoln Action censured & my Carriage justified' (Bodl., Wood MS E.4, fol. 28r).

26 D'Ewes, *Journal*, p. 132.

27 *Ibid.*, p. 186.

28 *Ibid.*, pp. 158–9.

29 TNA, SP 16/473/105.

30 *Extraneus*, p. 62.

31 Barnard, pp. 197–8. While Barnard does not specifically date this exchange, Vernon (116–17) locates it at the meeting when Heylyn and Williams resolved their differences, described in *Extraneus*, pp. 63–5. Heylyn's own account, as we have seen, makes vague allusions to 'expostulations . . . and honest defences' but does not refer specifically to this exchange.

32 D'Ewes, *Journal*, pp. 305–6.

33 TNA, SP 16/476/97.

34 See below.

35 *A Calendar of the Court Minutes . . . of the East India Company, 1640–1679* (11 vols, Oxford, 1907–38), II, p. 130.

36 WAM, Chapter Act Book II, fol. 77v (chapter meeting of 10 February 1641). Heylyn had been absent from previous meetings on 14 and 23 December 1640 and 25 January 1641 (fols 75r–77v).

37 A. G. Matthews, *Walker Revised* (Oxford, 1948), p. 184; Barnard, p. 199; *CA*, pp. 470–1.

38 J. Morrill, *The Nature of the English Revolution* (1993), p. 158; C. Russell, *The Fall of the British Monarchies, 1637–1642* (Oxford, 1991), pp. 411–12.

39 Others included Thomas Westfield (who had opposed the 'etcetera oath' and the sitting of convocation after the dissolution of the Short Parliament) and Ralph Brownrigg (who was married to John Pym's niece and had already played a notable role in opposing Laudianism in Cambridge University in the 1630s and in the Short Parliament convocation of 1640). *ODNB*, s.n. 'John Prideaux', 'Thomas Westfield', 'Ralph Brownrigg'; Russell, *Fall*, p. 110.

40 TNA, LC5/135, section 5, p. 4. Out of twenty-one preachers, non-Laudians include John Prideaux, Thomas Winniffe, Thomas Howell, Daniel Featley, John Young, Richard Love, John Hacket and John Bridgeman. Only two of these (Featley and Winniffe) had preached the previous year (LC5/134, p. 455).

41 Thomas Westfield, *A Sermon preached in the Cathedrall Church of S. Paul on the fourteenth Day of November 1641, in the Evening* (1641), pp. 11, 20–1.

42 George Morley, *A Modest Advertisement concerning the present Controversie about Church-government* (1641), pp. 18–19.

43 *A Copie of the Proceedings of some worthy and learned Divines* (1641), pp. 1–2.

44 See for example the defence of the Book of Sports in 'Of the Sabbath, written in satisfaction of a friend, June 1641': Bodl., Rawl. MS D.1350, fols 268r–295v.

45 Heylyn supposedly wrote a rapid answer to Hakewill's *Dissertation*: Vernon mentions this response as being in manuscript in 1641, and Wood lists it among Heylyn's writings, although Hearne notes that it does not seem to have been printed (Vernon, pp. 220–1; Wood, *Ath. Ox.*, III, col. 560). It seems clear that Heylyn suppressed the work. Vernon claims that he did this because Hakewill's friends called in Hakewill's book, but there is no other evidence for this, and it seems far more likely that Heylyn simply considered it unsafe to publish a self-defence at this time.

46 See the copy of the 1680 edition preserved in the Clark Library, UCLA, described in *The Center and Clark Newsletter*, 39 (spring 2002). I am grateful to Karen Harvey for this reference.

47 *CE*, p. 329.

48 *Horologia Anglorum, or, An Help to English History* (1641), preface.

49 Richard Dey, *Two Looks over Lincoln* (1641).

50 Russell, *Fall*, p. 247. It is often stated (even by modern scholars such as Walker) that this paper was published in the 1681 edition of Heylyn's works (and, indeed, the editor of that volume specifically claims on the relevant title page that the tract 'De jure paritatis episcoporum' was written in 1640 in response to the attempt to exclude the bishops from Strafford's trial). But it is quite clear from the very first sentence of this tract that it actually dates from the Restoration period, even if Heylyn may have been re-stating some of the arguments that he used in the earlier paper. The earlier paper itself, however, does not seem to have survived.

51 Williams did, however, emphasize the bishops' pre-Conquest parliamentary presence in one version of his speech: M. Mendle, *Dangerous Positions* (Birmingham AL, 1985), p. 159. The historical argument in defence of bishops sitting in the House of Lords was developed more fully in Gerard Langbaine's anonymously published *Episcopall Inheritance* (1641), which responded to Cornelius Burges's *Humble Examination of Printed Extract* and which Burges suggested was published around December 1641 (Cornelius Burges, *The Broken Title of Episcopal Inheritance* (1642), p. 2).

52 *Observations*, pp. 224–5.

53 Heylyn, *The Historie of Episcopacie* (1642), preface, sigs A4v–a1r.

54 Joseph Hall, *A Short Answer to the Tedious Vindication of Smectymnuus* (1641), p. 21.

55 One of the Smectymnuan authors was William Spurstow, who had been recipient of a gift in Rowland Heylyn's will (TNA, Prob. 11/161, fols 179r–181r).

56 Joseph Hall, *Short Answer*, p. 102.

57 Heylyn, *Historie of Episcopacie*, preface.

58 Hammond, *Dissertationes Quatuor* (1651); Spurr, *Restoration*, p. 139; Trott, 'Prelude', pp. 76–9.

59 Jeremy Taylor, *Of the Sacred Order and Offices of Episcopacy* (Oxford, 1642), pp. 190–97 (see also pp. 30–2, 99–100, 158–9, 166–70); *RP*, pp. 100–1, 132.

60 Vernon, p. 121. Walker (p. 170) notes that sheets were left over from this impression for reissue in the *Ecclesia Vindicata*.

61 Vernon, p. 121. The delinquent Dr William Watts was found to have a copy (TNA, SP 20/9, fol. 20v).

62 Kendall, 'Royalist scholar', pp. 209–10.

63 Heylyn did not sign for meetings of the Westminster chapter on 27 May, 5 June, 8 July and 21 December 1641, or 18 February 1642 (WAM, Chapter Act Book II, fols 78r–80v).

64 *PT*, pp. 367–95.

65 *Ibid.*, pp. 367–73, 390–1.

66 *Ibid.*, p. 391.

67 WAM, Chapter Act Book II, fols 77v–81.

68 Matthews, *Walker Revised*, p. 184.

69 Vernon, pp. 122–3.

70 TNA, C5/377/105. The accounts of both Barnard and Vernon are misleading on these matters, as they conflate the initial confrontation of Waller's troops in the summer of 1642 with the sequestration of Heylyn's estate by parliament, which was implemented only in late May 1644; see below.

71 Bodl., Rawl. MS D.353, fol. 103r–v.

72 *HQA*, postscript, sig. Ppp4r–v.

73 Bodl., Rawl. MS D.353, fol. 103r–v. Among the addressees is Arthur Lipscombe the younger, whose father Heylyn had crossed swords with earlier (see above, ch. 2).

74 J. Malcolm, *Caesar's Due: Loyalty and King Charles, 1642–1646* (1983), p. 131. But see Peacey, *Politicians*, p. 124. A specific form of pre-publication censorship was not introduced in royalist Oxford until 1644.

75 By far the best analysis of royalist factional and ideological divisions is David Scott's 'Rethinking royalist politics: faction and ideology, 1642–1649', forthcoming in J. Adamson (ed.), *Civil War and Rebellion in the Kingdoms of Charles I*. I am grateful to Dr Scott for letting me read his important article in advance of publication. For a presentation of royalist divisions as essentially being between 'constitutional royalists' and 'absolutists' see D. L. Smith, *Constitutional Royalism and the Search for Settlement, c. 1640–1649* (Cambridge, 1994), esp. ch. 7.

76 *Theeves, Theeves: or A Relation of Sir Iohn Gell's Proceedings in Darbyshire* (1643), p. 9; *A Letter from an Officer in His Majesties Army* (1643).

77 *Mercurius Aulicus*, week 1, 1 January, pp. 1–3.

78 *Ibid.*, week 38, 20 September, p. 529; *Memorial*, p. xxiv; Bodl., Wood MS E.4, fol. 28v.

79 N. Smith, *Literature and Revolution* (1992).

80 *Lord have Mercie upon Us* (1643), pp. 7, 49.

81 Vernon, pp. 123–4; *Memorial*, pp. xxiii–iv; P. W. Thomas, *Sir John Berkenhead, 1617–1679: a Royalist Career in Politics and Polemics* (Oxford, 1969), p. 33. Thomas suggests that after the fourth week only Nos 30–8 were edited by Heylyn alone. Heylyn would also take over editorial work again briefly in June 1644 when Berkenhead travelled with Charles to Worcester and Heylyn was, as he puts it, 'intreated to resume my old employment' (*Memorial*, p. xxiii), which he undertook in editing *Mercurius Aulicus* Nos 74–7 (26 May–1 June to 16–22 June 1644).

82 Barnard, p. 17.

83 Thomas, *Berkenhead*, p. 33.

84 *Memorial*, p. xviii; Bodl., Wood MS E.4, fol. 25v; R. Wilcher, *The Writing of English Royalism, 1628–1660* (Cambridge, 2001), pp. 41–2. Heylyn notes Digby's attacks on the church in *Extraneus*, p. 174.

85 Indeed, it is notable that Heylyn does not list Digby among those petitioning the king for him for the deanery of York in 1644, and it would appear to have been Digby's inertia that helped to prevent the publication of Heylyn's *Stumbling Block*: see above, pp. 130, 134.

86 *HQA*, postscript, sigs Ppp4v–Qqq1v.

87 Laud, *Works*, III, p. 246. I owe this reference to David Scott's unpublished paper ' "Our mongrel parliament": the Oxford parliament, 1644–1646'. I am grateful to Dr Scott for letting me see a copy of his paper in advance of publication.

88 Russell, *Fall*, pp. 278, 343, 475; Wilcher, *Writing*, pp. 41–2.

89 Sir Francis Wortley, Ελευθερωσις . . . *Truth asserted* (1641), p. 30.

90 Lord Falkland, *A Speech made to the House of Commons concerning Episcopacy* (1641), pp. 3–4, 6–7.

91 *ODNB*, s.n. 'Edward Bagshawe'.

92 Henry Hammond, *Considerations of present Use concerning the Danger resulting from the Change of our Church Government* (1645), pp. 1, 15–18.

93 Griffith Williams, *The Discovery of Mysteries* (1643), p. 2.

94 *Ibid.*, p. 104.

95 Henry Ferne, *Episcopacy and Presbytery considered* (Oxford, 1644), p. 1.

96 Hammond, *Considerations*, pp. 1, 3, 14–15.

97 There were parliamentarian attacks on Laud's speech – e.g. Joshua Hoyle, *A Jehojadahs Justice against Mattan, Baal's Priest* (1645) – but it is not clear that Heylyn was trying to respond to them.

98 Heylyn, *A Briefe Relation of the Death and Sufferings of the most Reverend and Renowned Prelate*, pp. 4, 12–13.

99 *Ibid.*, pp. 14–16, 24–6, 28–30; Walker, p. 210.

100 *Briefe Relation*, p. 2.

101 Heylyn, *Parliaments Power in Lawes for Religion* (Oxford, 1645), p. 26.

102 *Ibid.*, pp. 8–9, 12–13.

103 There is a good deal of confusion about the publishing history of this work. Heylyn states in *Ecclesia Vindicata* (1659) that it was written to give satisfaction to a particular party, and was so successful in this that some thought to have it published for use by others. But it was published only in a faulty and imperfect copy, so that Heylyn had it called in (*EV*, i. sig. A2v). Walker (pp. 213–16) suggests, however, that this must have been a 1653 edition of the same work which Wood refers to but which does not survive. The fact that no copies survive would support the idea that it had been called in, and Walker suggests that the 'occasion' was Barebone's parliament in that year.

However, this implies that Heylyn simply overlooked or forgot about the original 1645 edition. The references to the 'satisfaction of the party concerned' relate far more self-evidently to the individual's concern over Catholicism which is flagged so clearly in the title. It also seems unlikely that Heylyn would have achieved a complete recall of copies of one of his books in 1653. We have only Wood's word for the publication of a 1653 edition, and Wood is not always reliable on bibliographical matters. As the evidence is unclear, it seems to me safest to assume that Heylyn's comments relate to the one pre-1657 edition that we know exists.

104 N. Tyacke, *Aspects of English Protestantism, c. 1530–1700* (Manchester, 2001), pp. 284–7.

105 *PT*, p. 183.

106 *Ibid.*, p. 187.

107 *Ibid.*, p. 192.

108 *Ibid.*, pp. 185, 188, 192, 194, 200–2, 227, 230, 252.

109 *EV*, sig. b3v–b4r.

110 Vernon, p. 131.

111 M. Mendle, *Dangerous Positions* (Birmingham AL, 1985); C. C. Weston, *English Constitutional Theory and the House of Lords, 1556–1832* (1965), pp. 37–40.

112 E. Husbands, *An Exact Collection* (1643), pp. 324–5. The invitation to parliament to consider changes to the liturgy and government of the church (p. 325) would have particularly incensed Heylyn.

113 Heylyn, *The Rebells Catechism* (1643), pp. 21–2.

114 John Bramhall, *The Serpent Salve* (1643), pp. 34–5.

115 See *ibid.*, p. 20; John Doughty, *The Kings Cause rationally, briefly and plainly Debated* (1644), p. 27; Ferne, *Episcopacy and Presbytery*, p. 26. For rare examples of clerical supporters of the *Answer's* reading of the estates see Francis Quarles, *The Loyall Convert* (Oxford, 1643), p. 6, and Ferne's earlier *The Resolving of Conscience* (Cambridge, 1642), pp. 25–6.

116 *Observations*, p. 62; *SB*, pp. 226–7, 264.

117 *SB*, p. 267 (cf. pp. 38–9).

118 David Owen, *Herod and Pilate Reconciled* (Cambridge, 1610); Milton, *Catholic and Reformed*, p. 518.

119 TNA, SP 16/437/56.

120 *Rebells Catechisme*, pp. 15, 20, 21–3.

121 *SB*, pp. 4–5, 32–4.

122 *Ibid.*, pp. 143–226.

123 *SB*, pp. 147–51, 207–12. See also Williams, *Discovery*, p. 26; Gerard Langbaine, *Episcopall Inheritance* (1641), pp. 20–1; *Observations*, pp. 61–2. Williams treads more carefully in his *The Grand Rebellion* (Oxford, 1643), pp. 63–4.

124 *SB*, pp. 215, 307.

125 *Memorial*, p. xxiii; Bodl., Wood MS E.4, fol. 28r–v.

126 *Memorial*, pp. xxiii–iv; Vernon, pp. 126–7.

127 *Memorial*, p. xxiv.

128 Barnard, pp. 203–4.

129 *PT*, pp. 309–10. I am grateful to Dr Fincham for the point about the Lenten roster.

130 *Ibid.*, pp. 205–13. Heylyn's own account of his travels in the preface to his *Theologia Veterum* describes a more dignified series of relocations in which he continued his scholarly work. But in his 1650s published writings Heylyn always avoided referring to his mistreatment by parliament and the army. Barnard's account presumably relates the narrative of these years which Heylyn had told to his own family.

131 *TV*, sig. B3v; Matthews, *Walker Revised*, p. 185.

132 Vernon, pp. 141–2; *Articles concerning the Surrender of Oxford* (Oxford, 1646), pp. 6, 7.

133 *EH*, ii. pp. 199–200.

134 *Calendar of the Proceedings of the Committee for Compounding, 1643–1660* (5 vols, 1889–92), II, pp. 1481, 1509, 1526, 1565, 1586, 1593.

135 *TV*, sig. B3v; Barnard, pp. 213–14.

136 Bodl., Tanner MS 58, fols 453–6, 460, 461, 484a.

137 Wiltshire and Swindon RO, D1/18/5, Presentations 1645–46. I am grateful to Dr Fincham for this reference.

138 Centre for Kentish Studies, U120/C6, A18.

Chapter 5

Dealing with the Interregnum

The execution of the king sent shock waves through the royalist community. But it also posed important questions for the route that royalists should now take. With Charles II an absent and uncrowned monarch, and no prospect of negotiations with the newly created English republic, royalists faced a difficult dilemma as to what their course of action should be. Through its offer of the Engagement the new regime presented royalists with a means of affirming their loyalty to the new regime, while the 1652 Act of Oblivion pardoned all treasons and felonies committed before 1651.[1] Charles II's attempted alliance with the presbyterian Scots, on the other hand, made royalist clerics increasingly anxious regarding the lengths to which the new king might go to regain his throne. For a man like Heylyn who had always sought to provide services to the authorities the 1650s were a strange time. With no government or patron to serve or to write for, and with no immediate dependence, Heylyn's writings moved in a number of intriguing directions. As we will see, his attitude towards the Interregnum authorities was necessarily more complex and ambiguous than that of other royalist clerics. Indeed, in some respects one might even query whether the term 'royalist' is appropriate to describe Heylyn's position.

HEYLYN AND THE CHURCH OF ENGLAND IN THE 1650s

In the case of the clergy, and indeed of Anglicanism more generally, the usual picture presented of the 1650s is of a process whereby 'Anglicanism' was rebuilt. Freed of their obligation to be continually involved in affairs of state or absorbed in the secular aspects of ecclesiastical authority, royalist clergymen could instead focus on theology and devotional writing, and on building up a body of 'Anglican' spirituality which would regain popular support for the established church, and would eventually sustain the Restoration church.[2] This was also a period (we are told) in which clericalism was essentially renounced. Just as the clergy themselves adopted a more low-key and circumspect demeanour, far removed from the clerical excesses of the Laudians, so the 'Anglican' ideology of the 1640s and 1650s has often tended to be described in terms of moderation, rationality and erastianism. Historians have written of the 'transformation' of 'Anglicanism' in this period, and the growth of 'moralism'. Shorn of abrasive Laudianism, 'Anglicanism' emerged instead as a religion which was 'theologically prudent, socially deferential and liturgically restrained' – ready to become the understated, syncretic and quintessentially moderate 'Anglicanism' more readily recognizable to modern eyes.[3]

This humility and lack of clericalist pretensions is often summed up most powerfully in the famous images of suffering clergymen taking refuge in gentry households, writing improving works of practical divinity, and ministering to the needs of a local congregation devoted to the simple noncontroversial rhythms of the Prayer Book. It is Jeremy Taylor at Lord Carbery's Golden Grove, Henry Hammond in the Pakington household, Gilbert Sheldon making his home with the Okeover and Shirley families.[4] Or indeed the circle of clergymen – including Taylor again, Peter Hausted, Edward Martin and Peter Gunning – who enjoyed Lord Hatton as a patron at this time.[5]

This is not, however, a model which can be applied to Peter Heylyn. Crucially, he did not feel compelled to take refuge in the household of any gentry patron. Despite his work on the Order of the Garter, Heylyn had never displayed any capacity for forging links of patronage with the gentry or aristocracy. Moreover, after his wanderings of the mid-1640s, he was never again obliged to seek the hospitality of friends' houses. Heylyn fell back on his relatives, and as his nephew Colonel Heylyn had made his peace with the authorities, Heylyn was able to be based for several years at Minster Lovell, before moving to his own relatively comfortable dwelling of Lacey's Court near Abingdon.[6] While his ecclesiastical livings (which had provided the bulk of his income) remained under sequestration, Heylyn's compounding in 1646 nevertheless meant that he may have regained some of his temporal estate, which was not meagre. In the 1650s he was therefore able to fall back on income from family land and impropriate rectories that he either held directly or through third parties, while he was able to derive additional income for several years by farming his nephew's seat of Minster Lovell. As Heylyn summarized his situation in 1659, 'though my present condition be not such as to make me the subject of any mans envy, so neither is it so mean & despicable as to make me the object of any mans charity'.[7] This financial independence distinguishes Heylyn from most of his erstwhile colleagues, and enabled him to forge an independent path in the 1650s.[8] This is not to say that Heylyn had no links whatsoever with prominent royalist noblemen in the 1650s. He dedicated one of his books to the marquess of

Dorchester and another to the marquess of Hertford, but in neither case did this reflect an intimate existing connection.[9] This was reflected in the dedicatees' responses. Heylyn later noted that while he received 'a civil acknowledgement in curteous language' from one dedicatee (apparently Hertford), the other offered 'not so much as a verbal thanks', despite the fact that the book was delivered by Heylyn's young son. He contrasted this cold response with the fact that he had found 'more civility in this Kind, from a Noble Lady of Hertfordshire whom I never saw, and unto whom I never made the least application of this nature' – namely the literary patron Anne Sadleir, with whom he enjoyed an amicable correspondence at the end of the 1650s.[10]

Heylyn's relatively independent existence also seems to have extended to his public life. The 1650s were a time when two royalist clergymen in particular – Gilbert Sheldon and Henry Hammond – worked to preserve the ideological unity of the clergy in the face of the pressures of the Interregnum. Clerics who remained in England in the 1650s faced constant problems in attempting to remain true to the now disestablished church while also fulfilling their vocation and avoiding punishment. Several flashpoints emerged. For example, given that the use of the Book of Common Prayer was now illegal, was it permissible for clergymen to adapt its content? Also, given the rise of the Association movement in the 1650s, was it legitimate for 'Anglican' clergy to make common cause with presbyterian ministers in the face of the sectarian threat? These were matters where Hammond and Sheldon laboured to preserve a common front among the clergy.[11]

No evidence survives to suggest that Heylyn became involved in these internal debates within the royalist clergy. On a whole range of other issues that involved prominent royalist clergy in the 1650s – from Brian Walton and his colleagues' creation of a polyglot Bible to the anxious attempts to induce the surviving bishops to act to preserve the episcopal succession – Heylyn also seems to have played no role and to have expressed no concerns.[12] Perhaps most tellingly of all, he played virtually no direct part in the controversial pamphlets and exchanges that sought to map out the theology and historical claims of the Church of England in this period. Hammond and Sheldon had discussed the need to ensure that pamphlets attacking the Church of England always received an effective response, and tried to secure funding to encourage divines to assist in this polemical task.[13] It was Hammond who emerged as the main spokesman of the surviving church in England, while John Bramhall and John Cosin contributed on the Continent.[14] It is not clear whether Heylyn turned down invitations to contribute. Hammond reported having written to Heylyn in the mid-1650s about reprinting some of the early volumes relating to the Henrician Reformation (including *De Vera Obedientia* and the *Institution of a Christian Man*) but that Heylyn 'waved it', and he had therefore approached Clement Spelman instead.[15]

It is also possible that Hammond and Sheldon did not consider that Heylyn would be an effective controversialist for the cause, given his association with the personal rule and his notoriously acerbic style. If this was a fear in the early 1650s, it would doubtless have been intensified by the end of the decade, when Heylyn had conducted a voluminous and increasingly vitriolic series of published exchanges with serried ranks of opponents. One of these opponents, Henry Hickman, claimed that one 'Dr H.H'. (implying Henry Hammond) had said that Heylyn 'was an unhappy writer and marred every thing he medled with'.[16] Heylyn angrily denied the imputation, and an anonymous defender claimed that Hammond and Dr Humphrey Henchman 'are both the friends of Dr Heylin (as I am certified by some who are friends to both) and great applauders of his workes, and disclaim the having so much as given occasion to any slander'.[17] Nevertheless, the charge is not implausible, and similar sentiments can be found being expressed in the English exiled community.[18]

The sense that Heylyn operated at a remove from the other royalist divines is confirmed by other evidence. While Heylyn and Thomas Pierce found themselves acting as close polemical allies in combating the works of Richard Baxter, Henry Hickman and others, it is clear that they did not know each other (and this despite Pierce's links with Heylyn's college, Magdalen). Pierce wrote to Heylyn in July 1659 expressing his appreciation of the fact that Heylyn had shared the burden of answering Hickman 'notwithstanding my being a stranger'.[19]

The crucial fact that distinguished Heylyn from many other clergymen in this period, and which marked a significant change in his own daily life, was that after his sequestration he no longer possessed either a cure of souls or a licence to preach. While Vernon reports that Heylyn built 'a private Oratory' at his house near Abingdon where he daily read the liturgy and administered communion, nevertheless Heylyn seems to have avoided the exercise of a clandestine ministry that other royalist clergy attempted.[20] He did encourage the minister at Abingdon, Anthony Huish (who had studied at Magdalen when Heylyn was a fellow there), to continue to read public prayers, apparently from the Prayer Book, urging him not to be discouraged by having 'to pray in public with so thin a company as hardly will amount to a congregation'. He also implored Huish not to worry about the new ordinance against the use of the Prayer Book, because 'the Divine providence is still awake over that poor remnant of the regular and orthodox clergy which have not yet bowed their knees to the golden calves of late erected'.[21] When Huish did flee the parish, Heylyn seems to have secured the services of a number of temporary preachers. It was complained in 1658 that several members of the parish 'have at their owne will hired disaffected persons to preach and officiate to them, slighting and rejecting their own Minister a person godly able and well affected'. (This was the minister of the neighbouring parish of St Helen's, who was supposedly responsible for Heylyn's parish as well.)[22] There is of course a certain irony in the image of Heylyn the layman paying for his own 'disaffected' preachers (presumably ejected ministers) instead of the ministrations of the formally appointed minister – this was the behaviour that he always deplored in puritans.

As well as temporary preaching opportunities in Abingdon, Heylyn reportedly offered practical support and hospitality to other ejected royalist clergymen. These were not necessarily diehard Laudians. While Barnard lists Heylyn's old friends John Allibond and Thomas Levet, he also mentions among those who stayed for months at Heylyn's house George Ashwell, who was to be an admirer of the puritan Richard Baxter's Worcester Association.[23] Another visitor was Thomas Lamplugh, who was later attacked by Wood as 'a great cringer . . . to Presbyterian and Independents . . . [who] had made great compliance with the men of the times . . . not without great dissimulation'.[24] Lamplugh's patron in the 1650s was Robert Skinner, the Laudian bishop of Oxford, who had managed to retain one of his livings and (reportedly) a licence to preach.[25] Heylyn also seems to have enjoyed good relations with fellows of Queen's College Oxford – a safe haven of royalist episcopalian sentiment (albeit of a Calvinist character) under the tactful rule of Gerard Langbaine. Barnard also reports an improbable friendship with the strongly Calvinist fellow of Queen's Thomas Barlow (attacked by Wood as a turncoat and instinctive dissembler who had been close to John Owen), who allegedly provided Heylyn with books and whom Heylyn supposedly tipped for a bishopric.[26]

It should not be implied, however, that Heylyn was tacitly complicit with and accepting of the ecclesiastical regime. He wrote as if the established pre-1640 Church of England was still in existence, and usually used the present tense when describing its government and liturgy. Heylyn also nursed a profound sense of himself as one of the 'sufferers'. He deeply resented an insinuation made by an opponent in the later 1650s that he was a worldly pragmatist ('none fitter to describe the world, than he who all his life loved the world'). He demanded:

> hath he [Heylyn] lost such a fair Revenue, above 800 l. per annum in Ecclesiastical preferments, 1000 l. at the last in Books, Plate, & moveables, for the testimony of a good conscience? Hath his poor temporal estate been first brought under Sequestration, under a Decimation since, only for his adhesion to those sacred verities to which he hath been principled by education, and confirmed by study [?]

If he really were 'a right time-server' he would have burned his books and applied himself properly to 'the love of the World'.[27] Nor was Heylyn prepared to allow his opponent Thomas Fuller (who possessed a living and a preaching licence) to claim to be a fellow sufferer.[28] One of his last

controversial works, *Certamen Epistolare,* is dedicated to 'the poor Re-
mainders of the old Regular and Conformable Clergy of the Church of
England', whom Heylyn assumed were all ejected and sequestered.²⁹ The 1657
'Act for the quiet enjoying of sequestered parsonages', which settled the presbyterian intruders for life into the livings of the ejected clergy, undermined
Heylyn's own hopes of ever returning to his sequestered livings.³⁰ In another
of his late works Heylyn in passing complained bitterly about this new bill.
While the fifth part of the profits of the living could theoretically be given to
the ejected incumbent, he noted that ejected ministers would receive no benefit
if they had either £30 in real or £500 in personal estate 'by means whereof
many who have had some hundreds of pounds yearly to maintain their Families,
are tyed up to so poor a pittance as will hardly keep their children from begging in the open streets'. Heylyn clearly had himself in mind, as he must
have been rated at this sum to have been obliged to pay the decimation tax.
(He also complained that the fifth part could be insufficient for some, as it
did not take into account 'their Degrees, Families and ways of Living'.)³¹

However keen his resentment, however, Heylyn still sought to present himself and his fellow sufferers as meekly patient. Addressing the ejected clergy
directly in 1659, Heylyn urged them to behave with sobriety and moderation.
They should not be active in planning or hoping for relief: 'let us not suffer
our selves to be abused, by any flattering or deceivable hope of bettering our
condition by the change of times; but entertain Fortune by the day, and patiently
submit our selves to the appointments of that heavenly Providence'. The ejected
ministers, he claimed, patiently bore their present sufferings, 'neither repining openly at their own misfortune, nor railing malitiously on those whom
they know to be the Authors of them; nor libelling against the persons, *nor
wilfully standing out against the pleasure and commands of the higher Powers*'.³²
It was always crucial for the 'Anglican' clergy to convince the Interregnum
authorities that they posed no political threat, of course, but Heylyn's regular insistence on this point reflected a broader agenda, as we shall see.

In practice Heylyn was not quite as passive as his words might suggest.
He did live a relatively sheltered, withdrawn life in the 1650s compared
with his very public existence in the 1630s and 1640s. Nevertheless, he was
still prepared to play a role in public affairs. He reprinted his tithes pamphlet
in 1651, presumably when parliament was in the process of rejecting an additional ordinance to enforce tithe payment in the face of growing opposition.³³
Apart from this, however, Heylyn did not publish pamphlets on current affairs
or debates, but he still conducted a limited amount of lobbying and writing
of position papers. A surviving example of the latter is the paper of 'Considerations' which he presented 'to some Members of the House of
Commons' (according to Vernon). These are essentially a summary of his
complaints about the parliamentary bill to settle intruded ministers in

sequestered livings for life (which we have already noted), which Heylyn was hoping to block.[34] He appealed to government sensibilities by claiming that the bill subverted the ends for which the ministers had first been intruded into the livings: once the ministers were settled for life they 'will be apt when time and opportunity serves, to let fly all their fury at the present Government, as they did formerly at the other in the late Kings Reign'. He also noted that the bill necessarily deprived patrons of livings of their powers of presentation. He could not help adding self-referentially that the settling of intruded ministers permanently 'destroys many a learned, peaceable and Religious man without hope of remedy', who might still have entertained hopes because 'sequestration' had implied only a temporary punishment.[35] Heylyn also lobbied strongly to prevent his parish of St Nicholas Abingdon being merged with the neighbouring (and godly) parish of St Helen's. According to Barnard this involved many trips by Heylyn to London and the employment of 'divers solicitors; sometimes before committees, at other times before Oliver's Council' in pressing what was ultimately a successful suit.[36] For all that Heylyn often referred to his private, secluded existence in the country, he appears to have travelled to London reasonably regularly in the later 1650s.[37]

Heylyn did not completely retire from direct involvement in public affairs in the 1650s, then (and, as we will see, he could still envisage advising the government). But he did not become involved in any collective enterprise in this period, and continued to plough his own distinctive furrow. Especially in the first half of the decade this still amounted to something of a withdrawal from public life compared with his earlier activities, and it was also accompanied in the period up to 1656 by an apparent departure from controversial writing. But as we will see, this withdrawal was more apparent than real.

RETREAT FROM THE FRAY? *COSMOGRAPHIE* AND *THEOLOGIA VETERUM*

Heylyn's withdrawal from overtly controversial writing or commentary on recent events might appear to be exemplified in the two books that he published in the first half of the 1650s. The *Cosmographie* (published in 1652) is a vast geographical account of the world, while his *Theologia Veterum* (published in 1654) is a commentary on the creed that appears to have been the only overtly theological work that Heylyn ever wrote. Nevertheless, on further analysis these do not provide us with examples of a royalist clergyman retreating into contemplative 'Anglican' piety or dispassionate encyclopaedia writing. Indeed, as we shall see, these works were closely informed by recent events, and are very far from being ideologically neutral. In fact, they provide important early evidence of some of the ideas that would receive their fullest and more familiar expression in his later histories.

The *Cosmographie* is easily Heylyn's longest and most ambitious work. The subject matter and organization of the work are basically the same as *Microcosmus*, but the amount of material has been vastly expanded, with extensive additions and many major revisions. The original octavo volume has now become a huge folio volume, complete with a set of maps. Despite its enormous scale, the *Cosmographie* has often seemed to scholars to have least to do with Heylyn's ideas – and historians writing on Heylyn's thought have generally ignored it. It has been historical geographers who have most recently begun to identify the riches of this text.[38]

There are some obvious reasons why the *Cosmographie* should have been read as an uncontroversial encyclopaedia, and the first of these is that Heylyn himself presented the work in precisely that way. Heylyn later explained that he began work on *Cosmographie* in 1648 when 'by the importunity of some special friends' he was prevailed upon to revise his *Microcosmus* instead of proceeding with the nearly completed *Theologia Veterum*.[39] In the preface to the *Cosmographie* itself, Heylyn claimed that these 'special friends' were 'of no common quality', and that he was also urged by 'some Members of Parliament, whom I found loath to be denied, and . . . some others of great rank'. Heylyn emphasized that his importuners were not exclusively royalist or parliamentarian – indeed, those urging him to produce the work were of 'such different Interesses, that I wondered how they could al center upon the same Proposall'.[40] It is not entirely clear that Heylyn really encountered this universal pressure to write the book – the fact that he dedicates the work to the reader because he has no patron left would suggest that none of those allegedly urging the work upon him was really offering significant encouragement. Barnard hints that Heylyn needed money at the time – and it would make sense that the 'special friends' seeking to divert him to the work in 1648 were family and friends. The *Microcosmus* had gone through eight editions before the war and had proved to be easily Heylyn's most popular work, while in the late 1640s his finances were still precarious and he was dependent on the support of his nephew. A new edition of the *Microcosmus* would not in itself have restored his finances, but would undoubtedly have helped. Writing the *Cosmographie* seems to have occupied him during his entire stay with his nephew in Minster Lovell, with his wife doing his husbandry as well as housework to leave him free to finish,[41] and the income from the work may have helped the Heylyns to move to Abingdon in the year following the book's publication.

It is also possible that he did indeed receive some encouragement to proceed with the work from a broader range of people. The enormous scale on which the *Cosmographie* was written – involving some five different printers – suggests a degree of confidence on the part of both author and undertaker over the market for such a publication that might have been fuelled by the

expressed wishes of prominent people for such a work.[42] Whatever the truth
of the matter, it was important to Heylyn's overall intentions that the book
be presented as having been requested by the widest possible range of
opinion and party. Given his famous partisanship of the royalist cause, it was
vital that parliamentarians and anti-Laudians would not be deterred from
purchasing the book. Heylyn therefore deliberately presented the volume as
a retreat from controversial and confrontational work, and from religious
writing in particular. His preface to the reader recalls how, when called before
the parliamentary committee in 1640, he was confronted by 'a tall big
Gentleman' who 'thrusting me rudely from the wall' said in a hoarse voice,
'Geographie is better than Divinitie.'[43] Heylyn also told his readers that if there
was indeed partisanship in the book, it was the partisanship of a patriot –
there could be no more obvious way of trying to stake out common ground
with his erstwhile opponents.[44] Nevertheless, Heylyn also explained that
he had deliberately chosen to end his book's coverage of events in 1648,
so that he would not need to refer to recent events in England. He also
trod carefully when describing his own experiences: when mentioning his
own deprivation he avoided any allusion to specific human agents, describing it as happening 'by the unhappiness of my Destinie, or the infelicity
of the times'.[45]

Moreover, the *Cosmographie* generally seems to have been written deliberately to appeal to the general reader rather than the scholar or controversialist. There are only minimal citations, and the tone is light and popular,
The writing is spare and idiomatic, the analysis limited. There are witty turns
of phrase and frequent translations of poetry. There is still a large bulk of
basic factual material, but the tone is conversational, and there is a notable
absence of sarcasm and satire. In style at least, it marked a partial return to
the non-partisan Heylyn of the early 1620s.

The plan to present the *Cosmographie* as a non-partisan work would seem
to have succeeded. Secretary Thurloe was instructed in November 1652 to buy
a copy of *Cosmographie* for the council's use.[46] Nevertheless, this was very far
from being an apolitical work – in its enormous recasting and reworking of
the *Microcosmus* it is possible to identify some important new ideas, and some
insistent arguments. For all the author's sense of vulnerability, and of the
need to disarm the new government, the *Cosmographie* in fact reveals a far
more hostile, Laudian and conservative writer than the author of the 1620s
Microcosmus.

One advantage of the *Cosmographie* was that it gave Heylyn the opportunity to delete entirely sections of the *Microcosmus* which he had intellectu-
ally rejected many years before. He himself claimed that revisiting his
Microcosmus he became aware of so many mistakes and errors that he would
have felt bound to produce a corrected volume sooner or later regardless of

the added urgings of his friends. 'Being written in an age, on which the pride of youth and self-opinion might have predominancies, I thought it freer from mistakes than I since have found it', he commented. Heylyn stated that the mistakes had 'increased and multiplied' passing through the eight pre-war editions – six of which he had not supervised – so that 'I could no longer call it mine, or look upon it with any tolerable degree of patience'.[47] But these 'mistakes' were not (as he implied) simply errors of fact or later topographical slips – it is apparent from the changes made that there were whole sections of argument with which he no longer agreed.

Thus, Heylyn finally deleted the sentences on the Albigensians and Waldensians and the visibility of the church which had clashed so directly with his expressed views in the 1630s. He now stressed that he did not regard them as sources of the Protestant church, 'as some doe', and that on the contrary there were many tares among their wheat. He deplored their insolent behaviour and attacks on bishops, and suggested that they were 'bettered by affliction'.[48] Sections on Antichrist were also silently amended. While a passage in *Microcosmus* describing the pope's claims to temporal monarchy chiefly focused on prophecies of Antichrist and Babylon, the corresponding section of the *Cosmographie* is completely different in style and content, concentrating instead on the papacy's specific powers in the early church, and offering at times a guardedly positive assessment.[49]

One of the most striking and consistent differences between *Cosmographie* and *Microcosmus* is in their treatment of foreign Protestantism. Heylyn systematically removed all expressions of sympathy for and shared identity with the foreign Reformed churches and their leaders. This is particularly notable in his discussion of the Rhenish Palatinate. In place of his earlier celebration of the Elector Frederick, the winter king now barely merits a mention, except a perfunctory reference to how 'the poor Prince' was opposed by Lutherans and Roman Catholics because they disliked 'the active and restless Calvinian spirit'. If anything, Heylyn seems to side with Frederick's opponents (indeed, a paragraph which had attacked the duke of Saxony for opposing the elector palatine is now removed). Heylyn does, however, find time to introduce a new section condemning the introduction of Calvinism into the palatinate as having been merely to serve the ends of 'needy Statists' who raised money by attacking the church's tithes and glebe. The reintroduction of Catholicism in the palatinate is noted, but without any explicit comment or regret.[50] That other target of international Calvinist concern, the Huguenots, receive equally unsympathetic treatment, and Heylyn's critical comments are accompanied by a new section in which he emphasizes how far their situation has improved, and how much more tolerance they have received, since the king has destroyed their independence.[51] He was more interested in, and approving of, the Gallican church's independence and opposition to the pope, which was discussed in a new section.[52] When he turned to examine the exploits of the Protestant hero Gustavus Adolphus in the Thirty Years War, Heylyn discussed his campaigns in entirely political and military terms, making no reference to religion at all.[53]

This rejection of the 'Protestant cause' was combined with a newly hostile account of foreign Calvinist Reformations which would reach its outspoken climax in his later notorious *Aërius Redivivus*. In the case of each Reformed country, Heylyn's particular concern was to note attacks on bishops and the wealth of the church, and to associate the reformation with political sedition. In discussing the reformation in Bearn he now dwelt on how tithes, church land and the bishops' votes in parliament were all removed at the same time 'according to the Genevian way of reformation'.[54] When discussing Geneva itself, Heylyn unleashed a particularly hostile tirade. Where the *Microcosmus* had provided merely three sentences and the rather restrained comment that the presbyterian system had been implemented without 'mature considera- tion', the *Cosmographie* substituted a much longer, more acerbic and stridently anti-presbyterian assessment. Heylyn emphasized the dangerously populist nature of the presbyterian platform: it had been deliberately framed 'to con- tent the people' after the 'fickle multitude' had invited Calvin back to Geneva.[55] Heylyn was particularly keen to depict Geneva as a fomentor of rebellion elsewhere, and this led to one of his few direct allusions to the causes of England's recent civil war. He noted in a new section how great numbers of the young English gentry had resorted to Geneva and had been seasoned with seditious principles and had thereafter many times proved disaffected to English government on their return 'as well Monarchicall as Episcopall . . . to the great imbroilment of the state in matters of most near concernment'.[56]

Heylyn's concern to distance himself from the foreign Reformed churches may also be glimpsed in his more balanced assessment of the Lutheran churches. Not the least attraction of the Lutheran churches was their apparent retention of episcopacy. Heylyn thus noted Denmark's retention of what he termed 'bishops' (which he had never remarked on in *Microcosmus*) and provided details of the episcopal government in Sweden, noting pointedly that the Swedish 'bishops' still sat in parliament.[57]

Heylyn's attention to the issue of episcopacy was not accidental. If he might initially have conceived of the *Cosmographie* as offering a neutral account of countries, the failure of the English presbyterians may, however, by 1652 have encouraged Heylyn to be more assertive, and he explains with remarkable candour in his preface to the work that he has deliberately emphasized the importance of bishops in his account, and wishes to demonstrate that episcopacy had been accepted throughout the world. As with the Lutheran states, his accounts of Catholic countries and provinces always note the extent of the secular authority exercised by the bishops.[58]

All discussion of episcopacy was transparently intended as a commentary on recent events in England. Heylyn's section on England, while avoiding any inflammatory comments on recent events, also reflected the changed agenda evident in other parts of the *Cosmographie*. His list of celebrated divines removed Laurence Humphrey and retained John Reynolds and William Whitaker, but created a very different balance by finally including Richard Hooker, and then following him with a more exclusive list of Bilson, Whitgift, Andrewes, Laud and Richard Montagu.[59] His account of the English Reformation bears some notable changes of emphasis. Where *Microcosmus* had noted how 'tumultuously' the Reformation was received abroad compared with its 'mature deliberation' in England, the *Cosmographie* is more explicit in stating that its Continental reception was 'by the power of the People', while England's 'mature deliberation' was 'by the authority and consent of the Prince and Prelates'.[60] Heylyn's earlier note that there had been pressure to establish Calvin's presbyterian platform in England now bore a further reflection that episcopacy had been attacked in England only because of 'the Avarice of some great persons in Court and State, who greedily gaped after the poor remnant of their Possessions'.[61]

Heylyn's expanded coverage of countries in the *Cosmographie* also gave him more space to discuss forms of government, and for each country he normally notes the power and revenues of the monarch and the role of parliaments.[62] Nevertheless, he had to tread carefully when discussing England. In contrast to his discussion of other countries, he effectively dodges all issues of government: he does not describe the power of the monarch or the role of parliament, and while he notes the revenues of the kingdom, he provides no account of forms of taxation. Where he has to mention Charles I in his list of monarchs, he does not mention his death.[63] Nevertheless, in other sections he writes as if the English monarchy still exists. Thus, when discussing the Holy Roman Emperor, he notes that Bodin and others do not account him 'an absolute Monarch; such as the Kings of England, France and Spain, are confessed to be'.[64]

Heylyn's thoughts on politics and government in *Cosmographie* reflect his writings of the 1640s. He notably departs from the *Microcosmus* and repeats the argument of his *Stumbling Block* by claiming that William the Conqueror 'altered the antient Laws of England' and established those of Normandy instead, 'governing the people absolutely by the power of the Sword'.[65] More broadly, he distinguishes between absolutism and despotism. While calling Louis the most absolute king of France since Charlemagne, he describes French government as 'meerly Regal, or to give it its true name, Despoticall, such as that of masters over servants'. The French king had found the French parliament 'or Assembly of the three Estates' too prone to conflict, and had stopped making use of it, with the result that his power over his subjects was now 'so transcendent, it cannot be, but that his Forces must be very great'.[66] It should also be noted that Heylyn provides more overt discussion and praise of that great analyst of different political systems Machiavelli, whom he salutes as 'the greatest Politick of his times' and 'that great Master of State-craft'.[67]

While *Cosmographie* partly enabled Heylyn to spell out a number of his own *idées fixes*, it is worth pondering whether some of his reflections were aimed at the existing government. The *Cosmographie* repeats the claims made by *Microcosmus* that the historical scholar is the greatest servant to prince and country.[68] Heylyn does include some direct appeals to the state, most notably when discussing the need to attack Dutch fishing fleets. He prints extracts from Sir John Burroughs's manuscript tract 'The Soveraignty of the British Seas', and explicitly commends the policy 'to the care of the State'.[69] Heylyn's attacks on the iniquities of presbyterianism could have been welcome to the ears of prominent Independents, as well as providing an opportunity for Heylyn to let off steam. There may also have been a subliminal appeal for toleration of 'Anglican' clergy in Heylyn's apparently approving report of how the different religious groups in Switzerland had ultimately agreed upon a free exercise of religion, based upon due care of the public interest and the bond of peace (although he had offered far more muted remarks on this policy in his earlier *Microcosmus*).[70] We might also ponder Heylyn's decision at a very late stage (possibly as late as the spring of 1652) to insert the text of his earlier work *Augustus* into the *Cosmographie*. It does not fit naturally into the work, and was inserted without page numbers as it was too late to correct the existing foliation.[71] Did Heylyn intend to offer discreet advice to a potential usurper, on the basis of information suddenly received?[72] After his victory at Worcester Cromwell was an obvious candidate for personal rule, and there was already some enthusiasm being expressed in 1651 for Cromwell to be king. By late 1652 Cromwell himself was supposedly discussing with Bulstrode Whitelocke the possibility of his taking the crown.[73] Heylyn must himself have been acutely conscious that the last time he had published *Augustus* was at the beginning of Charles's personal rule.

Heylyn's *Theologia Veterum* is another work whose apparently innocuous form disguises a more radical content. It is a commentary on the creed, which developed out of Heylyn's initial interest in Thomas Bilson's *Survey of Christ's Suffering for Man's Redemption* (1604) – a treatise on the question of Christ's descent into hell. According to Heylyn, this initially engaged his interest, but the work grew into a vindication of the entire Apostles' Creed. He worked on the text from 1645, through his various movements to Wiltshire and finally to Minster Lovell, where he finished the book in 1648 but did not publish it until 1654, because of the interruption of working on the *Cosmographie* instead. Heylyn presents the book as simply a work of

scholarly retirement, implying that it was written merely for his own satisfaction. He would later maintain that he made no conditions with the
printer, and received only seven or eight copies of the work in payment. While
not a devotional piece (he stresses that his purpose throughout is to tackle
philological and historical issues, rather than 'practical' ones), Heylyn does not
present the *Theologia* as a controversial work either, and indeed emphasizes
that 'I never voluntarily ingaged my self in any of those publick quarrels,
by which the unity and order of the Church of England hath been so miserably distracted in these latter times'.[74]

It is true that in general terms Heylyn's *Theologia* is often muted in controversial matters, that plenty of the positions defended are fairly orthodox
and unremarkable, and that Heylyn is often happy simply to follow Bilson
and others in his arguments. He provides his readers with reassuring bouts
of anti-Catholicism – emphasizing how distinct his position was from the
Church of Rome on many issues, and equating Catholic conduct at one point
with Gentilism and devil worship. Indeed, his dedicatory epistle and epistle
to the reader make it clear that Heylyn intended the work partly to vindicate
himself against charges of favouring popery.[75] He also provides approving
citations of orthodox Calvinist divines such as Ussher, and even Calvin and
Beza.[76] Nevertheless, the *Theologia* is a consciously controversial work.
Heylyn's vindication of the Apostles' Creed was specifically provoked by the
attacks upon it during and after the Westminster Assembly among radical
puritans, and Heylyn's decision to delay publication until 1654 may represent not simply the interruption of the *Cosmographie*, but also concern to
see that more radical Independents would not gain control of government.
By 1654 and the failure of Barebone's Parliament (and failure to establish a
presbyterian system) Heylyn may have judged it less likely that he would meet
with serious opposition to his views.

Heylyn did not forgo the opportunity to attack many recent sectarian
positions, providing assaults on the views of Anabaptists, Familists and
Socinians. One section made a systematic refutation of Tombes's recent work
against the practice of infant baptism.[77] However, he also attacked more
mainstream puritan and Calvinist positions, partly on predestination, but
especially on church government.[78] He attacked the 'monster' of presbyterianism, and mocked the 'petty popes' and 'shopkeepers' whom it empowered,
although he reflected that the Independents had perfected its errors. He
particularly aimed at separatists. While condemning the papal supremacy, he
nevertheless reflected that it was better to have a church that was all head
than to have one which had no head at all. While the Romanists were 'out'
in their doctrine of the church, the modern Donatists were more so. He made
a point of attacking the congregationalism that he insistently identified as
originating in New England.[79]

Heylyn also revisits a number of disputed Laudian issues, emphasizing for example that the sacramental power of forgiving sins is judicial and not just declarative ('in this the Priest hath the preheminence of the greatest Potentate') and attacking the views of 'the Grandees of the Puritan faction'.[80] He also returned to the question of the location of the church before Luther, emphasizing that the Church of England had derived everything from the Roman church, and citing the Catholic Nicholas Harpsfield's 'Historia Wicleffiana' against Wyclif and the Albigensians.[81] Discussion of the authority of the church gave him the opportunity to recall again his conflict with Prideaux over the removal of part of the text of Article 20 from the Thirty-nine Articles.[82] He also deplored the 'Antichristian licentiousness' caused by the putting down of the church's holy days by 'the sons of the old Heretick A[e]rius' in 'these wretched times'.[83]

The most obvious difference from his Laudian pamphlets, however, is that Heylyn was not generally debating in the *Theologia* with people who necessarily accepted the authority of the Church of England, and therefore his treatment of evidence and authority is notably different.[84] In fact, while his controversial writings of the 1630s had already shown readiness to push the logic of his position further than most conformists were prepared to go, in the *Theologia* Heylyn was liberated still further, and sometimes delighted in musing in less orthodox directions, particularly when discussing the nature of faith and the church. Although Heylyn sought the approval of the deprived bishop of Rochester, John Warner, for the work, in his preface he admitted that, where he found the church had not determined an issue, 'I shall conceive my self to be left at liberty to follow the dictamen of my own genius . . . common opinions many times are but common errors'. He also announced that Protestant writers were in error on the issue of the sin against the Holy Ghost and chose instead to agree with Maldonatus, 'though he were a Jesuit'.[85] On the intercession of the saints Heylyn stated candidly that 'I shall venture a little further . . . than possibly hath been granted in the Protestant Schools'.[86] He was also sufficiently off-message to make the observation that the compilers of the King James Bible 'inclined too much' to Calvin's opinions.[87] In the speculative novelty of passages of the *Theologia* there is perhaps a parallel with Jeremy Taylor's increasingly heterodox musings on the doctrine of original sin.[88] When the 'Anglican' clergy retired to contemplation in the 1650s, then, they did not necessarily simply refine the piestisic core of 'Anglicanism', but could often go spinning off in more radical directions.

One final feature of the *Theologia* that must be stressed is the evidence of the practical deficiencies from which Heylyn was suffering. One was his lack of access to books, which leads to an uncharacteristic vagueness in his references. At one point he makes the surprising remark 'To which effect, though not so fully, I have read somewhere I am sure in St Jerome, but cannot well remember where'. At another point he mentions a pertinent discussion in Sir Thomas Browne's *Religio Medici*, but has to explain candidly, 'I have not now the Book by me to put down his words.'[89] These are very unusual admissions, and perhaps reflect his problems when writing the book, chiefly in the tumultuous period 1645–48, when he was living in a number of different places and his books had been seized by parliament. Is it perhaps also true that Heylyn felt less need to assemble all supporting references as he would in a controversial treatise? Certainly, his writings in the later 1650s are much more rigorous and confident in their citations. There was, however, another affliction that increasingly impeded his scholarship from now on – and that was his failing eyesight.

Heylyn was clearly having problems with his eyesight by the late 1640s. A letter that he wrote to Filmer in July 1648 thanks him for sending Heylyn a 'stock of eye-water'.[90] By 1654, his eyesight appears to have declined so far that he could no longer read or write effectively (although he firmly corrected a suggestion in 1659 that he was actually blind).[91] His first public allusion to this incapacity is made in the address 'To the Reader' in the *Theologia*. He admits towards the end that 'I have found of late (God helpe me) such great and sensible decay of sight' that it is now difficult for him to continue with his work. He also professed himself unable to use an amanuensis: 'for my part, I never had the facultie (as some men have) of studying by another mans eyes, or turning over my books by anothers hand; but have been fain to work out my performances by my proper strength without the least help or co-operation to assist me in them'.[92] There was of course a boast here about his own resourcefulness, but if Heylyn was not naturally suited to using an amanuensis he seems nevertheless to have availed himself of such assistance, and this may account for some of the inconsistencies and extreme utterances (unrevised first thoughts?) in his later works, as well as the sparse use of citations, especially in his later histories.[93] It also explains why Heylyn should have shown such an interest in the years following the *Theologia* in publishing all those works that he had written before his eyesight had failed him.

An early example of Heylyn's readiness to put into print some of his unpublished work under his own name in 1656 completes this impression of his tendency in the first half of the 1650s to publish works that were not *overtly* polemical. This work is his *A full Relation of two Journeys*, reissued as *A Survey of the Estate of France* in the same year of 1656. Manuscript copies of Heylyn's satirical account of his 1625 journey to France had been circulating for some years. Heylyn claimed that he only moved to publish the work because he had heard news that the bookseller William Leake was preparing to print an unauthorized edition of the same piece. In fact, Heylyn's publisher had entered the authorized edition at the press a month before Leake entered his, so it is possible that Heylyn was planning an edition anyway.[94] In his preface

Heylyn was apologetic that he had written the work when 'both my wits and fancies ... were in their predominancy' and since he was not at that point seeking preferment in church and state he had 'thought of nothing else then a self-complacency, and the contentment of indulging to mine own affections'.[95] Nevertheless, the volume may well have appealed to some of his *Cosmographie* readership. There was some acerbic material about presbyterianism in his letter to Laud, some hostile comments about the Huguenots, and some positive remarks concerning Roman Catholic ritual and church decoration amid much satirical scoffing, but Heylyn seems to have felt no need to censor these passages. Similar sentiments were to be found in the pages of *Cosmographie*, after all, and the choice of a non-polemical genre of publication may again have been assumed to have offered him protection from opponents.

However, the same year of 1656 saw Heylyn return to more controversial forms of writing. It is particularly notable that, when he did so, it was in an anonymous publication, of which he subsequently strove with extraordinary determination to deny his authorship. Before examining this work, it will be necessary to move ahead to 1657, to study one of the most remarkable of all Heylyn's publications, and one which raises the important issue of his relationship with the Interregnum government of Oliver Cromwell.

THE INCONSTANT ROYALIST: HEYLYN, CROMWELL AND THE STUARTS

In 1657 Heylyn made his most daring venture into print thus far. In a volume entitled *Ecclesia Vindicata*, he gathered together a series of works, almost all written in the 1640s, but which he had either published anonymously or had failed to publish before. None dealt directly with political matters – none indeed was an explicitly royalist work – but all represented defences of the established church (though none was a direct defence of the Laudian policies of the 1630s).[96] Having broken his habit of anonymous publication with his three overtly non-controversial works in the early 1650s, Heylyn now placed a series of his controversial works on public display under his own name. If the publication of these works was an audacious move on Heylyn's part, it was hardly more audacious than the alternative manuscript dedicatory epistle that he then inserted into a presentation copy of *Ecclesia Vindicata*. For the dedicatory epistle was addressed to none other than Oliver Cromwell.[97]

Why did the royalist Heylyn dedicate his work to the most famous regicide of all? There a number of possible reasons – including Heylyn's psyche, his view of the relationship between church and state, his perception of the course of events in 1657, and also perhaps his mixed attitude towards the Stuarts.

We may begin with Heylyn's own psyche. From 1625 onwards, Heylyn had always sought means of serving the existing political authorities. In this respect, when Heylyn signed himself at the end of his manuscript dedication to Cromwell 'your Highness most humble servant to be commanded', he was sounding a familiar note. As Cromwell's grip on power seemed increasingly assured, so it may have seemed more appropriate for the instinctive servant of the state to have made his addresses to the Lord Protector. After all, the Protectorate had increasingly taken to imitating the monarchical forms of the Stuarts. With the dissolution of the republic, and the re-establishment of the court at Whitehall, it was becoming possible for a monarchist to start to invest hopes in a Cromwellian dynasty.[98] *Ecclesia Vindicata* was first entered at the press in March 1655, when Heylyn may possibly have been encouraged by Cromwell's dissolution of the First Protectorate Parliament two months earlier.[99] Penruddock's royalist uprising in the same month, and the subsequent enforcement of the crippling decimation tax on ex-royalists whose estates had been sequestered for delinquency, or who had assisted the forces raised by Charles I or his son, would, however, have quashed such hopes. Heylyn reflects in his manuscript dedication to Cromwell that while great persons in the past have accepted dedications from people 'who differed in Opinion from them', yet 'then the times were better setled, & those great Persons more assured of their own Estates, then in a Medly of contending & unsatisfactory Interesses'.

Heylyn himself suffered from what his son-in-law dubbed the 'heathenish cruelty' of the decimation tax. The fact that Barnard refers to Heylyn being subjected to the decimation tax 'about the same time' that he published *Ecclesia Vindicata* has led a later scholar to assume that he was taxed *after* the book was published, and possibly as punishment for it.[100] But *Ecclesia Vindicata* was not in the event published until 1657, and there seems no reason to assume that the text initially entered at the press in 1655 played any role in Heylyn's being assessed for the decimation tax. Barnard's account of Heylyn's treatment implies that the decision to impose the tax on him was prompted by local officials who may have resented his apparent wealth, and the fact that his wife dressed well. The tax was only meant to be levied on individuals who either had a life interest in land, tenements or hereditaments worth at least £100 a year, or who possessed a personal estate worth at least £1,500.[101] It is quite probable that the legislation of November 1655, which imposed the decimation tax and also made the use of the Prayer Book illegal, led Heylyn to reconsider the advisability of publishing *Ecclesia Vindicata* at that point. Nevertheless, it is significant that by 1657 Heylyn had changed his mind and also seemed more confident that Cromwell would accept his overtures. A number of events may have prompted him to change his mind. It is always possible that Heylyn had successfully petitioned against his assessment for the tax, and that he had not been assessed for the second year that the decimation tax was levied (from June 1656 to June 1657). The lack of surviving assessment lists for Oxfordshire makes it impossible to verify this. Alternatively, the fact that the bill to extend the decimation tax beyond June 1657 had already been rejected in January of the same year may have reassured him that the authorities were no longer wishing to penalize ex-royalists.[102] Moreover, political events would have appeared still more auspicious in 1657: that was the year in which Cromwell was finally offered the crown.

If Heylyn was tempted towards supporting the protectorate he would not have been alone among former royalists. Even zealous royalist agents such as Edmund Waller, Abraham Cowley and John Cleveland had now made their peace with the Protectorate, while more lukewarm royalists such as James Howell, Andrew Marvell and Payne Fisher had long before opted to support the new regime.[103] The apparent futility of the latest royalist uprisings, and Cromwell's increasing readiness to imitate monarchical forms in his government, must have made royalist support for the lord protector seem a more natural choice. Justifications for pragmatic support for the Protectorate could also be found in royalist circles. Heylyn's friend Sir Robert Filmer had died in 1653, but before then had published a remarkable short treatise of 'Directions for obedience to government in dangerous or doubtful times', appended to his *Observations upon Aristotles Politiques*. Here Filmer – who had plainly shared his ideas and writings with Heylyn – maintained that patriarchal power could be usurped, and that the usurper should therefore be obeyed in everything. This obedience was due in all things – not only things lawful but also things indifferent – except in matters where it tended to the destruction of the person of the previous governor. Apart from this condition, obedience to a usurper is necessary and also, since it ensures the preservation of those who are subjects, is a form of obedience to the 'true superior'. It is a natural extension of the duty of subjection and obedience. Heylyn alludes in the later 1650s to having read the *Observations* (and therefore presumably the 'Directions'), and they may have helped him to rationalize his desire to address the increasingly monarchical Lord Protector.[104]

A number of royalist clergymen had also enjoyed sometimes cordial relations with the regime. Ralph Brownrigg, bishop of Exeter, James Ussher and other episcopalian clergy were on occasion summoned to conferences to discuss possible religious toleration, or managed to appeal in person to Cromwell.[105] Another especially notable example is the Laudian bishop of Oxford, Robert Skinner, who, recent research is suggesting, had suspiciously amicable relations with the Cromwellian regime, retaining a living and also allegedly a licence to preach. It also seems possible that Skinner had preached before none other than the lords of the privy council in December 1653.[106] For his part, Cromwell had always been keen to entice ex-royalists into his regime, although the uprising of 1655 had shaken some of his confidence in their reliability.

Cromwell's religious policy may also have given unrealistic 'Anglicans' some grounds for hope. The Book of Common Prayer was still officially banned, of course, but Cromwell was famously tolerant towards individual 'Anglicans'. An official toleration had been mooted in January 1652, and a practical toleration of use of the Prayer Book was rumoured in January 1654 (a month after Skinner's sermon). Even the savage attack on the sequestered clergy in the ordinance of November 1655, which prohibited the use of the Prayer Book for any purpose, was qualified by the promise that 'towards such . . . as shall give a real testimony of their godliness and good affection to the present government, so much tenderness shall be used as may consist with the safety and good of the nation'.[107] Moreover, the more that Cromwell apparently looked towards the establishment of monarchy the more there were rumours that he intended to re-establish episcopacy.[108] A monarchy (the logic ran) would require a hierarchical church to work in harness with Cromwell's regime, so that the many sects could be controlled and religious peace and unity re-established. The logic was spelt out directly by Heylyn in his manuscript dedication of *Ecclesia Vindicata* to Cromwell. He stressed that the book was offered to Cromwell so that

> in the settlement of the Civill State, there might be somewhat offered to your Consideration in order to the like Establishment in the Ecclesiastick. For certainly (my Lord) as long as Matters in the Church remaine unsetled, & that there be Liberty of multiplying into Sects and Factions, the Civill Peace will have no sure foundation to rest upon, & consequently must needs prove doubtfull, & of short continuance. It was the glory of Jerusalem to be like a city that was of unity in it selfe, which could not be expected, & much less presumed, when Preists were made out of the meanest of the People, or that the People were permitted to runne a madding after the Moulten Calves of their own inventions; when the *high places and the groves* were as much frequented as the holy Temple, the Nation miserably divided between God & Baal, the Scribes & Pharises attaining to a greater Empire over the consciences of their followers, then the Kings had upon their Persons. Which things (as the Apostle saith in another case) I have *transferred as in a figure for your sake* that in this Glass your Highness may beholde the face of the present times; in which there is neither *Unitie* in Doctrine, nor *Uniformitie* in Devotion, nor *Unanimitie* in Affections (the three great Bonds of publick Peace) to be found among us.

Heylyn explained to Cromwell that, in the book itself, 'Hints are offered towards the reestablishment of this ruined Church upon the first principles of her Reformation'. He would be happy if this work of reformation could be advanced either by the book's contents 'or otherwise within the compass of my weake Endeavours shall be found subservient'. He emphasized his 'honest zeal' and significantly signed himself 'Your Highness most humble servant to be commanded'.[109]

Even without this manuscript dedication (which is not in Heylyn's normal hand, and could conceivably be a forgery),[110] there is much in the text of the *Ecclesia Vindicata* that is pitched in a similar style. In the preface Heylyn denies categorically that James's famous dictum 'No bishop no King' can be reversed to imply 'that there can be no Bishop where there is no King'. On the contrary, Heylyn urges the examples of Naples, Venice and Florence to demonstrate that episcopacy could comply perfectly well with republican government. Heylyn's preface continually alludes to an intended reader 'advanced perhaps unto some eminent degree of Trust and Power in the present Government', and he declares that he lays the work 'with all humble reverence at the feet of those who are in Authority'. Heylyn also explicitly refers to his hope that 'our Affaires shall be reduced to a settled Government'.[111]

Heylyn's dedication to Cromwell does not hide the fact that they have different points of view. He notes that 'great Persons in all times, have graciously accepted the like Dedications from the hands of those, who differed in Opinion from them', and explains as one of the reasons for presenting the work to him 'that your Highness, seeing by what Rules and Precedents the distressed Party in the Church hath proceeded hitherto, may looke upon them with a favourable & more gentle eye; as Men not biased by selfe-love, or plungd into calamity by their own perversness, but acting on the warrant of so good Authorities'. Cleveland, too, emphasized his past devotion to Charles in order to assure Cromwell of his potential for selfless devotion to him.[112]

There is no need, therefore, for Heylyn's actions to be seen as reflecting any change in his attitude towards the church. Indeed, the first tract in *Ecclesia Vindicata* – an expanded version of his *Parliaments Power in Laws for Religion*, now entitled 'The Way and Manner of the Reformation' – offers perhaps the most wholeheartedly clericalist account of the Church of England and its Reformation that Heylyn ever wrote. If Heylyn was seeking Cromwell's patronage for himself and his church, this was still on emphatically Laudian terms.

The *Ecclesia Vindicata* is not the only example of Heylyn seeking to provide advice to the Cromwellian regime. He also printed separately in 1657 another of his unpublished works of the 1640s, the *Stumbling Block of Disobedience*. While admitting that the book was initially written for the Stuart cause, the preface insists that it is an appropriate time for it to be published 'to give warning to all those that are in Supreme Authority to have a care unto themselves, and not to suffer any Popular or Tribunitian Spirits to grow amongst them; who grounding upon Calvins Doctrine, both may, and will upon occasion, create new disturbances'. Heylyn gestured even more directly towards Cromwell in his suggestion that the book would help 'to preserve the Dignity of the Supreme Power, in what Person soever it be placed, and fix his Person in his own proper Orb, the Primum mobile of Government'.

Also notable is Heylyn's decision – unique in his published works – to translate every one of his Greek and Latin quotations into English, which could further boost the assumption that this was a treatise being directed at the Protectorate government.[113] Heylyn can also hardly have been unaware that his text invests supreme legislative authority in monarchs who gain their power by conquest. The application to current conditions hardly needed to be made. Perhaps because, unlike *Ecclesia Vindicata*, it was concerned with overtly political matters, Heylyn did not publish the book directly under his own name. But he used none of the elaborate pseudonyms to which he had resorted in the 1640s. 'P.H.' was a rather token effort at disguising his identity, reflecting his growing confidence.

Given Heylyn's apparent dedication to the Stuart cause, and his suffering because of it, his apparent courting of Cromwell needs also to be explained by his mixed feelings towards the Stuarts. The miserable condition of the Stuart cause at this point could easily have convinced a churchman that there was little chance of restoring the Church of England under a Stuart monarch. There would also have been a natural determination not to let the church fall because of the crown. In 1649 William Sancroft had written, 'the church here will never rise again, though the kingdom should', but Heylyn was presumably determined to make sure that this would not happen: that if a 'kingdom' should rise without the Stuarts, then the Church would rise with it.[114] He was emphatic in the introduction to the *Cosmographie* that the church needed a political sponsor.[115] Charles II's flirtation with Scottish presbyterianism was enough to convince a number of clergymen that the Stuarts were not necessarily the natural supporters of the Church of England, and Robert Payne would not have been alone among Sheldon's correspondents in being pleased by Charles's failure in 1651.[116] But there is also other evidence that Heylyn was far from impressed by the performance of England's first two Stuart monarchs. In his anonymous *Observations*, published in 1656, he made scathing attacks on both James and Charles. James received the most dismissive appraisal:

> It cannot be denied, but that he was an Universall Scholar . . . but that he was Great Britains Solomon, that is to say, either the wisest Man, or the wisest King of the British Nations, I am not Courtier enough to defend or say. It is true indeed, that he much pleased himselfe with boasting of his Kings craft, as he used to call it, but . . . I have heard many wise men say they could never finde what that King-craft was: It being no hard matter to prove, that in all publick Treatises and Negotiations, and many private Conferences and debates of Councell, he was outwitted, and made use of unto other mens ends, by almost all that undertook him. And one might say (I feare too truly) that by putting off the Majesty belonging to a King of England, that so he might more liberally enjoy himselfe; neglecting the affaires of State, and cares of Government, to hunt after pleasures; deserting the imperiall City, to sport himselfe at Roiston, Newmarket, and such obscure places

(which were to him as the Isle of Capre was to Tiberius Caesar) and finally by letting loose the Golden reines of Discipline, held by his Predecessors with so strict
a hand; he opened the first gap unto those confusions, of which we have since
found the miserable and wofull consequence.[117]

As if blaming James for the Civil War was not enough, Heylyn was too good
a classical historian not to have known how Tiberius was reputed to have entertained himself on Capri.

If his criticisms of Charles are less extreme, they are nevertheless a constant feature of Heylyn's *Observations*, and can be detected in other works of
Heylyn's later years. While less damning than he is of James, nevertheless
Heylyn regularly expresses his frustration at Charles's poor political judgement and lack of resolution. It has recently been suggested that Heylyn played
a major role in the development of the cult of Charles the martyr – indeed,
he has been described as 'the defender of cult orthodoxy' – but he was anything but that. In fact, his objections to Charles went to the heart of the cult's
rationale: he condemned the king for having divested himself 'of that Regall
Majesty which might and would have kept him safe from affront and scorn,
to relie wholly on the innocence of a virtuous life, which did expose him finally
to calamitous ruine'.[118]

There is an air of unreality – perhaps desperation – in Heylyn's hope that
Cromwell would establish a vigorously episcopalian church to defend his monarchy. But the idea was not entirely absurd. In the autumn of 1656 Ussher's
1641 plan for reduced episcopacy had been reprinted. This was, however, part
of a broader pattern of co-operation with the presbyterian Association movement, for which Heylyn would have had little sympathy.[119] At the same time,
there were rumours that the Protectorate might be contemplating a form of
episcopal government. Nedham reported that Cromwell intended 'to have taken
up a Church-form as like the Episcopal as might be, by mincing a Medley of
Bishop and Presbyter together; so that after all, we should have had Bishops
again; onely they were to have had a new Name, Superintendents . . . that is,
in plain English, a Chair-man to a Committee of Presbyters; that is to say, a
Bishop in Shackles'. Nedham also reportedly teased Cromwell in 1657 by telling
him that the current news was that 'Mr Nye should be Archbishop of
Canterbury, and Dr Owen of York'.[120] A bishop in shackles and a nonconformist archbishop – this was plainly not the sort of episcopalianism that Heylyn
had in mind. Despite being involved in lengthy criticisms of Ussher, Heylyn
had remarkably little direct to say in criticism of the proposals for reduced
episcopacy.[121] But while he may have felt it to be injudicious to mount a direct
attack on the policy and its promotion, it seems quite possible that among
Heylyn's motivations in publishing *Ecclesia Vindicata* was a desire to prevent
Ussher and his supporters from securing a religious settlement based upon

the model of reduced episcopacy. If Heylyn was hearing rumours that Cromwell was considering re-establishing episcopacy, it was all the more vital that he should be told what the right form of episcopacy was.

Heylyn's hopes that Cromwell might read his work may seem ridiculous and fanciful. But he may have nursed hopes that Cromwell was not entirely hostile towards the sequestered clergy – one of the very few references to Cromwell in Heylyn's published works from the 1650s suggests this.[122] Moreover, even if Heylyn apparently had no direct line of communication with Cromwell, he was not entirely lacking in connections with the Protectorate. In the middle of his controversy with Heylyn at the end of the 1650s, Thomas Fuller claimed that Heylyn '(as I am informed) hath his Friend in the Councel; and it is not long since, he had Occasion to make use of his Favour'.[123] The report is undoubtedly malicious in intent, but it presumably exaggerates a rumoured acquaintanceship rather than simply inventing it. The 'occasion' may relate to either of two events in the previous year of 1658 – Heylyn's endeavours to persuade the council to intervene to prevent his Abingdon parish being forcibly merged with its neighbour, or his attempts to ensure that his book *Respondet Petrus* was not burnt. The latter seems more likely. Heylyn himself later describes how, when he had heard a report that the Council of State had ordered his *Respondet Petrus* to be burnt, he 'applied my self to a chief Personage in the Council of State, from whom I might assure my self of all lawful favours'. Heylyn was quite confident that, if such an order had been made, he would be able within 'a day or two' to 'procure an Order from the Council for the reversing of that Judgment'. In the event, however, 'that honourable Person' on the Council of State reassured him that the council had given no such order, and that while an order from the judges had been received that the book be burned according to the 1644 ordinance for the better observation of the Lord's Day, the council had merely committed the whole matter to the Lord Mayor of London 'to be proceeded in according to his discretion'.[124]

Who, then, was the 'chief Personage in the Council of State' from whom Heylyn could expect 'all lawful favours', and whom Heylyn was confident could be trusted to effect a reversal of a council order? Heylyn's biographers never mention such an ally, and certainly the 'friend' on the council was not a sufficiently strong supporter to have ever been proffered a dedication of one of Heylyn's many works. If there was indeed a lukewarm contact of Heylyn's on the Council of State, a number of possible candidates suggest themselves. Either Sir Charles Wolseley or Lord Lisle would have shared Heylyn's political convictions, although in neither case has evidence of personal contact with Heylyn been unearthed.[125] Another possible candidate is Nathaniel Fiennes: this prime mover in the offer of the crown to Cromwell may have had brief dealings with Heylyn at this time as a member of the commission of inquiry into the uniting of the Abingdon parishes (the business of which is the probable reason why Heylyn was in London in June 1658), and was certainly considered approachable by the ex-royalist clergyman Thomas Fuller.[126] Another of the councillors, however, had known Heylyn for much longer. Henry Lawrence, Lord President of the Council of State, was the stepson of Heylyn's uncle, Robert Bathurst. Both Heylyn and Lawrence had featured in Bathurst's will – Heylyn as a beneficiary; Lawrence as an unrelieved debtor. This, and Heylyn's tangential involvement in the Star Chamber prosecution of Lawrence's mother, Lady Elizabeth, would have meant that family relations would have been strained, to say the least.[127] In religious terms, too, Heylyn and Lawrence would have been far apart: Lawrence had been a radical puritan since the 1620s, although he wrote against some of the more extreme sects. Politically they may have been somewhat closer by the 1650s: Lawrence was said to have strongly opposed the trial and execution of the king, and was a loyal supporter of the Protectorate.[128] Lawrence may not have been on close terms with his step-cousin, but nevertheless he seems the most likely candidate for Heylyn's mysterious contact on the Council of State, and may even have been a conduit through whom Heylyn hoped to engineer a presentation of *Ecclesia Vindicata* to the Lord Protector.

If the book was ever presented to Cromwell, there is no evidence that Heylyn ever received any response from the authorities to his approaches. With Cromwell's rejection of the crown, and his death the following year, royalist hopes of a Cromwellian monarchy were decisively ended, and as the regime crumbled royalists such as Heylyn could beat a track back to the reversionary Stuart interest as if nothing had happened. Heylyn would indeed appear to have moved with lightning speed, as in 1658 he anonymously published two works which seemed to reflect support for the Stuart cause – the *Short View of the Life and Reign of King Charles* and the enormous *Bibliotheca Regia*. Both works have been treated as simple Stuart hagiography – the latter partly because of the emphatically royalist iconography that is displayed on its frontispiece.[129]

Nevertheless, both works require more careful and critical study. *A Short View of the Life and Reign of King Charles* appeared as an introduction to Richard Royston's edition of Charles's works entitled *Reliquiae Sacrae Carolinae*; it was also published separately under its own title page.[130] While the *Short View* obviously offers a favourable account of Charles's life, it is not, however, a simple hagiography. In fact it offers a restrained political history of the king's life and times. The account of Charles's trial and execution is relatively brief and perfunctory, and does not compare with the elaborate account that Heylyn wrote of the execution of Laud in the 1640s.[131] This is emphatically not a contribution to the martyrological tradition – it concludes not with a quotation from the Bible but with one from Tacitus's life of Julius Agrippa.

It is a ruler who is being commemorated, not a saint or martyr.[132] Charles is also presented as a ruler who made mistakes. In his alliance with parliament for a war to regain the palatinate Charles followed Buckingham's emotionalism, and his desire to please the House of Commons, rather than the interests of the crown. If Charles had made peace with Spain after the initial failure of the fleet then he could have avoided further problems with parliaments and the rupture with France. He departed with all his powers and prerogatives in the early 1640s, and then missed an early chance to win the Civil War.[133] By contrast, Cromwell's military successes are mentioned, but the parliamentarian general receives no other mention or criticism.

It is notable that Heylyn chooses to draw attention to religious issues in the *Short View*, so that the sufferings of the church are noted as much as those of the king. The execution of Laud receives prominent attention – we are told that even his enemies returned from his execution full of tears. Heylyn also notes how in the Second Civil War Charles was still meditating on God's displeasure as a judgement for his earlier mistakes, and places in italics the section of *Eikon Basilike* where Charles confessed that 'worldly wisdome' had led him to permit improper divine worship to be set up in Scotland and to allow the bishops of England to be injured.[134] Heylyn presumably felt that Charles merited this self-reproof.

There are some more purple passages which reflect standard royalist hyperbole. A remark of stoical patience made by Charles when standing in the rain is described as 'a speech so heavenly and Divine, that it is hardly to be paralell'd by any of the men of god in all the Scripture'.[135] When Charles is sold by the Scots there is the inevitable comparison with Christ, a soldier who spits in his face receives 'Divine vengeance' shortly afterwards, and at his execution Charles exchanges his 'Crown of Thorns' for 'an immarcessible crown of Glory'. He is saluted as 'the meekest of Men and the best of Princes'.[136] But these are the only examples of such language in over 160 pages of text.

If the *Short View* presents a measured and not uncritical view of Charles, the same is true of *Bibliotheca Regia*. This collection of Charles I's papers (printed for Henry Seile) has usually been ignored by historians and commentators on Heylyn, but it offers important insights into Heylyn's historical thinking. It bears a frontispiece showing Charles guiding the ship of state and seated in state on his throne, which was clearly intended to send a strong message to pro-Stuart forces. Nevertheless, this is not a simple work of royalist hagiography. It must also be emphasized that it is no mere collection of documents. The selection has been made with care, sometimes in order to make some very specific political points. The editorial work does not end there. It is an annotated collection, and the editor's regular annotations take the form of detailed appendices to documents, sometimes up to three pages in length.

Sometimes these annotations simply provide background historical information, but they are also often used to gloss or comment on the documents and the political events that provoked them. Heylyn was determined to avoid what he saw as the main error of the previous collection of Charles's writings (in which his *Short View* had appeared) – the *Reliquiae Sacrae Carolinae* – which 'did rather represent his Majesty in his Personal, than his Political capacities; and rather showed his great abilities, as a private man, digesting his sad and solitary thoughts into Meditations, and managing disputes with particular men; than acting as a Free Monarch, and a Powerful Prince'. Heylyn was clearly not interested in the martyrological tradition, but even his treatment of Charles's kingship was not without its pointed criticisms.

There is insufficient space to discuss all of Heylyn's annotations in *Bibliotheca Regia* here. Nevertheless, two significant observations can be made. Firstly, as with the *Short View*, Heylyn does not offer an uncritical picture of Charles. The preface briefly refers to his political genius as 'a Master of Reason', but the rest of the preface swiftly undermines this. Heylyn is emphatic that Charles failed in Scotland 'either by the remissness of his resolutions, the infidelity of some about him, or his too great indulgence to that his Ancient and Native Kingdom'. It was the king's lack of consistency that encouraged puritans in England and Scotland to demand concessions which Charles in turn yielded too easily, so that Charles 'did but accelerate his own fall'.[137] In the body of the volume itself Heylyn gives a striking account of Charles's proclamation for dissolving the Glasgow Assembly, where he bound himself on the word of a king to protect the bishops and clergy, but proved unable to do so, and left his Scottish party destitute of all protection. Heylyn is most baffled by the provision that the king's declaration of grace 'shall notwithstanding hereof stand full, firm and sure to all our good Subjects in all time coming for the full assurance to them of the true Religion'. He remarks 'upon what considerations and reasons of State, his Majesty might be mov'd to commit that paper to be registred amongst the Acts of that Assembly is beyond my reach'. While proclamations of grace were regularly made by kings, they were not intended to stand on permanent record, and 'His Majesties condescensions had been large enough, and too much to the prejudice of his Crown and Dignity without this enrollment'. Similarly, Charles 'not seeing into what inconveniences he had plunged himself by these submissions to the lust and fury of his people, commended that submissive Letter which he had sent to the House of Peers in behalf of the Earl of Strafford, to be entred amongst the Records of that House, there to remain as a perpetual monument of those extremities to which he had reduc'd himself by his too much goodness'. 'I must confess', Heylyn concluded with heavy irony, 'I am not Oedipus enough for so dark a Sphinx, and must therefore leave this depth of State-craft to more able heads. Only I cannot chuse but note how little his Majesty got by those condescensions.' [138] In his preface Heylyn stated more baldly that Charles's behaviour in England and Scotland offered a warning example to other princes and supreme magistrates 'not to engage themselves in any action of concernment, but what they are both able and resolved to go through with. The doing of such work by halves, overthrows the whole.'[139]

Heylyn was also anxious to emphasize how far Charles had supported the Laudian church – presumably to send a message to those royalists who were anxious to downplay this association. For example, he made a point of including in his collection of Charles's works all of the canons from the 1640 convocation, which he insisted should be regarded to be as much Charles's work as his declarations and proclamations.[140] A 100 page section containing Charles's official statements and publications relating to the Church of England 'being in the state of her Ascendent' actually constitutes an annotated documentary history of Laudianism, placed now at the heart of Charles's works. A later section contains all the papers relating to Charles's concessions regarding the church and episcopacy 'in the state of her declination', especially in the second half of the 1640s. These are all reproduced without comment; after the reader had absorbed the message of the first half of the volume, no comment was really needed.[141]

The *Short View* and the *Bibliotheca Regia* are, then, manifestly the work of the same mind that had written the *Observations* and the dedication to Cromwell. They represented the best gloss that Heylyn could put on the life and works of Charles, and needed to appeal to a royalist audience (as well as seeking to guide it to the true message of Charles's fall). That these works did not represent unqualified endorsement of the Stuart cause is again demonstrated by another manuscript dedication that Heylyn wrote several months after the *Bibliotheca Regia* had been entered at the press (in September 1658). Once again, Heylyn wrote his dedication to a Cromwell, although this time he addressed Oliver's son Richard, the new (but short-lived) protector.[142] The volume does not bear the author's name on the printed title page or the manuscript dedication (which is not in Heylyn's normal hand), but it does have an engraving of Richard Cromwell pasted on the page facing the dedication.[143] It may be significant that Heylyn's step-cousin Henry Lawrence was the councillor who presented the oath of state to Richard Cromwell.

The work in which Heylyn wrote his dedication bears no sign of being tailored for its presentee, and the dedication is very brief, in contrast to that written for Richard's father.[144] The dedication to Richard Cromwell suggests, however, that he still regarded the Protectorate as compatible with his Laudian sentiments.[145] Even on the eve of the Restoration, then, Heylyn's exclusive commitment to the Stuart dynasty was not self-evident.

RETURN TO CONTROVERSY, 1656–1660

In the second half of the 1650s Heylyn became involved in an extraordinary series of interrelated print controversies, featuring no fewer than seven opponents, whom Heylyn encountered over the course of six different books, amounting to some 2,000 pages of text on Heylyn's side of the debates alone. It was these pamphlet controversies that sealed the image of Heylyn as a chronically argumentative, irascible polemical writer, always ready to misrepresent his opponent while subjecting them to unrelentingly hostile attacks. Yet these books are not ultimately typical of Heylyn's *oeuvre*. Heylyn had of course written against other authors, but in only one case had it been in the form of an exchange of arguments (Hakewill and Burton not being in a position to respond), and even then Williams's imprisonment had prevented his responding to Heylyn's second pamphlet against him. Heylyn's preferred form of writing, as we have seen, was the polemically charged history, and it was to these that he returned in the 1660s. The four years in which Heylyn engaged in these other controversies therefore constitute a curious phase in his writings, in which he briefly returned to a style of writing that he had not employed for some twenty years. We will therefore need to consider not only what the controversies were about, but also what the publications meant to Heylyn, and what they reveal about his ideas and behaviour.

The content of the controversies varied widely, taking in discussions of the political events of the 1620s and 1630s, church history, political authority, sabbatarian and predestinarian doctrine, and the events of Heylyn's own career. But all of the controversies were concerned to a varying degree with Laudianism, its meaning and its legacy. This was particularly true of the disputes with Heylyn's two most significant opponents, Hamon L'Estrange and Thomas Fuller.[146] Both had composed historical works which dealt with the Caroline period, and both had had critical observations to make about Laud and his followers, their innovations in ceremonies, and their role in provoking the Civil War that had overwhelmed the country.[147] In dispute with both authors, Heylyn sought to defend the policies and principles of the archbishop, and also to associate their criticisms with attacks on the power of both church and monarch. He was particularly anxious to correct their 'errors' on his favourite topic of the independent powers of Convocation, and parliament's encroachments upon them.[148] In the course of the debates, Heylyn branded both Fuller and L'Estrange as puritans: L'Estrange was 'a Semi Presbyterian at the least' and 'a Non-conformist' while Fuller was a dedicated friend of 'the Puritan party whom he acts for in all his work', whose writings embodied dangerous principles that would overturn both church and state.[149] But Heylyn would not have engaged with them if that were truly all they were – after all, there had been for many years an avalanche of puritan anti-Laudian writings which Heylyn had displayed no interest in refuting. It was the fact that both men had royalist credentials, and that they did not purvey a simple puritan or parliamentarian view of the period, which made their marginalizing and criminalizing of the Laudian movement such a threat to Heylyn. To combat it, Heylyn had to undermine their mainstream credentials, in very much the way that he had done when writing against Williams: even when L'Estrange indignantly protested his belief in *jure divino* episcopacy Heylyn professed himself unconvinced.[150] The readiness of L'Estrange and Fuller to report puritan complaints against Laud, or to entertain their own reservations, represented a dangerous indulgence and connivance with puritanism, similar to that of the 'popular prelates' whom Heylyn had so regularly condemned.

For all that he distorted and misrepresented their positions, there was a broader sense in which these authors threatened Heylyn's self-identity and his understanding of his recent experiences. For Heylyn, the catastrophes of the Civil War were the proof that he and Laud had been right all along – they had seen their puritan critics as seditious subversives who would destroy church and crown, and that was exactly what they had done. The catastrophe had of course been intensified by the temporary readiness of some future royalists to connive in the downfall of the principles and personnel of the personal rule in the early months of the Long Parliament. The Civil War and execution of the king demonstrated the disastrous mistake that this had been. Whatever his sufferings as a result, Heylyn could at least feel that he had been vindicated. In L'Estrange's and Fuller's readings of events, Laud and his followers had been provocative innovators who were partly responsible for their own fate, and had brought down church and state with them.

Heylyn's exchanges with Nicholas Bernard were partly related to these issues.[151] They were concerned in particular with the behaviour and writings of Archbishop Ussher, another of Heylyn's 'popular prelates'. As Ussher's supporters trumpeted his writings against Heylyn on the sabbath, Heylyn presented a series of doctrines on which Ussher differed from the Church of England, accused him of incorporating the heterodoxies of Calvin into the Irish Articles, and chided him with trying to ingratiate himself with the 'Sabbatarian Brethren', noting how he had always been feasted by the English puritans.[152]

The other controversies did not bear quite as directly on these themes. Heylyn's acerbic exchanges with the royalist historian Sir William Sanderson were not especially concerned with Laudianism at all. Heylyn freely admitted that he considered Sanderson to be 'of no ill affections to Church or State' and a far more orthodox opponent than Fuller, although he disagreed with his reading of the powers of Convocation and felt that he needed to take a stronger line in defending royal prerogatives.[153] There was no obvious ideological component to the acrimonious exchanges, however, and it was personal resentment of perceived insults that seemed to keep this pamphlet dispute going, as Heylyn corrected errors in Sanderson's *Compleat History* and Sanderson hurled personal abuse in return.[154] Heylyn's exchanges with Richard Baxter and Henry Hickman were of a different order again.[155] Both men were puritan parliamentarians, so that the polemical context of the exchanges was crucially different to that between Heylyn and Fuller and L'Estrange. In both cases Heylyn wrote to defend himself against particular charges relating to his earlier writings, and (in the case of Hickman) false reports of Laud's early career, and the exchanges broadened into defences of anti-puritanism and anti-Calvinism. A final controversy, with James Harrington (the author of *Oceana*), had little direct religious component (although Heylyn noted his 'prejudice against Divines'), but was instead concerned with matters of secular authority.[156] Unlike the other controversies it was Harrington who made the first intervention, and was therefore also able to set a tone of debate that was relatively dispassionate and respectful.

What did these various controversies mean to Heylyn? It should be emphasized that despite his voluminous contributions, and readiness to be engaging with up to five authors simultaneously, it is not clear that Heylyn enjoyed the exercise. Heylyn increasingly protested in his series of polemical pamphlets that he was reluctant to enter into controversies and wished to end them.[157] This could of course be interpreted merely as the rhetorical posturing that goes with polemical writing of this type, but it is just as possible that Heylyn's protestations were genuine. Heylyn undoubtedly aspired to the loftier writing of the true historian, but found it difficult to restrain himself from academic warfare once there was a *casus belli*. The debates themselves were not simply under his control – the controversies often snowballed of their own accord. His initial comments on L'Estrange's *Reign of King Charles* drew him into prolonged and unplanned controversies with Sanderson and Bernard. Where Heylyn undoubtedly started a number of these debates, it was usually because he had already been attacked in print (at least in passing).[158] As the disputes continued, so the language and the charges became more unpleasant. Commentators have been so transfixed by Heylyn's venom that they have sometimes missed the poison generated by the other contributors, who were keen to delve into Heylyn's own past and to use it to portray him as an unscrupulous, time-serving nonentity.[159] Fuller adopts a more peaceable polemical style than Heylyn, but still uses plenty of abusive language, attacking him as an 'Adventurous Empirick' who wrote 'poysoned papers' and 'a Malignant', trained in 'Billings-Gate Colledge', and making hostile anagrams of his name.[160] It should also be emphasized that *ad hominem* charges are almost the exclusive preserve of Heylyn's opponents. Heylyn could sneer, but he lacked the contacts or information to be able to respond in kind to a series of attacks and scurrilous insinuations about his early career, his finances and even his marriage. Small wonder that Heylyn commented that all of his opponents of the 1630s put together 'did not vomit so much filth upon me, as hath proceeded from the mouth of the Pamphleteers, whom I have in hand'.[161]

It therefore seems highly significant that Heylyn attempted to keep his contributions anonymous. The *Observations on the Historie of the Reign of King Charles* (1656) – his first truly controversial work since the Civil War – followed his practice in the 1640s by being printed anonymously. His attempted anonymity seems the key to explaining why this is by far his most outspoken tract (especially notable in his attacks on the Stuart monarchs). Heylyn anxiously sought to preserve his anonymity as long as possible. He denied his authorship of the *Observations* in his following work, *Extraneus Valupans*, which was also presented as the work of an anonymous 'Well-willer'. There is also clear evidence that he intended his next book, his response to Fuller, to be published anonymously.[162] Heylyn seems to have been prompted to de-anonymize, not just because his opponents were presuming his identity, but also because on that basis they were making personal attacks on Heylyn's past behaviour. The attempt to reply to these charges via an unnamed third party who reported Heylyn's responses rapidly became both cumbersome and pointless. Heylyn's reluctance to identify himself, and the shadow-boxing that resulted, are reminiscent of his exchanges with Williams in the 1630s, and can be partly explained by the fact that Heylyn felt as vulnerable now as Williams did then. Heylyn's exposed position became evident in 1658, when it was reported that his *Respondet Petrus* might be officially burnt because of its comments on the sabbath. Heylyn's desperate response to these rumours shows his anxiety to avoid one particular form of ignominy that he had previously been spared.[163] The compulsiveness with which he still continued these debates after such a fright suggests perhaps a deeper insecurity – that of the prickly, quick-tempered young fellow of Magdalen College, swift to take offence and expecting to do so, morbidly sensitive to issues of status and convinced that his opponents will not grant him the respect that he deserves.[164]

What should we make of Heylyn's contributions to these debates? It must be stressed that he does not present a coherent overall body of thought in the exchanges. Once they were joined in conflict, Heylyn and his opponents were each concerned to catch each other out on often minor points of detail in order to undermine each other's reliability, and as a result Heylyn's writing ranges too widely, disjointedly and opportunistically to provide an entirely coherent or consistent reading. These are also the most relentlessly polemical of all of his writings, far removed from the partisan but controlled form of his histories. This makes it hazardous to use stray remarks from his contributions to encapsulate his political or religious ideas. The immediate polemical context often determined whether Heylyn would express a positive or negative attitude towards the event or historical individual being discussed. He is notably inconsistent on a number of issues. For example, in *Examen Historicum* he reverses the trend of his previous and subsequent writing by suddenly defending the Elector Palatine's claim to the Bohemian throne as entirely legitimate, and condemning James for failing to support his son-in-law – simply (it appears) so that he could thereby correct his opponent Sanderson.[165] In *Extraneus Valupans* he seems temporarily to abandon his defences of absolute royal power and implacable hostility to popular rebellions by praising Jan van Oldenbarneveldt as a great man who tried to curb the Prince of Orange's powers which threatened to lead to 'the Suppression of the Publique Libertie'. Again the polemical context is crucial. In this case, Heylyn had sought to explain away James's support for Dutch Calvinism at the Synod of Dort by claiming that this was a matter of statecraft, from which L'Estrange had drawn the mischievous conclusion that Arminianism was therefore incompatible with the safety of the state. While elsewhere Heylyn wanted to depict Calvinism as a uniquely revolutionary force, in this case he was unable to deny the Arminians' opposition to the Prince of Orange, and was therefore obliged instead to defend the principle of popular opposition to overweening royal power.[166] Elsewhere, Heylyn maintains two flatly contradictory positions in two virtually contemporaneous pamphlets on the question of whether it was appropriate to use the term 'puritan' to brand Calvinist conformist clergy.[167]

The polemical context also means that the charges of semi-presbyterianism and covert republicanism that Heylyn brought against Fuller and L'Estrange cannot be read directly as indicative of a paranoid mind set – they were polemical weapons, and Heylyn was happy to cite the work of both authors elsewhere.[168] Nevertheless, Heylyn's distrust of Fuller's arguments seems more than a polemical device. When Fuller tried to close down the debate by suggesting that they agree it 'a drawn Battel' Heylyn was reluctant to see their dispute in such terms. He rejected Fuller's claims that he was a 'fellow-sufferer' and one of 'the same party in the Church', noting that Fuller had also written of Heylyn 'and all of his party' as a separate group. While the laity sought to broker a peace between the two, which Heylyn reluctantly accepted, there was still no suggestion that Heylyn accepted that the truce was based on an assumption that the two were writing on the same side.[169]

While Heylyn's contributions to the disputes are not sustained interpretative works, they do, however, at times preview some of the ideas, materials and preoccupations of the histories which he was already writing and would eventually publish in the 1660s. The final work within these debates, the *Historia Quinqu-Articularis*, in fact straddles the genres of the pamphlet controversy and the 'purposive history' of his other works. It is effectively a set of three separate, independent tracts – on the doctrine of predestination and its treatment in the English Reformation and by English divines up to 1625 – which are framed by polemical exchanges. The *Historia* is of particular interest as it represents Heylyn's first and only extended engagement with predestinarian issues. It is not, however, a work of theology; rather, it engages with works that had claimed Calvinism to be the orthodox doctrine of the Church of England by Heylyn's preferred style of 'purposive history' which claimed to demonstrate that the Church of England had always adopted an 'Arminian' position on the Five Articles. In the process, Heylyn provides a taste of two novel developments in his thinking which recur in his three post-Restoration histories, and which reflect the specific polemical needs of his treatment of predestinarian doctrines: the suggestion that the Church of England's Reformation shared many similarities with 'Melanchthonian Lutheranism', and the admission that the search for a succession of true doctrine in the late Elizabethan church necessitated the invoking of a silent, hidden congregation of true believers.[170]

Heylyn's controversial works of these years are also significant as marking his return to the public domain, albeit not in his preferred role of government adviser. It is clear that these volumes were not merely personal attacks and defences by isolated individuals that happened to acquire printed form. There is ample evidence that the pamphlet controversies were followed and sometimes actively promoted and encouraged by a broader public, which was often involved in egging on opponents, or offering ammunition.[171] Heylyn himself was not writing under the instructions of what passed for the authorities of the 'Anglican' establishment, and the *Short History* and *Bibliotheca Regia* may represent the extent of Heylyn's involvement in more collective royalist endeavours. Nevertheless, while his controversial books were mostly intended simply as acts of self-defence, his confrontation with Fuller was different. He claimed that 'clamours of wrong done came to his ears before the book', and his refutation of Fuller was urged upon him 'by Letters, Messages, and several personal Addresses; by men of all Orders and Dignities in the Church, and of all Degrees in the Universities'.[172] Allowing for exaggeration, we may still assume a large degree of interest in Heylyn's response. Moreover, it was pressure from a lay audience to the exchanges, in the shape of Fuller's patron Lord Berkeley, which forced an end to the dispute. In fact, for all their apparent immersion in personal squabbles, it was the very public nature of these disputational works which may have played a role in hindering Heylyn's promotion at the Restoration.

At the end of *Historia Quinqu-Articularis* Heylyn announced, 'I have now done with these polemical discourses and shall not easily ingage in a new adventure, unless invincible necessity, or some unsufferable provocation shall inforce me to it. In which case only it is possible that I may be tempted to the resuming of those armes which otherwise I would willingly hang up in the Temple of Concord: that I may spend the whole remainder of my time in more peacefull studies.'[173] While Heylyn would not return to this style of literature, he was not, however, ready yet to lay down his pen. Indeed, his 'peaceful studies' would not be quiet devotional works, but a series of histories that were in their own way quite as tendentious and polemical as the pamphlet exchanges that he had just completed, which had anticipated many of their arguments. In fact, the restoration of the monarchy opened up the prospect that Heylyn would be able to throw himself once more into offering his unique range of services to the authorities.

NOTES

1 Wilcher, *Writing*, ch. 12; P. H. Hardacre, *The Royalists during the Puritan Revolution* (1956), pp. 64–131.

2 The term 'Anglican' is here used not to imply the existence of a single religious ideology but rather to distinguish those divines who opposed the Westminster Assembly and its dismantling of the Elizabethan religious settlement from those presbyterians and independents who also advocated royalism. The danger, of course, is that the introduction of a new terminology can imply the emergence of a new body of thought: I hope to deal with problems of 'Anglican' terminology in more detail elsewhere.

3 J. W. Packer, *The Transformation of Anglicanism, 1643–1660* (Manchester, 1969); C. F. Allison, *The Rise of Moralism* (1966); D. Loewenstein and J. Morrill, 'Literature and religion' in D. Loewenstein and J. Mueller (eds), *The Cambridge History of Early Modern English Literature* (Cambridge, 2002), pp. 677–8.

4 C. J. Stranks, *The Life and Writings of Jeremy Taylor* (1952), pp. 67–70; V. D. Sutch, *Gilbert Sheldon: Architect of Anglican Survival, 1640–1675* (The Hague, 1973), p. 35; Packer, *Transformation*, pp. 37–8, 188–9; J. Spurr, *The Restoration Church of England* (New Haven CT, 1991), pp. 1–2.

5 J. P. Wainwright, *Musical Patronage in Seventeenth Century England* (Aldershot, 1997). I am grateful to Lynn Hulse for alerting me to Hatton's clerical patronage.

6 This sizeable building still survives within the grounds of Abingdon School.

7 *PT*, sig. B3r. Heylyn emphasizes that the dedication of this work to his kinsman Laurence Bathurst does not reflect either gratitude for any previous benefits or expectations of future ones (B2v–B3r).

8 Barnard, p. 216. Fragmentary evidence of Heylyn's income survives in Chancery suits from the 1650s, such as the dispute over the impropriate rectory of Norton, which Heylyn offered to one Thomas Fletcher (TNA, C400/112: 1653–54).

9 Like Heylyn, both Hertford and Dorchester had compounded under the Oxford Articles. Henry Pierrepont, marquess of Dorchester, had been a notable royalist nobleman in the 1640s, serving as a member of the Council of War and of the Oxford Parliament. He had spoken out in parliament in May 1641 in defence of bishops' right

to sit in the Lords and had maintained it was lawful for bishops to 'intermeddle' in temporal affairs (*ODNB*).

10 *CE*, p. 330 (Hertford lived in Wiltshire, and therefore was presumably the dedicatee identified here as professing a 'civil acknowledgement'). The correspondence with Anne Sadleir began inauspiciously with her complaints that Heylyn had maligned her father, Sir Edward Coke, as, noting that her brother Clement Coke had said in parliament that it was better to die by a foreign enemy than to be destroyed at home, Heylyn had described him as 'a true chip of the old block'. Initially Heylyn stood by and amplified the criticisms of Sadleir's brother and father, but having been better informed of the identity and principles of his correspondent he adopted a more obsequious tone: see Trinity College, Cambridge, MS R.5.5, Nos 37–41; BL, Add. MS 23206, fol. 27r; Add. MS 28104, fol. 8r. Heylyn does adopt a more restrained tone when discussing Coke in his subsequent *Cyprianus Anglicus*, where he praises Coke's integrity in refusing to betray his trust in Sutton hospital (which Sadleir had reported to him): *CA*, pp, 123, 148; Trinity College Cambridge, MS R.5.5, No. 37. It is not clear whether Sadleir's 'great favours' to Heylyn included financial assistance: Heylyn anxiously assured her in April 1660 that 'there is nothing poore or mercenary' in his writing to her, although he was worried that her favours could easily give the impression that he made addresses to her with such intentions (BL, Add. MS 23206, fol. 27r). A further letter written by Heylyn in March 1662 (less then two months before his death) mentions his having asked her favour in an unspecified affair (Trinity College Cambridge, MS R.5.5, No. 41).

11 Bosher, *Making*, pp. 1–48; Sutch, *Sheldon*; Packer, *Transformation*, pp. 129–71; Trott, 'Prelude', ch. 2.

12 Sutch, *Sheldon*, pp. 45–6; Bosher, *Making*, pp. 88–99. Heylyn does speak highly of the Polyglot Bible in the dedicatory epistle of his *Theologia*, but there is no indication that he played any role in the project: *TV*, sig. A2v.

13 Sutch, *Sheldon*, pp. 45–7. While Heylyn does defend the Church of England's position in the tracts collected in *Ecclesia Vindicata* (1657) these are not responding to any later opponents than Smectymnuus, and while his *Historia Quinqu-Articularis* (1660) defends the theology of the Church of England (as Heylyn sees it) it is more of a personal defence against Hickman's attacks on him.

14 Packer, *Transformation*, pp. 15–185; Bosher, *Making*, pp. 49–87; M. Keblusek, 'The exile experience: royalist and Anglican book culture in the Low Countries, 1640–1660' in L. Hellinga *et al.* (eds), *The Bookshop of the World* (Goy-Houten, 2001); Spurr, *Restoration*, pp. 115–16.

15 Macray, *Register*, III, p. 161.

16 Henry Hickman, *A Review of the Certamen Epistolare* (1659), p. 1.

17 *HQA*, sigs A4v–B1; M.O., *Fratres in Malo* (1660), p. 29.

18 See below, ch. 6.

19 Thomas Pierce, *The New Discoverer Discover'd* (1659), p. 262.

20 Vernon, pp. 146–54. It is notable that Barnard's comments on Heylyn's activities are even briefer than Vernon's, and make no reference to people outside the family attending prayers in the 'oratory' (Barnard, pp. 235–6).

21 Barnard, pp. 232, 234; Bodl., MS Gough Berks 5, fols 150v–152r.

22 A. E. Preston, *The Church and Parish of St Nicholas Abingdon* (Oxford, 1935), pp. 107, 109.

23 Barnard, pp. 216–17; Spurr, *Restoration*, pp. 25–6.

24 Barnard, p. 272; *Life and Times of Anthony Wood* (5 vols, Oxford, 1891–1900), I, p. 365.

25 K. Fincham and S. Turner, 'Bishop Robert Skinner and the Survival of the Episcopal Church of England' (paper delivered at St Anne's College, Oxford, 22 July 2006). I am very grateful to Drs Fincham and Taylor for kindly providing me with a copy of their important paper.

26 Barnard, pp. 221, 272; Wood, *Life and Times*, I, p. 364. Barlow's splenetic annotations in his copies of books by Heylyn which survive in the Bodleian library suggest a rather different relationship (e.g. Bodl., N.N.118 Th. – Barlow's copy of *Cyprianus Anglicus*). The claim that Heylyn felt that this 'man of learning' should be given a bishopric strains credulity. Barnard may have been seeking to capitalize on a lukewarm acquaintance between the two men in order to find ways of endearing himself to Barlow, who was then his diocesan. Barlow was apparently employed by the publisher to edit the life of Heylyn published in the 1681 edition of his collected works: *ER*, I, pp. xxiii–iv.

27 *Extraneus*, pp. 49–51.

28 *CE*, pp. 339–40.

29 *Ibid.*, sigs A2r–A8v.

30 *Acts and Ordinances of the Interregnum, 1642–1660*, ed. C. H. Firth and R. S. Rait (2 vols, 1911), II, pp. 1266–8.

31 *EH*, i. pp. 110–11; Vernon, p. 136. Heylyn would also have had his Westminster prebend in mind when he complained of how 'so many Bishops, Deans, and Prebendaries . . . have been thrust out of their Cathedrals without the allowance of one penny towards their subsistence', which he contrasted with the generous pensions granted to ex-monks by Henry VIII (*EH*, i. p. 110). It is not clear whether the example of a benefice rented at £250 a year for which the ejected clergyman 'to my certain knowledge' could obtain only £3 6s 8d (*ibid.*, i. p. 111) also draws on his personal experience.

32 *CE*, sigs A7v–A8v, p. 55 (my italics).

33 Vernon, pp. 140–1; W. A. Shaw, *A History of the English Church during the Civil Wars and under the Commonwealth, 1640–1660* (2 vols, 1900), II, p. 257.

34 Vernon implies (pp. 131–2) that the paper was written while Heylyn was at Winchester in the later 1640s, but its references to 'the late King', 'the Long Parliament' and the current bill for settling ministers in sequestered livings would seem to date it to the period when the bill was being debated between October 1656 and June 1657 (*CJ*, VII, pp. 431, 449, 459, 489, 560, 570–1, 577).

35 Vernon, pp. 132–7.

36 Barnard, p. 230.

37 For example, for the year 1658 Heylyn refers to being in London in June (*CE*, pp. 100–1 – presumably in relation to the St Nicholas case, which was being debated then: Preston, *Church and Parish*, pp. 109–10), to having business in London that detained him until the end of August (*CE*, p. 3) and also being in London for most of November (*ibid.*, p. 12).

38 See R. J. Mayhew, ' "Geography is twinned with Divinity": the Laudian geography of Peter Heylyn', *Geographical Review*, 90 (2000), pp. 18–34.

39 *TV*, sig. B3v.

40 *Cosmographie*, sig. A3r–v.

41 Barnard, pp. 213–16.

42 Walker, pp. 253–4.

43 *Cosmographie*, sig. A3v.

44 *Ibid.*, sig. A4r. Heylyn's patriotism had a Laudian inflection, however – most notably in his rejection of the country's ties to the Continental Reformed tradition. See below.

45 *Ibid.*, sigs A3r, A4v, A5r–v.

46 *CSPD 1651–52*, p. 476.

47 *Cosmographie*, sig. A3v.

48 *Ibid.*, i. pp. 192–3.

49 *Microcosmus* (1636), pp. 179–80; *Cosmographie*, i. pp. 87–8. A paragraph on the Whore of Babylon and the seven hills seems to be deleted entirely: contrast *Microcosmus*, p. 178, with *Cosmographie*, i. p. 86.

50 *Cosmographie*, ii. pp. 59, 92, 94. Contrast also the accounts of Christian of Anhalt in *Microcosmus* (1636), p. 318, and *Cosmographie*, ii. p. 104.

51 *Cosmographie*, i. pp. 147–8. Note the reworking of *Microcosmus* (1636), p. 79, in *Cosmographie*, i. p. 147.

52 *Cosmographie*, i. pp. 148–9.

53 *Ibid.*, ii. p. 147.

54 *Ibid.*, i. p. 180.

55 *Ibid.*, i. p. 139v; *Microcosmus* (1636), p. 134.

56 *Cosmographie*, i. p. 139r.

57 *Cosmographie*, ii. pp. 121, 140.

58 *Ibid.*, sig. A4v.

59 *Ibid.*, i. p. 267.

60 *Ibid.*, i. p. 266; *Microcosmus* (1636), p. 470.

61 *Cosmographie*, i. p. 266 (cf. p. 264); *Microcosmus* (1636), p. 470.

62 See for example his discussion of government in the Holy Roman Empire, where he notes that the Emperor is completely controlled by the Diet or parliament, but then notes how the individual princes exercise a supreme authority that would not be allowed the Emperor (ii. pp. 47–8, 118–19). See also his analysis of the question of the elective or hereditary nature of the Danish monarchy (ii. p. 137), and his observations on the creation of the Swedish absolute monarchy (ii. pp. 147–8).

63 *Cosmographie*, i. p. 321.

64 *Ibid.*, ii. p. 118.

65 *Ibid.*, i. p. 284 – contrast *Microcosmus* (1636), p. 483.

66 *Cosmographie*, i. p. 203.

67 *Ibid.*, p. 120.

68 *Ibid.*, sig. C4v.

69 *Ibid.*, i. p. 262 – note the much shorter complaints in *Microcosmus* (1636), p. 464.

70 *Cosmographie*, i. p. 140v; *Microcosmus* (1636), pp. 286–7.

71 Walker, p. 254.

72 *Cosmographie* was entered at the press on 30 December 1651 (Walker, p. 235).

73 A. Woolrych, *Britain in Revolution, 1625–1660* (Oxford, 2002), p. 525; J. Peacey, 'Nibbling at Leviathan: politics and theory in England in the 1650s', *HLQ*, 61 (2000), pp. 249, 253.

74 *TV*, sigs A4r–B3v; *CE*, p. 329.

75 *TV*, sig. A3r. See e.g. pp. 423–5, 457–9. Printed editions of the *Theologia* contain two different versions of the dedicatory epistle. One of these – a longer and more personal text – appears to have been intended more for presentation copies: see Walker, pp. 340–2.

76 E.g. *TV*, pp. 420–1, 457, 460.

77 E.g. *ibid.*, pp. 446–54, 463, 470, 477, 483.

78 E.g. *ibid.*, pp. 383–7, 431–3.

79 *Ibid.*, pp. 385–7.

80 *Ibid.*, pp. 455, 458, 459.

81 *Ibid.*, pp. 393–8. This was apparently the first time that Heylyn explicitly acknowledged Harpsfield as a source for his view of Wyclif. See also *HQA*, ii. pp. 8–9.

82 *TV*, pp. 400, 405.

83 *Ibid.*, pp. 202, 258.

84 For one brief example of a traditional Heylyn distinction between the testimony of Hooker and Jewel, as private writers, and the public testimony of the Church see *ibid.*, p. 445.

85 *Ibid.*, sig. B2v, B3v–B4r, pp. 440, 442.

86 *Ibid.*, p. 417.

87 *Ibid.*, p. 441.

88 Jeremy Taylor, *Unum Necessarium* (1655); Stranks, *Jeremy Taylor*, pp. 145, 149–57.

89 *TV*, pp. 453, 471.

90 Centre for Kentish Studies, MS U120/C6, A18, Heylyn to Filmer, 3 July 1648. I am very grateful to Cesare Cuttica for bringing this letter to my attention, and to the Centre for Kentish Studies for providing me with a xerox of it at short notice.

91 *CE*, pp. 336–7.

92 *TV*, sig. B4r.

93 On the limited schooling of his amanuensis and the problems that this created for Heylyn see *CE*, p. 313; *EH*, ii. p. 207.

94 Walker, pp. 359–61.

95 *Survey*, sig. a1v.

96 The works were *The Way and Manner of the Reformation* (an expanded version of *Parliaments Power in Lawes for Religion*), the *Historie of Episcopacie*, the *History of Liturgies*, the *Undeceiving of the People in the point of Tithes* and the *Brief Discourse* on the use of prayers before the sermon.

97 Bodl., 4o. Rawl. 152. This is not merely a dedicatory inscription but an alternative dedicatory epistle: the printed dedication (to Heylyn's schoolmaster) has been removed from this copy, and two sheets have been inserted in its place bearing the four-page dedication to Cromwell. While I came across this copy independently of Dr Walker, nevertheless his PhD thesis represents the first occasion when its existence was flagged in public. Walker reproduces most of the text of the dedication, and provides a photocopy of the final page of it, in his thesis, pp. xxxvii–xxxix.

98 R. Sherwood, *The Court of Oliver Cromwell* (1977).

99 Walker, p. 387.

100 Barnard, pp. 226–8; Walker, p. 387.

101 J. T. Cliffe, 'The Cromwellian decimation tax of 1655: the assessment lists' in *Camden Miscellany XXXIII* (Camden Society, 5th ser., 7, 1996), pp. 406–11.

102 *Ibid.*, p. 407.

103 *ODNB*; Wilcher, *Writing*, pp. 340–1, 346; John Cleveland, *Cleaveland's Petition to His Highnesse the Lord Protector* (1657); Peacey, *Politicians*, pp. 280, 282–3.

104 Filmer, *Patriarcha*, pp. 281–6; *CE*, p. 208 ('387'). Another royalist writer, John Hall of Richmond, had switched in 1656 to advocating submission to *de facto* powers: Peacey, 'Nibbling', p. 255.

105 Bosher, *Making*, pp. 9–10, 42; W. C. Abbott, The *Writings and Speeches of Oliver Cromwell* (4 vols, Cambridge MA., 1939), IV, pp. 69–70, 96, 102.

106 Fincham and Turner, 'Bishop Robert Skinner'; BL, Add. MS 20065.

107 Bosher, *Making*, pp. 9–10, 41.

108 See above, p. 168.

109 'to be commanded' has been added in a different hand to the rest of the dedication, as an afterthought.

110 The hand may be contrasted with that used (presumably by his amanuensis) in Heylyn's various letters to Anne Sadleir in the years 1659–62 (see above, n. 10).

111 *EV*, sigs a2r–v, d3r–v, e2r.

112 Cleveland, *Petition*. Cf. Lionel Gatford, *A Petition for the Vindication of the Publique Use of the Book of Common-Prayer* (1655), p. 53.

113 *SB*, sig. A3r–A4r.

114 H. Cary, *Memorials of the Great Civil War in England* (2 vols, 1842), II, p. 118.

115 *Cosmographie*, sig. A6; Walker, p. lxxiii.

116 Bosher, *Making*, pp. 15–16, 68–9.

117 *Observations*, pp. 13–14.

118 A. Lacey, *The Cult of King Charles the Martyr* (Woodbridge, 2003), pp. 69–70; Heylyn, *Observations*, pp. 28–30 (cf. pp. 48, 105–6, 109–10).

119 James Ussher, *The Reduction of Episcopacie unto the Form of Synodical Government received in the Antient Church* (1656); Spurr, *Restoration*, p. 26; Bosher, *Making*, pp. 45–6. For an excellent analysis of the wishful thinking behind the claims of common ground between Baxter and the moderate episcopalians see Trott, 'Prelude', pp. 33–9.

120 Marchamont Nedham, *A Second Pacquet of Advices and Animadversions* (1677), p. 6; Abbott, *Writings*, IV, pp. 69–70. I owe both these references to Blair Worden.

121 There are pertinent comments on Ussher's publication of *The Judgement of Doctor Rainoldes touching the Originall of Episcopacie* (1641) in Heylyn's response to Nicholas Bernard in *Respondet Petrus*. Heylyn reflects that Ussher would make himself 'no better then the President of the Presbyters within his Diocess' (*RP*, p. 102). But there is a remarkable absence of comment on Ussher's scheme for reduced episcopacy which the same Bernard had published two years previously.

122 *CE*, p. 35.

123 Fuller, *Appeal*, p. 13.

124 *CE*, pp. 107–8.

125 I am very grateful to Blair Worden for discussing this problem with me, and for these suggestions. He should not be held responsible for my own preference for Henry Lawrence.

126 Preston, *Church and Parish*, pp. 108–9. Barnard (p. 223) claimed to have seen Thomas Fuller 'make a fawning address' to Fiennes in presenting him with a copy of his *Church-History*. Fiennes was also a strong supporter of the offer of the crown to Cromwell. It is, however, difficult to imagine the ardently anticlerical Fiennes, who had spearheaded the attack on episcopacy in the Long Parliament, having much sympathy for Heylyn.

127 TNA, Prob. 11/142, fols 406v–407v. See above, ch. 1.

128 *ODNB*, s.n. 'Henry Lawrence'.

129 L. Potter, *Secret Rites and Secret Writing: Royalist Literature, 1641–1660* (Cambridge, 1989), pp. 198–202.

130 Seile was Heylyn's main undertaker at this point and was involved in the *Reliquiae* project (other editions of *Reliquiae* by other undertakers do not incorporate Heylyn's *Short View*). A separate issue of *Short View* was entered to Royston on 15 May 1658: Walker, pp. 402–4.

131 *Short View*, pp. 148–53; cf above, ch. 4.

132 *Short View*, p. 163. The title page also bears a quotation from Tacitus.

133 *Ibid.*, pp. 32, 42, 83–5, 109–10.

134 *Ibid.*, pp. 113–14, 141–3.

135 *Ibid.*, p. 107.

136 *Ibid.*, pp. 133–4, 149, 152, 161.

137 *BR*, sigs **1r–v, **3r.

138 *Ibid.*, pp. 169, 171–2.

139 *Ibid.*, sig.**1v.

140 *Ibid.*, sig. *5v

141 *Ibid.*, pp. 203–300, 301–59.

142 Cromwell resigned the protectorate in May 1659.

143 BL, shelfmark G.4681.

144 The work is Heylyn's *Examen Historicum* – one of the series of pamphlets that Heylyn wrote against a swelling number of his critics in the later 1650s (see below).

145 Walker, p. 431.

146 L'Estrange's *Reign of King Charles* was criticized in Heylyn's *Observations on the Historie of the Reign of King Charles*, prompting L'Estrange's *Observator Observed*, and Heylyn's response in *Extraneus Valupans*. Heylyn responded to Fuller's *Church-History* in *Examen Historicum*, which provoked Fuller's *Appeal of Injured Innocence*, to which Heylyn replied in his *Certamen Epistolare*.

147 *EH*, i. sigs b5r–b7r. L'Estrange's more direct criticisms are in the unpublished draft sheets of his *History* (described by Heylyn) and in *Observator*, pp. 17–19, 22–5, 26–30, 32–3.

148 *EH*, i. sig. b3r–v, pp. 71, 84–5, 95–103, 126, 139–41; *CE*, pp. 359–66; L'Estrange, *Observator*, pp. 34–5, 39, 40–1; *Observations*, pp. 263–6.

149 *Extraneus*, sig. A4r–v; *EH*, i. sig. A3v–A4r, p. 89.

150 *Extraneus*, pp. 153–61; L'Estrange, *Observator*, p. 36.

151 Bernard complained in his *The Life & Death of . . . James Ussher* of Heylyn's comments on Ussher in *Observations*. Heylyn responded in part of *Extraneus*, to which Bernard replied in *The Judgment of the late Primate of Ireland . . . of the Sabbath and Observance of the Lord's Day*. Heylyn's reply to this is *Respondet Petrus* (1658).

152 *RP*, pp. 53, 96–7, 116, 118–23.

153 *EH*, ii. sigs A3v–A4v.

154 Sanderson comments on Heylyn's exchanges with L'Estrange at various points in his *A Compleat History of the Life and Raigne of King Charles*. Heylyn's critical response is contained in an appendix to *Respondet Petrus* (to which Sanderson replied with *Post-haste: a Reply to Peter (Doctor Heylin's) appendix*) and in *Examen Historicum* (which also answers *Post-haste*). Heylyn did not deign to respond to Sanderson's further pamphlet *Peter Pursued*.

155 Heylyn responded to Baxter's *The Grotian Religion Discovered* (1658) in his *Certamen Epistolare*, in which he also commented on Hickman's *A Justification of the Fathers and Schoolmen* (1659). Hickman responded in *A Review of Certamen Epistolare*. Heylyn's *Historia Quinqu-Articularis* briefly replies in an appendix to some personal attacks in the *Review*. Hickman's *Historia Quinqu-Articularis Exarticulata* did not appear until 1673, although he published a critique of Heylyn's *Ecclesia Restaurata* in his *Plus Ultra* (1661).

156 Harrington's letter to Heylyn and Heylyn's reply are contained in *Certamen Epistolare*.

157 E.g. *EH*, ii. sigs a2v–a3r.

158 Heylyn's first response to Fuller is the only piece where he was not apparently pro- voked by critical comments on himself or his writings.

159 E.g. L'Estrange, *Observator*, p. 40; *CE*, pp. 136–8, 328–9; Sanderson, *Post-haste*; Hickman, *Review*.

160 Fuller, *Appeal*, i. p. 22, iii. pp. 33, 49, 61.

161 *Extraneus*, sig. A3v.

162 *CE*, p. 337 – note also *EH*, i. p. 77, and the variant copies of the *Examen* that survive without any author's name on the title page, although Heylyn's name appears at the end of the preface (e.g. CUL, shelfmark Sel.L*.10.46).

163 *CE*, pp. 100–10.

164 E.g. *Extraneus*, sig. A6r, pp. 52–3; L'Estrange, *Observator*, p. 40; *CE*, sig. A6v–A7r.

165 *EH*, ii. pp. 57–8.

166 *Extraneus*, pp. 229–30.

167 Contrast *CE*, pp. 4, 19–20, with *EH*, i. pp. 149–50.

168 See below, ch. 6.

169 *CE*, pp. 314–15, 339–42, 356, 392–6; Trinity College Cambridge, MS R.5.5: Heylyn to Anne Sadleir, 1 August 1659; BL, Add. MS 23206, fol. 27r, Heylyn to Anne Sadleir, 23 April 1660.

170 See below, ch. 6.

171 Fuller, *Appeal*, i. pp. 2, 7; *EH*, i. p. 282; *CE*, pp. 1, 115–16, 338.

172 *EH*, i. sig. b8r; *CE*, sig. A5v, p. 336. It seems that the only reference to Heylyn in Sancroft's voluminous surviving Interregnum correspondence is an allusion to *Examen Historicum* being in press: BL, Harl. MS 3783, fol. 220r, George Davenport to Sancroft, 1 October 1658. I am grateful to Ken Fincham for this reference.

173 *HQA*, postscript, sig. Qqq3r.

Chapter 6

Ecclesia Restaurata? Heylyn and the Restoration church, 1660–1688

SHAPING THE NEW SETTLEMENT, 1660–1662

The coronation of Charles II in Westminster Abbey – on St George's Day 1661 – was a splendid occasion that marked not only the restoration of the monarchy, but also the restoration of the Church of England. And in the abbey ceremony itself, presenting the new king with his sceptre before the eyes of the political nation, was the indomitable figure of Peter Heylyn.[1] This in some sense represented the final triumph for Heylyn, and for his understanding of the intimate link that could and should exist between church and state. And yet it was in many ways a mixed triumph. Whatever the symbolic trappings of the ceremony, and the apparent re-establishment of the Church of England, the return of the monarch was not immediately accompanied by the restoration of the Laudian church.

One notable indication that the Laudian church had not been restored was the conspicuous lack of promotion for one of its most doughty defenders, Peter Heylyn himself. He would never receive a higher post than that of sub-dean of Westminster – in a sense, he was no further advanced than he had been thirty years earlier. His lack of promotion was certainly commented on by contemporaries. His son-in-law recalled Heylyn's exchange with John Cosin (now appointed bishop of Durham). When Cosin exclaimed, 'I wonder, brother Heylyn, thou art not a Bishop; for we all know thou hast deserved it,' Heylyn's reported reply – 'Much good may it do the new Bishops: I do not envy them, but wish they may do more than I have done' – barely hides his own resentment.[2] The fact that the newly created bishops included old foes such as George Morley and Edward Reynolds can only have increased such anger.

Heylyn's lack of promotion has often prompted speculation among historians. He had certainly been considered as a possible recipient of further advancement: his name appears on a list made in 1658/9 of eighty-six men deemed worthy of promotion to vacancies (twenty-eight of whom received nothing, although some received posts in a second wave of appointments in late 1660).[3] Robert Baillie had feared that Heylyn would have a strong influence on the Restoration settlement, among the leaders of an episcopal party including Jeremy Taylor, Thomas Pierce, Henry Hammond, Herbert Thorndike, John Bramhall, and Matthew Wren. Heylyn was of the same generation as those clergymen – Gilbert Sheldon, John Cosin, John Earle and George Morley – who worked most closely with Hyde at the Restoration, and he had certainly held higher office in the pre-war church than two of them.[4] The afflictions of deprivation and the decimation tax meant that he bore his necessary battle scars, while his flood of publications in support of the pre-war church made him one of the most prolific clerical writers in the Restoration church (given the recent death of Henry Hammond).

Several suggestions have been advanced to explain Heylyn's lack of preferment.[5] One is that he was now virtually blind, and therefore not able to carry out higher ecclesiastical duties. While it is true that he could not read or write without the assistance of an amanuensis, nevertheless his son-in-law insisted that 'he was not so totally deprived of his sight (as some imagine) but could discern a body or substance near hand (though not the physiognomy of a face), so as to follow his leader, when he walked abroad'. He could also still sign his name, as the Westminster chapter minutes demonstrate.[6] Moreover, there was no sense that the enfeebled state of Bishops Juxon and Piers prevented their carrying out the duties of their office.

A more straightforward explanation is that there was too much competition for vacancies. There were certainly far too many possible claimants for the offices that were available. Moreover, preferment to office was an important weapon in the new government's armoury. Given the need to secure the maximum degree of public support for the new regime, it was vital that, where possible, offers of office were used to build a broad base of support for the government. In the church, this meant that bishoprics should be offered to ex-presbyterians such as Richard Baxter and Edward Reynolds. There were in fact very few Laudian appointments to bishoprics, and with the exception of Juxon those who had been Laudian bishops in the pre-war church – Warner, Piers and Wren – were not given further promotion.[7] Restoration England was full of embittered royalists who felt that they had not been properly rewarded at the Restoration, and their complaints spilled into pamphlet exchanges. Ultimately, if there were not enough rewards to go round, Charles and his ministers seem to have made the calculation that the one group he could afford to disappoint were the royalists. It was not until the mid-1670s that Charles II systematically favoured the supporters of Charles I and his sons.[8] Heylyn was one disappointed man among very many.

Heylyn may also have suffered because he did not have strong enough or sufficiently well placed supporters at court. He had no obvious links with the exiled court, although Secretary Nicholas would have remembered him from the 1640s. Neither had he developed close links with Gilbert Sheldon, John Barwick and the other clergymen co-ordinating the 'Anglican' network in the 1650s. He had also proved conspicuously unable to build links with the prominent lay people and aristocrats who flocked to the restored court.

Even if Heylyn had had his advocates, the most obvious reason for his being passed over for further advancement was that he was clearly regarded as too inflammatory a personality. Such was his notoriety as a vehement supporter of Laudianism that it was only three years since Heylyn himself had dared to start putting his name to disputational works again. The report that his fellow clerics had complained of his 'marring all' is all too likely to have been true. Fears of over-zealous clergymen were rife in royalist circles in the months prior to the Restoration. Hyde wrote in 1659 asking whether Bishop Wren thought that John Cosin had proceeded further than he needed to have done when responding to Thomas Fuller. This was an exchange that Heylyn himself had orchestrated, prompting Cosin to write a letter of self-justification for Heylyn to publish in his 'Animadversions' against Fuller.[9] Hyde's anxious response not only reveals government sensitivities, and their feeling that men such as Fuller needed to be accommodated within any Restoration church settlement, but also demonstrates that Heylyn's works were being scrutinized carefully by Charles's ministers in exile. A further letter in April 1660 expressed concern about impassioned royal chaplains whose hot spirits caused offence and threatened the settlement, and whose antics were making the king very worried.[10] This latter letter was referring to exiled chaplains who had recently returned to England, so cannot have intended Heylyn, but nevertheless reveals the government fears of zealous and inflammatory royal chaplains which would undoubtedly have included Heylyn himself in their notional list of dangerous men. After all, Heylyn's most acerbic public exchanges had just been with Richard Baxter, who was being earnestly wooed by the new regime, which was prepared to offer him a bishopric. The Restoration settlement passed by the Convention Parliament had at its core the Act of Free and General Pardon, Indemnity and Oblivion, which dictated that 'all names and terms of distinction' should be 'put into utter oblivion', and that anyone who taunted old adversaries with 'any name or names, or other word of reproach, any way tending to revive the memory of the late differences or the occasions thereof' would be punished.[11] It was difficult to see how someone like Heylyn would fit into such a settlement.

Moreover, even among ex-royalists there were many men who had been more than happy to see the defeat of Laudianism. That incorrigible royalist the earl of Newcastle was presumably not alone among royalist aristocrats in his emphasis that lay support would be forthcoming only on the condition of 'the Clergye not medleing in Laye Busines . . . & the Church not being proude, And Haughty, over the Layety, but Gentle & Curtious to them'. For Newcastle, this meant (among other things) no bishops being made Lord Keeper or Lord Treasurer, and no clergyman being made a justice of the peace.[12]

Hemmed in by the king's need to secure the broadest possible foundation for the church settlement, and fears of a return to Laudian clericalism, clergymen such as Sheldon had to move with great circumspection. It was the Cavalier Parliament that would provide the crucial momentum towards the establishment of a more unambiguously Anglican settlement, but only in 1662 did it became clear that there would be no compromise with the presbyterians. Before that time, the compromise settlement indicated by Charles's Declaration of Breda seemed very much on the cards. Not only might there be toleration of religious nonconformists, and reform of the liturgy to remove points of complaint, but the structure of church government might itself be an area for negotiation and compromise. Schemes for 'reduced episcopacy' were in the air once again, with Ussher's plan reprinted once again by Heylyn's opponent Nicholas Bernard.[13]

The first year following the Restoration was therefore an anxious time for men such as Heylyn who feared that crucial compromises might well be being made with their religious opponents, so that religious defeat would be snatched from the jaws of political victory. To counter this threat, Heylyn threw himself into a campaign to ensure that the Restoration settlement would not fall victim to unnecessary compromise or erastian instincts. His was not in a strong or influential position. Heylyn did not have the ear of the king, and despite the reports of some contemporaries and later historians he was not a member of the Savoy House Conference, which met from April 1661 and debated possible changes to the liturgy.[14] He played no formal debating role in the new settlement. But as we have seen, this was not Heylyn's preferred method of action. Moreover, unlike men such as Bernard and Gauden who published their proposals for moderation and reform, Heylyn did not resort to the printing press.[15] Instead, it is clear is that he was active behind the scenes, in lobbying, petitioning and private meetings, always seeking to ensure that a more Laudian settlement of the church would be achieved. He may not have attended the Savoy House Conference, but he did, however, sternly instruct Clarendon that he hoped that the selection of a few bishops and other lower clergy to debate points in the Prayer Book 'is not intended for a Representation of the Church of England, which is a Body more diffused, and cannot legally stand by their Acts and Counsels'.[16]

Heylyn's return to his old techniques of lobbying, petitioning, and offering advice in person and in position papers began early. Vernon reports that when the Restoration began to appear likely, Heylyn busied his active and searching mind in finding out several expedients for the restoring and securing of its Power and Privileges in future Ages against the attempts of Factious and Sacrilegious men. And the first thing that he engaged in, was to draw up several Papers, and tender them to those Persons in Authority, who in the days of Anarchy and Oppression, had given the most signal Testimonies of their Affection to the Church. In which Papers he first shewed what Alterations, Explanations, etc were made in the Publick Liturgy in the Reigns of King Edward VI, Queen Elizabeth, and King James; that so those who were entrusted with so sacred a Depositum, might be the better enabled to proceed in the Alteration and enlargement of it.[17]

Vernon also notes Heylyn's concern to ensure that a number of specific pieces of legislation were passed. One of these related to the issue which had first concerned him in his dispute with Henry Burton in the 1630s, and the threat from which had preyed on his mind when he had been conducting his further researches on the Edwardian Reformation. This was the Act made in the first year of Edward VI's reign whereby the bishops were required to perform their business in the king's name. It had been briefly revived in the first year of James's reign but then had lain dormant and, as Heylyn had reported to Burton in 1637, Charles had had the judges confirm in a proclamation that this act was no longer in force. But Heylyn, according to Vernon, considered 'that what the Judges did was extrajudicial, and that the Kings Proclamation expired at his Death'. He therefore solicited that the act of the first year of James's reign should be formally repealed. Another matter of concern to Heylyn related to a piece of legislation passed by the Long Parliament in 1641. This was the act passed in 1641 that disabled archbishops and bishops from administering oaths to churchwardens or sidesmen, thereby undermining all proceedings in church courts, making void all episcopal visitations, and subverting 'the whole Episcopal Jurisdiction'. Heylyn reportedly drew up a petition requesting that the clauses of the 1641 act be annulled.[18]

It is hardly conceivable that other Restoration churchmen were not alert to these problems, and Heylyn's biographers display over-eagerness to give Heylyn the credit for developments in Restoration ecclesiastical policy. Nevertheless, it is striking that, despite his blindness and frailty, Heylyn threw himself once more into lobbying hard for a restoration of Laudian principles in the new church settlement, and especially the re-establishment of the independent powers of the clergy. Another of his position papers related to the sitting of bishops in parliament. Despite the fact that the bishops had been restored to the House of Lords (resuming their seats at the opening of the second session of the Cavalier Parliament in November 1661, following the repeal of the Bishops' Exclusion Act the previous June), Heylyn learned that it had been insinuated 'that though the Bishops are admitted to be Lords of Parliament, yet they are not to be reckoned amongst the Peers of the Realm'.

In order to justify the bishops' claim to sit as peers of the realm, Heylyn dusted off his short tract 'De jure paritatis episcoporum', which he had initially composed in 1641. Citing historical records, case law and acts of parliament, Heylyn insisted that the bishops' sitting in parliament confirmed their status as 'Peers and Barons of the Realm', and added for good measure that the argument that they were not competent to sit in judgement on the death of a peer was 'a Trick imposed upon the Bishops by the late long Parliament' to exclude them from the trial of Strafford. This action was done, not with reference to ancient canons, 'but upon design, for fear, they might discover some of those secret practices, which were to be hatched, and contrived against him'.[19] It is not clear, however, that Heylyn's short tract was used by the Restoration bishops any more than it was by their predecessors in 1641.

Heylyn did not restrict his propaganda barrage to position papers. He also used the pulpit of Westminster Abbey, most notably in the sermon that he delivered on 29 May 1661 on the anniversary of the king's restoration and just a month after the king's coronation in the same venue. Alongside his magnifying of the king, Heylyn reflected on the past and delivered some very clear advice and warnings to the government. In a very direct allusion to his earlier clash with Williams, Heylyn defiantly applauded 'the Piety of these times' – twenty-five years had clearly done little to remove the scars of Heylyn's exchange with the former dean.[20] He lauded the attention that had been paid to the restoration of divine service and the bishops, and the splendid re-adornment of the chapel royal, particularly praising the revival of church music.[21] Nevertheless, Heylyn was alive to the ways in which 'the piety of these times' might not live up to the piety of Laudian times. In particular, he urged that the bishops should be restored to their secular, political powers. Without the full restoration of the bishops' powers and privileges, 'they must pass for Cyphers in the Church-Arithmetick, disabled from proceeding in the work of God; of less esteem amongst their freinds, and a scorn to their adversaries'. What Heylyn particularly had in mind was the restoration of bishops to the privy council. 'The State was never better served,' he claimed, 'then when the Messengers of Peace were the Ministers of it: when Kings asked Counsel of the Priests, and that the Priests were Counsellors, Officers and Judges'.[22]

Heylyn was particularly concerned with the fortunes of Convocation – whose history he had so carefully researched, and whose influence on the Reformation he had been so anxious to stress. He became particularly preoccupied with rumours that the new parliament that was being called would not be accompanied by a meeting of Convocation. Heylyn's anxieties about Convocation's future are understandable – just four years earlier he had published his 'Way of the Reformation' in which he had denied the accusation that the Church of England's Reformation had proceeded through parliament, and had gone to extraordinary pains to locate all the crucial activity in Convocation. He now urgently communicated with Clarendon and Juxon to try to prevent parliament assembling without a meeting of Convocation. Writing to Clarendon (whom he does not seem to have known personally), he reminded the earl of historical precedents. While some were reporting that the king felt it unwise to call a meeting of Convocation when the clergy were so divided, Heylyn stressed that the first year of the reigns of Edward VI, Mary and Elizabeth had all been 'times of greater diffidence and distraction than this present Conjuncture. And yet no Parliament was called in the beginning of their several Reigns, without the company and attendance of the Convocation, tho the intendments of the State aimed then at greater alterations in the face of the Church, than are now pretended or desired.' He offered the reassurance that, if the government was fearful of the divisions among the clergy, nevertheless since the clergy in Convocation were not allowed to debate anything without the king's commission, the king 'may tie them up for what time he pleases, and give them nothing but the opportunity of entertaining one another with the news of the day'. He therefore begged Clarendon 'to put his Majesty in mind of sending out his Mandates to the two Arch Bishops for summoning a Convocation (according to the usuall Form) in their several Provinces; that this poor Church may be held with some degree of Veneration, both at home and abroad'.[23]

In his attempts to persuade Clarendon of the need for a meeting of Convocation, Heylyn also returned to some of the arguments and preoccupations of his *Stumbling Block*. As the bishops were excluded from parliament at this point, he argued that attendance at Convocation was vital 'to keep up their Honor and Esteem in the eyes of the people'. But he particularly appealed to the rights and liberties of the lower clergy. If they were deprived of their right to meet to grant subsidies to the king, then they would instead be taxed and rated without having given their consent. Taxation without representation, he argued piously, was against Magna Carta and would leave the clergy with none of 'the Rights or Liberties belonging to an English Subject'.[24]

Heylyn also addressed his concerns in person to the new archbishop of Canterbury, William Juxon, whose visitation articles Heylyn had composed twenty years before. He was appalled to find that Juxon was ready to defer a meeting of Convocation 'longer than may stand with the safety of the Church'. He urged Juxon that 'questionless, some busy members of the House of Commons will thrust themselves into concernments of religion, when they shall find no Convocation sitting to take care thereof'. Juxon replied complacently that intimating that there would be a Convocation would be enough to prevent this happening. This response encapsulated the different perspectives of the two churchmen, and would have been all too reminiscent to Heylyn of the pusillanimity of the bishops in 1641 (of whom Juxon had of course been one).[25] Heylyn, not surprisingly, retorted that intimation of a Convocation would be more likely to hasten parliamentary involvement in a church settlement, 'and make them the more earnest to make use of their time before the prey would be taken out of their mouths by the coming together of so many divines'. A panicking Heylyn desperately urged Sheldon to act: 'Though there hath been much time lost since Monday last since I despatched the writ to Mr Wren, yet it may possibly be redeemed if such of the Lords the Bishops as are now in town would put themselves unto the charge of sending to the Deans and Archdeacons of their several churches messengers of diligence and trust, and that your Lordship would be pleased to do the like to such other bishops as are retired into the country'.[26]

In the event, Heylyn's worries were unnecessary, and the delay in calling Convocation helped to ensure that it was swelled by the ranks of returned Anglican ministers.[27] But the depth of Heylyn's anxiety demonstrates that, for all of his hatred of presbyterians, he was more exercised by the fear that the laity in parliament would gain a precedent for undermining the independent authority of the church. It was this, in the end, that was his greatest concern. When Convocation did meet, it took place in Westminster Abbey, conveniently close to Heylyn's own lodgings, and according to his son-in-law Heylyn was regularly visited by members of Convocation who came to him 'for his advice and direction in matters relating to the Church'. It is at least possible that Heylyn was behind the attempted revival of his 1640 plan to have a single uniform set of visitation articles.[28] Barnard averred that members of Convocation consulted Heylyn 'because he had been himself an ancient clerk in the old convocations', but it seems more likely that it was his expertise in the history and constitution of Convocation, rather than his very limited practical experience of convocations, that was being respected here, and it was in his capacity as a historian, rather than as a lobbyist or adviser, that Heylyn was destined to have his greatest impact on the Restoration church.

THE RESTORATION HISTORIES

It was in the 1660s that Heylyn completed the three historical works for which he has been most renowned in subsequent centuries. But Heylyn was not writing just for posterity. It makes sense to see these final works – and especially his history of the English Reformation – as further attempts to convey the urgent agenda for the Restoration church that he had already sought to disseminate by letters and position papers. It must be emphasized that these were not works that he had been commissioned, or even invited, to write by the authorities. They are not the work of a government propagandist. Nevertheless, Heylyn was attempting to warn government ministers and clergy, and to shape public policy. All of these final three books took his preferred polemical form of 'histories' rather than directly controversial works. Each of the books partly summarized the more long-term research and long-held positions that had also been reflected in his polemical works of the 1650s. But each also included some important and sometimes very recent changes of position. While they are often taken to encapsulate the Laudian viewpoint, it is important to recognise them as the end point of an intellectual journey that Heylyn had embarked upon in the 1630s.

The first of these works, and the one most directed at current policy, was the *Ecclesia Restaurata* – Heylyn's history of the English Reformation which he had been researching on and off for the best part of twenty years. As we have seen, he had already sent papers to prominent political figures that drew their attention to the method of reformation followed by earlier English monarchs, and his formal history of the Reformation should partly be seen as an alternative means towards this same end. That being said, the book was manifestly not simply written up for the Restoration – Heylyn had been hinting at the publishing of this 'great work' for several years, and had been amassing material for much longer.[29] Nevertheless, it is quite clear that Heylyn wanted its completed text to offer important advice to the architects of the Restoration church settlement. His dedication of the work to Charles II is quite unambiguous in this regard, urging him to note 'upon what rules of piety and Christian prudence the work was carried on by the first reformers. Which being once found, it will be no hard matter to determine of such means and counsels whereby the Church may be restored to her peace and purity; from which she is most miserably fallen by our late distractions'.[30]

That the history offered warnings against the behaviour of those presbyterians currently around the king was also made apparent. Noting his favourite parable of the tares, Heylyn remarked in his dedicatory preface that some tares had grown up almost immediately in the church, notable for their fruits of 'faction, schism, disorder and perhaps sedition'. He ended with the pious but pointed hope that God would so settle the king 'that no design of mischievous and unquiet men may disturb your peace, or detract any thing from those felicities which you have acquired'.[31]

There are a number of signs of haste in the text of *Ecclesia Restaurata*. It ends with surprising abruptness in 1566, and there are some indications that Heylyn had intended to carry the text further – certainly he had accumulated the necessary materials to do this. Both of Heylyn's biographers refer to his plan to write a history of the church in England *since* the Reformation[32] and while Heylyn sometimes alludes to two other works that were clearly in preparation which would contain some of his research on the later period, other remarks occasionally imply an intention that the text would have moved well beyond the 1560s.[33] There are some signs of haste in the final text of the first edition, including references within the text which have been left blank.[34]

Heylyn's blindness would explain his own failure to pick up these slips, but the relative lack of similar authorial errors in the books produced in the late 1650s when he was similarly afflicted imply that this text was being produced more hastily. This haste was presumably related to external events – either Heylyn's anxiety to produce a new work that would gain him promotion while posts were still available, or his concern that the volume should be able to direct government policy at a time when a new church settlement was being engineered.

This was a time when, for all the political manoeuvring involved, much discussion and debate was focusing on the precise liturgical, political and historical identity of the Church of England. Heylyn's *Ecclesia Restaurata* is a sustained attempt to locate a Laudian image of the Church of England at the very heart of its Reformation, while also painting a vivid picture of the forces that had always endangered this identity, and which were threatening to do so again.

Heylyn laid great emphasis on the original research that he had undertaken for the book. In his preface 'To the Reader' Heylyn explains that his sources include convocation registers, acts of parliament, 'not a few debates and orders from the council-table', 'some records and charters of no common quality', 'many rare pieces in the famous Cottonian library', and also 'many foreign writers of great name and credit'.[35] It is indeed possible to note his use of Convocation registers and Cotton manuscripts, but these are only occasional sources that are usually strongly flagged when they are used.[36] Foreign writers such as Sarpi and de Thou indubitably make their appearance at times.[37] But Heylyn's principal sources were clearly existing printed histories of the period. For all of his doubts about Foxe, the *Acts and Monuments* were the principal source for Heylyn's work, along with Speed's *Chronicle*, Francis Godwin's *Annals* and John Hayward's *History of Edward VI*.[38] He also made use at various points of Fuller's *Church History*, particularly when Fuller printed documents that were not available elsewhere. He cites Fuller without irony as 'the Church-historian' and adopts a generally respectful tone, not exploiting opportunities overtly to correct Fuller by name.[39] Otherwise, Heylyn makes a considerable fuss about making very laboured corrections of often very minor errors in other authors, usually on matters of chronology.[40]

He also makes significant and controversial use of Roman Catholic historians. He had already been using the works of Nicholas Harpsfield, especially the latter's *Historia Wicleffiana*, which strongly shaped Heylyn's reinterpretation of the orthodoxy of Wyclif.[41] Another influential Catholic historian whom Heylyn utilized was Nicholas Sander. Heylyn was certainly not uncritical of Sander's work, and could at times dub him 'Dr Slanders' and 'that malicious sycophant', and deplore 'the frequent falsehoods' of his 'pestilent and seditious book'.[42] Nevertheless, Heylyn does deploy him as an authority for a number of points, and had clearly read thoroughly Sander's *De Origine ac Progressu Schismatis Anglicani*, with its lavish use of the epithet 'Calvinist'.[43] He also made effective use of other Catholic writings, including Miles Huggard's *The Display of Protestants*.[44]

For all of his emphasis on his use of new sources, however, the bulk of Heylyn's interpretation was not built on new historical discoveries. Much of the text is actually reworked from existing historians. He was not, then, presenting a new interpretation based on new material; rather, it was familiar materials that were being read in very different ways.

Heylyn's perspective on the Reformation in *Ecclesia Restaurata* is perhaps best summed up in his interpretation of a passage from the Book of Kings: 'A great and strong wind rent the mountains, and brake in pieces the rocks before the Lord, but the Lord was not in the wind; and after the wind an earthquake, but the Lord was not in the earthquake; and after the earthquake a fire, but the Lord was not in the fire; and after the fire a still small voice [in which the Lord speaks to the prophet]'.[45] This scriptural passage had received various applications by English Protestant exegetes. In the hands of Peter Heylyn, however, it received a new application – to the English Reformation itself:

It may be feared that God was neither in that great and terrible wind which threw down so many monasteries and religious houses in the reign of King Henry; nor in that earthquake which did so often shake the very foundations of the state in the time of King Edward; nor in the fire in which so many godly and religious persons were consumed to ashes in the days of Queen Mary; but that he shewed himself in that 'still small voice' which breathed so much comfort to the souls of his people, in the most gracious and fortunate government of a virgin Queen.[46]

This represented a radical rethinking of the nature of England's Reformation. Before Heylyn, accounts of the Reformation had emphasized the heroics of the early days of reformation – the attack on monkish superstition, the rejection of idolatry, the godly reforms of Edward VI the young Josiah, the heroic testimony of the Marian martyrs. These were the heroes of Foxe's history, their achievements and martyrdoms the working out of a divine plan, and the enactment of the prophecies of the Book of Revelation. The accession of Elizabeth, who had herself suffered under Roman persecution, was of course presented as the final triumphant conclusion of this series of events. But there was no sense that her reign represented a contrast to the spirit of the early Reformation (except in those godly circles who deplored the fact that the Elizabethan church was only 'halfly reformed'), or that it was in the quietness of her reign that the spirit of God had truly spoken, rather than in the assault on superstition under Edward.

For many decades there had been writers who, in varying contexts, sought to emphasize and to praise the orderliness and stability of the English Reformation. They avoided the language of simple separation and stressed instead elements of continuity, representing the reformation in more pacific terms, as a rejection by Rome. This was not necessarily in direct conflict with the activist emphasis placed on the event by Foxe, although there were tensions.[47] The problems came when writers attempted to find sustained legality and restraint in the events of the Reformation. As we have seen, the efforts of writers such as Heylyn in the 1630s to defend the Laudian reforms by urging earlier precedents ran into the problem that they often seemed to run counter to the events and reforms of the Edwardian church.[48] In fact, the 1630s witnessed a number of attacks on aspects of England's Reformation – especially in its Henrician years – in sermons, manuscript tracts, letters and speeches by those associated with the Laudian movement.[49] These attacks were almost never made in print, however, and while Richard Montagu had clearly worked on an intended history of the Henrician reformation, no Laudian writer managed to produce a revised history of the Reformation that would make it clear how far these new attitudes and emphases required a revision of the familiar Foxeian account.

It is clear that Heylyn was actually at work on researching such a project in the late 1630s. He more than anyone would have been aware that the pamphlet debates of that decade had shown how far the proof texts and events of England's Reformation were susceptible to different readings, and how important it was that an authoritative replacement for Foxe should be written. His initial research – begun according to Vernon in September 1638 – may have been undertaken at Laud's request, and would seem to have focused on Cotton's library and the records of Convocation – a copy of his notes on the Convocation registers still survives.[50] It is possible that some of the fruits of his early research find expression in the court sermons that he delivered in the late 1630s and early 1640s – his application of the passage from the Book of Kings can be found first being made in a court sermon of 1642, for example – although it is equally possible that Heylyn adjusted the text of the sermons before publishing them in 1659 in order to fit his mature thoughts on these issues.[51]

The upheavals of the Civil Wars clearly put a stop to Heylyn's research. But they also may have prompted a radicalization of some of his views. The revival of iconoclasm, the rise of sectarianism, the overthrow of the established church and the fall of the monarchy could promote a more fundamental rethinking of the more evangelical and destabilizing aspects of the English Reformation. Tristram Sugge of Wadham College, Oxford (who may well have known Heylyn), presents a striking example of how far these tumultuous years could prompt an English Protestant into a conscious rejection of almost all aspects of the English Reformation.[52] Sugge kept his ideas in manuscript, but that was not Heylyn's way. He clearly continued his work on the English Reformation during the 1650s, although he no longer had access to his books or to the archives of the capital. His rethinking of the English Reformation began to spill out into a number of publications, such as his 'Way and Manner of the Reformation' in *Ecclesia Vindicata*, and in the series of pamphlet exchanges in the late 1650s.

Heylyn's sceptical attitude towards many of the deeds of the Edwardian Reformation had of course been anticipated in his pamphlets back in the 1630s, where he had already pointed the finger of blame at the greed of Edwardian courtiers and the malign influence of Calvin.[53] But it was only in *Ecclesia Restaurata* that these different themes were brought together and fully expounded. Heylyn does not flinch from the excesses of the Edwardian Reformation. Rather, he emphasizes them, the better to contrast them with the more orderly reformation of Elizabeth. Edward's reign is 'tumultuous' and 'defamed by sacrilege, and so distracted into sides and factions that in the end the King himself became a prey to the strongest faction'. Part of the blame for the excesses of the Edwardian reformation lies with the courtiers and councillors who sacrilegiously seized church property, but the rest lies with the malign influence of Calvin and his supporters who despoiled the church and forced an alteration to the liturgy.[54] As his dedicatory epistle to Charles II had implied, Heylyn wanted to offer warnings as well as a model for the next reformation. It was the Edwardian Reformation that was meant to provide the cautionary tale.

This partly explains why Heylyn has relatively little to say about the Henrician Reformation in *Ecclesia Restaurata*. When it is mentioned, it is described in essentially positive terms: the dissolution of the monasteries could be justified, and the increase in the number of bishoprics meant that Henry 'left the Church, in many respects, in a better condition than he found it'.[55] Heylyn's chief concern in *Ecclesia Restaurata* was not to criticize the Henrician reformation, but to warn the Restoration establishment of the dangers of Calvinist presbyterianism. This was best achieved by blaming it for the sacrilegious excesses and upheavals of the Edwardian Reformation, which could in turn be contrasted with the moderation and restraint of the Elizabethan settlement. Too much attention to the devastation to the church's property wrought by Henry would have frustrated Heylyn's purpose of identifying Calvinism as the root cause of all the destructive and politically radical aspects of the Reformation period.

However, the other crucial element in Heylyn's account of the Edwardian Reformation was the vindication of the reformers themselves. Heylyn was quite happy to condemn Edward's councillors, and even Edward himself. Indeed, Heylyn scandalized his contemporary readers by confessing that he could not consider Edward's early death to have been 'an infelicity to the Church of England', as he was 'ill-principled in himself, and easily inclined to embrace such counsels as were offered to him'.[56] Nevertheless, he did his utmost to present the Edwardian bishops as the voices of an authentically moderate, Laudian English Reformation, who had had to negotiate their way through the erastianism and foreign-inspired religious extremism that surrounded them. This model obliged Heylyn to work constantly to try to draw a distinction between the behaviour and ideas of the Edwardian bishops, on the one hand, and those of the king and his councillors on the other. This required some skilful footwork. One example among many relates to the event that Heylyn had previously debated with Williams in the 1630s – Bishop Ridley's orders for the taking down of altars in the diocese of London. Heylyn's position required this not to have happened. He therefore went to enormous lengths to suggest that Ridley had received an order from the privy council to that effect, and had been forced to carry out what he could not hinder, ignoring the fact that Ridley's visitation had actually *preceded* the letter from the privy council.[57]

Given how its coverage of Edward's reign ran so counter to the interpretation offered by Foxe and others, it is important to note that, when it came to Mary's reign, Heylyn's *Ecclesia Restaurata* still made some gestures towards the martyrological themes that had traditionally dominated accounts of her reign. The title page of the Marian section of the book is accompanied by several quotations from Hebrews which refer to the scourgings, torture and other torments to which the people were subjected.[58] Heylyn also lavishes more attention on some martyrs than even Foxe himself. When describing Cranmer's martyrdom, Heylyn follows Godwin rather than Foxe in reproducing the story that Cranmer's heart remained undamaged by the flames.[59] But Heylyn was actually very selective in his choice of Marian martyrs. The martyr bishops could provide testimony to the godliness of these individuals, and a vindication of episcopacy itself. The lay martyrs, however, are almost completely ignored – they may well have carried unhappy resemblances for Heylyn to the religious enthusiasts of more recent times. Heylyn did find time, however, to deliver a stinging attack on the false Protestant prophetess Elizabeth Crofts and her support for Wyatt's rebellion, which he treats as seditious.[60] Just as damaging was his suggestion that the 'exorbitancies' and 'madnesses' of some extreme acts of Protestant defiance were responsible for forcing a government 'exasperated by these provocations' to reintroduce the death sentence for heresy.[61] While the Marian lay martyrs are passed over, however, Heylyn lavishes attention instead on the divisions among the English exiles, and the attacks on the liturgy by the 'Franckfort schismatics'.[62] It is the Marian exiles who represent the malign influence of foreign Calvinist presbyterianism and predestinarianism in the Elizabethan church. Their time abroad exposes them to the worst of the international Calvinist conspiracy and when they return they are pro-grammed to undermine the moderate English religious tradition.

Heylyn's account of the Elizabethan settlement seeks again to depict a sim-ple division between a moderate English Protestant tradition, seeking a Laudian-style religious settlement, and the hostile interventions of returned Calvinist exiles. Once more he was required to do severe damage to the his-torical record in order to sustain this vision, and to grossly underestimate the Reformed objectives of the new Elizabethan episcopate.[63] Nevertheless he was able to present a picture of a principled, moderate Elizabethan settlement, though poised to be undermined by the presbyterian activists whose succes-sors had destroyed the Church of England entirely in the 1640s.

Given that Heylyn's history of the Reformation later became notorious for its hostility towards aspects of England's Reformation history, it should be emphasized that Heylyn's work is not an anti-Protestant rant fuelled by bit-ter anti-Calvinism and an uncritical reading of Roman Catholic sources. Heylyn is actually very carefully selective in the aspects of the Reformation which he condemns. His greatest ingenuity was expended in freeing the Church of England and its reformers from any responsibility for, or involvement in, the more radical courses that had been followed. In his attacks on Calvin and the Edwardian government, Heylyn may have been even more vigorous in his language and accusations than he had been in his earlier work, but did not depart significantly from the position that he had expounded in the 1630s.

But Heylyn was not finished yet. A further two works were also being completed by him in the early years of the Restoration, and both were clearly considered to be of a piece with the *Ecclesia Restaurata*. These were his life of Laud (*Cyprianus Anglicus*) and his history of Presbyterianism (*Aërius Redivivus*). Neither of these books was published in Heylyn's lifetime. It is possible that Heylyn was working on both simultaneously, and that he died before he had been able to put either of them into their final form for dis-patch to the press. However, it is also possible that both works encountered problems with the press, either before Heylyn's death or afterwards. Both works dealt with periods uncomfortably close to the present, and both were intended to show England's puritans in the worst possible light. This was not timely when England's parliament was busy passing the Act of Free and General Pardon, Indemnity and Oblivion. In the case of *Aërius Redivivus*, the chance survival of a report on the original manuscript, apparently written at Gilbert Sheldon's request, which strongly advises against the printing of the book, provides evidence that the publication of Heylyn's works may indeed have been inhibited by those in authority. There is a particular irony in the thought that Heylyn, in his pomp the spokesman for the Stuart government, was now being censored by the restored Stuart regime.

Cyprianus Anglicus is in many ways a continuation of *Ecclesia Restaurata* from where it left off in Elizabeth's reign. Heylyn had specifically cross-referenced the book in a marginal note in the first edition of *Ecclesia Restaurata* itself in a manner that implied the book was already virtually ready for publication. This lends some credence to the suspicion that the book's publication was blocked by the authorities; in the event it would not be published until 1668.[64] Laud was of course a highly controversial figure, and in the first delicate year of the Restoration, when attempts were still being made to appease presbyterian concerns, his was a dangerous figure to invoke. His reburial in St John's College Oxford was a surreptitious night-time affair, compared with the lavish ceremonial surrounding the burial of William Juxon a short time beforehand in the same college.[65] Some of his supporters planned to petition for the formal erasure of the parliamentary judgements that had been made against Laud at his trial for treason (as was performed for the earl of Strafford), but such an act may also have been deemed too inflammatory for the times.[66] Heylyn himself remarks at the beginning of the work that he writes knowing that there was 'more than an ordinary possibility of offending many; no expectation of Reward, nor certainty of any thing but misconstructions, and Detractings, if not dangers also'.[67]

Cyprianus Anglicus was a more worrying publication than a simple biography of Laud. Although in a sense it acts as a counter to Prynne's *Canterburies Doome*, and may well have been planned for a long time, Heylyn's *Cyprianus* is much more than a study of Laud's life. This point is encapsulated when, after forty-five pages, Heylyn finally arrives at Laud's birth in 1573, which he immediately comments was 'a year remarkable for the bustlings of the Puritan Faction'.[68] In fact, the book also offers both a broader history of the religion and politics of the early Stuart period, and an extended apologia for the policies and personnel of the Laudian movement. It lays out in systematic detail the alternative view of the pre-war church and state that had appeared in different forms in the various tracts that Heylyn had published against other royalist historians in the 1650s.

Not the least notable feature of *Cyprianus Anglicus* is the lengthy 'Necessary Introduction' to the work, which sets out to explain 'upon what Principles and Positions, the Reformation of this Church did first proceed'. Predictably, Heylyn's discussion begins with the Act of Submission of the Clergy and his emphatic insistence that this 'did no way prejudice the Clergy in their power of making Canons, Constitutions, and other Synodical Acts' and also did not in any way diminish the powers and privileges of the bishops.[69] Having safeguarded the authority of the clergy, Heylyn is free to embark upon a sometimes startling exposition of the alleged high ceremonialism and the doctrinal conservatism of the reformers. This is anything but a potted history of the English Reformation. In fact, Heylyn's analysis proceeds point-by-point through the policies of the Laudian period, revisiting his arguments in the altar and sabbath disputes, defending the church decoration, enhanced ceremonial and preaching restrictions of the 1630s, and also rehearsing his more recent arguments on the necessity of baptism and the doctrines of predestination and justification. In each case this required the provision of what are often very distorted readings in order to make the early reformers speak and act with a Laudian accent.[70] While a desire to 'Laudianize' the English Reformation is a clear subtext of *Ecclesia Restaurata*, the fact that the work is a detailed narrative history which often diverts into broader areas of civil history means that its polemical manoeuvring is less blatant than that of this 'Necessary Introduction'.

The 'Necessary Introduction' also provides a dimension to the English Reformation that is less apparent in the *Ecclesia Restaurata*, although it is hinted at in some of Heylyn's pamphlets from the later 1650s (especially the *Quinqu-Articularis*). This is Heylyn's insistence that the English Reformation was not entirely *sui generis*. While he affirmed (as he had done in his *Microcosmus*) that there was 'no regard had to Luther or Calvin' in England's Reformation, nevertheless Heylyn emphasized that 'the first Reformers . . . did look with more respectful eyes upon the Doctrinals, Government and Forms of Worship in the Lutheran Churches, than upon those of Calvins platform'. Heylyn claimed to discern a broader movement within the Reformation encapsulated in the figure of Philipp Melanchthon and the phenomenon that Heylyn dubbed 'Melanchthonian Lutheranism'.[71] This new enthusiasm for Lutheranism does not seem to have been based on any conspicuous knowledge of or interest in Lutheran theology on Heylyn's part.[72] As one of his critics complained, he presented the Lutherans as more quiet and better principled than the Calvinists 'for no other reason than that he fancied them such'.[73] Heylyn's 'fancy' may have stemmed in part out of his increasing obsession in his final years with the European scale of the disruption and ambitions of the Calvinist movement, which received its fullest expression in his *Aërius Redivivus* (which he was writing at the same time as *Cyprianus*). Rather than a mere destabilizing force in England, Calvinism was the principal source of instability in the whole continent. In this strange new version of the 'Protestant cause', it was anti-Calvinism that became the unifying cause, and a basic identity of interest could be assumed in all those who crossed swords with Calvinism. The Lutherans, of course, provided the added bonus of being non-Calvinist Protestants.

One of the most striking aspects of *Cyprianus* relates to the way in which Heylyn depicts the predominance of Calvinism in the late Elizabethan church. In his earlier writings he had constantly juggled the desire to uphold the continuity of the Laudian style of conformist thought with the need to explain the decay of the church's ceremonies, so that he could explain why their Laudian revival had the appearance of innovation. In his *Historia Quinqu-Articularis*, struggling to locate his anti-Calvinist tradition in Elizabethan Oxford, Heylyn had been reduced to writing of the hidden congregation of true believers, which he had strikingly compared to the debates over the location of the Protestant church before Luther. Having rejected in his accounts of the origins of the Reformation the notion of the succession of a hidden minority of true believers, secretly dissenting from the corruption around them, Heylyn now consciously re-embraced it for his own position.[74] That this did not simply represent Heylyn temporarily grasping at straws while under polemical pressure is demonstrated by a remarkable passage in *Cyprianus* which describes the virtual apostasy of the Church of England in Elizabethan Oxford:

> The face of that University was so much altered, that there was little to be seen in it of the Church of England, according to the Principles and Positions upon which it was first Reformed. All the Calvinian Rigours in matters of Predestination, and the Points depending thereupon, received as the Established Doctrines of the Church of England; the necessity of the one Sacrament, the eminent dignity of the other, and the powerful efficacy of both into mans salvation, not only disputed but denyed; the Article of Christs locall descent into hell . . . at first corrupted with false Glosses, afterwards openly contradicted, and at last totally disclaimed, because repugnant to the Fancies of some Forreign Divines . . . Episcopacy maintained by halves, not as a distinct Order from that of the Presbyters, but only a degree above them or perhaps not that, for fear of giving scandal to the Churches of Calvins Platform; the Church of Rome inveighed against as the Whore of Babylon, or the Mother of Abominations; the Pope as publicly maintained to be Antichrist, or the Man of Sin, and that as positively and magisterially as if it had been one of the chief Articles of the Christian Faith . . . the visibility of the Church must be no otherwise maintained, than by looking for it in the scattered Conventicles of the Berengarians in Italy, the Albigenses in France, the Hussites in Bohemia, and the Wickliffists among our selves.[75]

Of course, several items on this roll call of errors could be found in the works of a member of the Jacobean university – that is, in Heylyn's own *Microcosmus*. In a sense, Heylyn's own early writings were now evidence of the sink of error into which the university had fallen. Heylyn's account was in one sense entirely accurate, but the dominance of such views in Elizabethan Oxford reflected the fact that the Laudians' rejection of these points was not yet current at that point.

Heylyn's readiness to grant the total dominance of Calvinism in the Elizabethan church, which he had spent so much of his life trying to deny, partly reflected the specific requirements of his biography of Laud. Faced with the need at least to mention Laud's early struggles at Oxford, Heylyn seized on the opportunity to present the future archbishop as the lone hero having 'to oppose himself against an Army', battling against the forces of doctrinal and ceremonial error that had taken over the church.[76] In the genre of biography the Calvinist take-over of the church could serve a number of narrative functions that were not evident in Heylyn's other forms of polemic. It would be misleading, therefore, to assume that this image of complete Calvinist dominance of the Elizabethan church always lay at the heart of Heylyn's vision. As the biography proceeds, Laud can begin to act as the voice of the established order against the evils of puritanism, but it is the strength and ubiquity of the enemies of Laudianism that provide the suspense and narrative drive. And here, as in Heylyn's other works, it is the betrayal of the church's cause by 'popular prelates' that is his main theme, and Archbishop Abbot who performs the role of anti-hero, opposing Laud at every turn and releasing the puritan demon that Bancroft had managed to subdue.[77]

Heylyn deploys a variety of sources in writing *Cyprianus*. The book includes many details for which Heylyn is himself the main source. This is Heylyn's life and times just as much as (if not more than) it is Laud's. But, like *Ecclesia Restaurata*, Heylyn's *Cyprianus* is often dependent on other works for its details, which were liberally borrowed (although in this case much more frequently acknowledged). Two notable sources are those of Heylyn's erstwhile opponents L'Estrange and Fuller, whose arguments and information he is happy to cite without any allusion to their recent controversies.[78]

It is notable that in the text of *Cyprianus* Heylyn is rarely able to claim knowledge of Laud's thinking or intentions. Heylyn is often dependent on deductions made from published letters and papers, and from Laud's diaries. His richly detailed accounts of his own meetings with the archbishop partly cover up the fact that Heylyn was not really one of Laud's confidants.[79] These were manifestly meetings to conduct business, not friendly social calls, and we can perhaps assume from their absence from his text that Heylyn may never have received any personal letters from Laud. Lacking access to most of Laud's own papers in the original, Heylyn was therefore reliant on what was available in print. The problem here was that such sources were available only through Laud's opponents, most notably in the works of William Prynne (who had of course had unrivalled access to Laud's papers), specifically *Canterburies Doome* and Prynne's maliciously edited version of Laud's diary, the *Breviate of the Life of William Laud*. The net result was sometimes that Heylyn seemed to acknowledge many of the criticisms that had been made against Laud. An anonymous writer in the late seventeenth century observed that puritans were very glad to have Heylyn's life of Laud because it 'owns many things which others would denie, and which he would not own at his triall'.[80] Not the least of these admissions was Heylyn's willingness to countenance the suggestion that Laud may have facilitated the introduction of the papal agent Panzani to the court, and may also have been involved in the discussions over possible reconciliation with Rome. Heylyn was prepared to recognize what Richard Montagu (who had conducted enthusiastic negotiations with Panzani at the time) had clearly felt – that, if the terms being mooted for a reconciliation with Rome were to be genuinely observed, then it would in fact be entirely compatible with the logic of the Laudian position on the relationship between the Church of England and Rome.[81]

While not committing himself on the question of Laud's involvement in reunion projects, Heylyn was happy to project the idea that Laud's policies of ceremonial reform and opposition to extravagant anti-popery were partly intended as a way of attracting 'moderate Papists' back into the English church, although he had a conspicuous lack of direct evidence for such a reading.[82] Again, these reflections seem typical of Heylyn's final years, rather than being expressive of the principles upon which he had supported and justified the Laudian programme. It is also possible that Heylyn simply found the evidence of Laud's complicity compelling, and sought to place the most positive gloss that he could on the archbishop's actions. Perhaps too, in his final years, he was resolved not to pander to the anti-Catholic instincts of his puritan opponents. He had perhaps finally tired of a lifetime's switching to anti-Catholic polemic when he needed to disarm opponents' charges of popery.[83]

Another surprising feature of *Cyprianus Anglicus* is that, for all the work's obvious partisanship, Heylyn does occasionally gesture towards a more moderate and impartial position, which is all the more striking for the fact that he does not (as in so many of his other works) begin the book by pontificating about the duties of the historian to complete impartiality. Partly this reflected an emollience that Heylyn had to adopt towards a number of those whom he had criticized in his recent works – not least the previous two Stuart monarchs, but also previous royalist opponents such as Falkland.[84] But he also seems to make a point of providing detailed summaries of opposing views, whether they be puritan complaints against ceremonies or overarching critiques of Laud's strategies and temperament.[85] Heylyn also offers surprising qualifications. Thus he allows that 'otherwise very moderate and sober men' were offended by Cosin's *Private Devotions*, that some bishops provided good arguments against the 1629 Instructions, that Williams's client Osbaldeston was dealt with too severely, that it was poor strategy to advance Richard Montagu to a bishopric, and even that the sentences against Burton, Bastwick and Prynne caused 'a great trouble to the spirits of many very moderate and well-meaning men'.[86] The last comment is the most remarkable, as it is taken directly (though unacknowledged) from Fuller's comments on the event in his *Church History*, and Heylyn had particularly bridled at Fuller's invocation of 'moderate men' in *Examen Historicum*.[87] The inclusion of such passages forms a contrast with all Heylyn's other histories, most notably of all with *Aërius Redivivus*, which he was completing at the same time as *Cyprianus*. It suggests that Heylyn was consciously attempting something different in this work, and modelling himself (fitfully, at least) on a more lofty and dispassionate style of history. There may even have been a sense in which he hoped at least to pay lip service to the sensibilities of less ardently Laudian figures such as Fuller and L'Estrange, as well (perhaps) as their lay patrons such as Anne Sadleir.

Heylyn's final posthumous work was his *Aërius Redivivus, or, the History of the Presbyterians*. This is a highly coloured account of the political and religious activities of the so-called 'Calvinist' faction throughout western and central Europe from 1536 through to 1647, noting 'their Oppositions to Monarchical and Episcopal Government, Their Innovations in the Church; and their Imbroilments of the Kingdoms and States of Christendom in the pursuit of their Designs'. Like *Cyprianus Anglicus, Aërius* had been flagged in the text of the *Ecclesia Restaurata*. Heylyn alluded in the main text to his intention of writing on the terrible effects of the attacks on the religious hierarchy 'if God shall give me means and opportunity to carry on the history of those disturbances which have been raised by the Puritans and Presbyterians against the orders of this Church and the peace of Christendom'.[88] This implied an intention to focus solely on events in England. But as the *Ecclesia Restaurata* was going to the press Heylyn seemed both more determined to complete such a work, and also to have envisaged its scope going beyond England. The final page of some (but not all) versions of the first edition of *Ecclesia Restaurata* contains a paste-on addition to the text in which Heylyn comments that the doctrines, plots and practices by which the puritans 'did not only break down the roof and walls' of the English church 'but digged up the foundation of it' would 'better fall within the compass of a Presbyterian or Aerian History; for carrying on of whose designs since the days of Calvin, they have most miserably embroiled all the estates and kingdoms of these parts of Christendom – the realms and churches of Great Britain more than all the rest'.[89]

There can be little doubt that Heylyn's sense of the need for urgency in giving an account of the misdeeds of England's presbyterians was prompted by the degree to which the presbyterians seemed to be being reabsorbed within the restored Church of England. While he proudly recorded his status as 'royal chaplain' on the title page of his post-1660 works, Heylyn can hardly have been unaware that his fellow chaplains included two of the former Smectymnuans and his recent opponent Richard Baxter.[90] There is no doubt that his full-scale assault on presbyterian behaviour in *Aërius Redivivus* would have been seen as grossly inflammatory by those in power, and it is notable that Heylyn's book was not published until 1670. A critical review of the manuscript of *Aërius Redivivus*, apparently written by Jean Durel (the Jersey-born episcopalian divine and associate of Cosin), survives among Sheldon's papers, in which Durel urges Sheldon to prevent the publication of the work.[91]

In the book which we know as *Aërius Redivivus* more than one-third of the text deals with events in England alone. Indeed, it is the only work by Heylyn that covers the whole of Elizabeth's reign (albeit selectively), or that offers his sustained meditations on the sacrilegious upheavals of the Civil War. These accounts merely supplement and accentuate the vision of a successful puritan conspiracy against the English church and state that Heylyn charts in his other late works. But the main focus of complaint in Durel's report is Heylyn's depiction of Continental presbyterianism. Durel emphatically concluded that 'it would be very offensive, as it is very injurious, to the Reformed Churches beyond the Seas, and would gett no credit, either to him or those that should have a hand in the printing of it, if published, being so full of mistakes, passion and uncharitableness'.[92]

Heylyn offers a radical revision of the traditional Protestant account of events in France, the Netherlands, Germany and Bohemia. The earlier chapters present an account of the doleful influence of Calvin on the history of the church. Especial use is made of Calvin's letters to show his constant meddling in other countries, and Beza as following the same trend.[93] The rest of the book reveals the results as in a succession of countries the infusion of Calvinist doctrine leads inevitably to armed rebellion against the monarch, assaults on bishops, sacrilegious iconoclasm and the dissemination of puritan religious practice. It is not surprising to find Heylyn's customary attacks upon the Huguenots in these pages. What is more distinctive, and which probably reflects the specific polemical agenda of *Aërius Redivivus*, is Heylyn's readiness to think better of the presbyterians' Catholic opponents. The dukes of Guise and the Catholic League are treated with relative restraint and respect, whereas Beza is directly implicated in Guise's assassination and the authorship of *Vindiciae contra Tyrannos*.[94]

It is in the account of the Dutch Reformation and Revolt that the rigidly polemical structure of *Aërius Redivivus* served to brush away most strikingly the reservations and qualifications that Heylyn had habitually built into his analysis throughout his working life. In his earlier *Microcosmus* he had been anxious to reassure his reader that the Dutch revolt was emphatically not a war of religion, but was 'a warre of State, not Religion; the most part of the Hollanders being Papists, at the times of their taking Armes'. For all his subsequent courting of Laud and experience of presbyterian excesses and rebellion during the Civil War, in his *Cosmographie* of 1652 Heylyn had still preserved word for word the exposition of Dutch events that he had provided in *Microcosmus*.[95] In *Aërius Redivivus*, however, the Dutch Revolt appears as a religious revolt perpetrated by Calvinist extremists, and just another example of the truth that Calvinists were instinctively rebellious subjects. Heylyn's account of the revolt presents it essentially from the Spanish perspective. While he condemns the cruelty of the duke of Alva, he provides a sympathetic portrait of Cardinal Granvelle – a clerical statesman of Laud-like temper who was (revealingly) 'despised as an upstart by the Prince of Orange'. Indeed, the Prince of Orange is presented in an extremely poor light: a nobleman who rebelled simply out of ambition because he had not been appointed Supreme Governor of the Netherlands, and who was implicated in a Calvinist-inspired Association 'which' (Heylyn portentously adds) 'they called the Covenant'.[96] The prompt for Heylyn's rethinking of the Dutch Revolt would appear to have been the Jesuit Famianus Strada's *De bello Belgico*, which had been translated into English in 1650 by the ex-Benedictine monk Robert Stapylton, who had been like Heylyn an aspiring poet and hanger-on at the Oxford court.[97] Nevertheless, the polemical requirement for such a reading of events makes it unnecessary to posit a significant influence.

Heylyn's discussion of the Bohemian revolt marks his final rejection of the pro-palatine sentiments that he had earlier expressed in his *Microcosmus*. The Bohemian war is condemned as having been 'raised chiefly by the Pride and Pragmaticalness of Calvins Followers, out of a hope to propagate their Doctrines, and advance their Discipline in all parts of the Empire'.[98] The Bohemian revolt is marked by iconoclasm and the ransacking of religious houses, and the Elector Palatine's involvement in the 'rash adventure' goes against the wise advice of King James, who 'had a strong Party of Calvinists in his own Dominions, who were not to be trusted with a Power of disposing Kingdoms, for fear they might be brought to practise that against himself, which he had countenanced in others'.[99]

Here again we have Heylyn's new version of the international 'Protestant cause'. It was an international anti-Calvinist cause, where opposition to Calvinism became the unifying bond of all other churches and rulers, whether Catholic or Protestant. While an unfair exaggeration, Durel nevertheless in a sense put his finger on Heylyn's vision when he complained that 'Of the French he speakes iust as if he were hired by the house of Guise; Of the Dutch and of the Princes of Orange themselves: as if he were Chaplain to the Duke of Alva, or Cardinal Granvell; of the German, as if he were a Pensioner of the House of Austria; of the Bohemians and the late Prince Electour as if he were a Jesuit'.[100] But rather than Heylyn perversely taking the Catholic side, from his own perspective he was simply manifesting a comradeship in arms with the other forces involved in the anti-Calvinist struggle. It followed that if any English monarchs broke these common bonds by aiding the rebellions of foreign Calvinists against their natural rulers, they should be condemned. King Charles had therefore been punished for attempting to aid the Huguenot rebels in La Rochelle 'whereby he trained up his own Subjects in the School of Rebellion, and taught them to confederate themselves with the Scots and Dutch, to seize upon his Forts and Castles, invade the Patrimony of the Church, and to make use of his Revenue against himself'.[101]

There is a sense that his long-standing hostility towards the Huguenots, and his hatred of the damage which presbyterian forces had done to the Church of England in the 1640s, naturally predisposed Heylyn towards this line of argument. Nevertheless, it was possible for committed Laudians to have a very different view of the foreign churches. John Cosin had conquered his initial hostility towards the French Huguenots and had developed amicable relations with their congregation at Charenton during his exile.[102] To Cosin, it was axiomatic that the actions of the English presbyterians were unique, and abhorrent to the foreign Reformed churches. Heylyn, however, would seem to have found the idea of an international Calvinist conspiracy far too compelling. (It also of course helped to magnify the danger of native presbyterians by showing them as part of a foreign insidious force.) As Durel complained, Heylyn therefore falsely charged foreign Protestants with errors that were peculiar to the English presbyterians, such as the claim that the Dutch Reformation abolished Christmas.[103] It is notable, however, that it was only at the end of his life that Heylyn finally changed his perspective on the Dutch Revolt. It is impossible to know whether he would have changed and moderated his views once more, if perhaps it was the polemical need to condemn the English presbyterians that had prompted him characterisitically to overplay his polemical card on this occasion.

HEYLYN REDIVIVUS? 1662–1700

When Heylyn died on 8 May 1662 his anxieties about the limited secular powers of the Restoration church would still not have been entirely assuaged. But the fears about the betrayal of the church to the insidious forces of native presbyterianism which course through his *Aërius Redivivus* were being soothed. Within two weeks of Heylyn's death the royal assent had been given to the new Act of Uniformity, which sealed the victory over nonconformity in requiring all clergymen and teachers to conform to the Book of Common Prayer and to renounce the presbyterian Covenant, prompting the ejection of nearly 1,000 ministers.[104] The removal of the nonconformist canker from the church would doubtless have reassured Heylyn, although the surrender in the following year by Sheldon of Convocation's right to grant independent clerical subsidies would have confirmed his fears that the church's powers were being eroded by the forces of erastianism.[105] The rumoured revival of the Court of High Commission remained merely a rumour.[106]

Ironically, the period of Heylyn's greatest prominence as a writer still lay in the future. Amid the tensions of the restored Church of England, Heylyn's voice was increasingly heard from beyond the grave. In the heat of the religious tensions of the late 1660s and early 1670s, and again at the height of the Exclusion crisis, he was seized upon as an advocate of the Tory cause and a zealous opponent of the populist Whigs. Certainly, there no longer seems to have been a need felt to hinder his final works from publication. *Cyprianus Anglicus* finally appeared in print in 1668, and his controversial *Aërius Redivivus* appeared for the first time in 1670.[107]

That there was now a strong market for Heylyn's books is attested by the regular reprinting of his works. While *Aërius Redivivus* first appeared in 1670, the same year saw the republication of his *Ecclesia Restaurata*, and the following year saw a reprinting of *Cyprianus Anglicus*. *Aërius Redivivus* was republished in 1672, and two years later *Ecclesia Restaurata* was again published. Even his *Theologia Veterum* was published again in 1673. These regular reprintings are all the more significant as the works in question are substantial folio volumes. In 1681 Heylyn's continuing importance was recognized by the publication of a hefty volume of his collected works, accompanied by an engraved portrait and a biography.[108] The fall-out from the complicated and disputed creation of the biography contained in the collected works resulted in the publication of two further biographies over the following two years.[109]

Heylyn became an established author with a wide circle of readers of varying backgrounds. These included Samuel Pepys, who recorded in 1668 having *Cyprianus Anglicus* read to him and finding it a 'shrewd' book, 'but that which I believe will do the Bishops in general no great good, but hurt – it pleads for so much Popish'.[110] But Heylyn appealed to more than the general, disinterested reader. This late, posthumous blossoming of Heylyn's reputation and readership had everything to do with the increasingly bitter divisions in the Restoration church. The Act of Uniformity and the series of additional penal measures making up the Clarendon Code marked the end of the official comprehension of presbyterians within the Restoration church, and removed the need to accommodate them ideologically as well. Increasingly, too, men such as Sheldon, who had played a strategically moderate and watchful game in the early Restoration, began to embrace a more full-blooded ceremonialism that had its inspiration in Laudian policies.[111] When there was no longer a pragmatic need for emollience and toleration, and conformist forces sought to reject policies of comprehension and looked instead for the historical arguments to justify a more severe treatment of religious dissenters, Heylyn's histories provided the perfect weapon and justification.

Heylyn's history of the Reformation also appealed to those keen to re-examine the relations of the Church of England with the forces of Roman Catholicism. This had partly been a natural response to the traumas of the 1640s and 1650s (as we have already noted in Tristram Sugge). But the conversion of the duke of York to Roman Catholicism and the tensions of the Exclusion crisis lent all the more relevance to Heylyn's works. They certainly provided potentially valuable ammunition for Roman Catholics. It is clear that lay Romanists read Heylyn's works. For example, the Middletons – a recusant couple in Restoration Yorkshire – acquired copies of Heylyn's *Ecclesia Restaurata* and *Aërius Redivivus.*[112] Another more important couple who showed an interest in his *Ecclesia Restaurata* were the duke and duchess of York, and in both cases Heylyn's book allegedly prompted their conversion to the Roman church. The duchess said that after finishing Heylyn's book she could find no justification for the Reformation, opining that it had come about due to Henry's desire to divorce his wife, Northumberland's desire to plunder the church's land, and Elizabeth's need to justify her unlawful succession. James seems to have been particularly struck by Heylyn's description of the greed of the Edwardian courtiers, but failed to observe Heylyn's attempts to distinguish them from the principled Edwardian bishops. James commented that both courtiers and theologians had shown 'no resemblance to those who [sat] in the first Council at Jerusalem'. Gilbert Burnet described the duke of York showing him marked passages from the duke's own copy of Heylyn's *Ecclesia Restaurata* 'to shew upon what motives and principles men were led into the changes that were then made'.[113]

Certainly, Roman Catholic polemicists were happy to make use of Heylyn's work. George Touchet, in his *Historical Collections out of several Protestant Histories* made extensive use of Heylyn's criticisms of Henry VIII, his attacks on foreign Calvinist influence in the Edwardian Reformation and his relatively restrained depiction of Mary's reign. He also made particularly effective use of Heylyn's *Aërius Redivivus* to condemn Continental presbyterianism.[114] The Roman Catholic Thomas Ward made even more extensive use of Heylyn in his historical works on the English Reformation composed during James II's reign. Other Catholic authors found that others of Heylyn's works could also aid their anti-Protestant polemics. Thomas Godden, in his *Catholicks no Idolators* (1672), made use of Heylyn's *Cyprianus Anglicus* in order to dismiss as puritans those authors such as Ussher and Abbot whom Edward Stillingfleet had used to condemn the Roman church as idolatrous.[115] The only defence that Stillingfleet could find was to make the blunt statement that 'concerning Arch-Bishop Usher, Dr Heylin was known to be too much his enemy, to be allowed to give a Character of him'.[116]

Just as he had his enthusiastic readers, so Heylyn generated implacable opponents. The relentless Henry Hickman continued to attack Heylyn's various histories for more than ten years after Heylyn's death.[117] Heylyn's work on the Reformation received pamphlet criticisms, of which the most notable was the anonymous *K. Edward the VIth his own Arguments against the Pope's Supremacy . . . To which are subjoined some Remarks upon his Life and Reign, in Vindication of his Memory, from Dr Heylin's severe and unjust Censure* (1682).

This sought to restore the image of the godly king from Heylyn's shocking observation that it was fortunate that Edward had died as early as he did, before he could do more damage to the church. If Heylyn's monument in Westminster Abbey was probably defaced during the Exclusion crisis, this was also the time when his published works were similarly assaulted, especially at the hands of Whig authors. The extreme clericalism and anti-puritanism of Heylyn's histories made him a favourite target of writers such as Sidney and Locke, who used him as a spokesman for the high-church position. The need to attack Heylyn's interpretations also partly helped to shape Gilbert Burnet's own *History of the Reformation*, the preface of which made damning attacks on Heylyn's scholarship.[118]

Burnet's *History of the Reformation* comfortably superseded Heylyn's own in detail and scholarship, and the *Ecclesia Restaurata* would not be republished until the nineteenth century. For the erastian Burnet Heylyn's obsessive defence of clericalism represented a political and religious danger, rather than simply an example of scholarly malpractice, and the Glorious Revolution secured the victory of Burnet's principles. Heylyn did live on as a favourite bogeyman of Whig writers: a number of works in the 1690s noted the influence of Heylyn's *Ecclesia Restaurata* on the future James II.[119] This is not to say that Heylyn did not have his supporters among the high-church Tories. One anti-dissenter writer voiced the wish that Heylyn's works should be placed in churches instead of Foxe's *Acts and Monuments*.[120] His work defending the independent authority of Convocation as a vital bulwark of the church's survival and protection of its interests also provided important inspiration for Francis Atterbury's campaign at the turn of the century for the return of Convocation.[121] While Heylyn's *Ecclesia Restaurata* had envisaged a strong alliance between church and state, his insistence on the church's powers of self-regulation still appealed to those churchmen who were more sceptical of the state's intentions, and his writings were read and used by historians such as Laurence Echard and the non-juror Jeremy Collier.[122] While the actual reprintings of Heylyn's works conspicuously and permanently dried up in the 1690s, then, his influence did not disappear with them.

The diminutive, skeletal and partially blind figure who had barely lived beyond the Restoration, surviving just long enough to be disregarded in the ecclesiastical promotions and to have his last works apparently stopped at the press, ultimately enjoyed his most remarkable success after his death. The man who had striven always to serve the authorities had thus ultimately made his greatest contribution when he was already dead, through the printed histories that outlived him. His reputation as a government polemicist was secured for posterity, even though his most successful and influential histories had not been commissioned by the authorities at all.

NOTES

1 Barnard, p. 248.

2 *Ibid.*, p. 256.

3 I. M. Green, *The Re-establishment of the Church of England, 1660–1663* (Oxford, 1978), pp. 62–4.

4 Walker, p. ii.

5 Laurence Echard (*History of England* (1707–18), III, p. 94) suggests that it was his 'violent and inflexible Spirit, which had prov'd highly prejudicial to that very Church he had so often strenuously and nobly defended'.

6 Barnard, p. 262.

7 Green, *Re-establishment*, pp. 91–2.

8 J. Miller, *After the Civil Wars* (2000), pp. 164–8. See also the pamphlet exchange between Roger L'Estrange and James Howell: James Howell, *A Cordial for the Cavaliers* (1661); Roger L'Estrange, *A Caveat for the Cavaliers* (1661).

9 P. Barwick, *The Life of John Barwick* (1724), p. 422.

10 *Ibid.*, pp. 517–18, 520.

11 J. P. Kenyon, *The Stuart Constitution* (2nd edn, Cambridge, 1986), p. 342.

12 T. P. Slaughter (ed.), *Ideology and Politics on the Eve of the Restoration: Newcastle's Advice to Charles II* (Philadelphia, 1984), pp. 17–18.

13 *The Bishop of Armaghes Direction, concerning the Lyturgy, and Episcopall Government* (1660); Spurr, *Restoration*, p. 144. John Gauden and Heylyn's old foe Edward Reynolds were preaching reduced episcopacy to the Convention Parliament earlier in 1660 (*ibid.*, pp. 32–3).

14 Baxter's *Reliquiae Baxterianae* (1696) notes that Heylyn, Earle and Barwick never came to the Savoy House conference (implying that they were intended to come) (ii. p. 364). Carwithen (*History of the Church of England* (2 vols, Oxford, 1849) has Heylyn 'one of the Savoy Commissioners' (II, p. 311), citing White Kennet, *History of England*, III, p. 235 and J. Collier, *Ecclesiastical History*, Part ii, Book ix, p. 428.

15 Nicholas Bernard, *Devotions of the Ancient Church* (1660); John Gauden, *Considerations touching the Liturgy of the Church of England* (1661).

16 Vernon, p. 249. While Convocation first met in May 1661 it was unable to act because the Savoy House conference was still in session and had 'an antecedent commission' to convocation (Spurr, *Restoration*, p. 40).

17 Vernon, p. 242.

18 *Ibid.*, pp. 243–5.

19 *Κειμηλια Εκκλεσιαστικα: the Historical and Miscellaneous Tracts of . . . Peter Heylyn* (1681), pp. 739–45. (On the misdating of this tract by the editor of the 1681 collection see above, ch. 4.)

20 Heylyn, *A Sermon preached in the Collegiate Church of St Peter in Westminster, on . . . the Anniversary of his Majesties most joyful Restitution to the Crown of England* (1661), p. 39. It is notable that this phrase is italicized.

21 *Ibid.*, pp. 36–8.

22 *Ibid.*, p. 39.

23 Vernon, pp. 248–51.

24 *Ibid.*, pp. 246–7.

25 Heylyn had confessed to Hyde that it seemed inappropriate for one of his station to be writing to him to urge the calling of a convocation. But he was not convinced that the bishops were making effective representations: 'I know . . . how much better it had been, for such as shine in a more eminent Sphere in the holy Hierarchy to have tendered these Particulars to consideration. Which . . . they either have not done, or . . . no visible effect hath appeared thereof' (Vernon, p. 251).

26 Bodl., Tanner MS 49, fol. 146; Bosher, *Making*, p. 214.

27 Bosher, *Making*, pp. 213–15, 244–5.

28 *Ibid.*, p. 231; Barnard, pp. 255–6.

29 *EV*, sigs A1r–A3r; *TV*, sig. B4r. His *Certamen Epistolare* mentions that his history of the Reformation is almost finished: *CE*, p. 149.

30 *ER*, I, p. iii.

31 *Ibid.*, I, pp. iii–iv.

32 Barnard, pp. 174–5; Vernon, pp. 94–5.

33 E.g. the reference to Elizabeth's answer to the Polish ambassador in 1597, 'of which we may hear more in the proper place' (*ER*, II, p. 256).

34 E.g. *ER*, I, p. 110.

35 Heylyn also used a source which he describes as 'the register book of the parish of Petworth' (*ER*, I, pp. 132, 136), although this seems to have been a Latin history of the Reformation written by an individual.

36 E.g. *ibid.*, I, pp. 227–8; II, p. 63.

37 E.g. *ibid.*, II, pp. 60, 107, 209.

38 Other regularly recurring sources are Herbert's *Life of Henry VIII*, Raleigh's *History of the World* and Thomas Mills's *The Catalogue of Honour* (1613). Heylyn often fails to provide citations for his most frequently used sources, whereas he usually provides proper references for Latin classical adages or passages from Josephus. Some borrowings from historians such as Camden are hidden altogether (e.g. *ER*, I, p. 2).

39 *ER*, I, pp. 66, 77, 249.

40 E.g. *ibid.*, I, pp. 13, 16–17, 20, 95–6, 144–5.

41 *HQA*, ii. p. 8; Milton, *Catholic and Reformed*, p. 313. Heylyn was not alone in using Harpsfield: Fuller also admitted using him (*Appeal*, i. p. 37).

42 E.g. *ER*, I, p. 20; II, p. 310.

43 E.g. *ibid.*, I, pp. 31, 105, 164; N. Sanders, *Vera et Sincera Historia Schismatis Anglicani* (Cologne, 1628).

44 *ER*, I, pp. 225–6.

45 I Kings 19:11–12.

46 *ER*, II, pp. 224–5.

47 Milton, *Catholic and Reformed*, pp. 322–30.

48 See above, ch. 3.

49 Milton, *Catholic and Reformed*, pp. 331–6.

50 Vernon, pp. 94–5; LPL, MS WD 54, pp. 89–226.

51 *PT*, pp. 387–9.

52 N. Tyacke, *Aspects of English Protestantism, c. 1530–1700* (Manchester, 2001), pp. 284–7. On Sugge's possible acquaintance with Heylyn see above, ch. 4.

53 See above, ch. 3.

54 *ER*, I, pp. vi–ix, 302.

55 *Ibid.*, I, pp. 36–8.

56 *Ibid.*, I, p. ix.

57 *Ibid.*, I, pp. 204–5, 269.

58 *Ibid.*, II, p. 45.

59 *Ibid.*, II, p. 167.

60 *Ibid.*, II, p. 125.

61 *Ibid.*, II, pp. 148–9.

62 *Ibid.*, II, pp. 175–84.

63 On the distortions involved see Trott, 'Prelude', pp. 311–22.

64 See *ER*, I, p. 139, which refers to the legitimacy of the imposition of the Scottish Prayer Book with a marginal note 'See the book called Cyprianus Anglicus lib. 4 an. 1637' (see also 1661 edn, p. 67). See also II, p. 229. Sheldon was not necessarily hostile to the memory of Laud, who had been an early patron, and he later promoted editions of his works: see below, n. 107.

65 Wood, *Life and Times*, I, pp. 479–85.

66 Bodl., Rawl. MS D.660, fols 1–2. I am grateful to Julia Merritt for this reference.

67 *CA*, p. 46.

68 *Ibid.*, p. 46.

69 *Ibid.*, pp. 1–2.

70 See Trott, 'Prelude', pp. 329–36.

71 *CA*, pp. 3–4, 14, 30, 36 (cf. *CE*, pp. 154–5).

72 For a general discussion of the Laudians' perceptions of Lutheranism see Milton, *Catholic and Reformed*, pp. 440–6.

73 Bodl., Add. MS C.304b, fol. 75r.

74 *HQA*, iii. p. 280.

75 *CA*, p. 51.

76 *Ibid.*, pp. 53–5, 66–7.

77 *Ibid.*, pp. 63–4, 119–20, 170, 195, 201, 230.

78 *Ibid.*, pp. 67, 152, 156, 165, 168, 195, 251.

79 *Ibid.*, pp. 47–8, 175–6.

80 BL, Lansdowne MS 721, fol. 192v.

81 *CA*, pp. 412–17; Milton, *Catholic and Reformed*, pp. 353–73.

82 *CA*, pp. 229, 415, 417–19.

83 Heylyn had also argued for the legitimacy of pursuing reunion with Rome in *EH*, ii. pp. 261–3.

84 E.g. *ibid.*, pp. 130, 495–6.

85 *Ibid.*, pp. 202, 222, 538–42.

86 *Ibid.*, pp. 173, 185, 334, 346.

87 Thomas Fuller, *The Church History of Britain* (6 vols, 1843), VI, p. 118; *idem, Appeal*, iii. pp. 16–17; *EH*, i. pp. 215–17.

88 *ER*, II, p. 185. See also II, p. 323.

89 *Ibid.*, II, pp. 432–3. Note also the allusion to what 'may be shewn hereafter' in *AR*, p. 323.

90 Bosher, *Making*, p. 151. The Smectymnuans were William Spurstowe and Edmund Calamy. Another chaplain was Heylyn's old antagonist Edward Reynolds.

91 Bodl., Add. MS C.304b, fols 74r–79v.

92 *Ibid.*, fol. 79v.

93 *AR*, pp. 1–40.

94 *Ibid.*, pp. 59–60, 68, 72.

95 *Microcosmus* (1636), p. 252; *Cosmographie*, ii. p. 32. Heylyn had briefly included the Revolt in lists of Calvinist rebellions (e.g. *SB*, p. 26; *CE*, p. 75) but had not provided any detailed discussion of this reassessment before *Aërius*.

96 *AR*, pp. 83–120, esp. pp. 85–8, 92, 102.

97 *De Bello Belgico: the History of the Low-Countrey Warres. Written by Latine by F. Strada; in English by Sir Rob. Stapylton* (1650); *ODNB*, s.n. 'Robert Stapylton'. Durel accused Heylyn of following Strada (Bodl., Add. MS C.304b, fol. 75v). While Heylyn does not cite Strada explicitly in *Aërius*, he had clearly read the work closely, and quotes explicitly from it in *BR*, sig.*5r.

98 *AR*, p. 416.

99 *Ibid.*, pp. 413–15.

100 Bodl., Add. MS C.304b, fol. 74r.

101 *AR*, p. 423.

102 See my article in *ODNB*, s.n. 'John Cosin'.

103 Bodl., Add. MS C.304b, fol. 76r–v; *AR*, p. 118.

104 Spurr, *Restoration*, p. 43. The date of Heylyn's death differs from that given in Barnard: see *ER*, I, p. ccvi n.

105 P. Carter, 'Parliament, convocation and the granting of clerical supply in early modern England', *Parliamentary History* 19 (2000), p. 23; Spurr, *Restoration*, p. 51. Sheldon did secure in return the right of the clergy to vote in parliamentary elections – an issue which Heylyn had highlighted in his *Stumbling Block* – but the informal backstairs dealing involved would have confirmed Heylyn's fears about the ways in which Restoration religious policy was being formulated.

106 W. N. Darnell, *The Correspondence of Isaac Basire* (1831), p. 224. I am grateful to Ken Fincham for alerting me to this rather hopeful report of April 1663, which also predicted the repeal of all acts made in the Long Parliament and the return of the Court of Star Chamber.

107 Sheldon arranged for the publication of Laud's prayers as *A Summarie of Devotions* (Oxford, 1667), and asked Sancroft to prepare Laud's diary and his history of his trial for publication: J. Spurr, ' "A special kindness for dead bishops": the church, history and testimony in seventeenth-century protestantism', *HLQ*, 68 (2005), p. 332.

108 Κειμηλια Εκκλεσιαστικα.

109 *ER*, I, pp. xxi–xxviii.

110 *The Diary of Samuel Pepys*, ed. R. S. Latham and W. Matthews (10 vols, 1970–83), IX, pp. 291, 308, 373, 379. (I am grateful to Charles Knighton for these references.) See also D. R. Woolf, *Reading History in Early Modern England* (Cambridge, 2000), p. 119.

111 K. Fincham, ' "According to ancient custom": the return of altars in the Restoration Church of England', *Transactions of the Royal Historical Society*, 6th ser., 13 (2003).

112 M. Johnson and B. Maltby, 'A seventeenth-century recusant family library: Middleton of Stockeld', *Yorkshire Archaeological Journal*, 75 (2003). I am grateful to Lynn Hulse for this reference.

113 J. Callow, *The Making of James II* (2000), pp. 146–7; Gilbert Burnet, *History of his own Time* (Oxford, 1833), II, p. 24, quoted in *ER*, I, p. clxxiii; J. S. Clarke, *The Life of James II, King of England . . . collected out of Memoirs writ by his own Hand* (1816), I, pp. 630–1.

The other works alleged to have undermined James's allegiance, however, are Hooker's *Laws of Ecclesiastical Polity* and a treatise by 'a learned Bishopp of the Church of England'.

114 George Touchet, *Historical Collections out of several Protestant Histories* (1673); J. Champion, *The Pillars of Priestcraft Shaken* (Cambridge, 1991), p. 76.

115 Thomas Godden, *Catholicks no Idolaters* (1672), sig. (b)1r–(b)2v. However, where Godden cited Heylyn for denying that Rome was guilty of idolatry, Stillingfleet responded with apposite quotations from the *Parable of the Tares*: Edward Stillingfleet, *An Answer to several late Treatises* (1673), sigs g2v–g3r.

116 Stillingfleet, *An Answer to several late Treatises*, sig. liv.

117 Henry Hickman, *Historia Quinqu-articularis Exarticulata* (1673).

118 M. A. Goldie, 'John Locke and Anglican royalism', *Political Studies*, 31 (1983), pp. 66, 69–70. Champion, *Pillars*, p. 75, n. 89.

119 E.g. David Jones, *The Secret History of White-Hall* (1697).

120 *A True and Impartial Narrative of the Dissenters New Plot* (1690). I am grateful to Mark Knights for this reference. It is not entirely clear whether the author's comments on Heylyn are meant ironically.

121 For specific citations of Heylyn's works (especially his 'Way of the Reformation') see Francis Atterbury, *The Rights, Powers and Privileges of Convocation* (1700), pp. 165, 175, 177, 180, 514. On Atterbury's campaign see Spurr, *Restoration*, pp. 379–81; G. V. Bennett, *The Tory Crisis in Church and State, 1688–1730* (Oxford, 1975). Convocation had been recalled in 1689 but swiftly prorogued.

122 Laurence Echard, *History of England* (3 vols, 1718), III, p. 94; A. Starkie, 'Contested histories of the English church: Gilbert Burnet and Jeremy Collier', *HLQ*, 68 (2005), p. 338. An exception was the non-juror Thomas Hearne, who makes no mention of Heylyn at all when surveying church history in 1705: R. Mayer, 'The rhetoric of historical truth: Heylyn *contra* Fuller on *The Church History of Britain*', *Prose Studies*, 20:3 (1997), p. 16.

Chapter 7

Conclusion: religion and politics in Heylyn's career and writings

As a writer, Peter Heylyn seems impervious to doubt, ambiguity or change. Never less than emphatic in his views, he was often scathing in his attacks on more neutral or impartial authors. He was the spokesman for a body of ideas which are often perceived as fixed and intolerant – those of Laudianism and hard-line royalism. It is therefore easy to take him at his word – as an unquestioning upholder of what were for him unchanging verities. As the bogeyman of liberal and progressive thought, Heylyn has been depicted as an irredeemable bigot, expounding an extreme but coherent ideology which he never varied.[1] This book has tried to present a rather different picture. Instead of the rigid and uncomplicated extremist, it has instead argued that Heylyn was an individual whose ideas underwent substantial change and development over the course of his career. Most obvious is his abandonment in the late 1620s of the thought-world that is so evident in the 1625 edition of his *Microcosmus*, with its anti-popery, its strong confessional identity and its enthusiasm for the Protestant cause on the Continent. But even after Heylyn had thrown in his lot with Archbishop Laud, his printed ideas continued to change and develop through some thirty years of publications. Even his final, posthumous works sometimes point in new directions, or reflect revisions or even reversals of recent opinions. Partly these changes reflect the tumultuous times in which he lived, which radically altered the personal circumstances in which he wrote, and forced him to re-evaluate some of the presuppositions that had underlain his earlier views. But these shifts in printed opinion also reflect the type of writing to which Heylyn devoted his efforts. Heylyn was an instinctively polemical writer, his views always expressed with a clarity and dogmatism according to his immediate polemical requirements. But this mustering of the whole armoury of polemical weapons in each publication meant that, as his polemical needs varied from work to work, so inconsistencies could emerge across the range of his publications. The rigidity with which Heylyn expressed his views need not imply that they were not mutable. Heylyn is usually entirely consistent in his position *within an individual work*, when his polemical purpose is sustained against a particular opponent. But there are often inconsistencies between tracts, even if they have been written within months of each other.

In some ways, the writings of his later years can seem more coherent and clear in their claims than those which he produced during the 1630s. But the tendency for his particular judgements to vary from work to work did not disappear even then. It may also be the case that Heylyn's shifting arguments reflect inconsistencies which were inherent in the two ideologies of Laudianism and royalism for which he was an advocate. In this conclusion we will briefly note some of Heylyn's basic ideological stances and identify some of the tensions and ambiguities within them, before reassessing the reputation of this most controversial figure.

KING, CHURCH AND PARLIAMENT

Heylyn was famously a defender of absolute monarchy. He was also one of the few writers before the Civil War to employ the term 'royalist', and he used it as a positive appellation, accusing Williams of not being the royalist that he pretended to be.[2] In the 1630s he had insisted that kings had 'unlimited power' and that subjects owed them 'absolute obedience', which was not limited according to whether the king was acting in accordance with the positive laws of the realm.[3] In his later writings, freed from the need to avoid giving offence, and appalled by rebellions against the monarch, Heylyn became still more outspoken in defending the absolute authority of the monarch, and seemed to feel less need than ever to insert caveats.[4] In his *Stumbling Block* he insisted that kings alone make laws and that their authority derived from the Norman kings' absolute right of conquest.[5] In debate with James Harrington he reiterated this, and emphasized that laws and liberties would never have been freely granted by a king, but would only ever have been extorted.[6] He was not, however, a systematic political theorist: he toyed with the patriarchal ideas of his friend Filmer but not in a methodical fashion, and he admitted to Harrington that he had 'never managed' many of the 'Political Disputes' involved.[7]

Heylyn was not of course an advocate of tyrannical government – he insisted that Christian kings governed according to positive laws and the Law of God – although when writing anonymously he was happy to advocate radical political solutions in Machiavellian fashion, noting how the possession of a standing army could equip a king to override any concessions that he had granted to his subjects.[8] Otherwise, he was happy to invoke people's rights and liberties against the intrusions of parliament, his principal concern being to attack the ways in which liberties were invoked to dictate royal policy and infringe royal prerogatives, and the implication that the existence of these liberties implied the existence of an authority in the country that was independent of the monarch.[9]

Heylyn's main target was what he saw as the overweening power of parliaments. Parliaments did not exist in their own right and had no role in the practice of government; they were called to advise and petition, but not to collaborate in law making and had no independent privileges.[10] He depicted the 1620s as a time of constant infringements upon the rights of kings by parliaments claiming privileges that they did not have.[11] It was inevitable that parliaments and the people would extort further privileges from kings if they were given the opportunity: people would force a generous king to give away royalty itself.[12] The upheavals of the 1620s and 1640s therefore represented careful and cynical planning by subversive elements: the king was deliberately ensnared in a foreign war so that he became dependent on parliament's support and was forced to yield more power to it. The events of the 1640s were directed by republicans who had always intended to seize power. The Scottish uprising similarly reflected deliberate long-term plans to over-turn royal authority, and the best solution would have been to suppress the revolt early and subject the country to English rule.[13] Royal authority was therefore in a constant battle with other political forces that would challenge its sovereignty whenever the opportunity arose.

Heylyn's committed support for royal authority is a consistent feature of his career and writings, occasional polemical gestures towards popular liberties notwithstanding.[14] But this did not mean that he was uncritically supportive of the crown, or of the people who wore it. In fact, when he looked back on the disasters of the first half of the seventeenth century, Heylyn was constantly ready to place the blame for the problems at the feet of the Stuart monarchs: their deplorable misjudgements and misgovernment form one of the strongest and most persistent themes of Heylyn's later writings. King James receives a mixed report, sometimes praised for not yielding to parliament, but at other times blamed for his laziness, laxity and poor judgement.[15] It is Charles who is the monarch whose behaviour and judgement are most con-sistently condemned in Heylyn's many works. Nowhere is this stronger than in his *Observations* – the work where Heylyn (hiding behind his anonymity) is most candid, and makes scathing criticisms which he did not later retract when challenged in his debate with L'Estrange. The overriding theme of the whole book is of Charles's disastrous habit of 'vailing his crown' and sur-rendering his authority.[16] It is especially notable that Heylyn virtually never attempts to explain away Charles's policy failures by blaming poor or mali-cious advice; rather, it is Charles's own character which is at issue. Heylyn seems to have been quite convinced, for example, that Charles himself was the author of the disastrous concessions in the *Answer to the Nineteen Propositions*.[17] A key danger that Heylyn identified was that of 'popularity' – James and Charles were consistently guilty of seeking it, thereby endangering their own positions and encouraging their natural enemies.[18] In reviewing the catastrophes of recent times, Heylyn's constant insistence is that Charles was not a victim of events; he had the power to restore his position, but he never used it. The return of the Stuart monarchy in 1660 meant that Heylyn had to choose his words more carefully, but nevertheless there are still observable criticisms even then. Charles is still blamed for bringing his fate upon himself (and Heylyn may well have considered this to be useful cautionary advice for the new monarch).[19] There is also perhaps a sense not just of disapproval, but of resentment; it was not just Charles himself, but his followers who suffered for his mistakes (including, of course, Heylyn himself).

Essential to Heylyn's view of royal power, then, was his conviction that it needed to be exercised with strength and authority. Heylyn was a natural authoritarian; as he saw it, all political problems were the result of kings not exercising their power decisively enough. It is easy to see from this why it could make sense for Heylyn to make a pitch to support a powerful usurper like Cromwell who could exercise central power effectively (not least in his readiness to dissolve the Rump and the Protectorate parliaments), as long as Heylyn could be convinced that the protector would defend the church. It is notable that Heylyn seems to have dangled the carrot of his tract *Augustus* before both Charles and Cromwell.[20] Heylyn had an unshakable belief in monarchy, but not necessarily in the Stuarts. He may not have been the only royalist whose more implacable beliefs on the nature of royal authority made him potentially more amenable towards protectoral authority.

Another crucial source of power was that of the church, and it is the desire to protect and defend the independent authority of the church which increasingly emerges as an obsession in Heylyn's later writings. He had always shown readiness to defend the independence of the church from the power of parliament, both in its right to determine its own doctrine and ceremonies and also in its authority to grant its own subsidies through Convocation. It is the independent power of Convocation that becomes a prime theme of Heylyn's writings from the 1640s onwards, extending well beyond his occasional polemical need to defend the proceedings of the 1640 meetings in which he had been so closely involved. By the mid-1640s he was already depicting the English Reformation as solely the work of Convocation, and he was ever on the alert for any opponent's suggestion that it did not enjoy the rights and privileges that he claimed for it.[21]

What is not entirely clear is what all this meant for the authority of the monarch. At its most extreme, Heylyn's clericalism seems to remove most of the authority of the king from the church, making him little more than a rubber stamp for the decisions of Convocation. There had been no hint of this in Heylyn's 1630s writings. There was little need to make a case for the ultimate independence of ecclesiastical institutions when the church was acting in close alliance with a supportive king, and puritan opponents were attempting to revive the old canard that *jure divino* episcopacy was a challenge to the power of the monarch. In fact, Heylyn was ready to play with the idea that the king could dictate the internal furnishings of churches, and that his example should inspire ceremonial reform. Even in the 1650s Heylyn would defend the practice of touching for the king's evil.[22] But it is not always clear that he sees sovereigns as being imbued with religious power or authority (and in debate with Harrington Heylyn made it clear that he considered that the arguments of Aristotle (and Filmer) provided a better case for the divine right of kings than biblical examples).[23] He was not a keen adherent of the royal martyrology (partly because he disliked its passive connotations, which offended his ideas regarding the true exercise of royal power and majesty) and therefore the theme of the sacred nature of kingship is not very evident in his works. Historians may more generally have overestimated the importance of the image of sacred kingship in pre-Restoration 'Anglican' thought. The royalist cleric Herbert Thorndike, for example, also attacked the 'vulgar mistake' (of King James among others) that sovereign powers were called gods in scripture, and questioned the argument that Christian princes had the same rights in the church as the kings of Judah had in the synagogue.[24]

It may well be that it was the experience of the early 1640s that prompted Heylyn to consider the independent power of the church more fully. Royalists as well as parliamentarians had attacked the church, and the king had consistently shown himself unable or unwilling to defend the privileges of the clerical estate. Heylyn's insistence on the independent authority of the church is manifested most memorably in his 'Way and Manner of the Reformation' (published in *Ecclesia Vindicata* (1657)). Here he makes it clear that the royal supremacy over the church is a gift of the clergy. By their Act of Submission, the clergy transferred their power of self-government to the king and his successors, the king's religious authority was vested in him by the clergy, and therefore the king's acts of reformation 'had virtually the power of the Convocations'.[25] But could a power of self-regulation that had been invested in another also be taken back again (as parliamentarian pamphleteers argued in another case)? Heylyn's overwhelming desire to defend the independence of the church also makes a startling appearance in *Cyprianus Anglicus*, where Heylyn shows a sudden sympathy for and acceptance of the Scots presbyterians' complaint that Charles's attempt to impose canons on the Scottish church without the consent of the clergy was illegal.[26]

The restoration of the monarchy in 1660 offered the possibility of a triumphant alliance of church and state once more, and the clericalist extremes of Heylyn's writings in the 1640s and 1650s are less apparent in the 1660s. The alliance of church and state is what Heylyn had celebrated in his study of the 1630s in *Bibliotheca Regia* and what he proposed to the new king in *Ecclesia Restaurata*, and this was clearly Heylyn's ideal model for both church and state. (He was always emphatic that it was in the king's interest to defend an independent church.) But this was a partnership that was placed under considerable strain under Charles II and James II, and problematized still further by the Glorious Revolution. Heylyn's vision of the role of Convocation and the independent powers of the church did leave the door open for the church to dissolve its links with the secular authorities. This was something that had happened *de facto* in the 1650s, and some writers had justified the process in broader terms. The abolition of episcopacy had already driven writers such as Thorndike to reason that, as the temporal powers of the state had opposed religion and created schism, therefore the people should separate themselves from the state church and adhere instead to a stateless 'Society of the Church'.[27] This was also the route that the Nonjurors would take (some of whom were avid readers of Heylyn's works). The tension in the Laudian position between the support for monarchical authority and the defence of the independent power and identity of the church therefore becomes plain in Heylyn's varying advocacy.

THE IDENTITY OF THE CHURCH OF ENGLAND

Heylyn occupies an important place in the emergence of more exclusive ideas of the identity of the Church of England and of its Reformation. Indeed, he is credited with being one of the first writers to employ the term 'Anglican Church' (in *Ecclesia Restaurata*, I, p. 193). That being said, there are again some tensions and ambiguities in Heylyn's writings. Heylyn was not the ideologue of the *via media* of later Anglicanism; nor was he the simple opponent of the Continental Protestant Reformation that his opponents (both Catholic and Protestant) suggested. In fact, his ultimate reading of the identity of the English church is far from clear.

Heylyn undoubtedly defined ever more narrowly what he took to be the true doctrines of the Church of England, and compiled an ever larger list of doctrines and practices which he regarded as incompatible, foreign intrusions. These latter included the identification of the pope as Antichrist, the defence of the succession of the church through medieval heretical sects, 'Calvinist' doctrines of predestination, not defending episcopacy as a separate order for fear of offending the foreign Reformed churches, sabbatarianism, the rejection of the article of the local descent of Christ into hell, parish lectureships, metrical psalm singing, vestry authority, private fasting, hostility to the use of images, and any emphasis on private revelation.[28] Many of these ideas and practices were dominant in the Elizabethan and Jacobean church, and some indeed can be discerned in Heylyn's own earlier writings. What is most notable about Heylyn's contribution to ideas of the Church of England, however, is not his definition of orthodoxy (his lists of heterodox positions are fairly conventional Laudian ones, albeit with some of Heylyn's particular obsessions), but rather the historical identity that he constructed for the English church.

'Avant-garde conformists' and Laudians were faced with the problem of justifying their preference for elaborate high-churchmanship and distaste for Reformed doctrines and worship in the face of English religious opinion of a more evangelical, Reformed slant. While some invoked patristic authority, others urged the compatibility of their reforms in doctrine and worship with various documents of the English Reformation which were deemed to express the ultimate principles or purposes of the English church, be they the Prayer Book, the Book of Homilies, the Elizabethan injunctions or the 1571 canons.[29] This was inevitably a somewhat random, scatter-gun approach, and it was Heylyn's achievement to construct a more systematic interpretation of the history of the English Reformation which would explain why some aspects of it should be treated as authoritative while those not supportive of Laudian practices could justifiably be discounted. In the 1630s Heylyn had still conducted rather opportunistic raids on the sources of the English Reformation to support his arguments. More clarity began to emerge in the 1640s and 1650s, partly because Heylyn may have felt more freedom to slay some of the sacred cows of earlier Reformation history. Thus it is only in the 1650s that he specifically dismisses Wyclif and Tyndale as precursors of the English Reformation, and John Foxe as a reliable historian of it.[30]

In his *Ecclesia Restaurata* Heylyn completes the picture of a theologically restrained and orderly Reformation that earlier thinkers such as Overall had invoked but never documented. It is of course a very selective account, which systematically downplays the radical agenda of the Edwardian Reformation, and Cranmer's close involvement in pursuing it.[31] Instead, Cranmer and Ridley are clothed in moderate garb and presented as acting in fundamental opposition to the forces of Reformed theology and radical reformation. The more distasteful (to Laudian eyes) aspects of the Reformation are explained by the malign influence of foreign reformers, the first stirrings of puritanism and the rapacious anticlericalism of Edwardian courtiers. The later history of the sixteenth-century church can thus be the story of how the true, moderate Reformation was betrayed by the forces of puritanism, and the influx of 'Calvinist' divinity. 'Calvinism' is seen as a body of destructive ideas – destructive of worship and true doctrine but also of good order in church and state – and as the force that would drive the country into civil war. The fact that the Church of England becomes overwhelmed by Calvinism can then explain why the restoration of the true principles of the worship and discipline of the Church of England under Laud could have the misleading appearance of innovation.

There are, however, some important tensions and inconsistencies in Heylyn's presentation of the history of the Church of England. One major and problematic issue relates to the way that the church is seen as being overwhelmed by the forces of puritanism. In one rendering of his position, Heylyn wishes to present puritanism as an underground movement, kept under control by bishops such as Whitgift and Bancroft, and emerging to threaten the church only under the lax government of Archbishop Abbot. Heylyn's problem occurs when he wishes to describe the insidious influence of 'Calvinism' in doctrinal matters (particularly in relation to the doctrine of predestination). Here he is obliged to go back, not to the Edwardian, but to the Henrician Reformation and (perversely) to the King's Book in order to find a voice of the English Reformation which will coincide with his 'Arminian' position.[32] Moreover, on a range of doctrines – stretching from the doctrine of predestination to the pope's identity as Antichrist and the succession of the true church – Heylyn ultimately presents Calvinism as the dominant force in the English church by the 1590s, and is driven to writing of a tiny minority, a hidden succession of true believers in the doctrines of the Church of England, who finally emerge into the light of day in the 1620s and 1630s.[33]

This creates a fundamental uncertainty as to how one is meant to understand those Elizabethan and Jacobean bishops and divines who opposed puritanism but embraced the Calvinist doctrines which Heylyn depicts as intimately linked with the nature and objectives of puritanism. Heylyn never really resolves this question. In one of his last works, *Cyprianus Anglicus*, he jumbles together issues of doctrine and discipline, and the result is incoherent. The church is betrayed to puritanism only by Archbishop Abbot, and yet the church of his predecessors as archbishop, Whitgift and Bancroft, is one from which true doctrine has disappeared, and in which the Calvinist doctrines of the puritans are dominant. Heylyn speaks in almost the same breath of the activities of the 'Calvinian party' and the 'Puritan Faction', and it is far from clear that they are not the same thing. In Heylyn's dualistic picture of the forces of good and evil in the early Stuart church, the two are easily combined. Heylyn himself gives very different indications of his thinking on the topic of 'Calvinist conformity'. In a tract written against Fuller in the late 1650s he is emphatic that it is legitimate to brand those holding Calvinist doctrines as 'puritan', even if they are not advocating presbyterianism. But when accused by Baxter some months later of making precisely this point Heylyn denied it, affirmed his high regard for the bishops, deans and other clergymen who had held Calvinist beliefs while opposing puritanism, and accused Baxter of trying to sow division among 'us'. In *Cyprianus*

Anglicus he carefully repeats this caveat that not all Calvinists are puritans, but then seems to flout it in practice.[34]

Heylyn's basic problem was that his polemical requirements and preferred style of exposition drove him to create an image of diametrically opposed bodies of belief and practice. Not only did he define the orthodox practices and doctrines of the Church of England more narrowly, but he combined their opposites into a single body of divinity whose exponents formed a party committed to a subversive political and religious agenda. His determination to marginalize an enormous range of beliefs as belonging to a single puritan mind set made it impossible for him to account adequately for the identity of dominant modes of thought and behaviour in the establishment of the Elizabethan and Jacobean church. He created such an inflexible nexus of ideas that as a result a whole range of doctrines could be branded as 'presbyterian', including sabbatarianism, predestinarianism and the doctrines that the pope was Antichrist and that Christ had not descended locally into hell. Thus in *Aërius Redivivus* Bancroft's anti-puritan but Calvinist chaplain Gabriel Powel is dismissed as a 'stiff presbyterian' for writing in favour of the 'Calvinist' interpretation of Christ's descent into hell.[35] It also led Heylyn to insist on the heterodoxy of James Ussher, among others.

One way of partly explaining members of the established church who seemed to uphold 'Calvinist' ideas was in terms of 'popularity'. As we have seen, Heylyn was concerned throughout his career with the phenomenon of 'popular prelacy', incarnated in John Williams in his cynical raising of a popular party against the king, but also in other clergymen who spinelessly wished to keep on good terms with their congregations rather than support disciplinary actions against them. Just as Heylyn condemned it in kings, so he attacked 'popularity' in the church as a crucial means of explaining the catastrophe of the 1640s.[36]

Another issue where Heylyn's arguments were far from clear or consistent was that of how his preferred Laudian form of English Protestantism should be categorized. Had the Church of England followed a unique path compared with other churches? Here again Heylyn's position seems quite inconsistent. He seeks to blame errors in the English church on the influx of foreign Protestant ideas, and he does at one point gesture towards the idea of the Church of England occupying a *via media* between Lutheranism and Calvinism.[37] But Heylyn also at times invokes the English church's close links with Lutheranism. Lutherans are only briefly touched upon in his 1630s writings, and it is only in the 1650s that Heylyn seems to have become more enthusiastic in finding parallels with them, and also in emphasizing their influence on those aspects of England's early Reformation of which he approved. It partly seems to be a reflection of the demands of his doctrinal histories and his struggles to create an 'Arminian' lineage for the Church of

England that Heylyn developed an enthusiasm for emphasizing 'Melanch-thonian Lutheranism' as a crucial aspect of the English Reformation. Thus, in discussing 'the true and genuine doctrine of the Church of England' regarding predestination, Heylyn insisted that it was closest to the Church fathers and 'the famous Augustane *Confession*, the writings of Melanchthon, and the *Workes* of Erasmus'.[38] Also in another late work Heylyn makes the surprising concession that the revival of true English Protestant beliefs regarding divine grace was due to the inspiration and reading of books from the Dutch Arminian controversies.[39]

Heylyn's is not therefore an insular 'Anglicanism'. As in his late works Heylyn creates an increasingly extreme vision of a malign Calvinist international, so he tends to argue for much closer links across the confessions in opposition to it. This is true in doctrine just as much as in politics, where Heylyn creates a unity between 'the old English Protestants, the Remonstrants, the moderate Lutherans . . . [and] . . . the Franciscans'.[40] Necessarily, this involves a closer identity with the forces of Roman Catholicism.

We have noted that before 1640 Heylyn's moderation towards Roman Catholicism was more a function of his anti-puritanism. Throughout his career, after all, from 1627 through to 1659, Heylyn reserved the right to adopt anti-Catholic themes to vindicate his Protestant orthodoxy against his opponents.[41] But in the later 1650s he began to make more positive remarks about the Church of Rome. It is in his late works that Heylyn begins to argue that anti-popery was an insincere and dangerous weapon that had been used to undermine true English Protestantism.[42] He was prepared to adopt a positive perspective on reports of plans for reconciliation with Rome in 1630s, rather than simply dismissing them as fraudulent. This partly reflected polemical requirements, as usual, but it was also presumably because he did not see them as inherently improper, and he seems to have shared Richard Montagu's attitude that a potential reconciliation should not be spurned if the conditions being offered were reasonable. Towards the end of his life Heylyn also suggested on several occasions that Laud's policies in the 1630s had been partly intended to attract Roman Catholics back into the church.[43] Heylyn still never really discusses Roman Catholic errors in a manner that would make clear his overall position, and provides little discussion of the power of the pope. Also there is no obvious evidence that he enjoyed personal links with Roman Catholics (although plenty of Romanist polemicists would be grateful later for his anti-puritan diatribes). The later problems of James II and his declarations of indulgence meant that many of Heylyn's high-church successors were less keen than he to leave the door open for reconciliation with the Roman church, or to see anti-popery as inherently heterodox.

Heylyn's reading of the Reformation did, however, still have some importance in the longer term. This was not because other Laudians did not argue similar points, but rather because Heylyn provided a fuller historical justification for his position. Heylyn is most notorious, of course, for his condemnation of Foxe, his rejection of the Marian martyrs, his attacks on foreign Reformed churches, and his creation of a history of the English Reformation that was capable of converting James II to Roman Catholicism. But that is not really what Heylyn's history was attempting to do. His significance rather lies in his determination to *redeem* the early Reformation – to identify and magnify a distinctive *via media* amid the destruction, erastianism and radicalism of the Edwardian Reformation, and to winnow out and marginalize all aspects of Reformed thinking and behaviour from the actions of its martyr bishops. In this he managed to construct a remarkably successful and long-lived image of moderate 'Anglicanism' within a Reformed church settlement. His real successors were not the Tractarians, who were sometimes happy to cite Heylyn, but who ultimately decided to reject the early Reformers altogether when faced with the evidence (which Heylyn had struggled to disguise) of their radical Protestant convictions, and to return just to the primitive church (although a return to a purely patristic church order was always a potent tendency within Laudian writing). Heylyn's real successors were the pre-Tractarian high-churchmen such as Charles Daubeny – vehement opponents of low-church Evangelicals, who shared Heylyn's vision of a moderate native Reformation innocent of the puritanical principles of later nonconformists.[44]

The fundamental point, however, is that the ultimate picture that Heylyn presented of the Church of England's identity still had its tensions and ambiguities, for all of his taste for simple dualisms. It could still be taken in a variety of directions by later churchmen.

'THE PRAGMATICAL HEYLYN': REPUTATION AND INFLUENCE[45]

Heylyn has never wanted for detractors. Throughout his life, and well beyond it, he had been the recipient of extraordinarily intense vituperation. It may perhaps seem appropriate that a man who was happy to abuse his opponents has received more than his fair share in return. But, like Heylyn's own polemic, the charges against him have not been entirely fair and, more seriously, they have tended to distort interpretations of both his career and his writings.

One of the enduring myths about Heylyn is that he was Laud's chaplain. This error has proved remarkably resilient, despite the fact that there is not a shred of contemporary evidence to support it, and that it was never even hinted at by Heylyn himself or either of his early biographers.[46] It is easy to see where the assumption comes from, given Heylyn's enormous biographical apologia for the archbishop, his constant readiness to defend Laud's reputation and his descriptions of his private meetings with him. But while Heylyn's loyalty to Laud and his memory are certainly apparent, nevertheless the belief that Heylyn was Laud's chaplain has tended to encourage a number of distorting assumptions about Heylyn's ideas and writings. The chaplain's position, after all, is an inferior and servile one – a mere servant of a more important churchman. And this is partly why Heylyn himself is often written about as a second-rate inconsequential lightweight, a mere henchman of more senior figures. Historians have been happy to adopt the usage of some of his contemporary opponents in referring to him as 'Peter', whereas Laud is never just called 'William'. It is assumed that he can have had no ideas of his own; that he lived simply to anticipate the ideas and justify the actions of his patron. After his patron's death, his duty was to preserve his memory and to continue to defend those same ideas. Small wonder that it has often been assumed that Heylyn's ideas never changed.

An allied accusation is that Heylyn wrote for money. This was a favourite charge of opponents like L'Estrange and Fuller, and was repeated uncritically by later historians such as Hallam. There is, however, little evidence that Heylyn earned significant money from his publications. *Cosmographie* and the *Survey of France* may have been commercially successful, and he may have received a salary of sorts for editing Civil War newsbooks. But it seems unlikely that he received much money. This was particularly the case in the 1650s, when Heylyn met the accusations that he wrote for money with outraged denials.[47] Remuneration could of course come in more forms than monetary payment – Heylyn undoubtedly did well out of patronage in the 1630s in the form of grants of lucrative church livings. But these were not necessarily rewards simply for his writing – as we have seen, Heylyn performed a variety of services, and his more partisan polemical works of the 1630s were published after he had already received his main rewards. In almost the last thirty years of his life he received no significant promotion, and only one additional living. Most of Heylyn's publications – and almost all his more famous ones – were neither commissioned by the authorities nor written for money. It must also be emphasized that, while Heylyn undoubtedly received a number of highly profitable livings for his services, he was of independent means and he did not have to pursue the career of a professional writer. Heylyn wrote because he wanted to, and because he was good at it, and also because he wished to be of service to the authorities.

In this sense, L'Estrange's accusation that Heylyn was worldly ('all his life he hath loved the world') has some justification. Heylyn was not an other-worldly academic or theologian, and inevitably he will sometimes have pitched his ideas and arguments to suit what was required of him. But, equally, he was seeking to push his own agenda on the authorities. He spent a great deal more of his career doing this than being a paid hack. In fact, the one time when Heylyn did serve simply as a paid writer (in royalist Oxford) he clearly had a strong distaste for the assignment and was relieved to stop. Heylyn usually aspired to the loftier tones of the historian, and in his *Cyprianus Anglicus* he began fitfully to imitate the consciously impartial tones and methods of a historian like L'Estrange. Heylyn would presumably have drawn a distinction between journalism and polemical controversy. That is not to say that he did not value his polemical writing. Indeed, he saw it as performing a valuable religious function. He numbered among the noble deeds of the martyred fathers of the church how they had 'pleaded the Churches cause in their Apologeticks'. Sometimes an aggressive or satirical style could be necessary for this greater end: he noted that Martin Marprelate could ultimately be vanquished, not by learned scholarship, but only by the 'Sarcastical and jeering wit' Thomas Nashe.[48]

The charge that Heylyn wrote extremely partial history is a standard critique which cannot be denied. But this was a period when all historical writing was partial. Heylyn's *parti pris* may have been less disguised than others', and all of his history writing unquestionably served specific political ends, but that does not mean he was simply a fraud, or that he was consciously and cynically untruthful.[49] Heylyn was obsessed with the notion that history must be truthful and objective. It was a principle that he constantly invoked, and it is possible to make sense of his work and his protestations only if we accept the sincerity of his claims, however poor their application.[50] This did not, however, mean that partisan history was improper, or necessarily untruthful. As J. H. Preston has suggested, partisanship was not seen as the same as partiality. There was in Heylyn's work an 'exacting historical rigour' (as Bush puts it), even if it was often tendentiously applied. We should re-member that the insistence on the necessity of thorough documentation to support contested truth claims is not simply the creation of Enlightenment science or rational discourse, but is most obviously observable in the acrim-onious cockpit of adversarial writing, where every source could be picked over and every error identified and relentlessly mocked.[51]

The assumption that Heylyn was a mere chaplain or paid hack, 'an abso-lute creature of Archbishop Laud' and 'an obsequious tool of the persecut-ing authorities', also reflects the common presupposition that conservative positions are seldom defended because of ideological conviction but presumably from other, less pure motives.[52] This also leads to the assumption that his views did not change or develop. But, as we have seen, significant changes and developments – and some remarkable *volte-faces* and inconsistencies – can be observed in his works. As a strongly polemical writer, the context may often have determined the precise position that he adopted. This needs to be remembered whenever Heylyn is cited as the principal exponent and ideo-logue of the Laudian position. His views did change and develop, and his rendering of the nature and purpose of 'Laudianism' may have changed too. This makes for problems if any single work – such as *Aërius Redivivus* or *Cyprianus Anglicus* – is taken to encapsulate the sum of his views, or those of the Laudian movement as a whole.

Heylyn's mutability, and the apparent cynicism of his change of position in the 1620s, can also easily lead one to miss the fact that he suffered for his ideas. He was not a Marchamont Nedham. There were a great many more egregious side changers in this period, and there was no shortage of people who switched to support and then denounce the Laudian regime, or who changed sides in the Civil War. Heylyn may have kept his head down for much of the 1650s but he did not sell out to Cromwell or abandon his particular principles. For a worldly man, always after the main chance, Heylyn could easily have died in enforced retirement and obscurity were it not for the happy accident of the Restoration at the end of his life.

Moreover, Heylyn was not a uniquely aggressive and adversarial author. Withering satire and polemical unscrupulousness were typical of the period, and there is a danger that writers can be interpreted according to their chosen polemical style. Hooker and Fuller will always be perceived as moderate, judicious and forbearing because that is the polemical style that they adopted. Heylyn's choice of a more vindictive and destructive rhetoric means that he will always be seen as a more extreme figure. This is not entirely unfair – the choice of polemical and rhetorical styles undoubtedly reflects the personality of the author concerned to an extent. But not all of Heylyn's publications are aggressively adversarial in their presentation. His controversial writings of the late 1650s are not typical of his overall output. Heylyn was also capable of consciously varying his style of writing. He later explained that it was necessary for him to adopt a severe approach with Burton, but his use of vinegar did not contain malice, and he was obliged to use salt when dealing with 'unsavoury pieces of wit and mischief' like Williams and Fuller.[53] The actual ideas that Heylyn expressed (as opposed to the manner in which he expressed them) were not uniquely extreme. Especially on the topic of episcopacy, more radical positions may be discerned in the work of other contemporary authors who enjoy the reputation of being a more moderate figures, such as Henry Hammond and Jeremy Taylor.[54]

Heylyn's ultimate value for the study of Laudianism and royalism derives in part from his unquestioned status as an official spokesman for each cause in the 1630s and 1640s respectively. But his continuing writings in the 1650s and 1660s enable us to reassess the relative stability and coherence of royalism and Laudianism. His ambiguous attitude towards the Stuarts, his shifting position on the identity of the Church of England, his juggling of the powers of Convocation and the royal supremacy, and not least his hostility towards other royalist writers and churchmen, reveal the fluid and mutable character of both Laudianism and royalism, and remind us that these were invented and conceptually unstable ideologies.

Heylyn was undoubtedly 'pragmatical' in some senses. He was unscrupulous in using the polemicist's art, he enjoyed a long career of misrepresenting opponents, he sought out and gained Laud's and Charles' support in a calculating way, he told them what they wanted to hear, and acted as their agent when he could. He was also a commissioned propagandist for the royalist cause. Nevertheless, his pursuit of influence, his mastery of insinuation and invective, his sometimes jaw-dropping hypocrisy, and his vivid partisanship, do not mean that he did not have principles and convictions, which he suffered for. To make sense of Heylyn and the age that produced him, we need to move beyond the simple caricature of the aggressive cynic writing for money. *Pace* Carlyle, the 'human brain' needs to concern itself more with men such as Heylyn, and the other fellows of 'Billings-gate Colledge', if we are to understand the world in which they lived, which they exemplified, and which they also helped to create.

NOTES

1 E.g. Foster (*Notes*, p. 64) remarks that Heylyn 'spent the last twenty years of his life vindicating the opinions he had enunciated in the first forty'.

2 *AL*, i. pp. 2, 36.

3 *BMA*, pp. 26, 156.

4 Heylyn made some delicate adjustments to the text between impressions of the *Briefe and Moderate Answer* in order to avoid implying open-ended absolutist ideas, e.g. he altered a reference to the 'unlimited power which some give to Kings' to read 'unlimited power *as you please to cal it*, which some give to Kings' (my italics). See Walker, pp. 125–6.

5 See above, pp. 131–2; *EH*, ii. pp. 88–9.

6 *CE*, pp. 244–5.

7 *Ibid.*, pp. 208 ('387'), 211, 264, 273, 277.

8 *Ibid.*, pp. 282–4; *Observations*, p. 160. He also admitted to Harrington that 'late experience amongst our selves' had shown that a prince could not be an absolute monarch without a standing army: *CE*, p. 236.

9 See above, p. 123; *BMA*, pp. 25–41.

10 *SB*, *passim*; *CE*, pp. 243–5.

11 E.g. *EH*, ii. p. 87; *CA*, pp. 91–2.

12 *CE*, pp. 244–5.

13 *Observations*, pp. 151–6; *EH*, i. pp. 223–4, 227; ii. pp. 177–8.

14 See above, pp. 123, 131–2, 157.

15 E.g. *Observations*, pp. 13–14; *CA*, pp. 84, 90; *EH*, ii. pp. 63, 71–2; *Extraneus*, pp. 12–13.

16 *Observations*, pp. 28–32 and *passim*.

17 *Ibid.*, p. 62.

18 E.g. *CA*, pp. 128–9. Heylyn does, however, grant a correct form of 'popularity', which Queen Elizabeth displayed (*Observations*, pp. 108–10).

19 *Observations*, p. 105; *CA*, pp. 145, 149.

20 See above, pp. 32–3, 158.

21 See above, pp. 129, 174–5.

22 *Coale*, pp. 58–63; *EH*, i. pp. 47–9.

23 *CE*, p. 273.

24 Herbert Thorndike, *A Discourse of the Right of the Church in a Christian State* (1649), pp. 9, 214, CXIII.

25 *EV*, i. pp. 84–5. (Note also the significant alteration in *ibid.*, p. 28, to *Parliaments Power*, p. 20, where it is emphasized that the king's supremacy derives from the clergy.) Heylyn does, however, accept that clerical corruption can be dealt with by the king 'by his sole authority' and against the opposition of the whole body of the clergy, if necessary (*EV*, i. pp. 80–1).

26 *CA*, pp. 301–2; Trott, 'Prelude', p. 240.

27 Thorndike, *Discourse*, pp. 338–9.

28 For a useful partial summary see *CA*, p. 51.

29 A. Milton, ' "Anglicanism" by stealth: the career and influence of John Overall' in K. Fincham and P. Lake (eds), *Religious Politics in post-Reformation England* (Woodbridge, 2006).

30 *HQA*, ii. pp. 8, 9, 12.

31 Contrast D. MacCulloch, *Thomas Cranmer: a Life* (New Haven CT, 1996).

32 *HQA*, ii. pp. 21–3.

33 See above, pp. 179, 206–8; *HQA*, iii. pp. 90–2.

34 See above, pp. 178, 188n.167; *CA*, pp. 123–4.

35 *AR*, p. 348.

36 See above, pp. 29, 69, 175, 208; also *CA*, p. 170.

37 *PT*, p. 129.

38 See above, pp. 91–2, 179, 206; *HQA*, ii. p. 19.

39 *CA*, p. 127.

40 *HQA*, i. p. 73.

41 See above, pp. 22, 68, 91, 159.

42 E.g. *CA*, pp. 93, 129.

43 See above, pp. 208–9.

44 P. B. Nockles, 'A disputed legacy: Anglican historiographies of the Reformation from the era of the Caroline divines to that of the Oxford Movement', *Bulletin of the John Rylands Library*, 83 (2001).

45 'The pragmatical Heylin' is Trevor-Roper's phrase: see his *Archbishop Laud, 1573–1645* (2nd edn, 1962), p. 183.

46 For recent examples see R. Beddard, 'James II and the Catholic challenge' in Tyacke, *Seventeenth Century Oxford*, p. 921; S. Foster, *Notes*, pp. 42, 64. These may reflect the influence of Trevor-Roper's *Archbishop Laud*, in which Heylyn is consistently identified as Laud's chaplain (pp. 82, 108, 272). For an older claim see H. Hallam, *A Constitutional History of England* (3 vols, 1872), II, p. 38.

47 *CE*, pp. 328–9. Heylyn explains that he offered the first version of his animadversions on Fuller's *Church-History* to a printer for 'a peece of Plate of five or six pounds' and a number of copies of the book, and that his expanded *Examen Historicum* was finally published by another printer on these terms. He claimed to have made no conditions at all with the printer for the publication of the *Observations, Extraneus Valupans, A Help to English History, Theologia Veterum* and *Ecclesia Vindicata*, and to have received only between seven and twelve copies of the latter four books. (He presumably did not ask for copies of the *Observations* because he wished to preserve his authorial anonymity.) Heylyn's omission of *Cosmographie* and the *Survey of France* from this list would seem to indicate that they were more consciously commercial publications.

48 *PT*, p. 182; *AR*, p. 286.

49 This repeated suggestion mars the otherwise very perceptive analysis of Heylyn's later writings in Trott, 'Prelude'. Kendall ('Royalist scholar') perhaps goes too far the other way in arguing for Heylyn's credentials as a serious historian.

50 E.g. *Observations*, sig. A2v; *AR*, sig. A4r–v; *EH*, sigs A2r–A3r.

51 J. H. Preston, 'English ecclesiastical historians and the problem of bias, 1559–1742', *Journal of the History of Ideas*, 32 (1971); D. Bush, *The early Seventeenth Century, 1600–1660* (*Oxford History of English Literature*, VII) (2nd edn, Oxford, 1990), p. 224; A. Hughes, *Gangraena and the Struggle for the English Revolution* (Oxford, 2004), p. 438; D. R. Woolf, *The Idea of History in early Stuart England* (Toronto, 1990), pp. 220–1, 255.

52 Sir Richard Hill, *The Church of England Vindicated* (1770), pp. 14, 39–40.

53 *CE*, p. 31.

54 See above, ch. 4.

Bibliography of selected primary sources

MANUSCRIPTS

BODLEIAN LIBRARY, OXFORD
Add. MS C.304b
Claydon House MSS (microfilm)
Jones MS 17
Rawlinson MSS D.353, 660, 1350
Rawlinson MS E.21
Tanner MSS 49, 58, 65
Top. Oxon. C.378
Wood MS E.4

BRITISH LIBRARY
Additional MSS 23206, 28104, 46885A
Harleian MSS 3783, 6018
Lansdowne MS 721

CAMBRIDGE UNIVERSITY LIBRARY
Add. MS 4251 (B), No. 237

HUNTINGTON LIBRARY, SAN MARINO CA
Hastings MSS, HAF 12.10

CENTRE FOR KENTISH STUDIES, MAIDSTONE
MS U120/C6/A18

LAMBETH PALACE LIBRARY
MS WD 54
MS 577
MS 1030

MAGDALEN COLLEGE, OXFORD
MS 224
MS 312

THE NATIONAL ARCHIVES, LONDON
LC5
PCC, Prob. 11
SP16
SP20

SHEFFIELD UNIVERSITY LIBRARY
Hartlib MSS, 29/2, 29/3

TRINITY COLLEGE, CAMBRIDGE
MS R.5.5

WESTMINSTER ABBEY MUNIMENTS
WAM 1194
WAM 25095
WAM 53333
Westminster Abbey Chapter Act Book, vol. II, 1609–42

PRINTED PRIMARY SOURCES

Articles concerning the Surrender of Oxford (Oxford, 1646)

Atterbury, Francis, *The Rights, Powers and Privileges of Convocation* (1700)

Baillie, Robert, *Ladensium Aytokatakriσις: the Canterburians Self-conviction* (3rd edn, 1641)

Barwick, Peter, *The Life of John Barwick* (1724)

Baxter, Richard, *Church-History of the Government of Bishops and their Councils Abbreviated* (1680)

— *The Grotian Religion Discovered* (1658)

— *Reliquiae Baxterianae* (1696)

Bernard, Nicholas, *Devotions of the Ancient Church* (1660)

— *The Life & Death of . . . James Ussher* (1656)

Bernard, Richard, *A Threefold Treatise of the Sabbath* (1641)

Bramhall, John, *The Serpent Salve* (1643)

Britanniae Natalis (Oxford, 1630)

The Burford Records, ed. R. H. Gretton (Oxford, 1920)

Burges, Cornelius, *The Broken Title of Episcopal Inheritance* (1642)

— *An Humble Examination of a Printed Abstract* (1641)

Burton, Henry, *For God and the King* (1636)

Calendar of the Proceedings of the Committee for Compounding, 1643–1660 (5 vols, 1889–92)

Carlyle, Thomas, *Historical Sketches* (2nd edn, 1898)

Clarke, Samuel, *The Marrow of Ecclesiastical History* (1675)

Bibliography

Cleveland, John, *Cleaveland's Petition to His Highnesse the Lord Protector* (1657)

Collier, Jeremy, *An Ecclesiastical History of Great Britain* (9 vols, 1852)

Commons Debates for 1629, ed. W. Notestein and F. H. Relf (Minneapolis MN, 1921)

A Copie of the Proceedings of some Worthy and Learned Divines (1641)

Cosin, John, *The Works of . . . John Cosin*, ed. J. Sansom (5 vols, Oxford, 1843–55)

D'Ewes, Simonds, *The Journal of Sir Simonds D'Ewes, from the Beginning of the Long Parliament*, ed. W. Notestein (New Haven CT, 1923)

Dey, Richard, *Two Looks over Lincoln* (1641)

Documents relating to Proceedings against William Prynne in 1634 and 1637, ed. S. R. Gardiner (Camden Society, n.s., 118, 1877)

Dod, John, and Cleaver, Robert, *A Plaine and Familiar Exposition of the Ten Commandments* (19th edn, 1662)

Doughty, John, *The Kings Cause Rationally, Briefly and Plainly Debated* (1644)

Dow, Christopher, *Innovations unjustly Charged upon the present Church and State* (1637)

Echard, Lawrence, *History of England* (3 vols, 1718)

Falkland, Lord, *A Speech made to the House of Commons concerning Episcopacy* (1641)

— *The Lord Faulkland his learned Speech in Parliament, in the House of Commons, touching the late Lord Keeper* (1641)

Ferne, Henry, *Episcopacy and Presbytery Considered* (Oxford, 1644)

— *The Resolving of Conscience* (Cambridge, 1642)

Filmer, Robert, *Patriarcha and other Writings*, ed. J. P. Sommerville (Cambridge, 1991)

Fuller, Thomas, *The Appeal of Injured Innocence* (1659)

— *The Church History of Britain*, ed. J. S. Brewer (6 vols, Oxford, 1845)

Gatford, Lionel, *A Petition for the Vindication of the Publique Use of the Book of Common Prayer* (1655)

Gauden, John, *Considerations touching the Liturgy of the Church of England* (1661)

Godden, Thomas, *Catholicks no Idolators* (1672)

Gouge, William, *The Sabbaths Santification* (1641)

Hacket, John, *Scrinia Reservata* (1693)

Hakewill, George, *Apologie of the Power and Providence of God* (Oxford, 1627)

— *A Dissertation with Dr Heylyn: touching the Pretended Sacrifice in the Eucharist* (1641)

— *A Short but Cleare Discourse, of the Institution, Dignity and End, of the Lords Day* (1641)

Hall, Joseph, *A Short Answer to the Tedious Vindication of Smectymnuus* (1641)

— *The Works of . . . Joseph Hall*, ed. P. Wynter (10 vols, Oxford, 1863)

Hallam, Henry, *A Constitutional History of England* (3 vols, 1872)

Hammond, Henry, *Considerations of Present Use concerning the Danger resulting from the Change of our Church Government* (1645)

— *Dissertationes Quatuor* (1651)

Heylyn, Peter, *Aërius Redivivus: or the History of the Presbyterians* (2nd edn, 1672)

— *Antidotum Lincolniense* (1637; 2nd edn, 1637)

— *Augustus* (1632)

— *Bibliotheca Regia* (1658)

— *A Briefe and Moderate Answer, to the seditious and scandalous Challenges of Henry Burton* (1637)

— *A Briefe Relation of the Death and Sufferings of the Most Reverend and Renowned Prelate* (1645)

— *Certamen Epistolare* (1659)

— *A Coale from the Altar* (1636)

— *Cosmographie* (1652)

— *Cyprianus Anglicus* (1668)

— *Ecclesia Restaurata*, ed. J. C. Robertson (2 vols, Cambridge, 1849; 1661 edn)

— *Ecclesia Vindicata* (1657)

— *Erologia Anglorum or An Help to English History* (1641)

— *Examen Historicum* (1659)

— *Extraneus Valupans* (1656)

— *Historia Quinqu-Articularis* (1660)

— *A Historie of Episcopacie* (1642)

— *The History of the Sabbath* (1636; 2nd edn, 1636)

— *The Historie of St George* (1631; 2nd edn, 1633)

— *Κειμηλια Εκκλεσιαστικα: the Historical and Miscellaneous Tracts of . . . Peter Heylyn* (1681)

— *Lord have Mercie upon Us* (1643)

— *Memorial of Bishop Waynflete*, ed. J. R. Bloxam (Caxton Society, 1851)

— *Microcosmus* (Oxford, 1621; 2nd edn, Oxford, 1625; 7th edn, Oxford, 1636)

— *The Parable of the Tares* (1659)

— *Parliaments Power in Lawes for Religion* (Oxford, 1645)

— *The Rebells Catechism* (Oxford, 1643)

— *Respondet Petrus* (1658)

Bibliography

— A Sermon preached in the Collegiate Church of St Peter in Westminster, on . . . the Anniversary of His Majesties most joyful Restitution to the Crown of England (1661)

— The Stumbling Block of Disobedience and Rebellion (1658)

— Theologia Veterum (1654)

— Theeves, Theeves: or A Relation of Sir John Gell's Proceedings in Darbyshire (1643)

— The Undeceiving of the People in the Point of Tithes (1648, 1651)

Hickman, Henry, Historia Quinqu-articularis Exarticulata (1673)

— A Justification of the Fathers and Schoolmen (1659)

— A Review of the Certamen Epistolare (1659)

Hill, Sir Richard, The Church of England Vindicated (1770)

Historical Manuscripts Commission, De L'Isle, VI

Holles, John, Letters of John Holles, 1587–1637, ed. P. R. Seddon (3 vols, Thoroton Society, 31, 35–6, 1975–86)

Howell, James, A Cordial for the Cavaliers (1661)

Hoyle, Joshua, A Jehojadahs Justice against Mattan, Baal's Priest (1645)

Husbands, Edward, An exact Collection (1643)

Ironside, Gilbert, Seven Questions of the Sabbath briefly Disputed (Oxford, 1637)

Jones, David, The Secret History of Whitehall (1697)

Langbaine, Gerard, Episcopall Inheritance (1641)

Laud, William, The Works of William Laud, ed. W. Scott and J. Bliss (7 vols, Oxford, 1847–60)

Leighton, Alexander, An Appeal to the Parliament; or Sions Plea against the Prelacie (1628)

Leslie, Henry, A full Confutation of the Covenant, lately Sworne and Subscribed by many in Scotland: delivered in a Speech . . . 26th of September 1638 (1639)

L'Estrange, Hamon, A Caveat for Cavaliers (1661)

— Gods Sabbath before the Law, under the Law and under the Gospel (1641)

— The Observator Observed (1656)

— The Reign of King Charles (1656)

A Letter from an Officer in His Majesties Army (1643)

Mede, Joseph, The Works of Joseph Mede, ed. J. Worthington (1664)

Mercurius Aulicus

Morley, George, A Modest Advertisement concerning the Present Controversie about Church-Government (1641)

Morton, Thomas, A Sermon preached before the Kings Most Excellent Majestie, in the Cathedrall Church of Durham . . . the fifth Day of May 1639 (Newcastle upon Tyne, 1639)

Nalson, John, *An Impartial Collection of the Great Affairs of State* (2 vols, 1682–3)

Nedham, Marchamont, *A Second Pacquet of Advices and Animadversions* (1677)

Nicholls, William, *A Supplement to the Commentary on the Book of Common Prayer . . . To which is added an Introduction to the Liturgy of the Church of England* (1711)

O., M., *Fratres in Malo* (1660)

Oldmixon, John, *The Critical History of England, Ecclesiastical and Civil* (1724)

Parsons, Robert, *Judgment of a Catholicke English-man* (1608)

The Petition of the Inhabitants of Istleworth against William Grant (1641)

Pierce, Thomas, *The New Discoverer Discover'd* (1659)

Pocklington, John, *Altare Christianum* (1637)

— *Sunday no Sabbath* (1636)

Prideaux, John, *Lectiones novem de Totidem Religionis Capitibus* (Oxford, 1625)

— *Viginti-duae Lectiones de Totidem Religionis Capitibus* (Oxford, 1648)

Proceedings in the Opening Session of the Long Parliament, ed. M. Jansson (6 vols, Rochester NY, 2000–)

Prynne, William, *Canterburies Doome* (1646)

— *Histrio-mastix* (1633)

— *A Quench-coale* (1637)

Quarles, Francis, *The Loyall Convert* (1643)

Reportes of Cases in the Courts of Star Chamber and High Commission, ed. S. R. Gardiner (Camden Society, n.s., 39, 1886)

Sanderson, Robert, *A Soveraigne Antidote against Sabbatarian Errours* (1636)

— *The Works of Robert Sanderson D.D.*, ed. W. Jacobson (6 vols, Oxford, 1854)

Sanderson, William, *A Compleat History of the Life and Raigne of King Charles* (1658)

— *Post-haste: a Reply to Peter (Doctor Heylin's) Appendix: to his Treatise, intituled Respondet Petrus* (1658)

Stillingfleet, Edward, *An Answer to Several late Treatises* (1673)

Strada, Famianus, *De Bello Belgico: the History of the Low-Countrye Warres* (1650)

Sydenham, Humphrey, *Five Sermons preached upon Several Occasions* (1627)

— *Sermons upon Solemne Occasions* (1637)

Taylor, Jeremy, *Unum Necessarium* (1655)

— *Of the Sacred Order and Offices of Episcopacy* (Oxford, 1642)

Touchet, George, *Historical Collections out of Several Protestant Histories* (1673)

A True and Impartial Narrative of the Dissenters New Plot (1690)

Bibliography

Twisse, William, *Of the Morality of the Fourth Commandement* (1641)

Ussher, James, *The Bishop of Armaghes Direction, concerning the Lyturgy, and Episcopall Government* (1660)

— *The Judgment of the late Primate of Ireland . . . of the Sabbath and Observance of the Lord's Day* (1658)

— *The Reduction of Episcopacie unto the Form of Synodical Government received in the antient Church* (1656)

Visitation Articles and Injunctions of the early Stuart Church, ed. K. Fincham (2 vols, Church of England Record Society, 1, 5 (1994–98)

Votiva, sive ad Serenissimum . . . Jacobum . . . Regem . . . De auspicato . . . Caroli, Walliae Princeps, etc. in Regiam Hispaniam Adventu . . . Oxoniensium Gratulatio (Oxford, 1623)

Westfield, Thomas, *A Sermon preached in the Cathedrall Church of S. Paul on the fourteenth Day of November 1641, in the Evening* (1641)

White, Francis, *An Examination and Confutation of a Lawlesse Pamphlet* (1637)

— *A Treatise of the Sabbath-Day* (3rd edn, 1636)

Williams, Griffith, *The Discovery of Mysteries* (1643)

— *The Grand Inheritance* (1641)

Williams, John, *The Holy Table, Name and Thing* (1637)

— *The Work of Archbishop Williams*, ed. B. Williams (Abingdon, 1979)

Winthrop Papers, vol. 3 (Massachusetts Historical Society, 1943)

Wood, Anthony, *Athenae Oxonienses*, ed. P. Bliss (4 vols, 1813–20)

— *The History and Antiquities of the University of Oxford*, ed. J. Gutch (2 vols, Oxford, 1792–96)

Wortley, Francis, *Ελευθερωσις . . . Truth asserted* (1641)

Young, John, *The Diary of John Young*, ed. F. R. Goodman (1928)

Index

Note: 'n' after a page reference indicates a note number on that page

Index